ERDOGAN'S EMPIRE

ERDOGAN'S EMPIRE

Turkey and the Politics of the Middle East

SONER CAGAPTAY

To Tom,
with best wishes
Soner [signature]

I.B.TAURIS
LONDON · NEW YORK · OXFORD · NEW DELHI · SYDNEY

I.B. TAURIS
Bloomsbury Publishing Plc
50 Bedford Square, London, WC1B 3DP, UK
1385 Broadway, New York, NY 10018, USA

BLOOMSBURY, I.B. TAURIS and the I.B. Tauris logo are trademarks of
Bloomsbury Publishing Plc

First published in Great Britain 2020

Cover design by Charlotte James
Cover image © Sean Gallup / Staff / Getty Images

A catalogue record for this book is available from the British Library.

A catalog record for this book is available from the Library of Congress.

ISBN: HB: 978-1-7883-1739-9
       ePDF: 978-1-7867-3597-3
       eBook: 978-1-7867-2634-6

Typeset by RefineCatch Limited, Bungay, Suffolk
Printed and bound in the U.S.A. by Sheridan, Chelsea, Michigan

To find out more about our authors and books visit www.bloomsbury.com
and sign up for our newsletters.

In loving memory of my father . . .

CONTENTS

ACKNOWLEDGEMENTS

I am grateful to my assistant, Egecan Alan Fay, for his exceptional work on this book. Egecan helped me at each stage of writing this monograph, from drafting chapters to compiling endnotes. He has worked tirelessly with me, with dedication and passion for scholarship, and for this, I am forever indebted to him.

Furthermore, thank you to my research assistants and research interns, including Oya Rose Aktas, Antonia Boemeke, Lauren Fredericks, Kieran Hatton, Yagiz Sullu, Maya Yalkin and Deniz Yuksel, who have helped me during various phases of this book, from drafting an outline to fact-checking to digging for sources in libraries. Deniz and Yagiz assisted me especially in the final stages of the book, diligently helping me tie loose ends. Without their collaboration and that of other members of my research team, this book would not have been completed. I am also indebted to my former research assistant, Tyler Evans, and research intern, Cagatay Ozdemir, who helped draft portions of the initial chapters of this book. Tyler and Cagatay have great insight into Turkish politics and I would like to thank them for their invaluable role; I was able to start and then move this monograph through the publication process in a timely and swift fashion.

My thanks also go to the Washington Institute for Near East Policy research interns and assistants, Emma Bapt, Avichai Ozur Bass, Arjan Ganji, Kayla Harrington, Evan Lisman, Fiona Renezeder, Basia Rosenbaum and Alessandra Testa, who fact-checked and copy-edited various chapters of this manuscript. Their contributions improved the manuscript.

I am grateful to the Washington Institute for Near East Policy, which is the best place to work for a historian-cum-policy-maker. Since 2002, the Institute has strongly supported my scholarship on Turkey, its history and foreign policy. At least some parts of this book draw on my earlier analysis at the Institute, and in this regard, I am thankful to its Director, Rob Satloff, and Research Director, Patrick Clawson, who believed in my work and stood by it. I am also grateful to my colleagues, including Ambassador Jim Jeffrey, who reviewed an initial outline of this monograph, as well as to Sarah Feuer, Ben Fishman and Simon Henderson, who provided feedback on a number of the chapters of this book. My colleagues, Kori Francis, Mary Horan and Deniz Yuksel, helped produce various charts and maps that were used during the research and preparation of this book, and I am grateful to them for their assistance.

This manuscript would not be complete without the insights of my friends and colleagues, James Barnett, Dimitar Bechev, Ambassador Jonathan Cohen, Sir Michael Leigh, Alan Makovsky, Rich Outzen, Soli Ozel, Ambassador Eric Rubin, Sabri Sayari, Jesper Møller Sørensen, Aaron Stein, Sinan Ulgen, Ambassador Ross Wilson and Murat Yetkin, as well as to those who have asked to remain anonymous. They have reviewed different versions and chapters of this book, providing invaluable insight and corrections to me. Additionally, I am thankful to my editor at I.B. Tauris, Tomasz Hoskins, client manager Merv Honeywood, and copy-editor Roza I. M. El-Eini. Tomasz especially assisted me in conceiving this book, Merv shepherded the manuscript successfully during the production process for on-time completion, and Roza helped improve it during the editing process.

I would also like to thank Tony and Vanessa Beyer for their continuing dedication to my work and to the mission of the Turkish Research Program at the Washington Institute for Near East Policy. I am also indebted to Madeline and Michael Silverman for the support they have given me and the work of the Turkish Research Program.

Of course, all errors and omissions are mine.

I owe gratitude to my friends, Jen Moore and Yuri Kim, who have inspired me to write this book (and, of course, others). Finally, I would like to remember my parents, Mehmet and Sultan Cagaptay, who instilled in me a passion for books, scholarship and a dedication to make Turkey and the world a better place.

LIST OF
ABBREVIATIONS

A2D2	Anti-Access/Air Denial
AFAD	Disaster and Emergency Management Presidency
AKP	Justice and Development Party
AMISOM	African Union Mission for Somalia
ANAP	Motherland Party
AU	African Union
BRI	Belt and Road Initiative
BSEC	Black Sea Economic Cooperation
BTC	Baku–Tbilisi–Ceyhan Pipeline
CAATSA	Countering America's Adversaries Through Sanctions Act
CDU	Christian Democrat Union
CENTCOM	Central Command (US)
CHP	Republican People's Party
CSDP	Common Security and Defence Policy (EU)
CTP	Republican Turkish Party
DENK	Denk political party
DOST	Democrats for Responsibility, Solidarity and Tolerance
DP	Democrat Party (Turkish)
DPS	Movement for Rights and Freedoms

DYP	True Path Party
EC	European Community
EEC	European Economic Community
EU	European Union
EUCOM	European Command (US)
EUFOR	European Union Force
FDI	Foreign Direct Investment
FP	Virtue Party
FSA	Free Syrian Army
FTA	Free Trade Agreement
GCC	Gulf Cooperation Council
GDP	Gross Domestic Product
GERD	Grand Ethiopian Renaissance Dam
HDP	People's Democratic Party
HLSCC	High Level Strategic Cooperation Council (Turkish–Tunisian)
IHH	Humanitarian Relief Foundation
IMF	International Monetary Fund
IRGC	Islamic Revolutionary Guard Corps
ISIS	Islamic State in Syria and Iraq
KDP	Kurdistan Democratic Party
KDPI	Kurdish Democratic Party of Iran
KRG	Kurdistan Regional Government
MAD	Mutually Assured Destruction
MENA	Middle East and North Africa
MIT	National Intelligence Organization

MSP	National Salvation Party
MTTB	National Turkish Student Union
NAM	Non-Aligned Movement
NATO	North Atlantic Treaty Organization
NPSD	National Freedom and Dignity Party
NSC	National Security Council (Turkish)
OECD	Organisation for Economic Co-operation and Development
OIC	Organisation of Islamic Cooperation
PA	Palestinian Authority
PCDK	Kurdistan Democratic Solution Party
PiS	Law and Justice Party
PJAK	Kurdistan Free Life Party
PKK	Kurdistan Workers' Party
PLO	Palestine Liberation Organization
PPP	Purchasing Power Parity
PUK	Patriotic Union of Kurdistan
PYD	Democratic Union Party
RP	Welfare Party
SAC	Syrian Arab Coalition
SDF	Syrian Democratic Forces
SDP	Social Democrat Party (German)
SFG	Somali Federal Government
SNC	Syrian National Council
SOCOM	Special Operations Command (US)
SP	Felicity Party

TAF	Turkish Armed Forces
TANAP	Trans-Anatolian Pipeline
TESEV	Turkish Economic and Social Studies Foundation
THKP-C	People's Liberation Party-Front of Turkey
TIKA	Turkish Cooperation and Coordination Agency
TRNC	Turkish Republic of Northern Cyprus
TURKONFED	Turkish Federation of Entrepreneurs and Business World
TUSIAD	Turkish Industry and Business Association
TUSKON	Turkish Confederation of Businessmen and Industrialists
UAR	United Arab Republic
UAE	United Arab Emirates
UNHCR	United Nations High Commissioner for Refugees
YPG	People's Protection Units

PROLOGUE

Nations that were once great empires, such as Turkey, often have an inflated sense of their heyday. This, of course, leads to a readiness to be inspired, or a vulnerability to be manipulated, by effective politicians who are able to embody and speak to this narrative. Understanding the importance of Turkey's imperial past is essential to understanding modern Turkey. This is because a romantic view of the collapsed Ottoman Empire continues to shape the views held by Turkish citizens of their place in the world.

Enter Recep Tayyip Erdogan, the country's president, who has held sway since 2003. Erdogan, who has won thirteen nationwide polls, consolidating power in Turkey over decades, is the country's most consequential and powerful leader, probably since Mustafa Kemal Ataturk, who, in 1923, established modern Turkey out of the ashes of the Ottoman Empire at the end of the First World War.

The Romans measured time by *saecula* – the number of years that had to pass between the time of the occurrence of an incident and the death of all the people who were alive at the time of this incident. Ataturk's republic is not *yet* one *saeculum* old, and the shared, and malleable, memory of Ottoman greatness resonates deeply with Turkey's citizens.

For hundreds of years, the Ottomans dominated what are now nearly fifty sovereign countries – a quarter of the current UN member states – spanning three continents (Africa, Asia and Europe). However, starting in the eighteenth century, the Ottoman Empire went into a long and steady decline. Aware of their country's weakness, successive generations of Turkish leaders latched their country's foreign policy onto that of a global power or international bloc in the West, while waiting for Turkey's greatness to return.

Ataturk, a general in the Ottoman army, founded modern Turkey in his own image as a secular, European state. After he deposed the sultans, he turned Turkey's face further to the West. By copying European states, the great global powers of the interwar era, in statecraft, he aimed to place Turkey on a trajectory which would lead to the great nation status that was Turkey's birthright.

Inspired by European traditions, Ataturk's secularism mandated freedom *from* religion in government, politics and the education system. A Jacobin politician, Ataturk ran the country with an iron fist until his death in 1938. He left behind a secularist system of government based on his principles, also known as Kemalism. Ismet Inonu, who followed Ataturk as the country's second president, perpetuated his Kemalist legacy. But he ruled Turkey with an even stronger fist. It was not until 1950 that the country's first fully free and fair elections were held.

After Turkey became a multiparty democracy in 1950, Ataturk and Inonu's democratically elected successors for decades perpetuated their secularist legacy. These Kemalists believed that Ataturk's political system was durable, and should not be changed as the world changes.

Until Erdogan. Turkey's twenty-first-century leader hails from a tradition of political Islam, which seeks to blend a religious and political style that has been growing in the country during the late twentieth century, starkly opposing Ataturk's secularism. Since coming to power in 2003, Erdogan has revolutionised Turkish politics, and in doing so has proven the Kemalists wrong.

Ataturk ruled Turkey for fifteen years between 1923 and 1938. Erdogan has already governed from Ankara for over sixteen. He has successfully torn down, or recalibrated, much of Ataturk's legacy. In addition, under him, the country has reverted to an authoritarian style of government, ironically more reminiscent of the Ataturk and Inonu years than of late twentieth-century Turkey.

As the new 'Ataturk', Erdogan has recast Turkey top-down in *his* own image: as profoundly Islamic and socially conservative. Moreover, Erdogan's 'new Turkey' primarily faces not Europe, or the West, but the Middle East. Erdogan wants to see Ankara rising as a great power with and through influence over Muslims across Turkey's former Ottoman possessions – especially the Middle East, but also in the Balkans beyond.

Erdogan's quest to seek greatness for Turkey is not unusual, however. It is, in many ways, a continuation of the policies of the country's Turkish leaders, from the late Ottoman sultans to Ataturk, all of whom sought to revive Turkey's great power status. However, Erdogan's path is different compared to his predecessors. While they folded Turkey under the West to restore its global influence, Erdogan has picked an unorthodox model: his goal is to make Turkey great as a *stand-alone* power. First, in the Middle East and then globally.

A populist politician, Erdogan does not shy away from using this foreign policy vision to mobilise his right-wing base. The first four chapters of this book, beginning with the Introduction, explain Erdogan's rise and consolidation of power, and the nativist thinking that often, together with Ankara's national security concerns and historic patterns of Turkish foreign policy, informs his key international decisions.

Erdogan has delivered strong economic growth during the last decade, lifting many of his conservative supporters out of poverty, also creating a base of followers who adore him. Turkey's economic growth in the past decade has endowed it with increased regional influence. This is one reason for which Erdogan has pivoted the country towards the Middle East, as a way to enjoy the fruits of its newfound power, shown in Chapter 4. Chapter 5 details Turkey's simultaneously ebbing political relationship with Europe; and Chapter 6 describes Ankara's evolving relationship with Washington during the same timeframe, under presidents George W. Bush and Barack H. Obama.

The Kemalist constitution of Turkey, framed after Ataturk's thinking, remains however, and during the early years of the last decade, Turkey's secularist military and high courts loyal to Ataturk's legacy boxed in Erdogan and his political Islamist vision in government. Consequently, Erdogan then tried to implement a better version of late-Kemalist foreign policy, more tolerant, more European, more internationalist. For instance, he tried to unify Cyprus in 2004, supporting a UN-backed plan, which, nevertheless, failed (explained in Chapter 12).

Between 2008 and 2011, Erdogan took over the reins and complete power in Turkey. A referendum he won in 2010 allowed him to reappoint a majority of the judges to the high courts, without a confirmation process. Simultaneously, Erdogan defanged the secularist Turkish Armed Forces (TAF) with help of the Gulen movement, his ally at the time.

A religious order-cum-political network established in the 1970s by Turkish Muslim cleric, Fethullah Gulen, the Gulen movement played a key role in Erdogan's power consolidation. It helped build the kangaroo court Ergenekon–Sledgehammer cases (covered in the Introduction), alleging that there was a court plot against Erdogan, and then arrested a large number of generals, as well as Erdogan's secularist opponents, from journalists to university professors, thereby creating a 'republic of fear', in which opposing Erdogan became a crime.

In 2011, the military's top brass bowed to Erdogan and Gulen, resigning *en masse*. This ushered in a new dynamic: Erdogan and Gulen, each wanting to control Turkey by himself, split ways. This was the beginning of a long political fight that culminated in 2016 in the failed coup against Erdogan, in which Gulen-aligned officers seem to have played a key role.

Meanwhile, Erdogan's increasing power allowed him room to move forward with his foreign policy vision. During the ensuing second Erdogan era in Turkey between 2011 and the 2016 failed coup, Erdogan embraced an ambitious programme of neo-Ottoman and regional power initiatives, with help from his foreign minister-turned prime minister, Ahmet Davutoglu. The unfolding Arab uprisings at the time provided this vision with opportunities in the Middle East – as Erdogan and Davutoglu saw it. Most notably, during the Arab uprisings, Erdogan (and Davutoglu) supported the Muslim Brotherhood, a political Islamist movement. They also decoupled Ankara from Israel, and Erdogan tried to make peace with the Kurdistan Workers' Party (PKK) at home.

In its support for the anti-Assad rebels in Syria (covered in Chapter 7), Turkey butted heads with Russia and Iran, its historic adversaries. These policies refreshed threatening and old rivalries with Moscow and Tehran (covered in Chapters 8 and 9, respectively). Overall, Erdogan's Middle East initiatives left Turkey isolated and with no friends in the region, except for Qatar. Most notably, Ankara's ties with Egypt and Middle Eastern monarchies aligned with Saudi Arabia suffered severely because of Erdogan's (and Davutoglu's) support of the Muslim Brotherhood during the Arab uprisings (Chapters 10 and 11). Finally, the US–Turkish relationship started to zigzag in this period because of policy differences between Ankara and Washington regarding the Syrian Civil War.

The post-failed coup period

In 2016, a final and complete rupture between Erdogan and Gulen came, following the attempted coup against Erdogan. After the failure of the putsch, Erdogan not only pursued suspected coup plotters, such as Gulenists, but also used his post-coup state of emergency powers to carry out a more sweeping crackdown across Turkish society, consciously brutalising many of his opponents. Talks with the PKK collapsed in July 2015, casting Ankara and the group's Syrian offshoot, the People's Protection Units (YPG) as enemies in that country's civil war.

Further, in foreign policy, the November 2015 'plane crisis', in which Turkey shot down a Russian fighter jet that had violated its airspace from Syria, ushered in new problems. Following the crisis, Russian President Vladimir Putin slapped hefty sanctions on Ankara, and threatened to attack Turkish operations in Syria. Erdogan's call to have NATO missile defence systems placed in Turkey to protect it against Moscow failed to produce a strong show of support from Ankara's transatlantic allies – at least as Erdogan saw it.

Realising the risks of Turkey's complete isolation internationally, Erdogan fired Davutoglu in early 2016, launching an initiative to repair Turkey's ties with some of its neighbours, including Iraq and Israel (covered in Chapter 12), but also to make up with Putin, entering into negotiations with him to bring to an end Syria's war.

In another pragmatic turn, since 2017, Erdogan has tried to make a deal with US President Donald J. Trump regarding the many issues that continue to divide Ankara and Washington (Chapter 13). Recently, Erdogan has pivoted to new areas beyond the Middle East to offset his losses there, and to procure Turkish influence elsewhere – this time with some successes, most notably in East Africa (Chapter 14), as well as the Balkans, Black Sea Basin and Central Asia, i.e. the 'Bayram Belt' (Chapter 15).

The post-2017 environment also saw Erdogan's efforts to rebuild Ankara's links with Europe, underlining the importance of the deep financial and economic links that tie Turkey to the 'Strategic West' – i.e. the collective membership of NATO and of the Organisation for Economic Co-operation and Development (OECD) (Chapter 16).

A resource-poor country, and despite Erdogan's efforts, Turkey depends on the Strategic West to grow. Although Erdogan has recalibrated Ankara's political ties with Europe and the USA over the past decade, in terms of trade and incoming investment, the Strategic West still dominates in Turkey – and Erdogan relies on it to win elections. He has constantly scored victories at the ballot box, mainly on a platform of strong economic growth. In this regard, Turkey's economic slowdown in 2018 presents a challenge both to him and to Turkey, as does the alarming departure of educated citizens escaping his authoritarian grip – Turkey cannot become a great power, if smart and globally connected citizens leave in exodus and international capital avoids the country.

Last, the Kurdish issue, too, presents a challenge to Erdogan – and Turkey. The war in Syria has internationalised Turkey's Kurdish problem, linking the PKK in Turkey and the YPG in Syria. Erdogan should not, and cannot, leave the resolution of this problem to the USA or his adversaries, such as Assad, Iran and Russia, which have historic ties with the PKK.

Can Erdogan fix all these problems, and deliver Turkey back to safety, even greatness? What are the risks that lie ahead for him, and for the country? How can Turkey truly become a great power, fulfiling a dream shared by many of its citizens, the sultans, Ataturk and Erdogan himself? I have tried to provide answers to these questions in the concluding chapter of the book.

INTRODUCTION
A TRIP TO ISTANBUL

A mosque befitting a sultan

In September 2018, during a trip to Istanbul, I saw the construction site of the cavernous Camlica Mosque, a Muslim edifice built under the supervision of its patron, Turkish President Recep Tayyip Erdogan.

During my visit away from Washington, DC, as I woke up each day to the sound of the Muslim call for prayer pouring over Istanbul, I could pick out the Camlica Mosque almost instantly. Seen from miles away, the mosque's nearly 72 metre (236 feet) high dome dwarfs Istanbul's skyline. The mosque rises on the slopes of Istanbul's highest hill, measuring 268 metres (879 feet) at its highest point. I returned to Washington, convinced that the Camlica Mosque expressed Erdogan's grand political vision in physical form.

The Camlica Mosque is the first mosque of this magnitude formally sponsored by a Turkish leader in Istanbul since the collapse of the Ottoman Empire a century ago. At that time, Mustafa Kemal Ataturk, an Ottoman army general, liberated Turkey from Allied occupation.[1] He then established modern Turkey in 1923, as a republic, installing a secularist system of government. His secularism, borrowed from the French model, mandated no religion in governmental affairs, politics or education. Ataturk ruled Turkey with an authoritarian grip, until his death in 1938.

Istanbul is a city of mosques and the politics that surround them. Just as Erdogan is demonstrating his power by building *his* mosque in Turkey's biggest city, Ataturk did so as well by converting the Hagia Sofia Mosque, Istanbul's Byzantine-era cathedral church, transfigured into a mosque in 1453 by Ottoman Sultan Mehmed II, into a secular museum in 1935. Through this representational and political act of 'undoing a mosque', Ataturk signalled that he wanted religion out of politics. In another symbolic act, he moved Turkey's capital from Istanbul to Ankara, signalling – this time geographically and politically – his new republic's turn away from its Ottoman past. Subsequently, Ataturk pivoted Turkey to face the West, embracing European culture.

While Ataturk 'de-mosqued' Hagia Sofia to underline his vision, Erdogan's patronage of the grand Camlica Mosque, already dubbed so-called 'Erdogan's Mosque', in the former Ottoman royal capital, testifies to Erdogan's own vision. The 'new Turkey' Erdogan would like is a profoundly Islamic and socially conservative society, one that faces towards the Middle East. What is more, in this 'new Turkey', Islam is enmeshed in politics, instead of being firewalled from it – in even sharper contrast to Ataturk's vision.

Meet Recep Tayyip Erdogan

Following the tradition of Ottoman sultans, who built imperial mosques to adorn the seven hills of Istanbul's historic old city, Erdogan has constructed his mosque near modern Istanbul's highest point, creating a visual eighth hill for the Turkish megalopolis. Even more poignantly, the Camlica Mosque is adorned with six minarets, numerically competing in glory with the seventeenth-century Blue Mosque, the only other mosque in Istanbul with as many minarets. By physically soaring above the city's imperial mosques, the Camlica Mosque announces the ascent in the former Ottoman capital of a new sultan: Recep Tayyip Erdogan.

The Camlica Mosque sits at the geographic centre of greater Istanbul, a city of over 15 million people, and allows the Turkish leader to imprint his legacy permanently on the city of his birth and political ascent. It has been an extraordinary rise for the man elected mayor of Istanbul in 1994.

In June 2018, 24 years later, he won fresh parliamentary and presidential elections, with a slim majority, which fully put into place changes approved by an earlier 2017 referendum. Erdogan is now head of state, head of government, head of the ruling Justice and Development Party (AKP), de facto head of the Police (a national force in Turkey under the control of the Interior Ministry), and commander in chief of the Turkish Armed Forces (TAF).

Erdogan, who hails from a modest and pious family, was born in Istanbul in 1954, in the gritty and working-class neighbourhood of Kasimpasa. He entered politics in Istanbul in the 1970s, embracing political Islam at a time when Turkey was an officially secularist society, and starting his fight against the country's political system. Erdogan's rise to power was not smooth. During his ascent, he was briefly jailed in 1999 for reciting an allegedly incendiary poem that Turkey's secularist courts said undermined the country's political system.

Following the collapse of Turkey's traditionally secular parties during the country's devastating 2000–2001 economic crisis, Erdogan came to power through his AKP, which emerged as Turkey's leading party in the November 2002 parliamentary elections. Erdogan's brand as the pious, and therefore politically clean, guy from the other side of the tracks at a time when many of the secular parties he defeated in the 2002 elections were notoriously corrupt, played a key role in his victory at the polls.

He became prime minister in March 2003,[2] and has won numerous elections since, primarily because he delivered phenomenal economic growth, especially during his first decade in power. This has built him a base of loyal and mostly conservative supporters. He has won over a dozen elections since 2002 and consolidated immense power in his hands.

While I was a PhD candidate at Yale University studying Turkish and Balkan history, I worked as a tour guide in Istanbul in the 1990s to make ends meet. The sheer size of Istanbul's Ottoman-era mosques impressed me every time I guided tour groups through these historic landmarks.

I was always particularly awed when viewing another of Istanbul's glorious mosques: the Mosque of Suleyman I, the Magnificent. Suleyman I, probably the greatest of the Ottoman sultans, built this mosque in the sixteenth century at the height of Ottoman power. Signalling imperial glory, for centuries, the dome of 'Suleyman's Mosque', standing at 53 metres (174 feet), hovered over Istanbul's silhouette, and dominated the other mosques and monuments across the city's skyline, including the Hagia Sofia and the Blue Mosque.

At the time, I thought that an edifice matching Suleyman's Mosque could not be built in Istanbul – ever. In height, so-called 'Erdogan's

Mosque' easily surpasses Suleyman's Mosque. I returned to Washington, DC, thinking that Erdogan had outdone even Suleyman.

Inventor of twenty-first-century populism

Ataturk ran Turkey with an iron grip. A Jacobin politician, Turkey's founder shaped the twentieth-century country in his image as a Western staunchly secular society. Importantly, he did not eliminate or suppress Islam as a religion. Rather, he created a secularist system that essentially controlled religion and marginalised citizens, such as Erdogan later on, who identified primarily through Islam. Ataturk banished Islam to the private sphere, while removing the direct influence of religious institutions and leaders over politics.

Mustafa Kemal Ataturk and his followers – named 'Kemalists', after his original last name – were supremely self-assured in the secularist system they built. Their confidence was embedded in the Turkish Armed Forces (TAF), from which Ataturk hailed, and which saw itself as the protector of the country's secularist political system after the leader's death in 1938.

The secularist system Ataturk left in place was, however, modified by TAF following the 1980 coup. At that time, the generals' takeover aimed at curbing the rise of the leftist ideology in the country, as well as ending the developing civil war as fighting had broken out on the streets between left- and right-wing militia. Confined by these circumstances, the military decided to allow minimal, yet noteworthy, forms of Islam to penetrate the country's political and education systems. The generals believed that religion could stymie the rising tide of leftist sentiment in the country, 'inoculating' Turkish society against communism. In the 1980s and 1990s, these policies increased Islam's visibility in the public sphere in the country. Ironically, these dynamics, unleashed by the secularist generals, allowed political Islam to take root in Turkey. Again ironically, taking advantage of these dynamics to come to power in 2003, Erdogan has since recalibrated and dismantled Ataturk's secularism in just over a decade – and has done so with little mercy for his opponents.

Turkey is often considered a country that follows trends invented in the West and Europe. This has generally been the case since the early nineteenth century, when Ottoman sultans Westernised and Europeanised the Ottoman Empire. Therefore, while transitioning to the twentieth century, Ataturk and his followers looked to Europe and the West for clues in statecraft and foreign policy. In Erdogan's case, however, we see a unique interaction, in which a Turkish leader both turns East and sets a political trend for the West. Erdogan is *the* global prototype of populist leaders we are seeing in the twenty-first century – he can take credit for inventing a new breed of nativist politics, a trend which has been copied by effective populist leaders elsewhere.

Erdogan has brutalised and cracked down on demographic groups, from leftists to liberals, who are unlikely to vote for him. In order to build and boost his base, he demonises his challengers, often attacking those who oppose him, saying that they act as 'foreign proxies', who want to undermine him and, therefore, Turkey. This opposition, which constitutes nearly half of the country, simply loathes him. The strategy, however, has won him a loyal base of mostly conservative followers, demographics that includes centre-right, right-wing as well as political Islamist voters. Erdogan lifted many of these citizens out of poverty with his successful economic policies and, for that ,reason they adore him and want to keep him in power.

Enter the New Sultan

Erdogan's efforts to take over Turkey's political system have included tactful approaches, meticulous strategising, and patient steps. After coming to power, he delivered robust economic growth and, as a result, gradually built his popular electoral support. Following his second electoral win in parliamentary elections in 2007, and taking stock of his rising popularity (at the time, 46 per cent of the electorate voted for his party, AKP, up from 34 in 2002, constituting Turkey's largest electoral mandate in decades), he started to amass power, eroding democratic checks and balances.

Subsequently, he was able to take control of much of the media, using state watchdogs, and also the courts, following a 2010 referendum, which gave him the prerogative to appoint a majority of judges to high benches without a confirmation process.[3] Erdogan also started to crack down on his opposition at this time, beginning with the Kemalists, who wanted Turkey to stay on the West-facing and secularist path envisioned by its founder.

During a set of kangaroo trials between 2008 and 2011, he targeted, delegitimised and punished his secularist opponents.[4] The Gulen movement, which was established in the 1970s, and had gradually grown in power in the 1980s and 1990s, became a strong Erdogan ally after the 2002 elections, helping him in this process.

In 2008, Gulen's network of supporters in the country's police and judiciary helped Erdogan imprison nearly a quarter of Turkey's active duty generals and admirals in the secularist TAF, alleging that these officers were involved in the so-called Ergenekon coup plot to overthrow the government. Again, with Gulenist help, Erdogan jailed a number of prominent secular intellectuals, journalists and civil society activists, alleging in media, such as pro-Gulen daily *Zaman*, that these groups were part of the coup plot against him.[5] The prosecutors could not provide a convincing and persuasive account of the purported secularist coup, but the Ergenekon–Sledgehammer cases allowed Erdogan to jail dissidents, kicking off an authoritarian trend in Turkish politics, with him on top.

The generals caved in. Soon after the TAF's top brass resigned en masse in 2011, bowing to Erdogan's power, the courts started throwing out the indictments. Still, the Ergenekon–Sledgehammer cases permeated Turkish politics, producing the dangerous idea that opposing Erdogan equalled plotting coups.

This created an environment of intimidation, in which Erdogan and his allies, including Gulen at the time, could openly harass dissidents. The Ergenekon trials had sent a message to anyone opposing him that they could easily be jailed, their private phone conversations or emails could be leaked to the public, or they could be linked to coup plotters by the pro-Erdogan media. This made it infinitely more difficult for Turks of all stripes to oppose Erdogan, creating a 'republic of fear', enabling the leader's authoritarian style.

In control of Turkey, Erdogan has since flooded its political and educational systems with rigidly conservative Islam.[6] This is, paradoxically, Erdogan's 'Ataturk' side. Of course, Erdogan does not share Ataturk's values, just his methods. Just as Ataturk shaped Turkey in his own image, creating a secularist, European society, Erdogan is shaping a 'new Turkey', which is socially conservative and which embraces political Islamism as a key value – in *his* own image.

And the crisis of Turkey

In fact, however, Erdogan is an anti-Ataturk 'Ataturk'. Having grown up in secularist Turkey and faced social exclusion at a young age due to his piety and conservative views (explained in further detail in Chapter 2), he was motivated by deep-rooted animosity towards Ataturk's ways. Yet, he has dismantled Ataturk's system by using the very tools that Ataturk and the country's founding elites provided him: power of state institutions and top-down social engineering – both hallmarks of Ataturk's reforms. Erdogan has used Ataturk's means and methods to replace even Ataturk himself. The product is that now Turkey discriminates against citizens who do not primarily identify through Islam, more specifically, conservative Sunni Islam, to which Erdogan belongs.

However, Erdogan has a problem: whereas Ataturk came to power as a military general, Erdogan has a democratic mandate to govern. What is more, today's Turkey is split nearly in the middle between pro- and anti-Erdogan camps. Despite these facts, Erdogan desperately wants to change the country in his own image, and herein lies the crisis of modern Turkey: while half of the county embraces Erdogan's brand of politics, the other half vehemently opposes it. So long as Turkey is genuinely democratic, Erdogan cannot complete his revolution.

This has grown Erdogan's illiberal side: in order to push forward with his platform of revolutionary change against a split society, Erdogan has subverted the country's democracy. Instead of delivering more liberties for all, he has cracked down on his opponents and locked up dissidents, providing liberties only for his conservative and even much narrower political Islamist base.

Erdogan has accomplished this by playing the 'authoritarian underdog'. Building on his narrative of political martyrdom under the secularist system in the 1990s, including the brief jail term that he served in 1999, Erdogan now portrays himself as a victim who is, grudgingly, forced to suppress those conspiring to undermine his authority. He intimidates the media and the business community through politically motivated tax audits, and jails dissidents, scholars and journalists.

In addition, his police regularly crack down on peaceful opposition rallies. Accordingly, although Turkey's elections continue to be mostly free, they are increasingly not fair. These developments have compounded polarisation in Turkey: Erdogan's conservative base has zealously banded around him in his defence; the other half of the country, brutalised by Erdogan, holds a profound resentment against him. Increasingly, there is little common ground between these constituencies.[7]

However, he has managed to survive, winning thirteen nationwide polls since 2002. He scored victories in at least the first eleven of these elections, following fair races. By putting large parts of the media in the hands of his cronies and gaining nearly unfettered access to state resources, he was able to stack enough of the odds in his favour in the most recent April 2017 referendum and June 2018 presidential and parliamentary elections to eke out victories.

At this stage, it is implausible that the Turkish leader will be voted out. In other words, Erdogan, who has already ruled Turkey longer than Ataturk, is here to stay, as is his vision to reshape Turkey as a profoundly Islamic and socially conservative society. So is his foreign policy model for the country: a 'new Turkey', which faces the Middle East and Muslim-majority countries beyond, with a desire to rise with and through influence over Muslims – 'in the mould of the Ottoman Empire'.

1
OSMAN'S DREAM

The Ottoman Empire, established by Osman Bey (I) in 1299 as a *beylik* (minor principality) in today's north-western Turkey, quickly rose in the late medieval period to become a great power by the fifteenth century. For hundreds of years, the Ottomans dominated vast areas, spanning Africa, Asia and Europe. At the height of its power in the seventieth century, the borders of the empire stretched from Poland in the north, Somalia in the south, Morocco in the west and Iran in the east.

This memory, indeed, remains fresh in Turkey. The Turkish republic, established in 1923 out of the ashes of the Ottoman Empire, is not *yet* one *saeculum* old, and to this day, the memory of Ottoman greatness resonates closely with Turkey's citizens.

After the Turks constructed and profited from great power status, the Ottoman Empire went into a long and steady decline in the face of rising European powers in the eighteenth century. It took the sultans nearly a century to conclude that they had to reform themselves drastically in order to catch up with their European counterparts. The Ottoman quest for reform and Westernisation, which started in the late eighteenth century, was not an attempt at Europeanisation per se. Rather, this quest was driven by a desire to become great again – through learning and mastering Western military and engineering arts while simultaneously establishing alliances in Europe – optimistically anticipating the return of the Ottomans' global, hegemonic status.

Romanticising the collapsed Ottoman Empire continues to shape the view of Turkey's citizens of their place in the world. The long and painful collapse of the Ottoman Empire in the nineteenth and early twentieth centuries moulds modern Turkey in many ways, including its relationship with Europe and the West.

The emergence of the 'Eastern Question' in the early nineteenth century, when the future of the weak Ottoman Empire became a focal point of debate in international politics, suggested to the reigning sultans that the survival of the empire would best be guaranteed by seeking alliances with key European states, in essence, the global superpowers of the time.

Aware of their country's weakness, successive generations of Turkish leaders often latched its foreign policy onto that of a global power or international bloc. The policy was conducted informally until the Second World War, and formally at the beginning of the Cold War (following direct threats to Turkey in the mid-1940s from its historic enemy, Russia). Turkey's leaders made a strategic decision in order to safeguard the late Ottoman Empire and then the modern republic.

Throughout much of the nineteenth century, Istanbul informally allied itself with London, and to a lesser extent Paris, to stave off the Russian menace for what was left of the empire's territories. In fact, Great Britain and France fought alongside the Ottomans in the Crimean War of 1853–6 against the Russian threat to Istanbul.

Even with this new policy, the nineteenth century proved difficult for the enfeebled Ottoman Empire – the Sublime Porte's reliance on Great Britain or France never evolved into a formal alliance. Hence, for instance, the isolated Ottomans suffered another defeat at the hands of the Russians in 1878. Moreover, Franco-British pressure forced the sultans to recognise the autonomy, and in some cases de-facto independence, of various Ottoman provinces, ranging from Crete to Mount Lebanon. Considered the 'Sick Man of Europe' in the nineteenth century, the empire managed to claw its way into the twentieth century.

The rise of Germany in the late nineteenth century, which competed for global influence against Great Britain at the time, eventually undermined this delicate balance by slowly eroding British commitment to preserve the Ottoman Empire. By the turn of the century, Germany was making successful moves to win over the Ottomans and gain influence in the Middle East. This was unacceptable to Great Britain, which saw the Kaisers' influence in the Sublime Porte as a threat to its maritime access across the Mediterranean and through the Suez Canal to its most prized possession: India.

However, thanks to Sultan Abdulhamid II's shrewdness in playing off Germany and Great Britain against each other during his reign between 1876 and 1908, it took Berlin years to wean Istanbul completely away from London. The informal British policy of protecting the Ottoman

Empire completely ended only on the eve of the First World War. At the time, the revolutionary Young Turks, who had deposed Abdulhamid II in 1908 in a constitutional revolution, decided to throw in fully Istanbul's lot with Berlin in 1914 during the Great War against the Allies.

Enter Ataturk

This endeavour did not work out so well for the Ottomans. Losing the war, the empire collapsed in 1918, facing occupation and partition. However, Ataturk liberated Turkey following a successful campaign between 1919 and 1922, dubbed the Turkish Independence War, fighting against Armenia, France and Greece, the latter backed by Great Britain. Italy, which occupied parts of south-western Turkey at the time, withdrew its troops without war, convinced by the sheer power of Ataturk's forces to avoid fighting with them.

Turkey was a weak and inward-looking country in the 1920s, after Ataturk deposed the sultans and made it a republic. During this period, Ataturk was busy rebuilding the country, whose infrastructure and many key cities had been destroyed during decade-long wars, from the Balkan Wars of 1912–13 to the First World War, to his own campaign to liberate it.

Ataturk was Machiavellian in his foreign policy, especially in his approach to the Soviet Union. Most notably, he exploited the Soviet leaders' fascination with Turkey's War of Liberation, which the communists, naively, interpreted as an 'anti-imperialist' struggle, to secure Moscow's financial assistance to help in Turkey's reconstruction after the war – such as the building-up of heavy industries, including modern Turkey's first steel mill in the Black Sea region town of Karabuk, which opened in 1939.[1]

Once he firmly installed his secularist regime by the early 1930s, however, Ataturk was ready to throw in Ankara's lot with nations that really had his heart: France and Great Britain, two democratic superpowers of the interwar era in Europe.

And his Europeanisation project

Although he is often cast as an inward-looking leader, Ataturk, too, continued to pursue greatness for Turkey in the interwar period, by playing a more long-term strategic game. He fully embraced the Ottoman project of Westernisation, taking it to its logical extremes to make Turkey unconditionally European. Most notably, he borrowed Turkey's constitution from interwar Belgium, its civil code from Switzerland and its key principle of *laïcité* (Continental Europe's twentieth-century concept of secularism, which mandated freedom *from* religion in politics, government and education) from interwar France. Additionally, he imported Turkey's penal code from interwar Italy, and commercial code from interwar Germany.

Ataturk looked to Europe as a source of statecraft because the European states were the great powers of the world in the interwar era. He fully Europeanised Turkey in order to put it on track to become a major power again. If Brazil and Argentina had been key powers at the time, he would have probably followed a Latin American model of reform, statecraft and modernisation. At the same time, following late Ottoman sultans, Ataturk latched his country's security onto France and Great Britain, seeking their support in international affairs until the return of Turkey's great power status.

Turkey was weak in the interwar period, and felt threatened by its revisionist neighbours, such as Bulgaria and more importantly Mussolini's Italy, the latter of which possessed the Dodecanese Islands in the Aegean Sea, making it Ankara's maritime neighbour at the time. Ataturk overall sought good ties with Turkey's other neighbours. In 1930, he hosted Greek Prime Minister Eleftherios Venizelos in Ankara, kicking off an era of nearly two decades of good bilateral ties with Athens, until the emergence of the Cyprus issue in the 1950s undermined Turkish–Greek ties.

Ataturk also cultivated good ties with France and Great Britain to balance against Italian expansionist rhetoric towards Turkey by Mussolini. Famously, he hosted the British king, Edward VIII, in Istanbul in 1936, just over a decade after a long bloody war between his country and Great Britain, politely gesturing his interest in establishing meaningful ties with London.[2] Ataturk also sought Paris' friendship. In 1934, Ankara joined the Balkan Pact, backed by France, which aimed to push back against revisionism in South-Eastern and Central Europe. This policy bought Turkey security against threats from two revisionist interwar-era neighbours, Sofia and Rome. Accordingly, Turkey successfully fended off Mussolini's imperialism throughout the interwar period and during the Second World War, which began only months after Ataturk died.

Ataturk's successor, Inonu, embraces America

Turkish leaders, who followed Ataturk in the twentieth century, including the second president, Ismet Inonu, have embraced his model of seeking security in the democratic West.

Like Ataturk however, Inonu, too, was Machiavellian in his approach to foreign policy. Throughout the Second World War, he played Nazi Germany – which became Turkey's neighbour in 1941 after the Nazi occupation of Greece – and the Allies against each other. Inonu successfully kept Ankara out of the war, avoiding what would have been a potentially devastating German invasion, following a policy of 'active neutrality'.[3] For instance, on 18 June 1941, he signed the 'German–Turkish Non-Aggression Pact' with Hitler. Towards the end of the global conflict, however, anticipating the fall of Nazi Germany, Inonu dropped Turkey's anchor in the newly forming Western alliance: first, by declaring war on Berlin in February 1945; and then by moving close to the new global superpower, Washington.

Ankara's alliance-forming process with the United States accelerated in 1945–6, when Stalin demanded Turkish territory, including provinces along the country's north-east, adjacent to the Soviet Union, and basing rights along the Turkish Straits. The threat of Russia, the Turks' historic archenemy, sufficed to align Ankara with Washington for decades to come.

Inonu pivoted to Washington more fully when the USA emerged as a global superpower in the aftermath of the Second World War. Together with Western Europe during the Cold War era, the USA became Turkey's aspired model for greatness, as well as preferred foreign policy and security partner. Ankara sought and received US security guarantees and help against the Soviet Union. These included policy instruments, such as the USA issuing a formal declaration of protection through the 1947 Truman Doctrine, as well as providing financial assistance through the Marshall Plan that was initiated in 1948. Washington became a bulwark of Turkish foreign policy and security throughout the Cold War.

And his successors continue this tradition

Inonu, who ran Turkey with an iron fist between 1938 and 1950, not only allied Turkey with the USA, but also made it a democracy in the end. His historic role in regime change should not be underestimated. Had he wanted, he could have stayed in power until his death like Antonio de Oliveira Salazar did in Portugal (poignantly, Portugal was admitted to the North Atlantic Treaty Organization (NATO) in 1949, Salazar's authoritarian leadership notwithstanding). He saw democracy and alliance with the West as the Siamese twins of the future of the Turkish body politic, and his twentieth-century successors continued this tradition.

Accordingly, when Inonu lost Turkey's first multiparty and fully democratic elections in 1950, his successors, President Celal Bayar and Prime Minister Adnan Menderes from the Democrat Party (DP) took Ankara into NATO in 1952 – after they sent troops to fight alongside US forces in Korea, firmly cementing Turkey's Cold War alliance with Washington. In fact, the Turks were the fifth largest fighting force after the South Koreans, Americans, British and Canadians, out of over 20 nations that were engaged in anti-communist bloc operations on the Korean Peninsula in the 1950s.

There were later vicissitudes with Washington, most notably regarding the Cyprus issue. Problems started to brew on this island between Cypriot Turks and Greeks after the island gained its independence from Great Britain in 1960. The 1959 trilateral Zurich Agreement, signed by Great Britain, Turkey and Greece, made Cyprus independent. Furthermore, the agreement declared Great Britain, as well as Turkey and Greece as 'guarantor states', protecting Cyprus' sovereignty. The treaty effectively made Ankara the de facto guardian of the Cypriot Turkish community, and Athens the de facto guardian of the Cypriot Greek community. Following intra-ethnic violence between Turkish and Greek nationalists on the island in 1963–4, some feared Ankara would opt for a military intervention to protect the Cypriot Turks, the numerically weak community on the island.

In June 1964, US President Lyndon B. Johnson sent a letter to Ankara, warning Inonu, elected as prime minister in 1961 following the

1960 coup – modern Turkey's first TAF takeover – that had ousted DP from power. Johnson cautioned Inonu against any rash military moves regarding Cyprus. This memorandum sparked a crisis in bilateral ties, the first such crisis since the beginning of the Cold War.

The Cyprus issue haunted the US–Turkish relationship leading up to the next decade. On 15 July 1974, Greek military officers on the island carried out a coup, aiming to annex the island to Greece. Turkey sent troops to the island on 20 July to prevent a *fait accompli*. Turkish troops occupied nearly a third of the island, creating a homeland for Cypriot Turks. In February 1975, in the aftermath of the war, the US Congress slapped a hefty arms embargo on Ankara. Bilateral US–Turkish ties took a nosedive, only to recover following the 1980 coup in Ankara, where the generals in charge re-established their ties to Washington.

There were exceptions throughout the Cold War to the line of Turkish leaders eager to unconditionally latch Turkey's security onto Washington, such as the leftist prime minister, Bulent Ecevit, with his brief stints in government in the 1970s, including during the Cyprus War. The 1960s and 1970s witnessed the birth and rise of anti-Americanism in Turkey. However, overall, Ankara guaranteed its security throughout the Cold War by allying itself with Washington.

Following the end of the Cold War, Turkey's leaders stayed firm in their commitment to the USA. Most notably, Turgut Ozal, president at the time of the 1990 Gulf War, supported Washington during that first Iraq conflict, even at the cost of the resignation of the Chief of the Turkish General Staff, General Necip Torumtay, who objected to the war effort.

In return, NATO helped address Turkey's security concerns throughout the 1990s. The Alliance intervened in the wars in Bosnia and Kosovo in favour of Bosnians and Albanians, helping two of Ankara's predominantly Muslim friends in the Balkans. The United States also played a central role in the capture of Kurdistan Workers' Party (PKK) leader Abdullah Ocalan in Kenya in 1999, and by classifying Turkey's primary terror threat, PKK, as a 'Foreign Terrorist Organization' on a formal list kept by the US Government, as well as by encouraging NATO and some European countries to create similar designations.

This period also saw Turkey draw closer to Israel, most notably under then Prime Minister and later President Suleyman Demirel, and Prime Minister Tansu Ciller, Turkey's first female head of government, who served under Demirel when the latter became the country's president in 1993. Both leaders visited Israel and signed a number of trade and defence cooperation agreements in Jerusalem. Demirel even spoke to the Israeli Knesset during his visit there in 1996.

Overall in the 1990s, Turkey had tried to diversify its relationships within the West in order to decrease its dependency on Washington. In 1987, building on the 1963 Ankara Agreement that had established 'association' between Turkey and the European Economic Community (EEC), Ankara started pursuing more actively accession to the EEC's successor, the European Community (EC) – the EC itself would later be renamed the European Union (EU) in the 1990s. In addition to NATO and the USA, the EU vocation provided a third anchor in global politics to which to tie Ankara's fate in international affairs.

Diversification in the 1990s

At the same time, elated by the fall of communism, Ankara started to pursue a more multifaceted foreign policy in the 1990s. Following the (temporary) retreat of its historic nemesis, Moscow, in the 1990s, Turkey felt comfortable to build ties with both non-Western and non-European actors.

Turkish policy-makers also began reaching beyond the West in significant ways. Most significantly, Ankara boosted its trade links with the Middle East. In addition, following the fall of the Iron Curtain, under Demirel Turkey opened up to Central Asian and Caucasus regions, linking with Turkic and other states there. Turkish businesses and the Gulen movement followed suit into these areas, with mixed results for Ankara's power, as explained in Chapters 11 and 15.

Furthermore, in the late 1990s, guided by the pro-regional peace and integration vision of then Foreign Minister Ismail Cem, a social democrat-leaning politician, Ankara started repairing its historically tense ties with Athens. This resulted in significant rapprochement between the two NATO allies – Turkey and Greece appeared on friendly terms again for the first time since the 1950s, when the Cyprus issue had breached their ties. Cem drove the rapprochement, together with his Greek counterpart, George Papandreou, another leftist politician, who shared his vision.

Following the end of the Cold War, in trying to diversify its foreign policy, Ankara also carried out a putative Africa opening. However, this did not go very far in building the country's influence, or in allowing it a significant reach into sub-Saharan Africa. At the time, beyond Ankara's ties to the West, the vision of many Turkish diplomats was still constrained by Ankara's near abroad neighbourhood. In addition, successive economic crises during the 1990s sapped the energy of Turkish businesses to venture into distant markets, undermining Ankara's Africa opening.

In contrast, in the 1990s, Turkey extended its reach more successfully into the nearby Balkans by establishing strong ties with countries emerging out of Yugoslavia, such as Croatia and Macedonia, as well as Cold War-era adversaries on the peninsula, such as Albania, Bulgaria and Romania.

Ankara spent much of its energy during this period also in the adjacent Black Sea region. Working with Athens, they spearheaded a model of regional economic integration, named the Black Sea Economic Cooperation (BSEC). This organisation brought together all Black Sea littoral states (Bulgaria, Georgia, Romania, Russia and Turkey), as well as some nearby countries, such as Armenia, Azerbaijan and Greece, under a common umbrella – a historic first.

Although following Russia's resurgence under Putin in the next decade and subsequent conflicts between Moscow and Black Sea nations, such as Tbilisi, BSEC failed to usher in any serious regional political integration. Nevertheless, the initiative spoke volumes regarding Turkey's desire to engage with new foreign policy actors, beyond its traditional partners in the West, at the turn of the century. This, however, did not mean pivoting away from the West. Throughout this period, NATO, the USA, Europe and Israel remained Turkey's foreign policy bedrock. Although Ankara built close ties with new states, such as Azerbaijan and Georgia, these relationships were meant to complement its ties with the West.

Poignantly, therefore, Turkey worked in the 1990s with Baku and Tbilisi – but with Washington on board and supporting the Azerbaijan–Georgia–Turkey axis – to build the Baku–Tbilisi–Ceyhan (BTC) pipeline. This pipeline envisioned bringing Azeri oil through Georgia and into Turkey, from where it would be shipped into the global markets – all with US support and while bypassing Russia. More than anything, the BTC symbolises Turkish foreign policy in the 1990s: building new partnerships with traditionally non-Western actors, but working with the USA and the West.

Seeking greatness for Turkey – as a stand-alone power

Erdogan, becoming Turkey's prime minister in 2003, shared some of the budding thoughts at the time alongside a spectrum of nationalists, conservatives and political Islamists in Turkey: the unease felt towards the decreasing distance with the West as a foreign policy partner. He also shared, and this time with much wider constituencies, including business liberals and centrists, a desire to diversify Ankara's foreign policy relationships.

However, once in power, Erdogan eventually transcended these strains of thought, unfolding a rather revolutionary approach to international politics in the context of Turkish history, pivoting Ankara's attention away from the West.

Of course, before Erdogan, other Turkish leaders had turned Ankara's attention away from the West. Most notably, Ozal had engaged the Middle East countries in the 1980s, and Demirel had pivoted Ankara towards Central Asia and the Caucasus in the 1990s. Unlike the policies of Ozal and Demirel, however, Erdogan's vision for Turkey's foreign policy does not encompass Ankara as always being a loyal or obedient ally to the West. Erdogan sees foreign affairs through a balance-of-power lens, one that is often transactional.[4]

Before Erdogan took its reins, perceiving itself as a middle, and occasionally weak, power, Turkey believed it could secure safety in international affairs *only* by firmly siding with a superpower or a global bloc. Erdogan is not happy with Turkey's self-perceived middle-power, or weak, status. Recalling the memory of the powerful Ottoman Empire in Turkey, he wants to revive Turkey's greatness, and to this end, he is not afraid to shed the traditional Turkish policy of bringing the country into the Western-led security system for safety. Under Erdogan, Turkey no longer defines its national interest in tandem with the Western powers. Turkish national interest in Erdogan's thinking reflects a high degree of strategic autonomy.

He has therefore recast Turkey's ties with its neighbours and countries nearby, as well as with its traditional friends in the West, including the USA, NATO, Israel and Europe. He has appealed to his base through a scintillating promise to justify these changes in foreign policy. His goal: make Turkey a *stand-alone* power in the Middle East – and then globally, in the end reviving the country's Ottoman-era glory.

Erdogan believes that Turks will be respected around the world only if they build influence over Muslims. Accordingly, he does not mind distancing Turkey from the USA to boost his popularity, as he did with US President Donald J. Trump in the summer of 2018, during the 'Brunson Crisis' (explained in Chapter 13).

Erdogan also does not mind arguing with Ankara's traditional Western allies for more strategic reasons. This is especially the case when he concludes that these allies' policies challenge Ankara's interests, or that they hurt Muslims in the Middle East and globally. He wants to make sure that everyone respects Turks and Muslims, and that subsequently, through its protecting role over Muslims, Turkey is recognised as a global player.

Erdogan has also parted ways with a key tenet of Ataturk's foreign policy. Throughout the twentieth century, Turkish foreign policy was shaped by a mantra of the country's founder: 'Peace at Home, Peace in the World', a slogan that mandated non-intervention in the internal affairs of neighbours. There were exceptions to this policy, such as Turkey's 1974 military intervention in Cyprus, in which Ankara exercised its guarantor rights – as the Turks see it – but, by and large, the country's twentieth-century leaders avoided getting involved in their neighbours' conflicts.

However, Turkey's Muslim-majority neighbours and Muslims beyond Turkey's borders have a special place in Erdogan's vision: he believes that Turkey can become influential only if it gains influence over Muslim states near and far, so that *Muslims can be proud again under the leadership of Turkey – as a great power*.

Accordingly, Erdogan has sought to influence the affairs of Turkey's Muslim-majority neighbours, for instance by intervening in Syria's civil war, as well as by taking an active interest in the affairs of nearby Balkan states, to cite a few examples.[5] He has aimed to restore Turkey's Ottoman-era influence in the formerly Turkish-controlled Middle East, Balkans and beyond. These policies rest upon the idea that historical ties conditioned by shared geography form an immutable bond with neighbouring states and people – especially Muslims, constituting Turkey a sort of 'geocultural' capital, which Ankara can and should draw upon.

What every Turk wants: Osman's dream

In other ways, Erdogan's foreign policy is not so novel when compared to his predecessors. In fact, some of his key moves in the international arena are informed by the country's history, more specifically by generations of Turkish leaders and their quest to revive the country's great power status.

In the Turkish context, political Islam is just another reaction to the lost glory vis-à-vis Europe, not much different from Kemalism. However, Erdogan rejects the idea of bringing Turkey into the orbit of a great power while waiting for his country's greatness to return. In his vision, Ankara should deal with its traditional Western partners, such as the United States and Europe, while also seeking new partners, such as Russia and Iran. He has also pursued an aggressive economic and trade initiative with rising and otherwise important powers, such as Moscow and Beijing. Even though Ankara is still also anchored in NATO, in Erdogan's vision, Turkey ultimately stands on its own.

Animated by economic growth that he delivered in the first decade of the twenty-first century,[6] Erdogan is seeking greatness for Turkey, while also exploiting voters' interest in a more assertive role for Ankara in regional and world affairs. He is, furthermore, acting to secure Turkey's interests where other countries seem to stumble, such as in Syria, as he sees it.

As of 2019, Erdogan's policy has had mixed results. In the Middle East, he has failed to shape the outcome of events in Syria, where his opponent, the Assad regime, has overwhelmed Turkey-backed rebels, with support from Russia and Iran. He has also failed to shape the outcome of the conflict in Libya to Turkey's clear advantage. In addition, his pro-Muslim Brotherhood policy has put Ankara at odds with Egypt, Jordan, Saudi Arabia, the United Arab Emirates (UAE) and other countries, which see the Muslim Brotherhood (the Ikhwan in Arabic) as their greatest domestic threat.

Erdogan's support for Hamas, affiliated with the Muslim Brotherhood, continues to undermine Ankara's ties with Israel, as well as costing him dearly in the United States. Turkish–US ties are strained also due to a number of other issues, including policy differences over Syria. Finally, Erdogan's Middle East policy has also resulted in geopolitical troubles, putting Ankara at odds in Syria with Turkey's historic adversaries, Iran and Russia; the latter, of which, is increasingly coercing Turkish cooperation in Syria based on Putin's terms.

Accordingly, and ironically, Turkey has not only failed to earn star-power status in the region, but in 2019, Ankara is also left with no Middle Eastern friends – with the exception of Qatar.

Although Erdogan has had some success in building influence in Eurasia (especially across the Western Balkans and Black Sea Basin) and East Africa thanks to local dynamics in these regions (explained in Chapter 14 and 15, respectively), his policies have created a pattern of tension and mistrust across a number of regions, especially among policy elites. He has also compromised Turkey's position as a valued US and European ally. In Western capitals, he often invokes resentment for being a 'make-his-own-rules', and not always reliable, maverick in foreign policy.

However, Erdogan's political style is Janus-faced. He is both pragmatic and ideological in the way he approaches issues, including towards international affairs. Embracing his pragmatic side when he sees fit, Erdogan has proven himself capable of course correction in foreign policy. A case in point is Israel, where, after rupturing ties with Israel in 2010, he set out to re-establish them six years later (as explained in Chapters 6 and 12, respectively).

Nonetheless, because of domestic pressures – despite relatively strong economic growth until recently and his power consolidation notwithstanding, half of Turkey vehemently opposes him – Erdogan may find it tempting and simply easier to blame the West for Turkey's foreign policy (and even domestic) travails to avoid liability and maintain his popularity.[7]

Failed coup of 2016

The failed coup attempt of July 2016, a nefarious plot against democracy in Turkey, has enforced the latter trend. On a bustling Friday night in

Istanbul on 15 July 2016, a cabal of Turkish military officers attempted a coup d'état, which quickly collapsed amid poor planning and public resistance, resulting in almost 300 deaths. The attempt was among the most traumatic political events in Turkey since the fall of the Ottoman Empire. The bombing of the Turkish capital, Ankara, including the targeting of Parliament, terrified residents of the city and, in fact, the entire country. Ankara had not experienced a direct military attack in more than six hundred years, when the armies of Tamerlane defeated the Ottoman armies at the Battle of Ankara in 1402.

Although a clear and complete account of the coup is yet to be written, it appears that a group of officers in the Turkish Armed Forces, many reportedly aligned with the Gulen movement,[8] played a key role in the putsch effort. The coup plotters in the armed forces not only attacked the rest of the TAF, but also Turkey's democratically elected government.

Immediately following the coup attempt, much of the country rallied behind Erdogan. This is not because the opposition had suddenly decided that they liked their authoritarian leader, but rather because the citizenry and Erdogan chose to unite in their common trauma. At the very least, most opposition groups found the prospect of another military government an embarrassing one for Turkish democracy.

However, Erdogan has not used the coup to unify Turkey. In fact, the coup has ironically allowed Erdogan's grip on power to become tighter. Prior the coup, Erdogan had built a cult of personality as a kind of 'authoritarian underdog', portraying himself as a victim who is forced to crack down[9] on those conspiring to undermine his authority.

'Foreign enemies' and their 'domestic proxies'

The failed coup plot of 2016 actually gave this theory legs. Opposing Erdogan really does mean plotting a coup now. In the eyes of Erdogan and his supporters, conspiracies to overthrow him are more real than ever.

This is bad news for Turkey's democracy. Following the putsch attempt, Erdogan legitimately started to lock up alleged coup plotters, but also began prosecuting his opponents more vigorously. Erdogan's supporters, many of whom also blame Washington for the coup because its alleged plotter, Fethullah Gulen, is still residing in the United States, accept suppression – what its victims perceive as oppression – as the only way to legitimately prevent future coups. Meanwhile, Erdogan's opponents find it is increasingly difficult, if not impossible, to oppose him democratically.

Turkey's polarisation, driven by the narrative that Erdogan's foreign opponents are trying to oust him through coups supported by 'domestic proxies', fits neatly into Erdogan's claim that he is on a historic mission for Turkey and the Muslims.

The narrative, which has ample room for conspiratorial views, is as follows: Erdogan wants to make Turks great again as Muslims, but the West, which despises Muslims and does not want to see them flourish, tries to undercut him through insidious plots. His opposition, too, is deemed guilty under this narrative. In its efforts to stymie Turkey's rise, the West 'collaborates' with domestic Turkish proxies, that is to say Erdogan's opposition, which is responsible for helping the country's adversaries undermine Erdogan, but also Turks and Muslims.[10]

According to official documents issued by Turkey's prosecutors, the authorities in 2017 had investigated 11,985,000 out of Turkey's citizenry of 81 million people at the time – compared to 38,912 individuals investigated out of 68 million citizens in 2006.[11] Despite Erdogan's authoritarian grip, the unwillingness of half of Turkey's population, mostly constituting leftist-liberal-secularist groups and those disillusioned by Erdogan, to bow to his power has resulted in an even deeper political crisis.[12]

Erdogan's challenges

Today, in addition to a domestic crisis, Turkey also faces a hostile foreign policy environment – problems both of which are rooted in Erdogan's style of governance. More to the point, he has created huge risks and dependencies for Turkish foreign policy with relation to Ankara's historic enemy and natural competitor, respectively, namely Russia and Iran. The latter together have undermined his policies in Syria.

Russia, Turkey's historic arch-rival, has nearly geographically encircled it militarily after invading Crimea in 2014 and sending troops to

Syria in 2015. In 2019, Moscow has military bases as well as Anti-Access/Air Denial (A2D2) bubbles to Turkey's north in Crimea, east in Armenia and south in Latakia, Syria.

To make matters worse, at a time of increased encirclement by its historic adversary, Ankara cannot rely on the unconditional support of its traditional Western allies, such as NATO. Turkey is increasingly on its own in the global arena – for the first time since Ataturk's followers had Ankara join NATO.

2
RESTORING TURKS' DIGNITY – AS MUSLIMS

Ataturk, who was shaped by the sultans

Ataturk's followers, that is to say, Kemalists, often paint him as a semi-mythical revolutionary leader, who coined the idea of Turkey's Westernisation (he did not), and won battles against insurmountable odds to liberate the country at the end of the First World War (he did). The truth is that Ataturk was not a completely original thinker regarding statecraft. Many of his reforms to Westernise and secularise the country were rooted in the late Ottoman Empire, of which he is a product.

The Ottoman pivot towards the West that produced Ataturk grew out of a long period of soul-searching. The Ottomans, the dominant power in Europe until the sixteenth century, had stalled in the face of the emerging Christian powers by the late seventeenth century. The latter blocked Ottoman advance into Europe, dealing the sultans a crushing defeat at the gates of Vienna in 1683. This string of humiliating losses that started after Vienna prompted a process of Ottoman introspection.

Following nearly a century of soul-searching, the sultans decided to Westernise their state in an effort to catch up with the rising powers of Europe. In the late eighteenth century, Sultan Selim III (a contemporary of Napoleon I) gave initial life to these efforts by Westernising the Ottoman military, for example, by establishing European-style military academies. His successors in the nineteenth century continued to restructure the empire's bureaucracy, society, political and educational systems along European models. This gave way to progressive concepts such as: women's education; formal, legal equality for religious minorities; joining the European Concert of Nations; and establishing secular courts. Religious matters, already under state control, increasingly fell under a secular state of mind.

. . . in Ottoman 'New York City' . . .

These developments shaped the environment that produced the father of modern Turkey. Mustafa Kemal Ataturk was born in 1881 in Thessaloniki, called Salonika at the time of his birth, in what is now Greece. Thessaloniki was the cultural capital of the Ottoman Empire in the nineteenth century – an Ottoman New York City. In Thessaloniki, young Mustafa Kemal attended courses to learn French. The city's milieu exposed him to the current strains of European and French thinking at that time, including *laïcité*, which mandated freedom *from* religion in education, public policy and government affairs, as well as the philosophy of positivism. The latter, suggesting that all nations develop and progress linearly and that European nations had developed more than others, would later on shape Ataturk's pro-European reforms.

Young Mustafa Kemal attended European-style Ottoman military educational institutions at both high-school and university level in Bitola (then called Monastir) in today's Northern Macedonia and Istanbul, respectively, further exposing himself to Ottoman Westernisation at a young age. As a member of educational institutions on the cutting edge of Ottoman culture, Ataturk was a product of Ottoman Westernisation par excellence, not its creator.

. . . made Turkey completely secular

After he liberated Turkey, though, Ataturk took the sultans' quest for Westernisation to its logical extreme. This is where he deserves the credit which Kemalists give him. He pushed for revolutionary reforms to completely secularise Turkey. He abolished what remained of the Sharia in the Ottoman court system (there were already many secular courts), instituted a fully secular public education system (there were already secular schools, including Ataturk's own schools), and declared full legal equality between women and men (there was already a suffragist movement, led by Turkish novelist Halide Edip Adivar, among others).

In a break from the Ottoman approach (and this is where he deserves 'credit'), he banished religion to the private domain – although he kept state control over it, in line with the Ottoman tradition, but institutionalised this further through a newly established government department, today called the Diyanet.

Although Ataturk led a war of liberation against European powers, his views were not tarnished by anti-Western animus because he saw Turkey's place in Europe and the broader West. In foreign policy, he embraced the country's European identity even more openly than the Ottomans had done, pivoting it away from the Middle East. Shaped by his embrace of positivist thinking, Ataturk considered Europe the yardstick of 'contemporary civilisation'. At home, he employed state resources to mould the country in his own secularist image, and an education policy to raise pro-European youth. By the time Ataturk died in 1938, he had installed a strictly secularist political system. His Turkey was not democratic, and his follower, Inonu, too, pursued an authoritarian system of government.[1]

Turkey became a democracy only after the Second World War, at which time Inonu also pivoted to the United States. His turn to Washington meant paying greater heed to the loyal opposition in Ankara who had long been clamouring for more democratisation, arguing that Ataturk's vision of modern Turkey demanded it.

However, democracy was not quick to arrive in Turkey. In multiparty elections in July 1946, Ataturk's and Inonu's vehicle for power, and today's main opposition faction in the country, the Republican People's Party (CHP), managed to hold on to a large majority of seats in the legislature, due in part to vote-rigging by local CHP loyalists.[2] Nonetheless, in the 1950 elections, the party suffered a brutal rout, only holding on to 69 seats out of the legislature's total of 487.[3] The opposition Democrat Party came to power, and its leaders, Celal Bayar and Adnan Menderes, became the country's president and prime minister, respectively. From this point on, the debate regarding the role of religion in politics in Turkey would be between the CHP's brand of 'hard secularism', mandating absolutely *no* role for religion in government and public life, and the DP's and its successor centre-right parties' 'soft secularism', respecting secularism but allowing for *some* forms of public piety.

Representing the religion-friendly centre-right pillar of Turkish politics, Bayar and Menderes reversed some of the hard secularist reforms of their predecessors, such as reconverting the Muslim call for prayer (adhan) – traditionally chanted in Arabic, but chanted in Turkish starting in 1932 under Ataturk – into Arabic in 1950.

More importantly, the two leaders established religious Imam Hatip schools in 1951. Originally conceived as vocational schools to train Muslim religious leaders (imams) and preachers (hatips), these schools soon grew in number, evolving into publicly funded academic schools offering religious curriculum for students hailing from conservative families. Despite these changes, Ataturk's secularist system, perpetuated by generations of Turkish leaders that followed him, including Bayar and Menderes, who built a mausoleum-style tomb for Ataturk in downtown Ankara, Anitkabir, lasted until the rise of Erdogan.

Enter the guy from the other side of the tracks

Recep Tayyip Erdogan was born in 1954, less than a full generation after Ataturk's death and, symbolically, four years after the CHP's rout from power, in the gritty, working-class Istanbul neighbourhood of Kasimpasa. At the time of young Recep Tayyip's birth, Turkey was a poor, Third World country with a strongly secularist political culture and education system (with just over a dozen religious Imam Hatip schools, for instance, in the whole country, compared to hundreds of secular curriculum high schools, the latter offering no religious curriculum).[4]

Located in the heart of the city, Erdogan's neighbourhood of Kasimpasa sits at the bottom of a hill that ascends to Istanbul's bohemian Beyoglu district, and then to Nisantasi, the city's exclusive upper-crust, secularist and old-money enclave.

During Erdogan's childhood, Nisantasi was a refuge for the privileged few, Turkey's Kemalist elites, who would sip cocktails in high-end hotels and shop for expensive clothing on nearby leafy boulevards. The sights and sounds of Kasimpasa along the Golden Horn – a thin waterway that cleaves into the downtown European side of Istanbul – could not have been more different from Nisantasi, whose European and somewhat stuffy way of life has been memorialised in the oeuvre of Orhan Pamuk, Turkey's Nobel Prize laureate in Literature.

Erdogan vs Demirel

Erdogan grew up in a different environment than Pamuk, his contemporary who was born in 1952 in Nisantasi. Understanding Erdogan requires dissecting his upbringing in secularist Turkey as a pious man, the mistreatment he faced at the hands of the country's Westernised elites, and his subsequent rise to power by deploying – and, indeed, almost as the personification of – an ascendant movement: political Islam. Since he first entered national politics in the late 1980s, Erdogan cast himself as a 'poor pious man from the other side of the tracks', similar to Turkey's conservative leaders in the past, such as Suleyman Demirel. Erdogan's political identity has always been that he represents the voice of the common people, advocating their interests against the elites.

However, the reality is different. Like Erdogan, Demirel, too, was born to a poor and conservative (and rural Anatolian in his case) family, but the latter has a different political career. Demirel became an engineer and studied in the USA. His life story – where he took office seven times as prime minister between the 1960s and 1990s before becoming president in 1993 – epitomises Ataturk's success in providing upward mobility to poor and pious Anatolians. Demirel mostly perpetuated the Kemalist secularist system. Erdogan, who carries a chip on his shoulder against this system, decided to fight it, in the end bringing it down in all but in name.

Unlike Demirel, who embraced the centre-right brand of Turkish politics, promoting 'soft-secularism', Erdogan embraced political Islam aiming to suffuse society and politics with conservative Islam – at least as it is seen from the outside. Another key difference between the two leaders is that while Demirel hailed from a small village, Erdogan was born in Turkey's biggest city, an experience that he later used to build his unique political brand.

Dockyards of Istanbul

When Erdogan was born in Istanbul, his Kasimpasa neighbourhood was populated mostly by recent conservative arrivals to Turkey's biggest city from the Anatolian hinterland. Erdogan descends from a generation of Anatolian Turks, fleeing the grinding poverty of rural Turkey in an attempt to make a better life in Istanbul. His parents came to Kasimpasa as immigrants in the aftermath of the Second World War from Rize, a city along Turkey's far away eastern Black Sea Coast, near Soviet Georgia at the time.

Since its Ottoman past, when it was a popular area for sailors, Kasimpasa has been known for its culture of masculine bravado. To this day, the expression *Kasimpasali* ('of Kasimpasa' in Turkish) is used in Turkey to describe local street toughs who abide by a distinctive code of honour that values unapologetic bluntness. A *Kasimpasali* Turk will not shy away from humiliating his counterpart to undermine him: a characteristic Erdogan readily displays.

The Golden Horn, around which Kasimpasa is located, has been the hub of Turkey's industrial revolution since the late Ottoman sultans. By the time Erdogan was a child growing up along the Golden Horn, this inlet had become the most polluted area in Turkey. Open sewer and industrial waste flowed into the estuary. During the summer, the breeze from the Golden Horn would carry an overwhelming stench into the narrow alleyways of Kasimpasa. With every rainstorm, its rough cobblestone streets would fill with mud.

So much of Kasimpasa helps explain Erdogan. The experience of growing up in this rough-hewn, conservative area that was one of Istanbul's 'bad zip codes' would forever shape Erdogan's view of the 'other' – i.e. Turkey's elite, rich, Westernised communities and their secularist Kemalist ideology. Kasimpasa instilled in Erdogan an insight into the resentment towards elites, widely shared by many of Turkey's poor citizens. This dynamic would later become one of the main political engines of Erdogan's ascent, as well as putting 'Kasimpasa' in charge in Nisantasi and Istanbul – and then Ankara and all of Turkey.

'Bad' education

At the time of Erdogan's birth, though, Nisantasi and its citizens and values were in charge of Turkey. Ataturk and Inonu, whose family lived for decades in Macka, Nisantasi's sister neighbourhood in Istanbul, had together shaped a country, in which Erdogan grew up under their secularist principles and structures.

This legacy relegated religion to the private sphere, with the state strictly controlling it. Pious Muslims who wore religion on their sleeve did not feel welcome in the secularist Turkish society of the twentieth century. For those with strong attachments to their faith, like Erdogan's family, almost everything was an uphill battle.

For young Erdogan, for example, the secularist educational system served as a dramatic reminder of the barrier between religion and mainstream life. In 1965, when he was 11 years old, Recep Tayyip's pious father registered him as a student at Istanbul Imam Hatip School's middle school section. In Kemalist Turkey, the government could never completely quench the desire for religious education. Imam Hatip schools, established by Menderes and Bayar in 1951, gradually expanded in number, from 7 to over 400 by the middle of the 1970s, allowing students from conservative families, such as Erdogan's, to immerse themselves in religion.

At the time of Erdogan's upbringing, however, Turkey's secularist education system treated Imam Hatip schools as vocational schools, limiting their graduates to attend university only to study theology, where they could subsequently become imams or theologians. In a televised interview in 2012, Erdogan explained how he felt 'othered', along with his Imam Hatip peers, underlining how he was repeatedly told that his education would disqualify him from any profession other than washing the bodies of the dead, a task traditionally reserved for the clergy in Islam.[5]

Young Recep Tayyip had other plans, though. From an early age, he aspired to a life in politics, and he saw studying political science as the best preparation for this vocation. However, having an Imam Hatip diploma at the time would bar him from this academic path. In order to bypass this hurdle, he had to leave his school and friends and enroll in a public school with a secular curriculum in his final year of high school. This tactic undoubtedly left a scar of stigmatisation in young Erdogan's mind. Erdogan describes almost hiding his Imam Hatip pedigree because he could not use it in the outside world. As Erdogan once acknowledged accurately after going to an Imam Hatip in the 1970s, 'you could not easily attend university'.[6]

The 'Outlook' that changed Erdogan . . .

Young Erdogan's ambition to go into politics in the 1970s was rightly placed. Two decades later, in 1994, he became Istanbul's mayor, and nearly a decade after that, Turkey's prime minister, as head of the ruling AKP, which he established in 2001.

A self-declared moderate conservative movement, Erdogan's AKP grew out of the tree of political Islam in Turkey, namely the Welfare Party (RP), the original home of political Islam in the country in the 1980s and the 1990s. Turkey's constitutional court banned the RP on 16 January 1998 for violating the country's secularist constitution. On 17 December 1997, the RP cadres set up an alternative faction, the Virtue Party (FP), anticipating the ban against the RP, but Turkey's High Court banned the latter on the same grounds as the RP in June 2001. At this time, Erdogan broke away from the FP and established his AKP on 14 August 2001.

The FP and RP alike are rooted in the National Outlook (Milli Gorus), a nativist and anti-Western movement that emerged in the country during the 1970s. Erdogan was a subscriber to National Outlook and held membership of the RP and the FP later on. Espousing a message of nativism, social justice and grassroots organisation, National Outlook became Erdogan's intellectual home in the 1970s.

The debate that energised Turks during Erdogan's teenage and youth years was not, however, between secularism and political Islam. Rather, it was the Cold War contest between the communist left and nationalist right that provided the symbols, labels and language for political conflict in Turkey during those years.

It was then that Erdogan acquired his first taste for politics. His initiation into the tumult of student politics was a natural extension of his involvement in the religious Imam Hatip community. Erdogan and his conservative friends watched as Marxist left and ultra-nationalist right thrashed each other over their conflicting ideological visions, in a struggle that soon evolved into civil-war-like fighting on Turkey's streets in the 1970s. Erdogan and his friends found little to excite them in this contest or the fighting. The Marxist jargon of these leftist students was foreign and obscure. The ultra-nationalists, at least, claimed to stand for patriotic values and traditional morality. But, while many Imam Hatip youths were drawn into the ranks of these paramilitary gangs, the ultra-rights' relationship with political Islamists was a fraught one, and many pious youths felt they held little common ground with the nationalist paramilitaries who idolised the concept of 'Turkish race' over 'Islamic community'.

Amongst Erdogan's social circle, therefore, a different political message was gaining traction, that of National Outlook, which regards

Europe and the West as antithetical, and often adversarial, to Islamic polity. The growth of National Outlook in Turkey was in tandem with the rise of political Islam across Muslim-majority countries in the same period. Theorists like Sayyid Qutb in Egypt and Ali Shariati in Iran argued that the 'Muslim world' had taken a disastrous turn when it began to look to secular ideologies, whether nationalism or Marxism, for answers to society's most dire problems.

If the post-war decades had shown anything, it was that these ideologies had nothing to offer the Muslim nations but more of the same: poverty, political repression and cultural and political humiliation by the West. Returning to Islam – or rather, the version of Islam that this new movement's leaders were advocating – was the only way to lift the masses out of their misery.

Born in the Cold War milieu, the philosophy of National Outlook depicted the West (the 'Judeo-Christian world') as morally corrupt. National Outlook rejected leftist and rightist political movements as both being alien, contrasting the 'snake oil' of Western thought to the 'rich substance' of Islamic ideas. Snubbing capitalism and communism alike, National Outlook espoused a message of national sovereignty and denounced Turks who did not subscribe to this school of thought as 'proxies' for foreigners.

At times, National Outlook took a virulently anti-Semitic tone. The doyen of National Outlook, Necmettin Erbakan, also the founder and leader of the RP, through which Erdogan entered politics, argued:

> While the Turkish war of independence reversed their [Jews'] plans, the 1923 Treaty of Lausanne [which Ataturk signed with the Allies to end the war after he liberated Turkey] was introduced in order to create a state where the Turks would be alienated from their religion and all their institutions taken over by world Zionism. Thus, from that point onward, 'collaborators' in Turkey have tried to join the EU to remove Turkey from its own identity. Every force Turkey confronts – nay, every force in the world – is controlled by world Zionism and bent on the destruction of Turkey as a state, nation, and community.[7]

Turkey's salvation had to derive from the stock of traditions and ideas that had made the Turks great in past centuries – that is, from 'Islam', of course in the form that Erbakan understood it. Turkey could become a great power again, returning to its Ottoman glory, by breaking away from the West and the Jews, two adversaries who are constantly scheming to destabilise Turkey.

. . . and the poet who inspired him

While Erdogan followed Erbakan's lead in politics, his philosophical guru was Necip Fazil Kisakurek, an anti-Semitic Turkish poet and thinker, born in 1904 to an upper-class Istanbul family during the death throes of the Ottoman Empire. Kisakurek received his education from elite, Western-influenced schools of the empire and spent some time studying in France. Kisakurek, like Ataturk, was a product of Ottoman Westernisation. However, the two men evolved in opposite directions, with Ataturk strongly embracing the West and Kisakurek vehemently rejecting it, and then undermining Ataturk's legacy of Westernisation through his most famous disciple: Recep Tayyip Erdogan.

In the 1930s, while Ataturk was imposing his secularist reforms on Turkey, Kisakurek, a pro-Western thinker until that time, reacted against Kemalism, transmorphing politically. Kisakurek also had a strongly anti-secularist agenda, turning to the right, and choosing to adopt political Islam and anti-Semitism to refute Ataturk's legacy. During this period, Kisakurek published *The Protocols of the Elders of Zion* and Henry Ford's *The International Jew* and, with his commentary, 'praised both works effusively'.[8]

Throughout the rest of his career, Kisakurek promoted Islamic revolution, which, he argued, 'would enable the full reversal of Kemalism'. Adding that, 'When the state was guided by Islam, it would employ state institutions, law, and education as vehicles of revolution to create a new, pious youth.'[9] Kisakurek's prescription for Turkey was surprisingly 'Kemalist' in its methodology. Unwittingly inspired by Ataturk's top-down social engineering, Kisakurek suggested that not Kemalism, but political Islam should use state resources, education and government policy to shape the country's citizens in its image. Kisakurek also advocated for a strong presidential system, allowing the leader to shape the country in *their* own image.

This is exactly what Erdogan did. He won election after election, delivering strong economic growth and better economic governance than his predecessors had done, lifting many of his poor and conservative followers out of poverty, but also manipulating the kinds of political Islamist symbols Kisakurek had articulated – in the end, consolidating power in his hands.

After turning the tables on Turkey's Kemalist TAF, secular courts, media and businesses by using the Ergenekon–Sledgehammer court cases, referenda and politically charged tax fines and audits, respectively, to defang those actors, Erdogan took over the Turkish state, and then extended his reach over Turkish society. Following Kisakurek's recipe, he then went on to become an 'anti-Ataturk Ataturk'.[10] He dismantled Ataturk's system by using Ataturk's own means (state resources) and methods (top-down social engineering with education policy) to try to raise a 'pious generation' that shares *his* values – all on Kisakurek's advice.

Kisakurek is, without doubt, Erdogan's idol. In an interview in 2002, when asked which world figure had influenced and inspired him, his response was unequivocal: 'Necip Fazil Kisakurek [*sic*].'[11] In addition, in a speech he delivered as Turkey's prime minister years later, Erdogan told his audience how he 'had read [Kisakurek's] works, got to know him, and found the opportunity to walk in his footsteps'.[12]

The AKP comes to power

The AKP has been the primary vehicle for political change under Erdogan. A number of factors contributed to his party's dramatic rise to power in Turkey just a year after Erdogan established it in August 2001.

In fact, it took a perfect storm for the AKP to come to power in Turkey. Key among these was deep-rooted corruption within centre-right Turkish parties that preceded Erdogan's party. These conservative but secular-oriented factions had run Turkey, nearly uninterrupted, between 1950, when the DP came to power, and the AKP's rise in 2002. In the 1990s, corruption scandals and successive economic crises shook Turkey, tarnishing the image of the country's dominant centre-right forces, True Path Party (DYP) and Motherland Party (ANAP), both successors to the DP's legacy.

Moreover, between 2000 and 2001, Turkey suffered its worst economic crisis in modern history: the economy shrunk by nearly

10 per cent and unemployment jumped to an unprecedented 20 per cent. The electorate was ready for an alternative to the centre-right parties, which had ruled the country almost uninterrupted since 1950, now throwing it into economic ruin. At this time, Erdogan had branded his AKP as a 'conservative democratic' faction, similar to the centre-right parties, but also a 'clean party' – the AK Party's initials in Turkish 'ak' means 'white' in Turkish – in sharp contrast to the corrupt DYP and ANAP.

The AKP's political Islamist antecedent RP had won at most 21.4 per cent of the vote in the 1995 general elections. Erdogan split from the RP's similarly unsuccessful, immediate successor, the FP – it received only 15 per cent of the vote in Turkey's 1999 parliamentary elections – in 2001 when he established the AKP. The AKP was a massive success in the polls compared to its predecessors. Thanks to Erdogan's branding of it as a clean and centre-right force, coupled with his suggestion that it respected secularism, a plurality of Turkey's citizens at the time, many abandoning the DYP and ANAP, felt comfortable to swing to his AKP. Subsequently, the AKP received the most votes in the 2002 parliamentary elections, reaching 34.4 per cent of popular support.

Turkey's extensive 10 per cent national electoral threshold necessary for parties to enter Parliament further helped Erdogan at this stage. The threshold disqualifies parties that poll fewer than 10 per cent nationally from the legislature. This effectively barred a large number of parties from Parliament – almost 54 per cent of Turkish voters 'wasted' their vote by supporting minor parties. Key among them were the mainstream centre-right parties, DYP and ANAP, both stigmatised by corruption scandals in the 1990s, saw their popularity take a sharp nosedive in the lead-up to the elections. This was *the* perfect storm for Erdogan: the electoral system allocated most of the latter's' seats to the party winning most seats in the legislature: Erdogan's own AKP.

In a dramatic turn of events in November 2002, the AKP won a solid majority in the legislature (nearly two-thirds of the seats) with as little as just over a third of the popular vote. The gates of unchecked, and lopsided, legislative power had just opened for Erdogan, who became prime minister the following year. In due course, the Turkish leader would ensure that he would not lose this power, with grave ramifications for Turkey's democracy.

Ending 'Western subjugation'

Until Erdogan's rise, conservative Turks often felt like second-class political citizens in secularist Turkey. By mistreating pious citizens who wore religion on their sleeve, the Kemalist system, indeed, stripped many conservative Turks, who wanted to be pious in public, of their dignity. However, in this regard, the latter's distorted view of Kemalism has unfairly focused its resentment only towards Ataturk and his political system. Failing to note that Turkey's Westernisation and secularisation processes alike have roots stretching before Ataturk and to the Ottoman sultans, Kisakurek, Erdogan and many others, simply conclude that these two processes started with Ataturk, and ironically blame *only* him for their predicament.

Here, however, the liability falls on Kemalism. Revolutions need to portray themselves as representing a complete break with the past in order to justify their projects as the 'dawn of a bright new era'. Along these lines, Kemalism dismissed the Ottoman legacy of Westernisation and secularisation, suggesting instead that both processes actually started with Ataturk. Successive generations of Turkish pupils have been taught this false narrative, which has been internalised by conservatives and proponents of political Islam, together with their secularist counterparts.

Unsurprisingly, many conservative Turks today blame Ataturk and his Kemalist followers – as Erdogan often does – for Turkey's secularisation and Westernisation. Some of these conservatives also believe, wrongly, that after liberating Turkey from the Allied occupation at the end of the First World War, Ataturk's cohort of secular republican founders 'struck a deal' with the European powers, Westernising Turkey to keep them happy. The base concludes that the secularists subsequently subjugated Turkey under Western interests as a 'subaltern', ironically, in the words of Marxist and atheist Italian philosopher Antonio Gramsci.

To conservatives, Turkey lost its dignity during the transition from the Ottoman Empire to Ataturk's republic after the First World War. As a pro-Erdogan pundit stated recently, 'If your state has been overthrown and the new government has befriended those that destroyed your old government, then the creators of the new state are traitors, and your country is a colony.'[13] In the Erdoganists' view, the tradition of subjugating the people's will to the West continued under various secular parties that governed Turkey until the AKP and Erdogan took over eighty years later.

'Real children' of Turkey

Those who lived in Turkey during the 1970s, such as Erdogan and I, vividly remember the burning cars, violent rallies, assassinations and midnight gunfire of that decade as left- and right-wing militias battled each other on the streets.

Generations of conservative politicians in Turkey have drawn on these experiences to suggest that secular ideologies, divorced from Turkey's genuine roots, are bad for Turkey. Reflecting on those years in 2012, Erdogan described the 1970s as a time when 'symbols, slogans, and provocative actions eclipsed ideas'.[14] For them, the people who actually rolled up their sleeves to help the common man, the 'real children' of Turkey, had little concern with the fads of European political thought. It was the local boys, raised in the mosque, who were truly close to the people, and who had their best interests at heart.

Erdogan's musings on Turkey's secularist path, often rooted in Kisakurek's writings, reflect a tidy narrative that many conservatives view as common sense. The protagonists in this story are Turkey's Muslim communities. These ordinary folk, the 'real children' of Turkey, wanted nothing more than to lead a virtuous life, despite being constantly victimised by the Kemalist regime that denigrated them simply because they refused to turn their backs on Islam.

These heroes were brought to television screens across the country in 2016 under Erdogan, when Turkey's state broadcaster began airing a historical soap opera of the National Turkish Student Union (MTTB), a conservative pro-National Outlook political organisation, to which Erdogan belonged during the 1970s. The series opens with a flashback: the star, a handsome young leader of MTTB, painfully remembers how a military officer murdered his father in cold blood because he protested against the ban of the Arabic call to prayer. In the next scene, the left is portrayed when the hero finds himself protecting a group of young boys on their way to a circumcision festival – a traditional rite of passage for Muslim boys – against a band of leftist radicals who are torching the car of an American diplomat. The impressionable leftist youngsters in the show do not realise it, but they are acting on behalf of a dirty game of Western intrigue.

More than just prime-time entertainment, this characterisation of the left as a tool of international intrigue has been commonplace among political Islamists for decades. A key thread of political Islamist thought in Turkey concerns conspiracy theories that the West and the USA are tirelessly working to undermine good Muslims. 'For years, the West has been planning another military coup,' one of Erdogan's fellow politicians in the RP, Sevki Yilmaz, said at a political gathering back in 1991, a time of Erdogan's initial ascent in the RP. 'But, the CIA, the American agents, in these past years they have been unable to find the right conditions to carry it out.' The reason, according to Yilmaz, is that Muslim youth have thwarted the nefarious West. 'The seeds that were laid . . . have given fruit and now Imam-Hatip students are in the universities,' which was music to Erdogan's ears.[15]

Since good Muslims, alert to the sinister intent of foreign ideas, now make up a sizable chunk of the student population, added Yilmaz, 'anarchy has been prevented from entering the universities'. Islam has fortified Turkey against the West's tireless attempts to sow discord in the country and 'the West is disturbed by this!'

Jews are assigned a special and especially noxious role in this narrative as a group, which works with the West to undermine Turkey. Kisakurek scandalously even blamed them for the collapse of the Ottoman Empire, adding that, 'when the empire collapsed, the Jews orchestrated the "fake" liberation of Turkey from the Western powers on the condition that the nation and state be separated from Islam'.[16]

Echoes of Kisakurek's polemics resonate throughout the narratives deployed by Erdogan and his allies today. The axiomatic assumption that the West, the USA, the Jews and the latter's 'lobbies' (e.g. 'interest lobby', a term Erdogan uses) and cabals (i.e. 'mastermind', a term pro-Erdogan media uses to suggest the existence of a 'collective higher intellect') are scheming to destabilise Turkey and undermine its 'real' children appears frequently in speeches and rhetoric of today's AKP leaders and opinion-makers.[17]

Proud to see Islam in charge again

Erdogan has revolutionised Turkish politics since 2003, flooding the country's political and educational systems with conservative Islam. For conservative and pious Turks, he represents the end of the subjugation of the people's will in Turkey. The base loves him because they believe that he has restored their dignity through his embrace of Islam. Similarly, the base finds Erdogan's foreign policy rewarding and appealing. His pro-Ottoman slant in foreign policy (explained in the next chapter) offers to his supporters 'the semiotic allure of glory, power, and victory – a social identity that confers integrity, respect, and self-esteem', while dispelling 'the feelings of inferiority and marginalisation that animate a pervasive siege mentality, and validates Turkey's place in global politics'.[18]

Erdogan's ambition to make Turkey a great Muslim power also informs his decision to introduce religion into Turkey's domestic politics and foreign policy.[19] This judgement, together with strong economic growth into 2018, explains why Erdogan is wildly popular with his conservative base: his supporters love him because he has lifted them out of poverty, but also because they believe that he has restored their dignity – after eighty years of Kemalism.

The base loves Erdogan not only because he has helped Kasimpasa push back Nisantasi, but also because he has allowed Islam to be embraced by the government again, ending what the base sees as Turkey's subaltern-style relationship with the West. Erdogan has already made his supporters proud to be Muslims again.

3
'STRATEGIC DEPTH'

The 'perfidious West'

The legacy of the Ottoman Empire, including its painfully lengthy collapse throughout the nineteenth and early twentieth centuries, sheds light on contemporary Turkey's emotionally charged, and often conspiratorial, view of its relationship with Europe, and the West, a dynamic which Erdogan has taken advantage of in order to recalibrate Ankara's foreign policy.

Throughout the nineteenth century, rising nationalist movements among Greeks, Serbians, Bulgarians and other Ottoman subject-nations challenged the integrity of the multiethnic and religiously diverse empire. At this time, London's ambition was to prevent Moscow from accessing the warm waters of the Mediterranean through the Bosporus. Therefore, British policy overall helped preserve core territories of the Ottoman state, thus keeping Istanbul's status quo intact.

This did not mean, however, that the Ottoman Empire was safeguarded, or that London was keen on sustaining the former's complete territorial dominion. As the empire weakened, Britain seized chunks from the periphery of the dying Ottoman state, and did not mind if other European powers joined in – with British acquiescence, of course. Territorially, France emerged as the main beneficiary of this policy, seizing Algeria and Tunisia in North-West Africa during the nineteenth century. In 1878, Britain took Cyprus, which guards the entrance to the Suez Canal, leading to India. Furthermore, London wrestled for control of Ottoman possessions and vassal territories along the Persian Gulf and in southern Arabia, from Aden to Kuwait and the Trucial States (today's United Arab Emirates, the UAE) – again guarding the approaches to India.

Russia, acting on its own accord and distant enough to evade Britain's reach in the 1860s, subjugated the Ottoman northern Caucasus, after nearly half a century of wars against local Circassians and other Muslims there. The long and bloody Russian campaigns to subdue this region often ended with mass killings of Muslims and mass expulsion of nearly entire indigenous communities, such as the Circassians, from this region – policies which have left an enduring legacy of hostility towards Russia among the Balkars, Chechens, Circassians, Daghestanis, Karachays, Ingushes, and other northern Caucasus Muslim nations and their diasporas, mainly located in Turkey today.

The race for Ottoman territory often took an opportunist path, with European powers allying with Ottoman subject-nations against Istanbul, for example by supporting Greek and Serbian independence. European powers also competed for influence in post-Ottoman nations to maximise their leverage. After a portion of Greece gained independence from the sultans in 1821 with European support, for instance, it fell under the rule of three political parties, referred to as the 'Russian', 'British' and 'French' parties.

European powers employed a divide-and-conquer strategy in order to establish zones of influence within the collapsing empire. To rub salt into the wounds in a nineteenth-century version of the 'clash of civilisations', the former invariably sided with Christians in intra-Ottoman conflicts. For instance, Russia supported Bulgarian Christians against Bulgarian and Turkish Muslims in the south-eastern Balkans (large parts of Bulgaria were Muslim-majority in the nineteenth century); and Paris became a patron of the Maronites in Mount Lebanon against the Druze and Sunni Muslims in the region.

Through their policies, European nations also helped provide protection and autonomy for persecuted groups in the empire. Even then, these efforts had an overtly pro-Christian flavour, such as when European powers forced Sultan Abdulhamid II to appoint a Christian head of the newly autonomous government in Crete, a Muslim–Christian mixed island in the nineteenth century.

Overall, these policies accelerated the dismemberment of the empire. In due course, European intervention – which appeared to support *only* Christians against Muslims – led Turks and other Muslims in the empire to negatively and undeservedly label Christianity an 'alien faith', and a 'proxy of the West'. To this day, the footprint persists in Turkey, with grave ramifications for Turkish Christians and Christian missionaries in the country, including American Pastor Andrew Brunson, who was jailed for two years between 2016 and 2018 for 'spreading Christianity', among other charges, an incident that sparked off a major crisis between Erdogan and US President Trump.

The collapse of the Ottoman Empire did not end European power politics in the former Ottoman realms. Divide-and-conquer strategy shaped the Europeans' policies regarding former Ottoman lands now under their control. In British-ruled Cyprus, for instance, London employed Cypriot Turks disproportionately in security services on the island, to the consternation of Cypriot Greeks, who formed the demographic majority on the island. Thus, not only in Turkey, but also across former Ottoman lands and cities, from Athens to Basra, casting Europe and the West (to which the USA was added in the twentieth century) as 'perfidious' and 'only self-serving' became key components of both popular and elite *weltanschauung* during the collapse of the Ottoman Empire – and the years thereafter.

In Ataturk's republic, generations of pupils in schools were taught about how European powers tried to divide and conquer the Ottoman Empire – especially following the First World War, when the Allies signed the Treaty of Sèvres in 1920, dividing up Turkey among themselves, with the help of Armenian, Greek and Kurdish proxy states and entities. Ataturk successfully defeated the Allies, signing the Lausanne Peace Treaty in 1923 with them, ending the war and the Allied occupation of Turkey. This new treaty also abrogated the Treaty of Sèvres. Subsequently, the Treaty of Lausanne officially recognised the Republic of Turkey, and to this day, it is honoured as the country's founding document. A key square in Izmir, Turkey's third largest city, is aptly named Lozan (Lausanne) Square, recognising the role of this treaty in giving birth to modern Turkey.

The 'Sèvres Syndrome'

However, the defunct Treaty of Sèvres ironically became more notorious than its successor, the effective Treaty of Lausanne, despite the fact that Lausanne negated Sèvres. This is because the legacy of European machinations against the Ottoman Empire is actively amplified in Turkey's educational curriculum and political culture. The result is the 'Sèvres Syndrome', a viewpoint shared by many Turks that, despite what their leaders say, European nations and the West are ultimately out to divide Turkey through proxies, in the fashion of nineteenth- and early-twentiet- century European great power politics.

The United States did not play a key role in the collapse of the Ottoman Empire. Washington and Istanbul never formally declared war on each other in the First World War. However, in 1918, President Woodrow Wilson issued his Fourteen Points, in which, among other things, he called for the 'autonomous development and self-determination' of non-Turkish nations under the Ottoman Empire. At this stage, Kurds were the only sizable nation under Turkish rule, together with dwindling Greek and Armenian communities. Through the lens of the Sèvres Syndrome, Washington is often lumped in with Europe in Turkey under the rubric of the West. America's perceived role in this fiction is to divide Turkey – and attempt do so through the Kurds. The precise charge against Pastor Brunson in the 2018 case, for instance, was that he attempted to 'convert the Kurds in Turkey to Christianity to divide Turkey'.[1]

European foreign policy *leitmotifs* changed in the aftermath of the Second World War, and even more so towards the end of the twentieth century, when many European states adopted issues such as gender equality, trade promotion, environmental protection and human rights as their self-declared foreign policy objectives. The USA entered the global arena in the aftermath of the Second World War, with its self-proclaimed image as a country that promotes democratic values. Regardless of these changes, in the former Ottoman lands, which witnessed European power politics machinations first-hand during the long, bloody and painful collapse of the Ottoman Empire, the view of the 'perfidious West' has become entrenched as a key part of foreign policy perceptions among almost all segments of the population.

Enter 'Strategic Depth'

This salient view has provided an entrée for Erdogan's revolutionary foreign policy in Ankara, the basis of which is Turkey refusing to give into Western importuning.

In the first decade of the 21st century, while Turkey remained a member of NATO and gave high priority to EU accession, Erdogan started to signal the birth of a new wave of thinking in Ankara in terms of foreign policy patterns. Following the end of the Cold War, Turkish foreign policy elites had already begun envisioning a more robust role for Ankara in international affairs. Taking cues from this thinking since 2003, Erdogan has gradually parted ways with Ataturk's West-centric and inward-looking foreign policy model, instead embracing an activist and neo-imperialist foreign policy. Dubbed 'Strategic Depth' by Erdogan's advisor, and later foreign minister and prime minister, Ahmet Davutoglu, this policy sought to restore Turkey's Ottoman-era reach in the Middle East, Balkans and beyond – under the guise of good neighbourly relations.

No person deserves more credit for this vision than Davutoglu, who entered politics as an AKP advisor soon after Erdogan came to power. Previously a professor at the International Islamic University in Malaysia, Davutoglu argues that Turkey has multiple regional identities that cannot be reduced to a single unified character. He therefore advocates a multifaceted foreign policy to complement Turkey's various identities.[2] Davutoglu believes that Ankara made a mistake by turning its back for decades on Arab and Muslim-majority countries, therefore arguing that it was about time to revitalise Turkey's geostrategic potential by strengthening contacts with these countries.[3] He adds that the country can remain powerful and rise as a nation only if it utilises the 'Strategic Depth' of its neighbourhoods, for instance by developing better ties with those Muslim neighbours with whom it 'shares cultural affinity'.

The world, for him, is composed of 'geostrategic zones' – literally translated as 'basins' (havza) from Turkish. He classifies three geostrategic zones from which Turkey can derive advantage: the nearby land zones (the Balkans, Middle East and Caucasus); the nearby sea zones (the Black Sea, Adriatic, East Mediterranean, Red Sea, Gulf and Caspian Sea); and the nearby continental zones (Europe, North Africa, South Asia and Central and East Asia). Davutoglu asserts that Turkey needs to gradually expand its regional areas of influence in these zones in order to strengthen its global standing.[4]

Turkey's primary orientation should be towards the near land zones that surround it. He writes, 'Turkey, by means of its geographic location and cultural heritage, is an inseparable part of this near [land] zone . . .

Turkey's political, economic, and cultural weight internationally will . . .
depend on its activity and performance in this zone.'[5]

Davutoglu and Erdogan believed that Turkey in the twenty-first
century was strong enough to conduct multiaxial diplomacy, working
with different actors and poles in international politics, rather than being
bound by a primary to the (Western) axis. Davutoglu, therefore, does
not necessarily envision Turkey as completely abandoning the West.
Rather, he claims that Ankara's traditionally close ties with the West,
such as those with Israel, prevented Ankara from gaining the strategic
depth it could otherwise possess through good relations with its
Muslim-majority neighbours in the near land zone.[6] This was a rather
unconventional view in Turkey, considering that Ankara was the first
Muslim-majority capital to recognise Israel in 1949.

'Strategic Depth' implied a long-term vision, but Davutoglu's other
principle, dubbed the 'Zero Problems with Neighbours', created
immediate traction in Ankara. Taking cues from Turkey's foreign policy
thinkers in the 1990s, such as former Foreign Minister Ismail Cem who
improved ties with Athens, Davutoglu explains that in order to become
a great power, it is essential for Turkey to have good ties with all of
its neighbours. This means having good ties with not only Muslim-
majority neighbours such as Iran and Syria,[7] but also with Christian-
majority neighbours such as Bulgaria, as well as Armenia and Greece.

Accordingly, in the first decade of the twenty-first century, Erdogan
enhanced Turkey's ties with its Muslim-majority neighbours, especially
with Syria and Iran. Ankara tried to unify Cyprus, and attempted a
rapprochement with Armenia – both of which (explained in Chapter 12)
regrettably failed.

And its founding father: Davutoglu

Ahmet Davutoglu started his academic career as a professor of
International Relations in the 1990s in Istanbul after receiving his PhD in
Political Science and International Relations from Istanbul's prestigious
and liberal Bogazici University, with a thesis titled, 'Alternative
Paradigms', in which he compared Western and Islamic political
theories.[8] By 2005, when I met him for the first time, he had worked his
way to becoming an influential, yet still relatively unknown, advisor to

then Turkish Foreign Minister Abdullah Gul. Davutoglu soon rocketed up the AKP ranks to become Erdogan's chief foreign policy advisor, where he finally had a chance to apply his twin principles, 'Strategic Depth' and 'Zero Problems with Neighbours'.

Of course, Davutoglu did not invent the idea that Ankara would benefit from having good ties with is neighbours, or that it should deepen its links with neighbourhoods beyond the West. In addition to Cem's Greece opening, the country's diplomats and politicians in the 1990s, such as Demirel, built good ties with Central Asian and Black Sea nations.

In fact, just as the roots of Germany's recent pivot to Russia and Eastern Europe lie in the *Ostpolitik* (German for 'eastern policy') concept of its Cold War-era and leftist prime minister, Willy Brandt, the deeper roots of Turkey's own 'Eastern' pivot under Davutoglu can be found in the thinking of the country's own Cold War-era and leftist prime minister, Bulent Ecevit. In the 1970s, Ecevit promoted the idea of 'region-centric foreign policy', suggesting that Ankara would be better off diversifying its ties beyond the West, building links with Soviet Russia as well as with states in the Balkans and the Middle East.

But, there is also a revolutionary aspect to Davutoglu's thinking. When I met him in his modest office in a Kemalist-era government building in downtown Ankara, he struck me as a scholar with a deep knowledge of Ottoman history and a strong desire to transform Turkey into a regional, and then a global, powerhouse. However, if handed power, it seemed, Davutoglu would turn Turkey's traditional Western-oriented policy upside down. He did not appear content with simply diversifying Turkey's foreign policy partners. Rather, he wanted to prioritise Ankara's foreign objectives in the Middle East at the expense of its ties with the country's traditional Western partners, such as the USA. He even appeared ready to break rank with these partners. Eventually, as advisor to Erdogan and then as foreign minister, he did exactly that, rupturing ties with Israel in 2010, and breaking with the USA in Syria after 2013.

'Go East'

During our meeting, Davutoglu and I discussed a variety of foreign policy issues, including the role of Islam in Turkish politics, the legacy of

Ottoman rule and the responsibility this legacy entailed for Muslims previously under its rule. I recalled my scholarly work in the 1990s, when I had organised international academic conferences at Bilkent University in Ankara, trying to shed light on the suffering of the Bosnians during crimes committed against them in the Yugoslav Wars during 1991–5. Davutoglu, for his part, emphasised the Middle East, suggesting that Turkey had a responsibility to cooperate actively with the Muslim states in the area.

Of course, Davutoglu did not invent this trend in Turkish foreign policy-makers taking an active interest in the Middle East. In the 1980s, Prime Minister and later President Ozal pivoted to the Middle East, seeking business opportunities. And during the 'Oil Crisis' of the 1970s, the country's leaders reached out to Arab states in the Middle East, hoping to secure oil purchases from them at lower prices. Notably Necmettin Erbakan, deputy prime minister between 1974 and 1975, and Chair of National Salvation Party (MSP), a political Islamist faction that would be shut down by the generals following the 1980 coup, only to be recreated as the RP by Erbakan, aimed to pivot Ankara towards Arab-majority nations in the Middle East.

Among other goals, Erbakan hoped his pivot would secure cheap oil, stymieing the crisis of the Turkish economy in the 1970s, itself driven in large by the rising cost of energy imports at the time. That strategy did not help: the Arab states had no oil available at special prices for Turks or favours to make for their political Islamist leaders – a lesson that Erdogan would learn the hard way, three decades later. The energy crisis, among other problems, contributed to Turkey's economic collapse in the late 1970s, ushering in political stalemate and civil unrest, with fighting on the streets, ending with the 1980 coup.

Turkish governments also flirted with Arab states in the Middle East in the 1960s and 1970s to get them to adopt a more favourable stance at the UN and within the Non-Aligned Movement (NAM) towards Ankara's position in the Cyprus conflict. That opening, too, failed, with many of Turkey's Arab and Muslim-majority neighbours siding with the Cypriot Greek-controlled Republic of Cyprus, a NAM member. Even if Turkey's various Middle East openings often failed to deliver concrete benefits for Ankara, the fact is that despite official Kemalist policy of turning Ankara's back on the Middle East, in reality the country never completely severed itself off from the region. Even Ataturk, with all his

Eurocentrism but perhaps also because of it, could not ignore the Middle East next door. He most famously hosted Reza Shah Pahlavi of Iran, a Westernising leader and a fellow Turkophone, in Ankara in 1934. In addition, in 1937, Ataturk signed the Treaty of Saadabad, a pact of non-aggression with Iran, Iraq and Afghanistan.

'Samuel Huntington was right'

Just as he did not invent Turkey's pivot to the Middle East, Davutoglu also did not invent 'Ottomanism' in foreign policy. In fact, he is not the first Turkish politician to use the term. Ozal popularised this concept when he reached out to the Middle East, taking stock of Turkey's newfound economic prosperity during his term, to spread Ankara's influence. However, US-based Turkish scholar, Hakan Yavuz, argues that:

> [Ozal's] understanding of Ottomanism was simultaneously multicultural, pro-European, and Islamic. In *Turkey in Europe and Europe in Turkey* (1991), he sought to prove that Turkey belongs to Europe by way of the Ottoman legacy, rejecting American political scientist Samuel P. Huntington's conclusion in 'The Clash of Civilizations' that the Islamic world and the West are mutually exclusive and therefore engaged in inevitable conflict.[9]

Unlike Ozal's Ottomanism, Davutoglu's seems to believe in competition between civilisations. Here, Yavuz contends that Davutoglu's Ottomanism:

> pits East against the West. It places Islam at the core of the Ottoman identity, civilization, and polity ... It ... embraces a sense of responsibility toward Muslims of former Ottoman territories, especially toward the Palestinians. And it embraces Muslim hegemony and geopolitical power.[10]

According to Yavuz, this thinking 'has policy implications both at home and abroad. It is supposed to follow that Turkey has a right, if not a duty, to defend the rights of Muslims in former Ottoman territories.' Yavuz adds:

'It was Erdoğan [sic] who supported the independence of Albanian Muslims in the Republic of Kosovo, telling a cheering crowd in the capital of Priština that 'Turkey is Kosovo and Kosovo is Turkey.' His language is similar when it comes to the Palestinians: they, too, are claimed as Ottoman Muslims . . .' who need to be protected by Ankara.[11]

At my meeting with him, Davutoglu confirmed these conclusions, telling me that Turkey could become a great power only by reaching out to these Muslims in the former Ottoman lands, as well as by building bridges with other Muslims across the world, from those in South-East Asia to others in sub-Saharan Africa. Davutoglu, it dawned on me, was an Ottoman revivalist and Muslim nationalist, keen on eliminating Ataturk's legacy in Turkish foreign policy.

Caricaturing the Ottomans

Turkey's first president, Ataturk, had a mantra: 'Go West.' He and his successors, the Kemalists, wanted to turn Turkey into a European country, thinking that doing so would make it a great nation. To accomplish this goal, they needed to redefine the whole of Turkish civilisation – to jettison the Ottoman legacy in the Middle East and disavow the country's Muslim heritage. In its place, Turkey would embrace a new, secular national identity and an inward-looking foreign policy, rooted in 'non-interference' – that is, avoiding intimate ties with Middle Eastern states, especially Arab nations. They hoped that if Turkey faced the West exclusively, Europe would one day fully embrace their country.

Revolutions are often shaped by the legacy of systems they overthrow, even when they claim to be pure and to possess new ideological origins. Therefore, the Kemalists were not completely pure and wholesome in their embrace of the West. Ottoman greatness did inform their thinking throughout the twentieth century. Most notably, in 1953, Turkey's Kemalist leaders at the time organised massive public ceremonies, celebrating Istanbul's Islamic 'conquest' from the Christian Byzantines. At the same time, however, Kemalists genuinely embraced Turkey's Western vocation, as did Inonu in 1946 by pivoting Ankara to Washington, Menderes in 1952 by taking Turkey into NATO, and Ozal in 1987 by submitting Ankara's application to join the European Community (the parent of today's EU), and with both Ciller and Demirel in the 1990s by signing Free Trade Agreements and deepening ties with Israel.

Davutoglu is no Kemalist. When we met, he was a loyal member of the AKP, the backbone of political Islam in Turkey. The AKP leaders have often objected to Kemalism's top-down modernisation project and pro-Western stance.[12] However, the relationship between Kemalism and political Islamism in Turkey is not always antithetical. For instance, often characterised as authoritarian in nature, Kemalism has, in fact, carried out the modernisation that allowed Turkey to build democratic institutions.[13] Accordingly, growing within a democratic polity has differentiated AKP and Turkish political Islamists from other political Islamists in the Middle East. For example, Turkish political Islamists reject violence: in 1970s Turkey, most notably, these individuals eschewed violence, while left- and right-wing militias combatted one another with guns on the streets.

In addition, other political Islamist movements in the Middle East have to look deep into the annals of history for models of Islamic governments in their territories. As a result, they often pursue visions of austerity and obduracy. For instance, Saudi-backed Salafist movements harken back to the early seventh century, the period of Islam's birth, in their medieval values and goals. In Turkey, however, political Islamists need only look back to pre-Ataturk times, in other words, to the late-nineteenth- and early-twentieth-century Ottoman Empire. At home, this means idealising, but also, often unknowingly, distorting the legacy of the late Ottoman Empire.

Ironically, the roots of such idealisation extend back to Turkey's Kemalist past. In other words, Ataturk and his cohort are to blame for modern Turkey's and Erdogan's incorrect historical readings of the Ottoman Empire and legacy. In order to justify themselves, revolutions often portray the political systems they overthrow as useless, and so, in his revolution, Ataturk cast the Ottomans in an entirely different light. Ataturk and the Kemalist elites depicted the Westernising Ottomans incorrectly as religious fanatics, who were obsessed with Islam and who subsequently and consequently failed – this wrong interpretation, nonetheless, trickled down the echelons of Turkish society.

The Kemalists so negatively caricatured the Ottomans that the empire was almost a Turkish version of a Salafist state, a pre-modern version of Saudi Arabia. Kemalism, they argued, was all about progressive secularism, adding that it would enlighten Turkey. Between the 1920s and the rise of Erdogan's AKP's in 2002, for nearly eighty years, Turkey became one of the most secularly ideological Muslim-majority states, and such falsified ideas about the Ottomans were taught to generations of pupils and citizens, including Erdogan, who have internalised them. To justify their own foreign policy, the Kemalists had painted Ottoman foreign affairs as a complete failure. In its crudest form, Kemalist historiography caricatures Ottoman history to such an extent that Turkish school textbooks 'explain' the decline of the Ottoman Empire, suggesting this happened because many late sultans were 'crazy'.[14]

Counter-revolutions aim to rewind the political order back to the past, and this is what Erdogan, who has radically revised the legacy of Ataturk, is doing in Turkey. Now, Erdogan says, Turkey would be better off going back to its pre-Ataturk settings (except for the occupation by the Allies, of course!). Having internalised the teachings of Kemalism, Erdogan envisions the late Ottomans incorrectly as singularly pious and conservative Muslims, who led lives completely enmeshing religion with politics. Erdogan did not learn about late-Ottoman sultans who drank alcohol, partied, played classical music, travelled to Europe, danced with European empresses, listened to operas and even promoted reform. In other words, royals not much different from other European monarchs of their time. Instead, he inaccurately learned of sultans who were 'pious', 'fervent with Islam', 'crazy' and 'backward'.

Therefore, it is unsurprising that Erdogan's counter-revolution focuses on making Islam the centrepiece of Turkish politics, both domestically and in foreign policy. This is how Erdogan will bring to Turkey what he thinks the Ottomans had represented. The irony is that while trying to revive the pre-Ataturk Ottoman Empire, Erdogan is actually trying to revive the caricatured version of the Ottomans.

Europe's Muslim monarchs

The Ottoman Empire was a sophisticated, and nuanced, civilisation. Each example of the Ottomans as atavistic champions of Islam can be matched with multiple counterpoints of Ottoman pragmatism, such as

European identity in world politics and secular thinking. Ottoman rulers were Muslims, but overall, they were not singularly preoccupied with Islam, either in foreign policy or at home. From its inception, the empire saw itself as a European power. The Ottomans gained their first European territory only fifty-two years after the inception of their dynasty, and upon capturing Constantinople from the Byzantines in 1453, Mehmet II proudly added to his suite of titles that of 'Caesar of Rome', endowing himself with the prestige of the Roman and Byzantine Caesars who had come before him in Istanbul.

In the next century, Sultan Suleyman I (The Magnificent), who is usually considered the greatest among the thrity-six Ottoman sultans, envisioned himself as the Holy Roman Emperor, and competed against Christian European dynasties for the designation.[15] Geopolitically, the Ottomans were an integral part of the European system of politics, playing deftly on the European chessboard. Beginning with a pact between Suleyman I of the Ottomans and Francis I of the House of Valois, the Ottomans often allied with France to balance against the power of the Hapsburgs in Spain and Austria.

Similarly, with exceptions, farsighted political leaders in the Ottoman government knew that prosperity lay not with rigid adherence to an imagined past, but by looking outward and toward the future. That is why, in the midst of the decline of the Empire, the sultans and caliphs embarked on a programme of intense reforms to remake the Ottoman Empire in the Western image to match up with the European powers. To this end, the caliphs of Islam – ironic as it sounds – established institutions of secular education, subsequently paving the way for women's emancipation by enrolling them in those schools. The sultan-caliphs also ran secular courts and Western-style military schools by the nineteenth century. Young Mustafa Kemal was once a cadet in these Ottoman schools that took religion out of education.

The irony for political Islamists, who today embrace the Ottomans as paragons of 'virtuous, conservative, and Islamic lifestyle' is that by the time the Ottoman Empire was ending, the sultan-caliphs embodied Western life and values for Ottoman Muslims from Sarajevo to Sana'a. For instance, the last Ottoman caliph, Abdulmecid Efendi, whom Ataturk exiled in 1924, after abolishing the monarchy and the caliphate, was an established painter, known for his nudes. Today, Abdulmecid Efendi's paintings sell for about $1 million at auctions.[16]

Problem pivot

The sultans' vision was to keep their state a Muslim and European power, even as their power greatly waned in the nineteenth century. Missing these facts, Erdogan (and Davutoglu) subscribe to the opposite of the (distorted) version of Ottoman Empire foreign policy, taught to them by Kemalists.

Rejecting a revolution built on the denunciation of the purported religiosity of the Ottomans, Erdogan, with guidance from Davutoglu, launched a foreign policy counter-revolution after coming to power that has cast Kemalism as the destroyer of the Ottoman Empire's identity as a benevolent Islamic empire. In short, Erdogan has embraced the straw man and has dedicated himself to the task of making that straw man real.

Insisting on Islam as the centrepiece of Turkish politics, he identifies the country's foreign policy role with Muslim causes. This, Erdogan thinks, is how he will bring the Ottoman glory days back, and how he will make Turkey a great power again. Accordingly, he has assigned a central role to Islam in Turkish foreign policy, blending it with his domestic emphasis on political Islam and Turkish nationalism. The product has been an ahistorical, political Islam-oriented, and often patronising, foreign policy concoction, an outgrowth of Davutoglu's 'Strategic Depth' and 'Zero Problems with Neighbours' principles.

Imagine if Turkish greatness could be revived

Taking advantage of the momentum gained from Turkey's strong economic growth under his reign, and embracing these principles, Erdogan re-engaged Ankara with the former Ottoman lands in order to rebuild Turkish power – through imperial benevolence, Islam, Turkish national pride and soft power. Subsequently, Turkey pivoted gradually toward the Middle East, seeking rapprochement with its Muslim-majority neighbours, including Iran, Iraq and Syria, as well as paying more attention to the Palestinian cause. Erdogan also reached out to the Gulf monarchies, while building good ties with Muslim-majority countries further away, such as Sudan. The number of these openings rose, based on his and Davutoglu's belief that that these policies would build Turkish influence in regional capitals, helping establish Turkey as a Middle Eastern power.

Another tenet of Davutoglu's doctrine, power revival, draws even more directly on the late Ottoman Empire, but this time from an understanding closer to reality. Davutoglu's reference here is to the foreign policy pursued, first by Ottoman Sultan Abdulhamid II in the late nineteenth century and then by his successors, the Young Turks, until 1918, just before the collapse of the Ottoman Empire and the dawn of Kemalism. Although Abdulhamid II and the Young Turks opposed each other in power, their foreign policies revolved around a common goal: reviving Ottoman greatness. In other words, Davutoglu's revivalism is itself rooted in a period of revivalism.

Building Turkish–German friendship

By the late nineteenth century, Germany, the rising power of Europe and contender to British imperialism globally, found an opening in Istanbul to help its foreign policy agenda. In 1898, German Kaiser Wilhelm II visited the Ottoman capital, bringing an expensive and heavy gift: the German Fountain built in Germany and transported, piece by piece, to Istanbul, to be assembled on the site of the old Roman-era hippodrome in the heart of Istanbul's Old City.[17] Holding great symbolism politically, the Fountain is crafted in the neo-Byzantine style, making a poignant reference to the Ottomans' imperial identity as the inheritors of Rome and Byzantium.

The Kaiser's visit to Istanbul in 1898 and German delivery of a powerfully symbolic political gift in 1901 (it took nearly three years to ship the massive fountain to Istanbul and assemble it at the heart of old Constantinople) signalled the steady ascent of Ottoman–German friendship in the late nineteenth century.

Abdulhamid II was shrewd enough not to be enamoured by a fountain. However, the sultan could still admire the Germans – their sly tactics, notwithstanding. They were alone among the major European powers of the time, in the sense that they had not thrown their support behind Ottoman minority nationalities against Istanbul, or openly set their eyes on Ottoman territory.

The seeds of historic Turkish–German ties were sown during the late Ottoman period. Germany's 'clean record' vis-à-vis the Ottoman Empire during its collapse has strongly resonated in Turkey ever since.[18] To this day, Germany regularly ranks top in surveys in Turkey regarding the views of Turkish citizens about European and Western nations.

Abdulhamid II, for his own part, found some inspiration in the Germans. Perhaps encouraged and inspired by the Kaiser's outreach to win him as an ally against Great Britain and Russia, the opera-watching and rum-drinking caliph pragmatically employed Islam as a foreign policy tool against London, and the Turks' eternal foreign policy nemesis, Moscow. He sent emissaries throughout the Indian subcontinent and Central Asia, to agitate among and organise local Muslim populations against London and Moscow in order to undermine Great Britain and Russia as imperial powers. Abdulhamid II's ultimate goal was to build up proxies and support overseas. This strategy worked, up to a point: at the end of the First World War, when British forces occupied Istanbul, the subcontinent's Muslims organised a massive fundraising campaign to support the faltering Ottoman Empire and help the caliph.[19]

Davutoglu: Grand Vizier or Young Turk?

Like Abdulhamid II, but perhaps with less pragmatism, Davutoglu had envisioned running a country with a reach not just across the Middle East, but also throughout Muslim-majority lands. Early on, as foreign minister, he tried to assume the mantle of the protector of Muslims, from the Philippines and Somalia to Myanmar and Bosnia. Accordingly, Turkey has emerged as a staunch supporter of aid programmes for Muslims everywhere, giving new life to organisations such as the Turkish Cooperation and Coordination Agency (TIKA), the Turkish version of USAID. This agency, a small outfit that had only around a dozen offices overseas before the AKP came to power, ballooned under Davutoglu. As of early 2018, it has 55 offices overseas, at least 29 of which are in Muslim-majority countries and territories, including the Palestinian Authority, Pakistan and Somalia.[20]

Davutoglu, Erdogan and the AKP cadres care deeply for Muslims around the world and see Turkey as their advocate. Following this vision, in 2004, Turkey also took over the presidency of the Organisation of Islamic Cooperation (OIC). This was an unusual step for a country with a secular constitution – but ultimately a success for Erdogan and Davutoglu: Ankara had tried in the past to take over the OIC presidency, but failed. A Turkish OIC presidency fit well with Davutoglu's vision of building influence among Muslims in order to revive Turkey's status as a great power.

For better or for worse, Davutoglu has also borrowed a page of impetuosity from the Young Turks' book. The latter not only ousted Abdulhamid II, but also gave birth to Kemalism with their secularist thinking. The Young Turks were mostly composed of idealist Ottoman soldiers and bureaucrats, who, in 1908, declared the empire a constitutional monarchy, after overthrowing the sultan. Impatient revolutionaries as they were, three Young Turks leaders, namely, Enver, Talat and Cemal pashas, respectively 27, 34 and 36 years old at the time of the 1908 Revolution, were far more rash in their pursuit of Ottoman greatness than was the sultan. Thanks to his calculating style in international politics, cultivating the Germans but never completely breaking with the British, Abdulhamid II had, for decades, avoided drawing Turkey into a major war involving the great powers.

However, the Young Turks triumvirate, which took the reins of the empire, were quick to fall for the German siren song of making the Ottoman Empire great again. In October 1914, when Berlin offered Istanbul vast territories from the Russian Empire in return for allying with the Central Powers, the three pashas eagerly accepted, subsequently dragging the empire into a major war against more than one great power at a time – for the first time in nearly a century since the Greek independence.

The Ottomans had to fight long battles on multiple far-flung fronts, ranging from Galicia in the Ukraine to the Sinai in Egypt, against indomitable adversaries, Russia, France and Great Britain – three powerful armies of the time. Drained, tired and feeble, the Ottoman Empire collapsed like a house of cards in 1918. At one point, the sophomoric pashas even deployed ill-equipped Arab recruits from the Syrian Desert, some of whom had not seen snow before, to battle against the Russians on the ice-laden 3,048 metre (10,000 ft) high Caucasus plateau: tens of thousands of Arab Syrian troops died from the cold before the Russians could get to them.[21]

Davutoglu's policy in Syria bears an eerie and sad resemblance to the foreign policy moves of the Young Turks pashas. When the uprising in Syria against the Assad regime started, Davutoglu spent a few months of fruitless diplomacy to cajole reforms out of Assad. When these efforts failed, Davutoglu, who thought he had solid and unwavering US support in Syria, was quick to call for Assad's ouster, failing to realise that US President Obama had other ideas regarding how to move forward in Syria.

To be fair, Davutoglu was far more concerned about the plight of the neighbouring Muslim populations affected by his policies than were the Young Turks: under Davutoglu, Turkey was gracious to Syrians, this time saving many lives during the uprising in that country by welcoming refugees into Turkey. To date, Ankara has provided shelter to more than 3.5 million registered Syrian refugees – plus possibly another million unregistered individuals – with only limited international assistance. Yet, Davutoglu's policy in Syria has also proved itself ill-conceived. He and Erdogan hoped that assisting and then arming the anti-regime rebels would be enough to trigger Assad's downfall.

Here, the blame also partly goes to Washington: as explained in Chapter 6, Obama encouraged Turkey to take a more active stance against Assad, only to pull back later on. Erdogan and Davutoglu wrongly believed that they had America's military backing to oust Asssd. That turned out to be erroneous, unfortunately for Turkey, and for the suffering Syrian people – and for Davutoglu – in 2013.

Forever foreign policy

Obama's vacillating policies notwithstanding, Davutoglu's 'Zero Problems with Neighbours' and 'Strategic Depth' principles, with their adopted imperial-esque attitudes disliked by Turkey's neighbours, have failed.

Davutoglu's Middle East policy has been quite different from that of Ataturk and his successors. The Kemalists accepted that the Ottoman Empire was over and that it was no longer coming back. In fact, many of the Kemalists were happy to see the Middle East territories, which they viewed as an albatross, gone.

Ataturk tried to shape Turkey to be great as a republic. In contrast, a vision of imperial restoration shapes Davutoglu's and Erdogan's foreign policy. To this end, the two men have cast the Ottomans, who followed a self-serving, often Machiavellian and imperial foreign policy, instead as the practitioners of an Islam-guided, and therefore benevolent, foreign policy. So benevolent that they have led themselves to believe that former Ottoman subjects yearn for the return of *Pax Ottomania* – while, in reality, for 'the forty-five states that the Ottoman Empire once ruled, Ottomanism connotes oppression, brutality, conquest, Islamic hegemony, and a pervasive source of economic and political backwardness'.[22]

In any case, Turkey's nearby neighbours, such as the Greeks and Arabs, have a different memory of Ottoman rule than that of Erdogan. These neighbours view the past through their own nationalist historiographies, which negatively depict the Ottomans as colonial overlords – in stark opposition to Erdogan's vision of the Ottomans as benevolent rulers.

Davutoglu's model has not turned out to be a good fit for Turkey. 'The size of the county's economy, its reliance on Foreign Direct Investment (FDI) to grow, and historical "antibodies", such as, hostile sentiments among its neighbours, as well as push back by Iran and Russia have undermined Erdogan's and Davutoglu's great power ambitions for Turkey.'[23] Similarly, this model has not been good for Ankara's ties with Europe and the West. 'With a much heavier emphasis on Islam and the Ottoman past, this foreign policy has confirmed to many of Turkey's Western allies that its deep-rooted values and moral compass are not aligned with the West.'[24]

4
BUILDING SOFT POWER

If Erdogan needed evidence in the first decade of the 21st century, to convince Turkey's citizens that they need not worry about problems in their country's ties with the West, and that their country could, as a stand-alone nation, have an impact on the Middle East, Ankara's growing soft power at the time provided initial proof.

'Soft power' can be defined as a country's ability to instill their beliefs and values in a designated country in a way that influences that country's behaviour. From brokering peace deals to cementing trade agreements, a country with soft power can punch above its weight on the international stage.[1] With prodding from Davutoglu, Erdogan maintained that Turkey could regain the regional leadership role it had lost in the Middle East and other areas, following the dissolution of the Ottoman Empire. This goal would be best accomplished not through displays of military force, but rather by the establishment of soft power across the Middle East.

Just as Erdogan (and Davutoglu) did not invent Turkey's Middle Eastern pivot, they also did not create Turkey's soft power from scratch. Following the fall of communism, for instance, Turkish companies were among the first to penetrate the markets of Central Asian and Caucasus states, which had just gained independence from Moscow. Similarly, Turkish companies, and TIKA, established a formidable presence in the Balkans, following the fall of communism in the 1990s. In addition, as Afghanistan convulsed with violent conflict in the 1990s, Turkish companies were bravely doing business across that country.

However, the real score in Turkish soft power was due to the dramatically improved living standards domestically in the first decade of the twenty-first century. This was accompanied by Ankara's increasing commercial, economic and cultural might in the Middle East and beyond. Both of these developments are linked to Turkey's burgeoning economy under Erdogan. As proof of this success, the country became a majority middle-class society for the first time in its history, a fact the CIA recognised in 2010 by listing it as a developed economy.[2]

Recently, the Turkish economy slowed down, triggering a currency crisis in 2018 and two consecutive quarters of decline, signalling a recession. Nevertheless, the country still has an impressive economic story under Erdogan that needs to be told in detail.

Much of the growth in the last decade has come from a strong export sector. Turkish products – from heavy-duty trucks to canned tomatoes – have found happy consumers across the Middle East, bringing Turkey regional influence in the same way that cars did for Japan in the 1970s and 1980s across the world. Turkish soap operas, once obscure dramas, produced solely for local audiences, are now beamed into living rooms across the Middle East, from Aden to Casablanca. To name just one example, *Magnificent Century* (*Muhtesem Yuzyil*), a classic historical fictional drama, based on the life and court of the Ottoman sultan, Suleyman, The Magnificent, has enthralled 200 million viewers. Such soap operas earned Turkey about $130 million in foreign sales, mostly from Arab countries, compared to a mere $1 million in 2007.[3] A study conducted by Interpress Media Services, a monitoring company in Turkey, shows that viewers in nearly 100 countries watched Turkish TV dramas in 2017. Furthermore, Turkey now ranks second in the world, after the USA, in overall export of general TV dramas, with $350 million in revenue.[4]

Netflix, the online video streaming service giant in the USA, has also recently caught onto the wave of Turkish soap operas. It has not only licensed to show *Magnificent Century* to the US audiences, but also, in 2018, commissioned a multimillion-dollar Turkish TV series titled, *The Protector*, an action drama, with Istanbul serving as its backdrop, for the US market – a first.

Although its entry into the United States market is recent, Turkey's movie industry has for nearly two decades now helped dramatise the country's trends for an Arab audience. Turkey's first breakout soap-opera success in the Arab world, *Nour* (*Gumus*) in 2005, was a sensation, drawing a viewership of 85 million across Arab countries with its series finale. These Turkish *telenovelas* work from safe storylines, likely to win a wide audience in the Middle East and beyond. Viewers can cheer on paragons of womanly virtue as they struggle against adversity to protect their families (i.e. *The Day My Destiny was Written* and its

Turkish title of *Kaderimin Yazildigi Gun*; and *Rebel* and its Turkish title of *Asi*); or, if they prefer, they can revel in testosterone-fuelled fantasies of violent revenge against crime lords, American soldiers, Jews and other perceived villains (i.e. *Valley of the Wolves* with its Turkish title of *Kurtlar Vadisi*). In addition, just as important as the story, is the scene: these dramas play out against the backdrop of a Turkish society that is effortlessly Islamic, affluently middle class and politically stable.

For a time, Turkey's quest for influence, and its apparent success as an affluent, well-functioning Muslim-majority society, seemed to be having the effect desired by Ankara across the Middle East. In 2011, in a Brookings Institution poll of the citizens of five Arab countries, Turkey ranked first among countries believed to have played a 'constructive role' in the Arab uprisings. In the same survey, Erdogan's popularity towered above that of other world leaders, including Obama; and Egyptians wished for their country to look more like Turkey than any other nation, including any other Arab or non-Arab state.[5]

'Quran Belt'

Commercial considerations, namely yearning for Arab wealth (denominated commonly in dinars in oil- and gas-rich Persian Gulf economies), also influenced Erdogan's foray into the Middle East. Some of the AKP's most stalwart supporters come from the business community in Central Anatolia, one of the most conservative parts of the country. Whereas other parts of Turkey, such as the eastern Black Sea Coast remained Christian and came under Ottoman rule only in the late fifteenth century, central Turkey faced relatively early Islamisation and Turkification – in the late eleventh century under the Ottomans' predecessor, the Seljuks, hence the region's deeply conservative nature.

Cities such as Konya and Kayseri, located along the 'Quran Belt' in Central Anatolia, are among some of Turkey's most conservative urban centres. In these cities, religious brotherhoods and the mosque grease the wheels of commerce. Just as in the Calvinist communities of early modern Europe, in Kayseri and Konya and other cities in this area, too, capitalism and piety are tightly woven together into the social fabric of the local business community. For decades, the spiritual bourgeoisie in these cities had felt they were locked out of the commanding heights of the Turkish economy by the well-connected and pro-secularist large businesses and families. These individuals, with their European habits located in Turkey's big cities such as Istanbul and Izmir, also had cozy ties with the bureaucratic and military elites.

When Turkey's economy abruptly opened its doors to liberalisation during the mid-1980s under Ozal, the burgeoning cities in Turkey's Anatolian hinterland more so than the established, risk-averse and mostly Istanbul-based companies looked to the Middle East for untapped markets and opportunities for investment.

Labelled 'Anatolian Tigers', Kayseri and Konya, as well as other inner Anatolian cities such as Gaziantep and Malatya, really took off economically in the last decade when Erdogan started to promote trade and the movement of people within the Middle East. The results were dramatic. Between 2002 and 2010, alone, the share of Turkey's total exports going to the Middle East doubled from 10 to 20 per cent, with total Turkish exports to the region rising from $3 billion to $23 billion.[6] Turkish brands filled the shelves of supermarkets and department stores, and Turkish contractors brought the experience they acquired in Turkey's construction boom to eager clients in Arab-majority countries.

Turkey profited monetarily and in terms of prestige. That an avowedly Muslim government seemed to be leading its people to prosperity was an alluring selling point for Turkey's brand in the Middle East. Just as the Arab uprisings were occurring, the Turkish Economic and Social Studies Foundation (TESEV), an Istanbul-based think tank, conducted a survey across the Arab world. The 40 per cent of those surveyed cited the economy as the most urgent issue facing their country, and Turkey topped the list as the country that most people believed could be a regional leader.[7]

'Globally yours'

Turkey built soft power across the Middle East and beyond through its service sector as well. Perhaps no company is more emblematic of the Turkey's global outreach under Erdogan than the country's flagship carrier, Turkish Airlines.

Ankara established the airline in 1933, as part of the Kemalist programme of state-led economic development. For decades, it lived up to the mediocre reputation held by most state-owned airlines in developing countries. In the 1980s, the airline got a boost, improving its service and quality under Turkey's pro-free market leader, Ozal. Then, in 1990s, the company was swept into Turkey's 'Wild West-style' privatisation frenzy and was opened to private investors. Erdogan accelerated the sell-off of the airline in 2006, but the government kept its golden share. Service and quality rose at a pace with the rate of private ownership, and today, Turkish Airlines ranks among the top European carriers.

As the country's flag carrier, Turkish Airlines helped spread Ankara's political wings around the globe. In 2002, just as Erdogan's AKP came to power, they flew from Istanbul to about 100 destinations, many of them domestic routes inside Turkey.

In the Middle East, between 2003 and 2018, the airline increased its destinations from about ten to about thirty,[8] and the number of passengers it carries from about a half a million to over 4 million.[9] Via its hub in Istanbul, it has become a major carrier for passengers from all over the world, including those travelling on Muslim pilgrimage (*hajj*) and visits to the holy city of Mecca (*umrah*).

The airline's reach is not limited to the Middle East. By 2018, it connected five Spanish and ten Italian cities to Istanbul and, therefore, the rest of the world. The airline now has up to twelve flights a day to the Greek capital, Athens.[10] The carrier has made Istanbul not only a transit hub for travellers to and from Southern Europe, but also for faraway places such as Ulan Bator, Mongolia. In 2018, it launched daily flights to Caracas, Venezuela, from Istanbul, both tapping into an underserved market, as well as underlining Erdogan's claim to be the voice of the global south. The airline offers frequent flights to Israel, making Tel Aviv the destination with the greatest number of connections from Istanbul.

The airline's network is, indeed, vast, stretching even to mid-sized cities of many countries. In 2018, the carrier flew to seven scheduled destinations in Saudi Arabia and ten in the Ukraine, compared to one each in 2002.[11] Today, the airline services over 300 routes, many of them in the Middle East, Eurasia and Africa. Together with Erdogan, Turkish Airlines has, indeed, become Turkey's second global brand: currently flying to more countries than any other airline in the world.[12]

African openings

Perhaps more than any other part of the world, Africa has become the test case for Erdogan's global and soft-power ambitions, aptly demonstrated by the increase in Turkish Airline flights connecting the continent to Turkey and the world. By 2018, the carrier was flying to fifty-five destinations in thirty-seven countries in Africa, offering more connections to the continent than Air France – flag carrier of Africa's once dominant coloniser, France – making it a leading airline for this continent.[13]

Before Erdogan, aside from a few pro forma ties, Turkey had virtually no links with sub-Saharan Africa. In 2002, Ankara had only a dozen diplomatic offices to cover the entire continent (nearly half of them in North Africa).[14] Both trade and cultural exchange with the broader continent was minimal. Eyeing sub-Saharan Africa as an untapped field for Turkey's influence, Erdogan announced his intention to build ties with African countries, declaring 2005 the 'Year of Africa',[15] and inking a formal partnership with the African Union (AU) in 2008.[16]

The year 2005 also marked the formal beginning of Turkey's accession talks with the EU. Despite this, Erdogan (and Davutoglu) chose to focus much of Ankara's foreign policy energy on Africa the same year. With German Chancellor Angela Merkel and French President Nicolas Sarkozy taking measures to slow down, and eventually block Turkey's EU accession, perhaps it was fair that the two men were losing patience with Europe during the EU membership talks that soon became an international kabuki dance.

A product of its foreign policy environment, Turkey's Africa pivot only strengthened after talks with the EU came to a halt. When a famine struck Somalia in August 2011, Erdogan sprang into action. Visibly moved by the catastrophe, he gathered his top ministers, his wife and daughters and flew out to Mogadishu.

The optics of the visit were nothing short of brilliant: images of Erdogan and his wife walking in refugee camps in Mogadishu, Erdogan barking orders to his ministers to build whatever seemed necessary for the refuges, while his wife compassionately conversed with locals. All of this told a story that continues to shape the narrative of Turkey's involvement in Africa. Unlike the faceless aid agencies of the big powers, Erdogan seemed to take a personal interest in the Somali plight. He travelled to Mogadishu at a time when no other non-African head of state would do so, and he called upon the rest of the world to follow his example.

In private, seasoned international aid workers had misgivings about this ersatz approach to aid work, worrying that it might sow confusion and disorganisation. Concerns also arose over Turkish contractors hiring local warlords and corrupt power brokers to provide security and gain access to business.[17] However, these wrinkles were invisible compared to the dramatic imagery of the visit itself. Taking hold of this momentum, Turkey ramped up its diplomatic presence across Africa, with Erdogan making official visits to twenty countries on the continent, visiting many on multiple occasions, especially following his first-time election as president in 2014.[18] These efforts overall helped Ankara penetrate Africa: in 2018, Turkey had nearly forty embassies there.[19]

Falling behind neighbours and former subjects

Although Erdogan has built influence for Turkey in faraway countries such as Somalia and Mongolia, the most dramatic and radical shift that he has ushered in is the momentum to rebalance Turkey's standing compared to its neighbours.

Modern Turkey has nearly a dozen neighbours in Europe, located around the Balkans, the Black Sea, Caucasus, and the Middle East. Ankara's position in its near abroad was not always at a point of strength. This was most apparent during the collapse of the Ottoman Empire, a period that informs many key trends of contemporary Turkish politics. During the First Balkan War of 1912–13, for instance, the Ottomans suffered a crushing and humiliating defeat at the hands of their European neighbours, Bulgaria, Greece, Montenegro and Serbia – all former Ottoman subjects. In less than eight months of warfare, from 1912 to 1913, the Ottomans lost nearly 83 per cent of their territory, and 69 per cent of their population in Europe.[20]

After Ataturk liberated Turkey at the end of the First World War, Turkey remained weak, especially in financial terms. The peace treaty that ended the war also included terms for the payment of the Ottoman Empire's debt – the late sultans, in their efforts to modernise the empire, had borrowed large sums from European states and investors[21] – by its successor states, much of it falling on modern Turkey's shoulders.

Ankara continued to pay the Ottoman Debt until 1954.[22] According to the official Turkish Statistical Institute in Ankara, the total amount of loans paid between 1923 and 1938, alone, amounted to $320 million at the time.[23] Between 1929 and 1938, the debt repayment ratio as a percentage of export earnings for Ankara was 38.2 per year, on average.[24] Coupled with the destruction of much of Turkey's infrastructure and many of its key cities during the two Balkan Wars of 1912–13, the First World War and Ataturk's liberation campaign of 1919–22, the payment of Ottoman debts severely limited Turkey's ability to invest in domestic projects, stunting growth.

To put it simply, interwar Turkey was poor to the core, inconsequential internationally and underpopulated. Not only these facts, but also those concerning its neighbours, many of them former Ottoman subjects, dwarfed it at the time – economically as well as demographically. In the 1920s, for instance, Turkey's population was just over 13 million, compared to Greece's population of 6.2 million and Bulgaria's 5.5 million during the same decade.[25] Just two of its immediate neighbours in Europe had almost as many inhabitants as did Ataturk's Turkey.

The demographic imbalance did not improve during the interwar years. According to the United Nations *Demographic Yearbook* of 1948, Turkey had a population of 17 million in 1937.[26] Four nearby Balkan countries, namely Greece (7 million in 1937),[27] Bulgaria (6 million in 1937),[28] Romania (16 million in 1937)[29] and Yugoslavia (15 million in 1931)[30] – all former Ottoman subjects – together surpassed Turkey's population by over 250 per cent in the 1930s.

Among Turkey's other neighbours during this period, Iran matched its population with nearly 16 million citizens.[31] In addition, in 1926, Russia had a population of 147 million citizens, about seven times Turkey's population that same year.[32]

Its European neighbours overshadowed Ataturk's Turkey also in the economic sphere and on on a societal level, human development indicators being a case in point. A shocking 79 per cent of Turkey's population in 1935 was illiterate, for instance, compared to only 41 per cent in Greece in 1928, 31 per cent in Bulgaria in 1934 and 55 per cent in Yugoslavia in 1931.[33]

Lingering power disparity between Turkey and its neighbours in the 20th century

The economic and demographic balance between Turkey and its neighbours shaped Ankara's foreign policy in the interwar era, leading the country to establish friendship treaties with most of its neighbours and nearby countries, ranging from the 1934 Balkan Pact in the west with Greece, Yugoslavia and Romania, to the 1937 Saadabad Treaty in the east with Iran, Iraq and Afghanistan. Except for taking advantage of opportunities in interwar-era European politics (explained in Chapter 7) to wrest control of Hatay (Sanjak of Alexandretta) from French-governed Syria, Ankara generally behaved as a pro-status quo power in the interwar period.

Following the Second World War, with the Ottoman Debt paid off, the country's Gross Domestic Product (GDP) increased from around $14 billion in 1960 to almost $70 billion in 1980 – a fivefold jump.[34] However, Turkey's economic growth spurts in the 1950s, late 1960s and 1980s only tangentially narrowed the discrepancies between Ankara and its neighbours. This is since many of its neighbours were growing faster than Ankara during this period. By the late 1960s, the size of the Soviet economy had reached $5 trillion, for instance.[35] In 1970, the Soviet Union had almost seven times Turkey's population and nearly 50 times its GDP.[36] In 1980, while Turkey's population had reached 44 million citizens and its GDP was nearly $69 billion, Greece, with only 10 million people, had a GDP of close to $57 billion. Iran, with 6 million fewer citizens than Turkey at the time, surpassed Turkey's GDP by nearly 36 per cent (with a GDP of $94 billion), just at the onset of the Revolution in Tehran.[37]

No longer overshadowed by its neighbours

Population boom without economic growth means poverty. Turkey's most recent economic spurt, especially in comparison to its poorly performing neighbours,[38] coupled with the Eurozone crisis of 2008, wars in Syria and Iraq and Iran's economic stagnation since the 1979

Revolution, have together refashioned the twentieth-century economic balance of power between Turkey and its neighbours.

Contemporary Turkey has twelve neighbours, when including nearby maritime neighbours. Eight of them lie across by land (Armenia, Azerbaijan, Bulgaria, Georgia, Greece, Iran, Iraq and Syria), and four across the sea (Cyprus in the Mediterranean, and Romania, Ukraine and Russia, around the Black Sea, a closed maritime basin, where access to international waters goes through the Turkish Straits). The Turkish Republic of Northern Cyprus (TRNC), recognised only by Ankara, can be considered a thirteenth neighbour.

With 82 million citizens in 2018, Turkey is demographically larger than eleven of each of its neighbours (twelve, including the TRNC), except for Russia. Furthermore, Turkey and Iran have nearly identical populations but, using current prices, Ankara's economic output is 1.2 times greater than Tehran's. Turkey is economically larger than eleven of each of its neighbours (twelve including the TRNC), except for Russia. Moreover, it is wealthier, based on Purchasing Power Parity (PPP)-adjusted income, than each of its neighbours, except for Cyprus (after lagging behind Greece in wealth for decades, Turkey has finally caught up with the latter: in 2018, the two countries have nearly identical per capita incomes, measured in current prices). Even more impressively, Turkey's 2018 GDP (again, measured by current prices) is larger than nine of its neighbours (Armenia, Bulgaria, Cyprus, Georgia, Greece, Iraq, Romania, Syria and Ukraine – ten if including the TRNC), put together.[39]

Furthermore, Turkey's 2018 population is larger than eight of its neighbours (Armenia, Azerbaijan, Bulgaria, Cyprus, Georgia, Greece, Romania, Syria – nine with the TRNC), put together at 81 million.[40] Just adding up the populations of Turkey's four former Ottoman subjects in the Balkans, namely Bulgaria, Greece, Romania and former Yugoslav republics, relays the dramatic shift in balance between Turkey and its European neighbours since the collapse of the Ottoman Empire. In the interwar period, those four countries surpassed Turkey's population by 250 per cent; today, Turkey surpasses the population of these states and their successors by 150 per cent.[41]

The demographic and economic rebalancing towards Europe and Russia is, indeed, impressive. In 2017, Turkey surpassed Germany to become the largest population in Europe (excluding Russia). Using current prices, Turkey has recently overtaken Spain to become Europe's fifth-largest economy after Germany, France, Great Britain and Italy, and is on course to surpass Italy before the end of the 2010s. What is more, once dwarfed by Russia demographically, Turkey's population today is only 45 per cent smaller than Russia's, and its economy, once completely overshadowed by that of the Soviet Union, is more than half of Russia's in 2017.[42]

Finally, but importantly, Erdogan's Turkey now boasts a near universal literacy rate.[43] This new demographic and economic balance, with the positive course moving forward for Ankara, inevitably influences Turkey's foreign policy and attitude towards its neighbours.

No longer dwarfed by its neighbours, Turkey is now seeking to wield influence over its neighbours, many of them former Ottoman subjects. As this growth increases, so will Ankara's leverage, prestige and power in the region, alongside growing weariness from neighbours. Turkey, after hundreds of years, appears to be standing on its own two feet again.

Dinner in Damascus

Turkey's economic achievements in the last decade propelled Erdogan's (and Davutoglu's) belief that Ankara could become a stand-alone power in the Middle East by using its soft power. Ankara flaunted its perceived influence in the region by advertising the 'Shamgen Zone' idea – a play on the EU's Schengen Area of free travel and Sham, the traditional name for Syria in Arabic – that would cover the Levant (minus Israel).

Erdogan, brimming with confidence from the attention bestowed on him by US presidents George W. Bush and Barack Obama, and a strong current of opinion in Ankara, held that Turkey had played a secondary role to Washington and Brussels for too long in the Middle East. Turkey could become a regional power only by going its own way, even if this sometimes meant diverging from pro-Western foreign policy goals.

For a while, it seemed as if Turkey's newfound economic influence had, indeed, brought Ankara the long-anticipated political greatness in these regions, especially the Middle East. That, Erdogan (and Davutoglu) believed, would be best accomplished not through displays of military force, but by building up soft power.

In May 2011, just as the unrest of the Arab uprisings was beginning, Ibrahim Kalin, a key foreign policy thinker within the AKP, and a spokesperson for Erdogan in 2019, wrote that Turkey had become a bona fide 'soft power' in the region, by dint of its successful synthesis of 'Islam, democracy and economic development'.[44] At the beginning of Arab uprisings, a point of pride in AKP circles was that they had concocted a new style of foreign policy, providing an antidote to the traditional way of doing politics, specifically in the Middle East, where the 2003 US-led war in Iraq was a case in point of how the traditional powers were failing.

These convictions drove Turkey's diplomatic outreach at the onset of Arab uprisings. In rapid succession, Erdogan forged stronger diplomatic ties with all of Turkey's neighbours in the Middle East. High-level visits to Baghdad, Damascus, Tehran and other regional capitals became routine. Between November 2002 and April 2009, for instance, the Turkish foreign minister made at least eight trips to Iran and Syria, alone.[45] In addition, Turkey opened scores of new diplomatic missions across Arab-majority countries. These provided the country with increased visibility in the region that had been absent since the Ottoman era, after which the Turks had turned to Europe and the Arabs fell under British and French rule. Erdogan especially hit it off with Syrian dictator, Bashar al-Assad, who came to power three years before Erdogan. In 2008, the families of the two leaders even vacationed together at the resort town of Bodrum, along the Turkish Riviera.[46]

In early 2006, I toured Syria's Crusader-era castles, Mameluke mosques and Byzantine churches. One chilly winter evening, in Damascus' old city, I met up with a high-ranking Turkish diplomat for dinner at a Damascene restaurant that was converted from a Mameluke-era mansion. My interlocutor, who had close ties to the Erdogan administration, told me that the Turkish leader believed he had a special bond with Assad. He added that Ankara hoped to pry Assad away from his over-reliance on Tehran, if not to replace it completely as an anchor for Syria – and, in so doing, draw Assad toward the West, thereby reducing regional tensions.

The diplomat friend added that Erdogan and Davutoglu both believed that Ankara was in a position to single-handedly shape Syria's future, catapulting Turkey to become a Middle Eastern player. This pivot was rooted in the two men's belief that Turkey's EU accession path was closed – later developments would, unfortunately, prove them wrong, except regarding Turkey's EU journey.

5
EUROPE'S SLAP

In hindsight, if Erdogan needed a good reason to remind Turkey's citizens why Turkey should turn away from Europe to the Middle East, where they would be respected, the EU was quick to hand him what he needed.

As an early member of NATO (1952), an early member of the Council of Europe (1949) and a founding member of the Organisation for Economic Co-operation and Development (OECD) (1961), Turkey has been associated with integration into the Western and European system for decades. The first step of synchronisation was taken in 1959, with the intent of establishing an eventual customs union between Ankara and the EU. Accordingly, Turkey concluded an association, the Ankara Agreement, creating a framework for cooperation with the EU's predecessor, the EEC, in 1963, and finally paving the way for a customs union in the 1990s.[1]

Turkey and the EU: Always dating, but never tying the knot

The Ankara Agreement, signed between the EEC and Turkey in 1963, left the door open for Turkish membership to the European club in the future. Back then, in the Cold War context, the Europeans did not seem to doubt that Turkey, a NATO member, firmly belonged to 'the West'. During this time, however, the Turkish economy, which had a large agricultural sector and rural population, was not sufficiently developed to join the European project.[2]

Following Turkey's intense industrialisation and urbanisation drive under Ozal, the EU goal suddenly seemed more achievable. In 1987,

Ozal submitted Turkey's formal application to become a member to the EEC's successor and the EU's predecessor, the European Community (EC). Nevertheless, for over a decade, Ankara failed to become a candidate country for accession talks after it entered the EU Customs Union in 1996. The European Union repeatedly delayed accepting Turkey's application for membership, postponing the opening of negotiations on Turkey's accession.

One reason was the dispute over Cyprus, and another was Turkey's human rights record. The latter deteriorated significantly during the 1990s as Ankara fought the PKK and many of Turkey's Kurdish citizens got caught up in the crossfire between the government and the terror group, subsequently suffering human rights abuses, as well as terror attacks by the PKK. The long list of Eastern and Central European countries applying to enter the EU crowded the playing field for Ankara, undermining its chances of speedy accession. Suddenly, Turkey was not the only candidate waiting in the EU's triage room, but one of the many.

In December 1997, the EU rejected outright Ankara's application for membership. In the words of Jean-Claude Juncker, then prime minister of Luxembourg and president of the European Council for that half-year: 'It cannot be that the representatives of a country in which torture is still going on can sit at the table of the European Union.'[3] However, it should be noted that Ankara was not alone in being chided by the EU for its democracy during this period. Brussels issued negative opinions in other cases, too, including, for instance, towards Bratislava for its human rights abuses under then Slovak Prime Minister Vladimir Meciar. And five other East European countries were also denied the possibility of starting accession talks until they met the EU's democratic requirements.

Meanwhile, Brussels went ahead and concluded a far-reaching customs union agreement with Turkey, allowing industrial goods to be freely traded between Turkey and EU members without tariffs. This development forced Turkey's businesses to become competitive in the EU markets and globally, later helping ignite Erdogan's economic boom, but also cementing economic contacts between Turkey and the Union.

Economic rationale drew Turkey and Europe closer at the time. In December 1999, the EU dramatically changed its position regarding Ankara's membership, following democratic reforms in Turkey and elaborate diplomacy, whereby Germany and Greece accepted Turkey as a candidate on the understanding that it would contribute to a comprehensive settlement of the Cyprus problem. US lobbying on behalf of Ankara with EU member states also helped shape Brussels' decision. Most famously, in 2002, US President Bush personally called a number of EU leaders, including, for instance, fellow conservative and Danish prime minister, Anders Fogh Rasmussen, asking them to support Brussels decision regarding Ankara's membership.[4]

Considering the hesitations about Turkey's application, especially among Christian Democrat and centre-right parties in the EU, and about its ability to fulfil the EU's political criteria for accession, including respect for and protection of minorities (i.e. Kurds in the Turkish context), it was a major achievement that Brussels accepted Turkish candidacy.[5] As a result, when Erdogan founded the AKP in 2001, the idea of gaining entry into the EU seemed a possibility for Turkey.[6]

When Erdogan voiced his support for EU accession in Turkey's 2002 parliamentary election, his rhetoric did not mark a shift in Ankara's EU policy, but rather solidified his self-declared moderate stance for the AKP. At the time, EU accession had wide public support. According to a 2002 survey conducted by Yuksek Strateji Merkezi and Input Arastirma ve Iletisim Sirketi, a Turkish research and polling firm, 64 per cent of the respondents wanted Turkey to join the EU, while only 28 per cent said they did not.[7]

By favouring EU programmes in public, Erdogan crafted a convincing case for political moderation. His message was simple: as seen by its embrace of Turkey's EU vocation, his AKP could not be considered a political Islamist faction, opposing the West and its values. The AKP was moving away from the political Islamist Welfare Party (RP)'s and its anti-EU successor Virtue Party's (FP) narrower popular base and brand of politics. This, together with other factors explained in Chapter 2, helped Erdogan succeed in appealing to a broader range of voters.

A plurality of Turkey's citizens felt comfortable voting for Erdogan's AKP. Hitherto considered a political Islamist and a fringe politician in the context of Turkish politics, Erdogan had just passed the test to be accepted as a centre-right politician again in the Turkish context, thanks in no small part to his embrace of the EU process, opening the gates of power for him.

Crushing the generals and their secularist allies

In 2003, as a democratically elected leader, though, Erdogan faced genuine threats, namely the secularist TAF and its allies, including similarly secularist Turkish courts, as well as large parts of the media and business community.

For many decades, the Turkish military had exercised control over the country's democracy. Following the 1995 parliamentary elections, in a series of events later dubbed the 'Soft Coup', and with help from the courts, the media and the business community, the generals had played a role in destroying Erdogan's former political home, RP, after it entered into a coalition government with the True Path Party (DYP) in 1996.

At the time, the TAF orchestrated a civilian protest movement to eject the democratically elected RP (also known as 'Refah') from government. This worked, and, faced with rising protests and threatening warnings from the TAF, the DYP-RP coalition government caved in. In 1997, Tansu Ciller, head of DYP, resigned from her post as prime minister, together with RP leader, Necmettin Erbakan, who vacated his post as deputy prime minister. Turkey's constitutional court shut down Refah in 1998 for violating the country's secular charter. The courts also sentenced Erdogan, Istanbul's mayor from RP at the time, to a ten-month term in jail for reciting a poem that allegedly undermined Turkey's secular constitution.

Only four years after his release from jail in July 1999, Erdogan assumed power as Turkey's prime minister in March 2003. Needless to say, the memory of the recent events was fresh in his mind. He was rightly worried regarding the next steps of the generals and their powerful allies across Turkish society. Erdogan had in mind the Refah experience. He knew that it was not a matter of if, but when, the military would move against his party, as well. His strategy was to be pro-active, isolate and then undermine the generals so that they could not crush the AKP the way they had crushed Refah.

Enter: the EU accession process. Erdogan first sought to prove his domestic and international democratic credentials by aggressively pursuing EU accession and reforming Turkey with that goal in mind. Subsequently, Ankara adopted a liberal penal code and strengthened civilian control of the military, receiving a green light for accession talks in 2005.

A perfect storm developed, helping Erdogan. Soon after the accession talks started, Brussels told Ankara it needed to 'uphold the rule of law', which meant the EU wanted the generals subjected to civilian control. Erdogan happily obliged, carrying out reforms, including rebalancing the TAF's role in politics, such as the power they emitted through Turkey's National Security Council (NSC), a top decision-making body in all aspects of Turkish politics and policy-making, until Erdogan's rise. Following the EU reforms, the Turkish NSC, controlled by secularist generals for decades and dominating the country's politics, became a civilian-controlled body in 2004. The generals grudgingly agreed to this change lest they be seen as blocking Turkey's EU accession, overwhelmingly supported by nearly 80 per cent of the country's population at the time.

The baton in Turkish politics passed from generals to the civilian government also because the TAF did not play its hand well. In 2003, the former intentionally abandoned the policy court, letting Erdogan make Ankara's decision concerning Turkey's position in the US-led 2003 Iraq War. The generals hoped that if they allowed Erdogan handle this unpopular war in Turkey, he would end up in hot water: either he would support the war and anger the Turkish public, or he would stand against it, angering Washington. However, Erdogan was lucky. As explained in detail in the next chapter, although a majority of AKP legislators voted to authorise Turkish support for the war, the vote failed in the legislative chamber on technical grounds, when it did not receive support from a majority of the quorum.

Erdogan not only survived the test of the Iraq War, but soon after, he filled in the policy court left vacant by the generals. He started consolidating political power in his hands, and soon eclipsed the Turkish NSC, which subsequently faded away as a key policy-making institution.

Erdogan's next step was to send shock waves through the military. He knew that he had to act fast to pre-empt another 'soft coup', i.e. the Turkish military working behind the scenes in the same way as they had done in the 1990s to oust his party, and then ban it through a decision of the country's constitutional court. Erdogan's worst fears were confirmed in April 2007, when the TAF issued a warning on its website, threatening him and his AKP. This threat, dubbed the 'E-Coup', was coupled with a case launched in the country's constitutional court on 14 March 2008, in which the public prosecutor asked that the AKP be banned.[8] All this signalled to Erdogan that he had to move fast in order to undermine the military and its secularist allies.

To this end, he used the Ergenekon–Sledgehammer trials during 2008–11 (explained earlier in the Introduction of this book) to arrest, intimidate and silence the generals – but also his broad secularist opposition, including journalists and university presidents – with help from the Gulen movement.[9] The EU criticized the arrests of journalists and scholars from the sidelines.[10]

The EU process had been extremely useful for Erdogan: 'the guy from the other side of the tracks' had just managed to undermine 'the track-guard' of Turkey's political system, successfully neutering the generals, with, unwitting, help from the EU process. Later developments would prove Erdogan's lack of commitment to Turkey's EU vocation. All he needed now was for the EU to turn its back on Turkey so he could sail away from Brussels, with Turkey's citizenry in tow.

Unwilling partners: Turkey's (sad) EU accession story

The EU was quick to hand Erdogan what he wanted. A problem with Ankara's EU accession has been that some member states themselves have not been too serious about Turkey's membership. In this regard, a key driver was the lack of broad public support for Turkey's EU vocation among the citizenry of member states. With the exception of a few countries, such as Great Britain, public support for Turkey's accession was not strong among key member states such as France and Germany, even as Ankara received a green light from Brussels (endorsed by EU governments) to start membership talks. In addition, in most countries, Great Britain again being among the exceptions, support for Turkey's membership often split along partisan lines, with left-leaning voters usually backing it and right-leaning parties generally opposing it. This meant that support for Ankara's entry into the Union would vacillate even after the talks commenced due to the changing political identity of governments in the member states following elections.

Notwithstanding the doubts and hesitations regarding the prospect of Turkish EU membership that significant segments of their populations expressed, France and Germany agreed to the opening of accession negotiations based on Turkish commitments to make further efforts at satisfying the EU's political accession criteria, including 'respect for and protection of minorities' (e.g. rights for Kurds in Turkey) and 'rule of law' (e.g. ensuring civilian control of the military). Greece, too, agreed to open talks with Turkey, despite continuous tensions, including military tensions in the Aegean Sea.[11]

However, even then, Turkey's accession path would not be a smooth ride. Here, the blame ought to be split between Ankara and its EU counterparts. Soon after France and Germany agreed to accession negotiations, the EU Commission, the top body overseeing the accession of new members, issued a recommendation that membership talks begin. Despite growing doubts, member states consented to the Commission's attempts to fully engage with Ankara, in the hope that Turkey's performance on the rule of law, democracy and human rights would improve. In truth, it trended in the opposite direction.[12]

Senior EU officials whom I met at the time were already worried about democratic backsliding in Turkey. At the same time, France and Germany began to turn against Turkish membership, once the talks started in earnest. The obstructive nature of the objection by Paris and Berlin to Ankara's membership hardened after the accession process started, with both the European capitals actively placing hurdles in Turkey's path.

Then, the French president and right-wing politician Nicolas Sarkozy, who opposed Turkey's bid for EU membership, urged Ankara to pursue 'partnership' with the EU, instead.[13] In Germany, in November 2005, Angela Merkel from the Christian Democrat Union (CDU) replaced leftist Gerhard Schröder from the Social Democrat Party (SDP) as chancellor. Berlin's position regarding Ankara's membership shifted. Merkel endorsed the policy of her party, offering Ankara 'privileged partnership', continually emphasising that accession negotiations with Turkey never promised membership, despite the fact that accession talks with all previous candidate countries had concluded with membership offers from the EU.[14]

However, there was thinking inside the Commission at the time that: 'accession negotiations had an inherent value of their own in promoting political and economic reform in Turkey, whether or not they eventually led to membership'. What was more, other member states, including the UK and Sweden, 'strongly supported the goal of Turkish membership and the EU position was a compromise among its then twenty-five members'.[15]

Just as Turkey started accession talks, helped by EU dogma stating that each country proceeds in accession negotiations according to its own merits, Brussels decoupled Turkey's accession process from that already undergone by former candidates, applying substantive new bureaucratic hurdles for Ankara (as well as other incoming countries, such as Croatia) as part of the EU's 2006 'Strategy for Enlargement' document. In this document, the Union drew lessons from its previous enlargements, consequently deciding to tighten the conditions of accession to increase requirements of aspiring members. Turkey just happened to be in the wrong place at the wrong time for EU accession, but for Erdogan, who already extracted what he wanted out of the EU process – a defanged Turkish TAF – the situation presented the right place and time to be.

Erdogan did not see a problem in dropping the ball on Ankara's EU accession efforts. Brussels, with a push from EU member states, had already made the talks a Sisyphean ordeal, subjecting Turkey and other incoming states to modified procedures. The 35 'chapters' of policy issues to be addressed during membership discussions with candidate countries, and which required the consent of all EU members (then 25 states), now had attached benchmarks needed to open and close these chapters. In effect, when it entered accession talks with the EU in 2005, Turkey faced 1,750 potential vetoes, i.e. the sum of potential 'no' votes Ankara could face, with the EU's 27 members each holding two blocking votes to open and close each of the 35 accession 'chapters', respectively.

Newly established benchmarks for opening and closing the 'chapters', indeed, became an explicit, transparent way for member states to block Turkey's membership talks. Erdogan failed to implement the additional protocol to the 1963 Ankara Agreement between the EU and Turkey for Cyprus-related reasons. The additional protocol required Ankara's commitment to open its ports and airports to all EU member states' ships and airplanes, including those of Cyprus.

Turkey and Cyprus, represented by the Cypriot Greek-dominated southern part on the island, did not recognise each other, but Cyprus had become an EU member in 2004. Erdogan had pushed hard to unify Cyprus in early 2004, but this effort had failed due to Cypriot Greeks overwhelmingly voting against unifying the Turkish and Greek sections of the island. As an EU member, Cyprus was in an advantageous position compared to Turkey. The game was on: EU including Cyprus versus Turkey. Erdogan, who has appreciated nationalist sentiments in Turkish society, knew that he needed to avoid the perception of offering a win to Cypriot Greeks after their snub to the Turkish side to unify the island. Subsequently, Ankara said, 'no' to opening its ports and airports to Cypriot Greek vessels. This decision consequently allowed countries opposing Turkey's accession, such as France, to freely veto accession chapters with Turkey at will, using the Cyprus issue as a convenient alibi.

Of the 35 'chapters' of accession talks to be negotiated between Turkey and Brussels, the first 33 must be opened for talks and closed after satisfactory progress in order to move Turkey's accession process forward. The last two chapters, respectively entitled 'Institutions' and 'Other Issues', are opened following the closure of the first 33. These two chapters include provisions about issues not covered under any specific chapter and the candidate country's anticipated proportion of representation in EU institutions. Once negotiations are completed on all 35 chapters, a 'Treaty of Accession' is signed between the candidate country and all member states.[16]

So far, Turkey and the EU successfully opened and closed one chapter, 'Science and Research', which requires implementing measures to ensure that the candidate state is able to participate in the EU's 'Framework Programmes for Research and Technological Development'.[17]

Of the remaining 32 'chapters', whereas 15 have been opened, the EU General Affairs Council, an executive body that brings together foreign ministers of EU member states, blocked 8 in 2006 in a decision backed by France.[18] In its judgement, the EU cited the relevancy of these chapters to Turkey's restrictions against Cyprus, evidenced by Turkey's blocking of Cypriot Greek ships and aircraft entrance to Turkish territory. These restrictions violated the additional protocol to the EU–Turkey association agreement, which expanded the EU–Turkey customs union to ten member states, including Cyprus.[19] Accordingly, the EU General Affairs Council has blocked another six 'chapters' with Ankara, based on requests, this time directly by the Cypriot government.[20]

At the same time, Turkey did not meet the opening benchmarks for three 'chapters' in 2018, despite the absence of blockage by Cyprus, France or the EU on political grounds. This time, the blame falls more directly on Ankara.

The first of these 'chapters' concerns public procurements, which Erdogan objects to since upgrading Turkey's public procurement policy endangers generous business deals and contracts he often awards to his supporters. The second 'chapter' Erdogan seems uninterested in opening focuses on competition policy, to which he objects for similar reasons. Finally, Ankara has not met the benchmarks for the 'chapter' regarding social policy and employment, which requires ensuring full trade union rights, including the right to strike and the right to bargain collectively both in public and private sectors, and the submission of an action plan for the enforcement of relevant EU rules with regard to the entire labour force.[21] Similarly, with its judicial independence under assault following the Ergenekon-Sledgehammer trials, Turkey failed to make progress to move forward with Chapters 23 (Judiciary and Fundamental Rights) and 24 (Justice, Freedom and Security) of the accession talks.

Unsurprisingly, while no substantial progress has been made on Turkey's EU negotiations, Croatia deservedly became a member in 2013.

How many people died in the First World War, and what are their names?

These hurdles and hoops that the EU created for Turkey to jump through and achieve membership undoubtedly undermined Turkish support for EU accession.

A joke about Turkey's EU accession, as told by my friend and Turkish columnist, Soli Ozel, encapsulates the disappointment Erdogan and the Turks felt, correctly or not, at the EU's refusal to treat Ankara's accession equally alongside previous candidate countries' membership talks. The joke is that after dealing with a number of accession countries for several years, the EU becomes sick and tired of the talks and calls in candidate countries, Serbia, Montenegro and Turkey, for a test on European history. The EU tells the three countries that they will be asked one question. If they get the answer right, they can join the EU; answer wrong, and they will be rejected. The Serbs are offered the question: 'When did the First World War begin?' This is an easy question, and the Serbs answer: '1914.' Doors open, bells ring and Serbia joins the EU. Then, the Montenegrins are asked: 'When did the First World War end?' This, too, is an easy question. The Montenegrins answer: '1918.' Doors open, bells ring and Montenegro joins the EU. Finally, the Turks are asked: 'How many people died in the First World War, and what are their names?'

Democracy problems

The simplistic takeaway of this joke for Turkey's citizens is sad and clear: the EU treats them with double standards because they are Muslims and 'different'. In the policy world, however, other factors played an even bigger role in slowing down Turkey's membership process, as once top EU official in charge of Turkey's accession, my friend, Sir Michael Leigh, put it for me:

> To be sure, the fact that Turkey has a predominantly Muslim population is an issue especially for Christian Democrats – though it has always been robustly rejected by Socialists and other political groups and by the EU's institutions as a reason for opposing Turkey's eventual membership. Other reasons for doubts include size, standard of living, large agricultural sector and implications for the EU's structural funds and budget, geographic location, and, of course, failure to meet the political criteria for membership. For years, the Commission bent over backwards to give the most objective and generally favorable analysis possible in its annual reports of Turkey's 'progress' in meeting the political criteria. It was only when Erdogan's slide into authoritarianism became blatant that the Commission ceased to repeat every year that Turkey 'sufficiently fulfills' the political criteria for membership.[22]

This was, indeed, the case toward the end of the last decade. I wrote for *The Washington Post* in February 2009:

After six years of AKP rule, the people of Turkey are less free and less equal, as various news and other reports on media freedom and gender equality show. In April 2007, for instance, the AKP passed an Internet law that has led to a ban on YouTube, making Turkey the only European country to shut down access to the popular site. On the U.N. Development Program's gender-empowerment index, Turkey has slipped to 90th from 63rd in 2002, the year the AKP came to power, putting it behind even Saudi Arabia. It is difficult to take seriously the AKP's claim to be a liberal party when Saudi women are considered more politically, economically and socially empowered than Turkish women.[23]

According to the World Economic Forum's Global Gender Gap Report, published in 2009, measuring women's empowerment using criteria such as economic participation, political empowerment and educational attainment, Turkish women actually lost economic and political power between 2006 and 2008, with their empowerment score dropping by 0.0022 points. In 2008–9, that number dropped by 0.0025 points, rendering Turkey the country with the biggest gender gap among all upper-middle income countries.[24]

Women have been among the groups that under the AKP have suffered most, politically, even during years of high Turkish economic growth. Women's employment dropped by 0.8 per cent between 2003 and 2007, while men's employment increased by 1.8 per cent, according to research conducted by the Turkish Federation of Entrepreneurs and Business World (TURKONFED), a lobby group that serves as a voice for small and medium-sized Turkish businesses.[25] The decrease in women's employment was significant despite an average 1.1 per cent annual increase in employment during this period. By 2010, the takeaway for those analysing democracy in Turkey was simple: Erdogan increasingly failed to satisfy the EU's political criteria, i.e. strong liberal democracy and respect for egalitarian values needed for EU accession.

Bad endings

In the case of Turkish and European ties, it is a two-way street. Many states in Central and Eastern Europe – some of them not exactly beacons of democracy in the late 1990s – had entered the Union in 2004, just as Ankara was about to start accession talks. Additional states would join the Union in the following years, with Turkey remaining a 'candidate country', while the debate on whether Christianity was a core value of the EU became prominent among right-wing parties in certain EU states such as Germany, France and others. What is more, the 2008 global financial crisis and its repercussions inside the EU, with successive Euro crises, too, added to enlargement fatigue, further eroding support for Turkey's membership among EU member states.

These disappointments have left a bitter taste in the mouths of Turkey's citizens. Consequently, many Turks soured towards the membership process, with public support for accession dropping precipitously. According to a recent poll, public backing for EU accession dropped from 61.8 per cent in 2016 to 48.4 per cent in 2017 – a nearly 13 per cent drop in one year alone.[26]

As Europe ignored Turkey, Erdogan felt free not only to drop the ball on membership talks with the Union, but also to swivel Turkish foreign policy more overtly towards the Middle East. Turkey turned away from Europe following what it saw as a Brussels and Franco-German bloc's slight, and then the floating of the previously mentioned 'Shamgen Zone' idea in 2011.[27] The EU effectively lost Turkey as early as 2005, when it failed to offer Ankara a fair accession process, such as the implied promise of close-ended talks it offered to all candidate countries, which came before Turkey.

Limp power

What is worse, the EU has overall played an unwitting role in helping contribute to dynamics that have also catalysed the demise of democracy in Turkey. Many member state leaders failed to appreciate the nature of Erdogan's nativist and populist political movement, which is not much different from the far-right parties that have recently emerged on the European continent.

The hope of joining the EU became a key driver of Turkey's democratisation process in the 1990s, with the prospect of membership providing an incentive for major liberalising reforms. For instance, the EU's 1999 promise to open accession talks with Turkey if it fulfilled the

Union's political expectations led to the elimination of capital punishment from Turkish law, as well as efforts to eliminate torture from the country's police stations and jails.[28]

When Europe shows a serious commitment to Turkey, it responds by liberalising. In 2000, although public opinion in Turkey supported capital punishment for Abdullah Ocalan, jailed leader of the PKK, the Turkish government, thanks to the EU's luring power, selected maintaining the possibility of membership, and refused to execute the leader of an organisation that had killed thousands of Turkish citizens. The EU subsequently failed to provide Turkey with a fair and realistic-looking accession process. It has also failed to use its soft power, which could have helped further democratic consolidation in Turkey.

One could, of course, also argue the opposite, that authoritarianism has always been alive and well in Turkey and that Erdogan's bent toward it reflects that fact. In other words, the problem has less to do with the EU than with Turkey.[29]

Whichever explanation one adopts, the EU's reluctance toward Ankara has permitted many Turks to turn away from the negotiations. This has allowed Erdogan to dismiss criticism from the EU. If the EU had been delivered stern repercussions, such as the threat to suspend talks and cut off Foreign Direct Investment and development funds from Turkey to undermine Erdogan's electoral success, it would have forced him to be more serious and, most likely, would have mediated his authoritarian tilt.

How Europe got Erdogan wrong

Perhaps more consequentially, Brussels insisted on curtailing the Turkish army's power as one condition for EU membership instead of ensuring that Erdogan simultaneously put strong democratic checks and balances in place. The Union rightly expected to see civilian control of the military in Turkey, as was the case in member countries. The EU was right to insist on the TAF's exit from politics in order to consolidate Turkey's democracy; however, it was wrong to expect that a movement with illiberal antecedents would execute the latter task.

With notable exceptions, EU officials and politicians in member states seemed to think the military was the main obstacle to democracy in Turkey. Further developments proved them completely wrong. Once he neutralised the generals during the Ergenekon–Sledgehammer trials, Erdogan no longer felt it was necessary to please Brussels. In fact, there is a direct correlation between Turkey's slide regarding democratic freedoms, which started around 2007–10, and the defanging of the TAF and its allies during the Ergenekon–Sledgehammer cases in the same period.[30]

Missed opportunity

After helping Erdogan force the military out of his way and catalysing EU-favourable political change, Brussels still had a chance to help save Turkey's democracy. If it wanted to, in the last decade, Brussels could have played a role in tempering Erdogan's power grab, but it missed that opportunity as well.

In the last decade, Erdogan's electoral wins were fuelled by record amounts of FDI flowing into the country, mostly due to Turkey's status as a country in accession talks with the EU. Had Brussels sternly called Erdogan's attention at the time, for instance, by suspending or threatening to suspend accession talks, he *would* have listened and his democratic transgressions would have certainly been tempered. However, the EU did not act, and Erdogan moved forward.

In 2010, Erdogan won a referendum, which gave him the prerogative to appoint a majority of judges to Turkey's high courts, without a confirmation process, thereby endangering judicial independence in the country, and yet the EU did nothing. When the head of Poland's ruling Law and Justice Party (PiS), Jaroslaw Kaczynski, and his ally, Poland's President Andrzej Duda, tried to do the same in their country in 2018, passing legislation that allowed them to stack the high courts with their own, hand-picked, judges, the EU sued Poland, also threatening Warsaw that it could lose its voting rights in Brussels. These credible threats forced Kaczynski and Duda to rewrite legislation to comply with EU law: Brussels successfully made Poland come to heel.[31]

However, with member states such as Germany and France objecting to Turkey's full membership and making the process look unrealistic in the eyes of many of Turkey's citizens, as encapsulated by the joke from Ozel above, Brussels could, perhaps, not use the credible threat of suspending talks to nudge Erdogan into a democratic course correction. To put it simply, the EU could not suspend what it did not offer – with big thanks to France and Germany. This dilemma left Erdogan free to sail in his own direction at home – once he had brought the TAF to its knees, the courts stacked with his hand-picked judges and the media and business communities intimidated through politically motivated tax fines and audits.

Cruising east

The EU's mishandling of Turkey, including the often conflicting positions between Brussels and member states toward Ankara's accession process, the member states' shifting views of Turkey's membership and the Cyprus blockage in foreign policy, subsequently also encouraged Ankara to look away in its foreign policy. Erdogan started to cultivate warmer ties with its Muslim-majority neighbours to the east and the south. Though Turkish–EU economic ties remain robust thanks to the Customs Union, and the key role that European trade plays for the Turkish economy, and Turkey's cooperation with the EU on controlling migration, politically Ankara continues to pivot away from Europe.

Washington-based Turkish scholar Kemal Kirisci once told me he thinks of Turkey's foreign policy course as being similar to that of a giant oil tanker slowly changing shipping lanes in the ocean. Europe gave fuel to Erdogan's gradual shift in foreign policy away from the continent. From 2005 onwards, just as Turkey's accession talks were put on ice, he gradually rolled out a new foreign policy agenda, departing from Turkey's traditional orientation of focusing on Europe.

To this end, Erdogan had fuel to burn: Turkey's newfound soft power in the Middle East. This eastward wind encouraged him to test Ankara's traditional ties also with Washington, and then gradually to navigate the country away from Europe and the West.

6

AN AMERICAN AFFAIR

Together with the slow end of Turkey's EU dreams, zigzagging US–Turkish ties shaped Ankara's relations with the West during the first decade of the twenty-first century.

At this time, Erdogan's (and Davutoglu's) conviction that, equipped with soft power, and by taking stock of its recently found clout in the Middle East, Turkey could afford to act independently of its Western allies to influence its Muslim-majority Middle Eastern neighbours. Simultaneously, however, Erdogan, who felt threatened by the secularist TAF at the time, wanted to make sure he had Washington's backing against the generals. Therefore, he did his best to avoid crises with Washington – a stark difference when compared to his policy towards the USA and in the Middle East, including in Syria, in the 2010s – right after he had defanged the secularist military in 2011.

The Iraq War debacle

The Iraq War of 2003 was Erdogan's first test with the United States. In early 2003, Ankara was under significant pressure from Washington to cooperate in the event of an American attack on Iraq. When then US Vice President Dick Cheney visited Turkey in 2002 (just before the AKP's ascent to power in the November elections later that year), he asked Ankara for permission to open a northern front against Saddam Hussein. Bulent Ecevit, Turkey's prime minister at the time, rebuffed the United States.[1]

Washington saw a potential for AKP success in the approaching November election polls, which predicted the latter would win. It saw this chance materialise when the AKP won the election. The US Government invited Erdogan to visit Washington in December 2002, though he held no official position in Turkey at the time. On 5 February 2003, the new prime minister and AKP member, Abdullah Gul – who briefly took the country's helm between November 2002 and March 2003 while Erdogan waited to run in the February 2003 by-elections to join the Turkish parliament and qualify for prime minister – declared support for military action in Iraq. Gul also asked Parliament to open military bases to American troops, reluctantly (he and Davutoglu were working behind the scenes to make sure that Parliament would not approve the war).

Erdogan, who controlled the AKP as its chair, though he was not yet prime minister at the time, allowed his party's members in the legislature to 'vote their consciences' on the legislative motion to permit US troops to open a northern front in Turkey.[2] This was a departure from the tradition of 'whipping' in parliamentary democracies, where parties enforce factional discipline in legislative votes. In a historic vote on 1 March 2003, with many AKP and opposition Republican People's Party (CHP) deputies voting against it, the motion received 264 votes for and 250 against, with 19 abstentions. However, since Turkish law (as interpreted by the country's Constitutional Court) requires the majority of all present members to vote for a motion to authorise deployment of foreign troops inside the country, the motion was rejected despite receiving more votes because it technically failed to garner the required 267 votes of the 533 deputies present. Although initially raising hopes in Washington, the new AKP government ended up refusing to aid the United States in the Iraq War.

Erdogan found himself between a hammer and an anvil, leading up to the vote: public opinion opposed the war; Washington, whose support he wanted to retain, expected him to support it. As mentioned earlier, the generals simply sat on their hands at the time, letting Erdogan call the shots, hoping that he would engage in poor decision-making and anger either Washington, the Turkish public or both. But, the legislative vote fixed this dilemma, while also addressing Erdogan's challenge. He could inform Washington that blame for Turkey's failure to support the US war fell on this technical glitch in the vote in the country's Parliament. And for the public, what mattered was that, in the end, Turkey did not enter the war. An astute politician, and with the help of some well-timed luck, Erdogan had just passed his first big test, firming his position at Turkey's foreign policy helm, while successfully navigating between the secularist generals, Turkish public opinion and the United States. The Iraq vote in Turkish Parliament also made Turkey popular on Arab streets. Balancing foreign policy challenges and crises with domestic opportunities and political calculations would later become Erdogan's trademark – the 2003 Iraq War is where he learned to master it.

. . . and the mess that followed it

The Turkish Parliament's Iraq War vote, nevertheless, strained US–Turkish relations. Many in Washington took a hostile view of Ankara for not supporting the United States in the war, some even unfairly blamed Turkey for the 2005 Iraqi insurgency.[3] Most Turks felt slighted by the fact that Washington launched the Iraq War despite a democratic vote in a country that was, at the time, a staunch NATO bastion.[4]

From the Turkish perspective, there were also several key issues that Washington did not address during its request to deploy troops to Turkey. For one, Washington did not provide the Turks with sufficient guarantees against threats potentially arising from US military efforts in northern Iraq. During the ally-enforced no-fly zone in northern Iraq in the 1990–1 Gulf War, the PKK (which is responsible for the death of almost 40,000 Turkish citizens over the past several decades) was able to entrench its presence along Turkey's borders. As northern Iraq became a staging ground and safe haven for the PKK, Ankara pushed for guarantees that Iraq's territorial integrity would be protected during the war. In October 2001, then Prime Minister Ecevit stated that an independent Kurdistan along Turkey's borders would furnish, without a doubt, a *casus belli* situation.

As Ankara saw it, Washington never shared a credible end goal or exit strategy regarding Iraq with Turkey. Ankara also did not see any relevant security threat to Turkish interests from the Saddam regime in Baghdad. While Saddam Hussein was perceived as a difficult neighbour with whom Turkey managed to live for more than three decades, he would not – despite his tyrannical bent – dare bother Ankara.

Additionally, Turkey and Iraq shared a robust economic relationship, heavily benefiting the former. In 2001, Turkey suffered a calamitous economic crisis that left hundreds of thousands of people unemployed, shrinking its economy by nearly 10 per cent. Erdogan knew that in the event of a campaign against Saddam, the country could also suffer significant financial damage through loss of tourism and trade revenues, endangering its fragile economy and jeopardising its recovery, and undermining his tenuous hold on power at the time, with only 34 per cent of popular support. In order to alleviate Turkish concerns about the US Government promising financial aid to Turkey for allowing the Americans to stage troops in the country, the US Congress passed legislation providing Ankara with $1 billion in loan guarantees. Four weeks after the early March vote, although Turkey never took advantage of this loan offer, the decision was a token of US willingness to support Ankara financially.

However, Erdogan was not ready to break from the USA. Therefore, following the failure of the vote in Parliament, he granted the United States fly-over rights across Turkish airspace. At the same time, however, his government embraced a policy of hammering Washington, which carried grave ramifications for future US–Turkish ties.

The 'Hood Incident': Anti-Americanism and anti-Semitism go mainstream

Anti-Americanism has existed in Turkey since at least the late 1960s and 1970s, when many leftists took issue with the country's support for the United States during the Cold War. However, following the Iraq War, the AKP government brought anti-Americanism to Turkey's centre of gravity, causing it to go mainstream to an extent not seen before.

In July 2003, in what was perceived in Ankara to be retaliation against Turkey's decision not to enter the war in Iraq, US troops detained and hooded Turkish Special Forces who were operating covertly in the Iraqi city of Sulaymaniyah and allegedly targeting an elected official of US ally Patriotic Union of Kurdistan (PUK). This event was later dubbed the 'Hood Incident' and depicted in the Turkish box-office hit, *Valley of the Wolves: Iraq*. This movie later went on to become an all-time hit in Turkey. Anti-American views spread in Turkey like brush fires, often fuelled by pro-government media at this time. Another film, *Metal Storm*, a thriller adapted from a novel, alleged that the Iraq War was a US-led organ-harvesting operation benefiting Jews and Israel, and became an all-time success as well. After attending the premier viewing, Erdogan's spouse, Emine Erdogan, expressed her pride in the movie.[5]

Opinion polls such as a BBC survey carried out in January 2005, showed that 82 per cent of Turks opposed the Bush administration.[6] It was, indeed, true that Turks became more critical of US foreign policy during this time. Moreover, such sentiments, previously expressed vocally mainly by fringe political Islamists, socialist and Marxist leftist constituencies, now pervaded nearly the entire political landscape, uniting political Islamists, nationalists, leftists, rightists and centrists on a common platform.

Erdogan's administration was surely also not the first in Turkish history to criticise Israel harshly. Most notably, in 2002, then Prime Minister Ecevit asserted, 'Israel carried out genocide against civilians/ Palestinians.'[7] Where Erdogan's administration differs, however, is in the way in which it utilised anti-Israeli rhetoric to make anti-Semitism mainstream, once unacceptable in centrist political circles in Turkey. During the Gaza war in 2006, for instance, Istanbul's AKP-run city government put up oversized billboards, depicting a burnt child's sneaker, with the words, 'Humanity has been slaughtered in Palestine', written above it. Under the sneaker, in large print, the billboard quoted the Old Testament commandment, 'Thou shall not kill,' adding, 'You cannot be the Children of Moses.' The billboards were prominently placed in Istanbul's mixed Muslim–Jewish Nisantasi neighbourhood. The next day, vigilantes distributed fliers calling for a boycott of Jewish businesses in Nisantasi, prompting some Jewish businesses in the neighbourhood to take down their name signs the following day.

In another example of government efforts to mainstream anti-Semitism and anti-Americanism, the Istanbul city officials opened a cartoon exhibit in the city's central Taksim Square metro station in early February 2009. The station is a government-owned public service, and Taksim Square is to Istanbul what Times Square is to New York City. Tens of thousands of commuters pass through it each day. The exhibit included cartoons depicting bloodthirsty Israelis killing Palestinians with American help. One such cartoon showed a satanic-looking Israeli soldier washing his hands with blood from a faucet labelled, 'The United States'.

Such propaganda has not been without consequences. A 2008 Pew survey found that 76 per cent of Turks maintained a negative view of Jews, marking a 49 per cent increase from 2004.[8] During the Gaza war in 2006, Israelis (including Israeli teenagers visiting Turkey to play volleyball) faced attacks. Shopkeepers plastered signs on their windows saying, 'Americans and Israelis may not enter.'

Despite incidences of anti-Israel and anti-US sentiment at this time, in terms of Ankara's engagement, Turkish–Israeli and Turkish–US ties were at one of their historic best.[9] The irony is that, although Erdogan maintained good ties behind closed doors with Israel and the United States, his rhetoric demonised the two countries (and also the EU), often lumping all under the rubric of the 'perfidious West'. He has, for instance, often and repeatedly labelled Israeli policies as 'genocidal' and castigated the West for 'being immoral'.[10] In a speech in 2014, he said, 'They look like friends, but they want us dead, they like seeing our children die. How long will we stand that fact?'[11]

Israel often received the most severe criticism from Erdogan. He gave an early warning sign of the brewing storm regarding ties with Israel at the 2009 World Economic Forum summit in Davos, Switzerland, when he chided Israeli President Shimon Peres, stating: 'One minute! . . . When it comes to killing, you know well how to kill.'[12] Before that moment, many Israeli policy-makers had ignored Erdogan's anti-Israeli rhetoric. Peres, in fact, had been one of Erdogan's greatest fans, telling me at a Washington Institute meeting in 2007 that he 'had great hopes' for him.

Erdogan has often used anti-Israeli rhetoric to mobilise his nativist base for domestic political gains. For instance, his 'One Minute' episode with Peres was repeatedly recycled on media friendly to him in the run-up to the 2010 referendum, which allowed him to stack the country's high courts with his hand-picked candidates.

With some exception, not only Israelis but also some of my US Government friends, who worked in the Bush administration at this time, dismissed Erdogan's rhetoric as politicking. Once considered harmless, Erdogan's collective remarks eventually led to severe political consequences: few people in Turkey today care for the West, many oppose EU accession, many more hate America and almost no one likes Israel.

Canary in the coalmine

Erdogan, nevertheless, cultivated good ties with Israel in the early years of his tenure as prime minister. Most notably, he built a positive rapport with Israeli Prime Minister Ehud Olmert, and also offered to negotiate disputes between Israel and Syria, where he hoped to bring his perceived influence over Assad into the talks. However, his Israel policy was Janus-faced. For instance, in 2006, he reached out to Hamas, an anti-Israel, violent, political Islamist faction linked to the Egyptian-based Muslim Brotherhood. Hamas had just won a resounding victory in the 2006 Gaza elections for the Palestinian Legislative Council.[13]

This latter development signalled a see-saw change to come in Turkish–Israeli ties. Ankara had recognised Israel in 1949. Until Egypt's recognition of Israel at Camp David in 1978, Turkey was the only Muslim-majority state to have diplomatic ties with the Jewish state. For decades, Ankara maintained good relations with Israel and Palestinians alike. For example, while it signed many cooperation agreements with Israel, enhancing bilateral political ties, it also allowed the Palestine Liberation Organization (PLO) to open an office in Ankara in October 1979 (though only after the PLO received observer status at the United Nations in 1974 and received recognition as the representative of the Palestinian people). In the balancing act between the Israelis and the Palestinians, Ankara attempted to establish itself as an honest broker. For a while, both the Israelis and the Palestinians appeared to respect its position. For instance, in 2007, both Israeli Prime Minister Shimon Peres and Palestinian President Mahmoud Abbas spoke at a Turkish parliamentary meeting. This perception notwithstanding, Erdogan increasingly signalled stronger support for the Palestinians, especially Hamas. Turkey adopted a very critical view of Israeli actions against Hamas and its leadership. In 2004, Erdogan labelled Israel's targeted assassinations of Hamas leaders Sheikh Ahmed Yassin and Abdel Aziz al-Rantisi 'state terror'.[14] Similar negative commentary from AKP leaders further dampened the relationship. However, Erdogan and then Turkish Foreign Minister Gul's visit to Israel and the Palestinian territories in early 2005 partially alleviated the problems.

The visits by Erdogan and Gul assured both sides of Turkey's continued desire to act as a just mediator, but in 2006, Khaled Mashal, a Hamas military-wing leader, appeared in Ankara.[15] Despite fierce debate in the Turkish press and objections from secular-minded foreign policy elites in the Turkish Foreign Ministry, Mashal's visit received backing from Erdogan and his AKP government. Thus, Mashal was hosted at the AKP offices instead of the Turkish Foreign Ministry.

Mashal's visit was, nevertheless, important because it allowed Davutoglu to launch his long-awaited 'Strategic Depth' policy towards the Middle East. By inviting Mashal to Ankara, Erdogan and Davutoglu took the first step towards their vision of distancing Turkey from Israel (and the West as they saw it) in order to curry favour with Turkey's Muslim neighbours in the region. The Mashal invite signalled the coming rupture in Turkish–Israeli ties over Hamas and Gaza, which many Israeli policy-makers chose to ignore at the time. Having so few friends in the Middle East, Israel could not imagine that Erdogan or a Turkish leader in Ankara would one day become a key regional opponent.

Even if some in Washington, including US Vice President Cheney, were perturbed by the fact that Erdogan had not been honest with them regarding plans for Mashal's visit, others saw it as a potentially positive development. Washington and Jerusalem hoped that as a 'moderate political Islamist' politician, Erdogan would help moderate Hamas.

However, as a democratically elected head of a political Islamist party, Erdogan felt an affinity with Hamas' electoral win in Gaza and offered it unyielding support, even as Israel and its allies took steps to isolate the latter internationally. Erdogan's unwillingness to budge regarding Hamas, and later on the broader Muslim Brotherhood in the Middle East, of which Hamas is an offshoot, suggests that solidarity with the Muslim Brotherhood, the Ikhwan in Arabic, has a close place in his heart. Regardless of Hamas' use of violence, Erdogan became one of its greatest defenders. His unconditional support for political Islamist parties (especially those linked to the Ikhwan) became one of the most recognisable parts of his international political brand.

Every US president's Rorschach test

Overall, the Bush administration ignored Erdogan's pro-Ikhwan tilt. This is because Bush interpreted Erdogan's politics through the prism of his own 'Rorschach test' of Muslim politics, giving Erdogan a hall pass, as did his successor Obama – but at least in one instance, not Trump.

Bush saw in Erdogan a faithful Muslim, with whom, he, a faithful Christian, could do business. Bush, and policy-makers around him, also viewed Erdogan as a 'moderate political Islamist' leader, who ran in democratic elections and accepted democratic legitimacy – a welcome antidote to al-Qaeda's brand of violent political Islamism. This was a comforting assessment, considering Erdogan became Turkey's prime minister less than two years after the attacks of September 11, 2001.

Erdogan's initial embrace of EU accession helped support these conclusions. In fact, until recently, Erdogan has been a master in reading and exploiting the international zeitgeist. By embracing the EU process right after the September 11 attacks, he made a case that there should be no cause for international concern over the AKP's illiberal antecedents in the National Outlook, Welfare Party or Virtue Party. His narrative suggested that, on the contrary, Turkey's friends in the West should embrace the AKP as a 'democratic antidote' to al-Qaeda – enter the 'Turkish/Erdogan model' of 'moderate Islam' in the early part of the first decade of the twenty-first century (a view also held by Obama).

Europeans were further enamoured with Erdogan's strong pro-EU tilt and viewed him and his policies through a pair of extra rose-tinted glasses. When I asked a West European diplomat friend of mine what he thought of Erdogan in 2003, he told me he 'wished all Muslims in Europe supported leaders like Erdogan'. A 'Muslim leader who embraced the EU' could simply not cause concern, neither in Brussels nor in Washington, my friend added. Ironically, many of the same EU politicians and bureaucrats would unite a decade later in their efforts to block Erdogan from carrying out campaign rallies or setting up pro-AKP parties across Europe.

Not all European bureaucrats and politicians viewed Erdogan as a positive ally. Most notably, some on the right, such as Rasmussen, the Danish prime minister between 2001 and 2009, did not trust Erdogan. Nor did Rasmussen see Erdogan's party simply as a benign and 'Muslim Democrat' movement, parallel to the European Christian Democrat parties.[16]

Similarly, US policy-makers did not necessarily view Erdogan entirely naively. Rather, they also took into account Ankara's strategic value to Washington. While Turkey's neighbours, including Iran, Iraq, Syria and Russia, have presented key challenges to Washington starting in the late 1940s, US presidents have historically aimed to cultivate Turkey and its leaders. This policy overall guided Bush's and Obama's approach to Erdogan. Trump's economic sanctions against members of Erdogan's cabinet in retaliation for Ankara's detention of American Pastor Brunson in 2018 were an exception to the traditional approach of US presidents towards Turkish leaders, not the norm.

Bilateral ties (always) improve when Washington helps Ankara against the PKK

A key problem between Bush and Erdogan was the latter's disappointment with Washington's lack of support for Turkey's campaign against the PKK camps inside Iraq. By 2007, domestic pressures amidst a series of PKK-led attacks on Turkish soldiers prompted Erdogan to toughen his stance. Ankara threatened a cross-border invasion,[17] targeting Iraq-based PKK camps from where the organisation had been launching attacks into Turkey. At the time, with Iraq going through an al-Qaeda-led insurgency and suffering hundreds of bomb attacks and deaths across the country every month, Iraqi Kurdistan remained a uniquely peaceful part of the country. A Turkish invasion there threatened to destabilise the relative calm.

Washington reacted by reaching out, and Bush's ties with Erdogan gradually improved, after deteriorating in 2003–5. At the time and at the onset of his 2008 standoff with the secularist generals in the Ergenekon–Sledgehammer trials, as well as the case in the Turkish Constitutional Court to shut down the AKP, Erdogan had his own interests to improve ties with Washington. He recognised that maintaining America's support meant he could stand firm against the generals. In November 2007, Erdogan met Bush in Washington, demanding concrete action from the White House against the PKK. The event also functioned as a perfect photo opportunity for Erdogan to be seen with the leader of the most powerful nation in the world only months before taking on the generals. During the meeting, Erdogan asked the United States to commit to increased military cooperation and intelligence sharing against the PKK, as well as to blocking money movements to the group.[18] Following the meeting, Bush agreed to increase the flow of 'actionable intelligence' to Turkey in its fight against the Kurdish separatists, and his administration urged the Iraqis to crack down on the group.[19] Baghdad complied, shutting down the offices of a political party associated with the PKK.[20]

Kurds in Turkey: Divided three ways

When Bush decided to strengthen US support for Turkey against the PKK, my journalist friends called to ask: 'What do the Kurds in Turkey think of US policy targeting the PKK?'

My answer was: 'Which Kurds?' Kurdish citizens, who constitute around 15 per cent of Turkey's population, are not a monolithic bloc. They are divided roughly three ways into political blocs of descending size.'

Just over a third of the Kurds are secular and leftist, mostly supporting the pro-PKK People's Democratic Party (HDP), a liberal-Kurdish nationalist alliance that in 2019 has 65 seats in the country's 600-member legislature. A little less than another third of Turkey's Kurdish citizens lean conservative, and many of them support Erdogan. The final, smallest bloc of the Kurdish population is integrated into the broader Turkish population through marriage, migration and experience of living in mixed neighbourhoods and cities, and generally shies away from ethnic identification in national politics.

This being the case, what do the Kurds in Turkey, and for that purpose, the country's broader citizenry, think of US policy regarding the PKK? Large segments of the country's population, including quite a few pro-Erdogan Kurds, oppose, and in some cases even despise, the PKK. US policy to assist Ankara against the PKK has near universal support in Turkey, with an overwhelming majority of the country's population viewing the PKK as a terrorist entity or a generally undesirable group.

Increased US support for Turkey against the PKK under Bush, therefore, jump-started a new era of cooperation between Ankara and Washington. In return, Erdogan began working closer with Washington, garnering further support for US stabilisation efforts in Iraq by urging the Iraqi government to accept the 2008 Security of Forces Agreement that oversaw the status of US forces in Iraq.[21]

Obama's 'window to the Muslim world'

With Bush leaving office in early 2009, the newly elected US President Barack Obama made his first historic overseas country visit to Turkey in April 2009 – of course, this is not including a sojourn in next-door Canada and attending bilateral summits. Obama turned a new page in the bilateral US–Turkish relationship.

Whereas Bush and Erdogan started their relationship with the Iraq War crisis, Obama experienced a much more positive start with Erdogan. Many of Erdogan's AKP colleagues welcomed the new Obama presidency. Some were even convinced Obama was Muslim, nicknaming him 'Our Huseyin.'[22]

Like Bush, Obama approached Erdogan through the prism of his own 'Rorschach test' of Muslim politics. Obama, mistakenly, saw Erdogan not as a right-wing politician who had just started locking up his opponents in the Ergenekon–Sledgehammer case, or eroding women's political power, but rather as a 'window to the Muslim world'. Obama approached Erdogan, hoping that Ankara would help broadcast and amplify his message to Muslims that America was not at war with Islam.

Obama's historic trip to Turkey, which he framed as part of his outreach to the Muslim world,[23] caused his popularity to skyrocket within AKP circles and Ankara. In a great show of symbolism, he picked Turkey as the destination of his first overseas trip after Canada and bilateral summits in Europe. The AKP officials considered Obama visiting Turkey an acknowledgement of the party's successes rather than recognition of modern Turkey and the country's status as a US and NATO ally.

During his visit to the Turkish Parliament, Obama stated:

This is my first trip overseas as President of the United States. I've been to the G20 summit in London, and the NATO summit in Strasbourg, and the European Union summit in Prague. Some people have asked me if I chose to continue my travels to Ankara and Istanbul to send a message to the world. And my answer is simple: Evet – yes. (Applause.) Turkey is a critical ally. Turkey is an important part of Europe. And Turkey and the United States must stand together – and work together – to overcome the challenges of our time.[24]

It seemed for a moment that Obama had caught Erdogan in the right place. It was as if, by casting Turkey as a model country, Obama had found a platform from which to speak to Muslims and a partner to broadcast his message of moderation, peace, democracy and tolerance to the nearly 2 billion Muslims in the world.

Crippled by the flotilla

Obama's dreams for Erdogan notwithstanding, the 2010 'Flotilla Incident' between Turkey and Israel and Turkey's 'against' vote at the UN Security Council on Iran sanctions backed by Washington both proved that Erdogan could be more elusive than Obama had hoped.[25]

Turkish–Israeli relations faced a watershed moment on 31 May 2010, from which bilateral relations have never fully recovered. Towards the end of May in 2010, six civilian aid ships titled the 'Gaza Freedom Flotilla' left Turkey and Greece in an attempt to break the Israeli blockade on Gaza and deliver aid to the Palestinian territory. Israeli commandos ambushed the ships loaded with Turkish aid workers (all non-governmental organisation representatives) in international waters. Of the six, the Turkish *Mavi Marmara* resisted and violent clashes between Turkish aid workers and Israeli soldiers broke out, with activists reportedly using wooden clubs and kitchen knives. The violent ordeal resulted in nine Turkish citizens and one Turkish–American dual-national being killed by the Israeli forces.

With harsh injuries inflicted by both sides, the boats were forced to dock in Israel. Nearly 700 activists were detained after they refused to sign deportation papers and remained in prison until their eventual release.[26] Although the UN High Commissioner for Refugees (UNHCR) considers the blockade illegal, then UN Secretary-General Ban Ki-moon's investigation into the event, dubbed the 'Palmer Report' – after Sir Geoffrey Palmer, a former prime minister of New Zealand and the lead UN investigator into events on the main flotilla ship, the *Mavi Marmara* – found that Israel was justified in upholding the blockade, much to the disappointment of Ankara.

Needless to say, the *Mavi Marmara* incident completely demolished Turkish–Israeli ties. Ankara downgraded its diplomatic relations with Israel, which followed suit. Bilateral military cooperation, the bedrock of the relationship, was also frozen. In June 2011, the flotilla's conservative Turkish co-organiser, Humanitarian Relief Foundation (IHH), began planning 'Gaza Freedom Flotilla II'. However, this attempt never materialised due to heavy international pressure against it.

During a private phone conversation between Erdogan and Netanyahu in 2013, the latter apologised and offered $20 million in compensation. The negotiations, brokered by Obama led to an agreement to return ambassadors, which was finalised, after another three years of talks, in 2016. However, bilateral Turkish–Israeli military and intelligence ties never fully recovered after 2010.

Shifts views of Turkey in the US military

The Flotilla Incident had deep repercussions also in Washington, fundamentally undermining Turkey's image in the US Department of Defense as a rare Muslim-majority country that could get along with Israel, a key US military ally. This development cost Ankara dear support within the Pentagon. Together with the debacle of the 2003 Iraq War, the Flotilla Incident negatively remoulded the US military's image of Turkey.

The Pentagon, Turkey's greatest friend in Washington for decades until Erdogan's rise, would subsequently, and gradually, switch to become his and Ankara's chief adversary in the US capital. And later policy differences between Ankara and Washington during the Syrian Civil War and in the war against the Islamic State in Iraq and Syria (ISIS) (explained in Chapters 7 and 13) would only further erode Turkey's image within the US military.

But comes with a reward for Erdogan

This being the case, the rift with Israel came with a silver lining for Erdogan, earning him accolades among political Islamists and Ikhwan-related movements in the Middle East. Overall, regardless of Washington's mediation and the urges of the Obama administration, Turkey and Israel, two US allies, pivoted away from each other following the events of 2010, with Israel taking a negative view of Erdogan for his continued support for anti-Israel groups like Hamas.

Iran vote crisis at the UN

Indeed, 2010 was the year of crisis in US–Turkish ties. In spring 2010, the AKP's opposition to sanctioning Iran's nuclear programme emerged in stark contrast to the international consensus Washington was building around the issue. By mid-summer, US–Turkish relations were in tumult, with disagreements on a number of issues – such as Turkey's relations with Israel and how to deal with Iran's growing nuclear ambitions – undermining Washington's historical bond with Ankara.[27]

In the 2009–10 term at the UN, Turkey became a temporary member of the UN Security Council. During a critical vote to sanction Iran over their nuclear programme in June 2010, Turkey and Brazil voted against the resolution. This was a squandered opportunity for both parties in the Obama–Erdogan relationship. At first, Obama encouraged Ankara (and Brasilia) to negotiate a nuclear deal between Tehran and Washington. The USA, which was intently focused on passing Security Council sanctions against Iran, then, however, rejected the deal, dubbed the 'Tehran Agreement', and which it considered weak, brokered by Erdogan and Brazilian President Luiz I. Lula da Silva.

In turn, despite a phone call from Obama asking Erdogan to abstain, Turkey voted against sanctions at the UN Security Council, where Ankara had secured, by way of its soft power, a non-permanent seat for the first time since 1961.[28] With close Turkish ties to Iran more apparent than ever, the United States felt that their NATO ally's decision undermined US national interests and a rift soon emerged. As a result, former US Defense Secretary Robert Gates commented, 'I'll be honest, I was disappointed in Turkey's vote on the Iranian sanctions.'[29]

The AKP leadership used intense rhetoric to defend Tehran's programme after the vote, suggesting that Ankara did not perceive Iran's nuclear growth to be as worrisome as Israel's nuclear arsenal. For about two months, it looked as though this vote would sever US–Turkish ties completely. Along with Turkey and Israel's 'Flotilla Crisis', the Iran vote contributed to the deterioration of US–Turkish ties in 2010.

Obama makes up with Erdogan

Setbacks notwithstanding, Obama would simply not give up on Erdogan or Turkey. There was also positive news from Ankara at this time, including Turkish efforts to normalise ties with Armenia, a prospect holding enormous value for Obama given US domestic political dynamics, including the large number of Armenian-Americans voting for Obama's Democrat Party. After an intense debate inside the US government on how to properly handle Ankara, a frank and straightforward conversation between Obama and Erdogan on the sidelines of the G20 summit in Toronto in June 2010 improved the dynamics between the two leaders – at least for a while. At that meeting, Obama reportedly told Erdogan how upsetting Turkey's UN vote had been to him, asking Erdogan to halt anti-Israeli invectives. His candour helped clear the air between the two leaders. Turkey's Iran policy soon shifted: Ankara stopped defending Tehran and insisting that the United States recognise the stillborn 17 May 2010 nuclear fuel swap deal that Turkey had brokered with Tehran and Brazil.

The United States and Turkey entered a period of calm in late 2010, with Obama and Erdogan enjoying probably the best relationship between a US president and a Turkish prime minister in years. When Turkish media outlets reported that after Erdogan's mother died, Obama was among the first world leaders who called him, the two 'spoke for 45 minutes about their feelings'.[30] The two leaders began chatting often – at least a dozen times in 2011, alone – and began to agree on policy more frequently. Just a couple of months prior, Turkey's relationship with Washington had been wavering and Ankara's Iran policy was oscillating. Now, however, Erdogan and Obama seemed to have struck the right balance in relations between their two countries. What is more, in January 2012, Obama described Erdogan as one of five leaders with whom he had established 'bonds of trust'.[31]

Beautiful (early) days of the Arab uprisings

The uprisings in Tunisia, Egypt and Libya offered Ankara and Washington a welcome opportunity to cooperate, though only after some initial hesitation.

Prior to the 'Arab Spring', Erdogan and Davutoglu had cultivated ties with former Ottoman lands in the Middle East and beyond, ignored by Ankara's elites for much of the twentieth century. In 2010, as the uprising started in Arab countries, Erdogan appeared ready to promote a softer form of secularism in these states, one that allowed for freedom of religion in government, politics and education, much different from the Kemalist model of the past in Turkey.

The 'Erdogan Model' appealed to socially conservative Arab countries, where quite a few of them traditionally regarded Turkey's Kemalist-era secularism, which mandated *no* religion in government and education, as an anathema. Erdogan's embrace of religion made Ankara a good fit for Obama's thinking, as the US president was busy searching for partners with whom to navigate the tumultuous waters of the Arab uprisings.

Turkey's embrace of a Muslim identity and the new Turkish middle-class society, midwifed by Ozal and brought to maturation by Erdogan, cast Ankara as a better partner for Obama. Thanks to Erdogan's 'economic miracle', Turkey had become a relatively wealthy, functioning Muslim-majority country during the first decade of the twenty-first century. At the onset of the Arab uprisings, Obama could not find a better possible model to promote than that presented in Erdogan's Turkey.

In reality, however, Ankara was initially lukewarm toward the Arab uprisings. It was concerned about disorder and instability in its backyard – hence its tactical transition from caution to attempting to curb or manipulate the inevitable disorder and instability in Arab-majority countries in its favour.[32] Turkey initially warned others when protests started in Tunisia in December 2010. It brought attention to the Libyan and Egyptian protests, stating support for 'reforms and democratization . . . [through] peaceful transformation, not through violence, attacks against civilians, or by . . . creating instability'.[33] However, Erdogan started to coordinate his policies with Obama after Ankara concluded that dictators such as Libya's Mu'ammer Gaddafi would eventually fall, and only after Turkey evacuated the nearly 10,000 Turkish workers and engineers who had relocated to Libya since the 1980s in larger and larger numbers to take advantage of booming opportunities for Turkish businesses there.

Erdogan adopted caution also towards Syria. He moved to oppose Assad some five months after the revolt against Assad started. At this

time, Washington and Ankara alike aspired for a 'soft landing' in Syria
– an end to Bashar al-Assad's rule without descent into chaos. Disorder
in the Middle East, now at Turkey's doorstep in Syria, suddenly looked
menacing to Turkish interests. The US–Turkey convergence was so
apparent that in September 2011, Turkey abandoned its rhetorical
hedging that Iran 'has the right to pursue nuclear energy research for
peaceful purposes', and joined NATO's missile defence shield.[34]

Yet, Erdogan and Obama saw different potential gains from the Arab
uprisings. Once shunned by outsiders as an 'Islamist', Erdogan saw his
AKP as an evolutionary model that could help Ikhwan-affiliated political
Islamist parties transform during the Arab uprisings. According to his
logic, parties linked to the Ikhwan, such as those in Egypt and Syria,
could moderate and come to power through democratic elections, as
the AKP had done in Turkey when it had split from the FP. Such an
outcome would offer the added benefit of creating natural regional allies
for Turkey. With the Ikhwan's initial rise to power in Egypt, Erdogan's
vision seemed to be coming to fruition. Likewise, in Syria, Ankara began
supporting the faction to help it emerge as the leader of the country's
opposition. Erdogan pursued similar strategies in Tunisia and Libya,
although with mixed results for Turkish power and reach across North
Africa.

Obama, on the other hand, was more of a realist: he vacillated
between supporting democratic movements and regime stability during
the Arab uprisings. Erdogan, too, vacillated, delaying joining the US
effort in Libya, and then getting out in front of a US effort in Syria. This
would eventually bring the former and latter back into conflict.

Fallout

The most dramatic period in the two leaders' relationship arrived
between May and July 2013. First came the best part. On 16 May 2013,
Obama hosted Erdogan and his family in Washington. This was a truly
genuine welcome: the US president opened up Blaire House to the
Erdogan family, hosting them in the warmest way possible in Washington,
and the two leaders presented themselves at a friendly news conference
on 16 May at the White House Rose Garden – against the backdrop of
colourful spring blooms.

Sadly, however, after this spring crescendo, came the free fall in the Erdogan–Obama relationship. The first roadblock emerged only days after Erdogan and his family returned to Turkey: the liberal Gezi Park protest movement against Erdogan in Turkey swept the country.

On 28 May 2013, Turkish police cracked down on a group of pro-environment protestors, who had camped in Istanbul's downtown Gezi Park to prevent the government from digging up the park to build a shopping mall instead. This particular incident inspired normally uninvolved citizens to mobilise and support the protestors. Soon, images of police violence careened across social media. Istanbul was consumed by an insurrection, with further protests occurring throughout the country until the end of the summer. Erdogan responded on 30 May 2013 with a bloody crackdown.[35]

On 2 June 2013, the White House criticised Ankara's violent crackdown on the Gezi Park demonstrators, saying, 'we expect Turkish public authorities to act with restraint'. On 23 December 2013, for the first time since Erdogan's rise, the press in Turkey began calling for the American ambassador to leave.[36] Unsurprisingly, these calls came from pro-Erdogan newspapers such as *Star*, *Yeni Safak* and *Aksam*. The events underlined a growing dynamic: the Turkish government using its media to target Washington.[37] Needless to say, Obama was very unhappy.

The second roadblock between Obama and Erdogan arrived following their disagreements over the fall of Egyptian President Mohamed Morsi between June and July in 2013. Egyptian dictator Hosni Mubarak was ousted from power on 11 February 2011, following mass rallies against him. A candidate from the Egyptian Ikhwan, Morsi then won the country's presidential elections in June 2012. For Erdogan, who backed the Brotherhood in Egypt, it appeared as though he had just won the jackpot, by gaining a new ally at the head of the most populous Arab state.

Morsi's hold on power, however, proved tenuous, and he was toppled just as quickly as he gained it. In June 2013, anti-government protestors took to the streets, demonstrating for the ousting of Morsi. By early July, a coup led by the military-made Defence Minister Abdel Fattah el-Sisi successfully deposed Morsi and placed Sisi as the new president. Appalled by Morsi's fate, Erdogan denounced the coup, despite Obama's suggestions that it was time to move forward and treat Sisi as the new head of Egypt. While Obama accepted the new reality in Cairo with General Sisi's government, Erdogan resolved not to recognise the status quo in Egypt, or a coup against a fellow political Islamist leader.

Erdogan blamed Obama for the coup in Egypt,[38] and continued doing so even after Obama asked Erdogan during a phone conversation to shy away from making such allegations. The end of Obama's political love affair with Erdogan came when the latter refused to stop accusing the US for Egypt's new government. During this time, Ankara and Washington also diverged on Syrian policy, when Turkey threw its support behind the Brotherhood affiliate there, without apparent success.

From that point until leaving office in early 2017, President Obama was less enthusiastic towards the Turkish leader. Tellingly, when Erdogan came to Washington in March 2016 to inaugurate a Turkish government-sponsored mosque complex in the Maryland suburbs, on the outskirts of Washington, DC, Obama ignored Erdogan's requests to dedicate the mosque together.

The most consequential decision by an American president regarding Turkey

Erdogan, too, started to cool towards Obama when the latter was in his second term, during the course of their relationship. Starting in 2014, this was due to the latter's budding fascination and growing relationship with the PKK offshoot, the People's Protection Units (YPG).

Desperately seeking allies in Syria with which to counter and defeat ISIS, but committed to doing so without putting US boots on the ground, in 2014–15 Obama was urgently looking for fighters willing to combat ISIS on behalf of the US.

Taking a cue from the YPG's battlefield successes against ISIS in Mt Sinjar, Iraq, in the summer of 2014, and then in Syria in the fall of the same year, Obama gradually decided to forge a relationship with YPG to combat ISIS. After the siege of Kobane (explained in detail in the next chapter) ended in October 2014 with a successful YPG-led defence against ISIS, the YPG's utilitarian value increased in Obama's eyes. However, the PKK and YPG share overlapping command structures and are closely linked and intertwined. Obama's slow pivot to the YPG caused the biggest crisis ever witnessed in the US–Turkey relationship – at least this was the perspective from Ankara, which felt it could not get its message regarding the PKK–YPG relationship across to Washington.

To be fair, Obama did look for alternatives. In June 2015, the United States initiated a $500 million programme, entitled 'Train and Equip', to arm and train moderate Syrian rebels, including segments of the Free Syrian Army (FSA) to fight ISIS.[39] However, this failed bitterly. The programme yielded only a handful of graduates, who quickly perished or were captured on the battlefield, in Syria. A clandestine programme run by the US government in southern Syria fared better, but even then, the forces that it built were unprepared to stop ISIS. In 2015, Obama embraced the YPG even stronger, with the US military leading, and many others in the US government following him in this gradual and incremental approach.

Obama then made incremental moves to support the YPG, to the point where Washington decided to provide weapons to the YPG – through proxies. Turkey, the USA and NATO recognise the PKK as a terrorist group, but only Turkey designated the YPG as a terror entity as early as 2014. Nevertheless, because Washington wanted to avoid risking providing weapons to an offshoot of a terrorist entity, it needed fig leaves. Enter umbrella organisations such as the Syrian Arab Coalition (SAC). In October 2015, the YPG rebranded itself as part of the Syrian Democratic Forces (SDF), itself consisting of an alliance of a number of smaller Syrian factions, such as the SAC. The YPG, of course, remained the dominant faction inside the SDF.

When Erdogan objected to the USA's October 2015 decision to provide weapons to the SAC (that ended up in the hands of the YPG), Obama informed him that the United States would proceed, regardless.

Obama's decision to start an arming programme that helped the YPG in Syria through proxies (even if to combat ISIS) is one of the most consequential decisions by a sitting US president regarding Turkey in recent memory, and may have irreversibly poisoned US–Turkey ties. An overwhelming majority of Turkey's citizens, including many Kurds, oppose the PKK and see anyone who helps it as an enemy. In 2019, US policy to work with the YPG had helped Washington push back against ISIS, preventing further attacks against the American homeland as well as US allies. Turkey understands the need to defeat ISIS, but will never accept working with the YPG towards that end. An overwhelming majority of Turkey's citizens and policy-makers (including those opposed to Erdogan) will remember Obama as the American president who 'gave weapons to the PKK'.

Turkey or the Syrian war or ISIS no longer presented Obama with daily problems at the end of his term in 2016, but Syria's bloody civil war has ushered in severe security challenges for Ankara. As the 'Arab Spring' morphed into the 'Arab Winter', Erdogan's Middle East aspirations stalled. To make things worse, he could no longer call his once favourite US president for help.

7
THE SYRIAN DISASTER

Starting in 2013, Ankara and Washington slowly slid into opposition and misunderstanding on Syria that has deeply compromised their broader relationship.

Even more problematic for Turkey, when Erdogan authorised the arming of the anti-Assad rebels early in the Syrian Civil War to oust the Assad regime, he almost certainly misread the risk to Turkey's newly established soft-power nation status in the Middle East, as well as opening Pandora's box against a raft of enemies, among which were the YPG, the Assad regime and his international supporters, Russia and Iran, two key powers that are Turkey's historic nemesis and competitive adversary in foreign policy, respectively.

Erdogan's hostile stance towards Damascus also meant that Ankara was abandoning a key element of its traditional Middle East policy that it had followed since the fall of the Ottoman Empire: neutrality in regional politics. In any case, Erdogan's entanglement in Syria had the result of butting Ankara against its problematic neighbour, yet again.

Enter modern Turkey's most problematic neighbour

Except for brief periods, Turkey's relations with Syria have been tense since the latter broke away from the Ottoman Empire. Ruled by Ottoman Turks between 1517 and 1918, Syria has presented Turkey with almost persistent security challenges – more than any other of Ankara's neighbours for nearly a century.

Following the collapse of the Ottoman Empire, Syria fell under French Mandate rule in 1920. Throughout the interwar period, the new government in Damascus provided a safe haven to anti-Ataturk groups from Turkey who fought against his regime in Ankara.[1]

In the 1920s, large numbers of Kurds from Turkey crossed the border into Syria, mostly as refugees, following a number of failed Kurdish uprisings in Turkey, as well as to avoid the Turkish nationalist campaign of Ataturk and his successors. Not keenly liked by the locals, especially the more indigenous Arab populations, these Kurds settled in large concentrations along Syria's north-eastern border with Turkey, joining other Kurds already living in the region. Later on in the 1960s, the Syrian government disenfranchised large numbers of Syrian Kurds, including many originally from Turkey, stripping them of their citizenship, but also subsequently channelling their anger towards Ankara. For decades, the Syrian Kurdish community became an exceptionally disproportionate recruitment pool for the PKK, which Damascus has used as leverage against Ankara.

Almost without exception, successive Syrian governments had their reasons to be hostile towards Ankara. The roots of this hostility lie largely in the issue of the Sanjak of Alexandretta that has undermined Turkish–Syrian ties ever since the end of the Ottoman Empire – *sanjak* was an administrative district in the Ottoman Empire.[2] Following the First World War, the Sanjak of Alexandretta, then a multiethnic Ottoman district with a sizable Turkish community – known today as Hatay Province in Turkey – came under French Mandate rule within Syria. Nonetheless, the 1920 Ankara Treaty, which ended the Franco-Turkish War, stipulated that the Mediterranean-littoral sanjak would be governed by a special regime designed to protect the cultural and linguistic rights of the Turkish community there.

In the late 1930s, as France was preparing to end its colonial rule in Syria, the future of Alexandretta became an issue. To keep Ankara on its side against the rising Nazi German threat, Paris agreed to spin the sanjak completely out of Syria, making it an independent state. During the first week of September 1938, the sanjak was christened as the Republic of Hatay. This, however, proved to be a short-lived political entity as the Parliament of the nascent Hatay Republic voted to join Turkey on 29 June 1939. Successive Syrian governments never got over the loss of the sanjak to Turkey and, to this day, official maps of the Syrian Arab Republic show Turkey's Hatay Province as part of that country.

During the Cold War, Turkish–Syrian ties were further strained. In 1957, the two countries came to the brink of war. At the time, Syria joined forces with socialist Egypt and South Yemen to form the United Arab Republic (UAR). Threatened by the rise of a socialist giant next door, Ankara massed troops on its border with Syria in response. Though a war was eventually averted, Cold War politics cast Ankara and Damascus as regional adversaries.

In 1963, following a coup led by members of the Arab socialist Baath Party rule in Damascus, the two countries found themselves at even further opposing ends of the Cold War divide, with Turkey staunchly aligning with NATO, and Syria emerging as one of the Soviet Union's most reliable allies in the Middle East. Problems only increased and Syria's rejection of Turkey's annexation of Hatay became more vociferous after the Assad family came to power in Damascus in 1970. The Assad dynasty hails from Syria's Alawite heartland, along that country's northwest Mediterranean Coast, just across the border from Hatay.

What is more, Hatay happens to be home to a large and strongly left-leaning Arabic-speaking Alawite community, which has traditionally supported opposition forces against successive Ankara governments. (Turkey is a mainly right-wing dominated country: between 1950, when it became a multiparty democracy, and until 2019, the left has ruled the country – on its own – for only 17 months.) During the Cold War, a number of Alawites from Hatay joined radical leftist groups, including the radical and violent People's Liberation Party-Front of Turkey (THKP-C), which enjoyed the backing of Damascus against Ankara.

The Hatay issue deeply resonates in Syria. In 2006, during my visit to Damascus, I was impressed to discover the apparent strength of ties between the Assad regime and Ankara back then. For instance, Turkish diplomats in the Syrian capital were given royal treatment by the Syrian authorities. However, during the same visit, I was also surprised to see maps in the offices of Assad regime officials, showing Hatay as part of Syria. I left Damascus, convinced that Assad's show of friendship towards Erdogan was not genuine, and that it was not a matter of if, but when, Turkish–Syrian ties would suffer again.

Damascus–PKK nexus

Following the civil war in Syria, not surprisingly, through its offshoots and with Assad's permission, the PKK has returned to undermine

Turkish–Syrian ties, providing Damascus with a lever against Ankara. As mentioned earlier, the PKK has strong and historic ties to Damascus. The Assad regime played a key role in helping to prop up the group against the backdrop of Cold War dynamics.

During the Cold War, Turkey was the soft underbelly of the Soviet Union. In fact, Turkey's 531 kilometre (330 miles) border with the Soviet Union represented the only physical point of contact between a NATO member and Moscow, excluding Norway's much shorter border with the Soviet Union, north of the Arctic Circle.

Throughout the Cold War period, Moscow backed the PKK, a Marxist–Leninist group, to use it as leverage against Ankara, then a staunch US ally. Enter Damascus, with Cold War proxy war dynamics in play: the first PKK training camps were established in 1982 in Lebanon's Beqaa Valley, conveniently occupied at the time by the Soviet ally, Syria. The Assad regime provided the PKK with logistical support throughout the Cold War. It harboured the group's members for decades, and the PKK leader, Abdullah Ocalan, lived in Damascus during the 1980s and the 1990s.

Following the end of the Cold War, the Syrian government adjusted its policies regarding Ankara and the PKK. At the time, Turkey was building a number of large dams across the Euphrates River. Syria, which, as a downstream country, relies on irrigation from the Euphrates for much of its agricultural production, used the PKK as a bargaining chip in negotiations with Turkey over water rights of the Euphrates River – but also in the long game regarding the Hatay issue. With a majority of Syrian Kurds disenfranchised and stateless under the Baath regime, many of whom were refugees from Turkey a few generations ago, Assad also saw the PKK as a useful tool with which to further direct the Syrian Kurds' nationalist anger away from himself and toward 'the enemy'.

Recognising the potentially destabilising impact of a Syria-based PKK insurgency across its longest land border, Ankara took bold steps against Damascus in September 1998, threatening invasion unless the regime stopped harbouring the group.[3] Turkish pressure worked, and in September 1998, Bashar al-Assad's father Hafez al-Assad kicked Ocalan out of Syria and signed the Adana Protocol with Turkey, officially ending his support for the PKK.[4]

Following his expulsion from Syria, Ocalan went on an international tour to find a safe haven. In February 1999, Turkish officials caught him in Kenya – with US assistance – and brought him to Turkey, where he was put on trial. A Turkish court sentenced him to death in June 1999. However, as a consequence of Turkish reforms to qualify for EU membership, which included eliminating capital punishment, his sentence was commuted to life imprisonment. To this day, Ocalan remains in jail on Imrali Island, Turkey's Alcatraz, on the Sea of Marmara, an isolated and punishing rocky outcrop, popular in the past among Istanbul's former Byzantine emperors, who sent their fallen princes there after gouging out the royals' eyes.

'Turkish Spring' in Damascus

Ocalan's expulsion from Syria drastically changed Turkish–Syrian ties. Ankara's relations with Syria, strained since the 1920s, recovered after 1998. Remarkably, Turkish President Ahmet Necdet Sezer attended Syrian President Hafez al-Assad's funeral in 2000. Relations further improved in 2003, after Ankara refused to take part in the United States' invasion of Iraq. For the first time in decades, Ankara and Damascus were aligned on a regional issue. Bashar al-Assad, who succeeded his father as Syrian president in 2000, made a presidential visit to Turkey in 2004, signalling the start of a new chapter in Turkish–Syrian relations.

In line with Davutoglu's 'Zero Problems' policy, Erdogan went out of his way to court Assad. Assad reciprocated for his own reasons. At this time, the assassination in February 2005 of Lebanese Prime Minister Rafic Hariri in Beirut, with the alleged involvement of the Syrian regime, had put Assad in bullseye internationally. The latter was more than happy to appear to be good friends with the NATO ally, Turkey, a strategy that, among other reasons, helped him avoid severe international consequences for the Hariri assassination. Assad took Erdogan's hand and shook it even more strongly. Subsequently, Turkey and Syria signed a Free Trade Agreement (FTA), held joint cabinet sessions and Erdogan lifted visa restrictions for Syrians travelling to Turkey. Ankara even briefly facilitated dialogue between Syria and Israel, upon the request of both countries, but this effort failed after its own relations with Israel started to deteriorate.

Assad's game

When Assad launched his crackdown on the anti-regime demonstrations in the spring of 2011, Erdogan thought he had built enough influence over Damascus to stop him from killing civilians.[5] Then Turkish Foreign Minister Davutoglu even flew to Damascus in early August 2011 to advise the latter to refrain from using violence against the crowds and form a new government, which would include members from Syria's Muslim Brotherhood.[6] However, only hours after Davutoglu's departure, Assad sent tanks into Hama, a centre of the rebellion, snubbing the 'Zero Problems' policy, Davutoglu and Erdogan.[7]

Whereas Erdogan believed he was building people-to-people bridges with Syrians, for example by lifting travel visa restrictions, the Assad regime had a different vision of this 'rapprochement'. Throughout the first decade of the twenty-first century, Assad took advantage of his developing ties with Ankara, a member of NATO, to gain legitimacy internationally – all while oppressing his people and letting Erdogan believe he was the new sheriff in Damascus. My impression regarding the hollow nature of Erdogan's influence over Assad, gathered during my visit to Syria in 2006, turned out to be correct.

The Arab uprisings ended this kabuki dance. When Assad snubbed Erdogan, this demonstrated that there had never been any true rapprochement between Assad and Erdogan, and nor had Ankara built any real power over Damascus. Ankara's influence in the Middle East proved to be more Fata Morgana than reality. This interplay also revealed Turkey's true intentions for Syria, they were really advocating for the Muslim Brotherhood to take power in Damascus.

Erdogan flips against Assad

Ankara's stance against Damascus reversed in August 2011, after Erdogan's plea for the Assad regime to halt its violent repression went unheeded. Erdogan went from being Assad's 'friend' to becoming his chief adversary.[8] At this time, Obama encouraged Erdogan to press hard against the Assad regime – though, later on, Washington dialled back against Damascus, and this would become part of Ankara's grievances against the USA.

In 2011, Erdogan also had his own reasons to act against Assad's pique. Appalled by the latter's refusal to take his advice and outraged by Assad's brutal crackdown on civilians, Erdogan decided to back the uprising, opening Turkey's borders to anti-regime rebels, including, soon after, an increasing number of radicals. Erdogan's goal was to prove that Turkey called the shots in the Middle East, while exacting revenge on Assad for betraying his friendship. He simply believed that the Syrian Muslim Brotherhood would replace Assad.

But, without a 'Syrian army' at bay

Ankara sheltered Syrian activists and allowed them to form the Syrian National Council (SNC), a coalition opposing Assad and largely dominated by members of the Syrian Muslim Brotherhood. With US assistance, involving a clandestine arming programme initiated in early 2012, Turkey also started to provide weapons to the rebels. The rebels included mostly rural Sunni fighters, many of whom identified with the Muslim Brotherhood, hardly a representative cross section of Syrian society.

Ankara failed to build broad ties with representatives of Kurdish, Alawite, Druze, Shi'ite, Assyrian, other Christian and secular Sunni groups in Syria. Given Syria's diversity – non-Sunni Arabs constituted nearly 40 per cent of Syria's pre-war population – the SNC struggled to get off its feet against the Assad regime. Further complicating Erdogan's plans, relatively few defections from the Assad regime took place among the groups mentioned above. Ankara failed to build a truly 'Syrian army' to oppose Assad.

And goes for regime change in Syria

By the end of the summer of 2011, following Obama's cues – in August 2011, the USA called for Assad to resign – Ankara, likewise, was calling for Assad's ouster.[9] A senior Turkish diplomat told me at the time that this led Erdogan to believe he had Washington's unconditional backing to go full force into Syria.[10] Having worked with the United States and other NATO allies to overthrow the Gaddafi dictatorship in Libya (though after initial foot-dragging), Erdogan believed that cooperation was possible in Syria against Assad.

The Turkish leader hoped that if he boosted the rebels enough, he could eventually convince the USA to establish 'safe havens' in northern Syria, protected by 'no-fly zones' enforced by Washington, guarding rebel-held territories, paving the way for a final assault on Damascus to oust the Assad regime.

From the beginning, this ambitious policy faced hurdles, some Syrian-made and others manufactured in Turkey. In 2011, Syrian army dissenters who fled to Turkey founded the Free Syrian Army, a loose network of brigades fighting the Assad regime. Since then, the group's leadership has been based in Turkey,[11] with dozens of members allowed to coordinate attacks from sites inside Turkey, heavily guarded by the Turkish army and in cooperation with Turkey's National Intelligence Organization (MIT).[12] Yet, despite efforts to support the Syrian opposition, Turkey's inability to broaden the political arm of the FSA and the FSA's struggle to stand on its own two feet against Assad in the initial years of the war, meant that the Ankara-backed rebels failed to become a formidable force against Assad in the civil war. The FSA eventually got on its feet in 2015, but by that time, al-Qaeda's Syrian affiliate had already infiltrated its cadres.[13]

Other factors played a role in the FSA's general initial weakness. At first, the Turkey-based leadership of the FSA did not have easy access to units stationed in Syria. Unlike other Syrians settled in refugee camps along the Turkish–Syrian border, Ankara settled these FSA officers deeper inside Turkey and exercised a greater level of control over them. As the rebel group seized territory along the Turkish–Syrian border in 2012, it eventually gained access to supply routes and communication channels to connect them to the leadership based in Turkey.[14]

As Assad increasingly proved to be a formidable force, Ankara shifted its calculus. By early 2012, Turkey began to turn a blind eye to weapons transfers across the border. Hundreds of rocket-propelled grenade launchers, Kalashnikov rifles, machine guns and ammunition, reportedly supplied by Saudi Arabia and Qatar,[15] were distributed to groups fighting in Idlib, Hama, Homs and in the outskirts of Damascus.[16]

Also without getting America firmly on board in the end

Erdogan had to secure American assistance for his campaign against the Assad regime to make sure that the regime would be ousted. The rebels' lack of progress towards Damascus risked prolonging the conflict – and only Washington could change the equation, by establishing a US–protected no-fly zone in northern Syria, providing a launch pad for a major assault against the Syrian capital. Indeed, the infusion of American power by arming the rebels or enforcing a no-fly zone would change the military and regional dynamics, helping to unite the often squabbling 'Friends of Syria' countries that opposed Assad internationally behind American leadership, including Turkey. Only direct American military engagement would rally the disparate parties wanting to act against Assad into unified action, Ankara reasoned.[17] However, to Erdogan's dismay, this and his much wanted no-fly zone idea never came to fruition.

Indeed, Ankara had depended on US support when taking a decisive stance against Assad in 2011. However, as the war dragged on, Obama ignored Turkey's constant requests for a more decisive stance against Damascus and the establishment of a no-fly zone by the US–led coalition. Simply put, Obama wanted no part in direct military involvement in Syria. Obama, perhaps inadvertently, misled Erdogan in Syria: he had never intended to become directly involved in Syria's war.

Erdogan, on the other hand, mistakenly ascribed Obama's unwillingness to act in Syria to the 2012 US presidential elections. He believed that after Obama was re-elected, the latter would be free to take up a larger role in the Syrian war, including implementing the no-fly zone idea.[18] This was a wrong assumption, more wishful thinking than reasoned analysis. In fact, while many in the US government had made clear their support for an increased American role in the conflict, Obama himself feared getting bogged down in another Middle East war. Especially following his decisive 'Rose Garden Walk'[19] on 31 August 2013, in the aftermath of which he decided he would not follow through on his threat to punish Assad militarily – instead throwing the decision to a Congress that he knew wanted no responsibility for it. He ordered them to weigh in against robust military options against the Assad regime.[20] And, although Obama expanded the clandestine programme to arm the Syrian rebels, he repeatedly vetoed the no-fly zone idea, ultimately ensuring that the Assad regime and his allies would eventually quash the rebels. From this point on, it became certain that Erdogan was mostly on his own against Assad.

Together with the related problems of Gezi Park, Egypt and the YPG, the rift in Syria brought to an end the political romance between Erdogan and Obama. The three-year period of calm in US–Turkish ties from the summer of 2010 until the summer of 2013, guided by the personal rapport between the two countries' leaders, soon faded away. From this point forward, Erdogan knew he was not only going to have to act increasingly without Washington in Syria, but also often to butt heads against his ally and former friend, Barack Hussein Obama.

Assad's counter-move: Use the PKK (once again) against Turkey

Erdogan only pushed more aggressively against Assad when he realised that US support was not coming. More weapons started to flow to the anti-Assad rebels in Syria, with the conflict taking a particularly bloody turn after 2013. Seeing Turkey's growing and increasingly open support for rebels aiming to overthrow him, Assad brought the PKK back into the game – against Turkey. Although Assad's father had cracked down on the PKK, this had not been a complete shutdown. I saw numerous Ocalan posters and PKK banners in public during my 2006 visit to Kurdish areas in northern Syria – another reason I had left Syria at the time, convinced that Assad was playing Erdogan.

Having been allowed to recruit members and disseminate propaganda in Syria for decades, the PKK had gained a strong foothold in the country, including sleeper-armed cadres. In 2012, just as Erdogan started allowing foreign fighters to cross into Syria, the Assad regime vacated Kurdish-majority regions of the country along its border with Turkey, moving some troops from these areas to places where its authority was being directly challenged. The YPG, staffed by local Kurds – many from Turkey and others who are descendants of emigres in the early twentieth century and therefore holding a deep grudge towards Ankara – quickly filled the vacuum, also emerging as a threat to Ankara.

Assad now had a hand equal to that of Erdogan: while Erdogan was harbouring anti-Assad rebels in Turkish provinces, such as Hatay and Sanliurfa, across the border with Syria, Assad was harbouring the PKK offshoot in Syrian cities such as Kobane and Qamishli.

'A language is a dialect with an army and a navy'

The YPG was quick to take over areas vacated by the Assad regime because it maintained a network and presence in these areas. In 2003, as Erdogan was taking office, the PKK created regional proxies in the Middle East outside of Turkey, including one in Syria, to avoid embarrassing the Assad regime lest he be seen as harbouring the PKK, just as Erdogan was getting ready to extend him a welcoming arm.

Subsequently, the PKK launched a Syrian franchise named the Democratic Union Party (PYD), as well as Iranian and Iraqi offshoots: the Kurdistan Free Life Party (PJAK) and Kurdistan Democratic Solution Party (PCDK), respectively. Of these three franchises, however, only the Syrian progeny of the PKK truly flourished, confirming my observations regarding the deep-rooted and tolerated presence of pro-PKK networks in Syria during my 2006 visit there. After 2003, the PYD simply took over the PKK networks and cadres in Syria, successfully becoming the latter's Syrian offshoot, sprouting openly in 2012.

In addition to a tolerant political environment, the PYD's success in Syria as the PKK's branch can also be explained through similarities between Turkish and Syrian Kurds, including close idiomatic affinities. Linguist Max Weinreich wrote, 'A language is a dialect with an army and a navy.'

The Kurds as a nation speak three main, yet mutually non-intelligible, 'dialects': Kurmanji, Sorani and Zaza, and a number of pocketed minor 'dialects', spoken by small populations. The main 'dialects' are as different from each other as perhaps are Spanish, Portuguese and French within the Romance language family. Whereas Zaza, the most distinct and smallest of the three main Kurdish 'dialects', is spoken only by Turkish Kurds, Iraqi and Iranian Kurds speak Sorani. Some Iraqi

Kurds speak Kurmanji, as well. On the other hand, Syrian Kurds speak Kurmanji, the most widely spoken Kurdish 'dialect', which is also the dominant 'dialect' among the Turkish Kurds. These linguistic differences help explain the historic permissibility of the 'Turkish' PKK and its ideology among the Syrian Kurds, and the less hospitable reception to its ideology among the Iraqi and Iranian Kurds.

The PYD, which quickly moved in, taking control of the Kurdish areas of northern Syria vacated by the Assad regime – with his blessing – subsequently established three self-declared cantons in these areas, namely Afrin, Kobane and Qamishli. Kurdish-dominated areas were not contiguous, contained large populations of non-Kurds and had their own Kurdish opposition (non-PYD/PKK) elements. The PYD's military wing, the YPG, ruthlessly eliminated such opposition, establishing itself as the chief authority in the cantons. Collectively and informally known as 'Rojava', these PYD- and YPG-held areas soon became Erdogan's enemy in Syria – just what Assad hoped.

Erdogan retaliates against Assad: Enter more foreign fighters

Beginning in 2013, just after Assad had allowed the PKK to surface in Syria, and at the time he started to accept that the USA was not going to help him oust Assad, Erdogan allowed larger numbers of foreign fighters to cross into Syria to join various rebel groups, but also al-Qaeda affiliate Jabhat al-Nusra. There was no ideological test: all those willing to fight Assad were welcome to move through Turkey. In 2013 alone, according to one source, about 30,000 militants, most of them radicals, reportedly travelled through Turkey to Syria.[21]

At that point, the Turkish–Syrian border became merely a line on paper. Much of the border runs through the flat stretches of northern Mesopotamia. Drawn up at the end of the First World War by the French authorities and Ataturk's government, the border nearly follows a straight line for much of its length. In the absence of any clear geographic features to help delineate it for much of its length, Paris and Ankara drew most of the frontier line so that it followed the Middle Eastern portion of the Berlin–Baghdad railway (built with German financing during the late Ottoman Empire to provide Berlin with access to the

Persian Gulf). Accordingly, most of the Turkish–Syrian border runs across flat terrain: there are no physical barriers such as mountains, rivers or lakes for nearly three-quarters of its expanse of 911 kilometres (566 miles).[22]

The PKK had used this permeable border in the 1980s and 1990s to launch numerous cross-border attacks into Turkey, until 1998, when, following pressure from Ankara, the group's open targeting of Turkey from Syria ended. After 2011, the Syrian rebels took advantage of this terrain and Turkey's lax policy to criss-cross the border and establish smuggling networks to move people and weapons. The situation became a concern for Ankara with the rise of ISIS in 2014.

ISIS recruiters reportedly set up offices around Turkey to reach the youth, while crossing through Turkey into Syria. Some of the recruits were even seen buying supplies in border towns before crossing into Syria.[23] Despite Turkey's denial of tacit support for ISIS, Turkish media reported on wounded ISIS fighters receiving free treatment in hospitals in south-eastern Turkey before returning to Syria to fight Assad.[24]

Erdogan was discouraged by the decrease in Washington's already insufficient level of support for the rebels. To offset this, he continued to serve as a safe haven for the rebels, including radicals, further angering Obama. At least some of the fighters who crossed into Syria morphed into ISIS, joining forces with the 'core ISIS', al-Qaeda and former Baath Party members from Iraq.[25] Ankara's inability to predict and pre-empt the jihadist surge added to Washington's concerns about Turkey. Accordingly, some in Washington, especially in the Pentagon, started to view Turkey as a country that works with America's adversaries in Syria.

By August 2015, following intense US pressure, Turkey agreed to tighten its borders, but by then, thousands of foreign fighters had already reached Syria and Iraq.[26] These better funded and better armed radicals soon became the dominant faction in the country. Ankara did not intend for these extremists to gain the upper hand in Syria. In fact, Ankara believed that supporting all opposition groups indiscriminately and allowing the transfer of arms and fighters across the border would guarantee Assad's defeat. In a worst-case scenario, Ankara believed that it could control these radical forces, once unleashed.[27] Both turned out to be terrible fallacies.

The Battle of Kobane

The rise of ISIS in 2014 gradually engendered a new threat to Ankara. Nevertheless, the siege in 2014 by ISIS on the PYD-held town of Kobane across the Turkish border did not necessarily result in Turkey running to fight the jihadi group.

This is because, in Kobane, Turkey's YPG policy overwhelmed its ISIS policy and, as a result, shifted the entire dynamic between Ankara, Washington, the PKK and its affiliates (PYD and YPG) and ISIS in the power game for northern Syria.

When the PYD first took control of parts of northern Syria in 2012, Turkey was initially not openly hostile to the group. As mentioned above, at the time, Ankara was in peace talks with the PYD's mother organisation, the PKK. Accordingly, for instance, Salih Muslim, a key political leader in the PYD, was formally hosted in Ankara, establishing direct contact with the Turkish government. In 2013, Ankara also tried, and failed, to integrate the PYD into the Free Syrian Army. Erdogan's goal was to pressure the PYD to end its bid for autonomy in Syria and to cut their ties with the PKK and the Assad regime.[28] This effort, however, fell apart: in mid-July 2012, Turkish-backed rebel forces began clashing with the armed wing of the PYD, the YPG.[29]

In September 2014, ISIS launched a campaign to capture Kobane, the critical city belonging to the PYD's self-declared Kobane canton in northern Syria. As ISIS laid siege to dozens of villages near the town, tens of thousands of refugees fled across the border to Turkey.[30] The YPG appealed to the United States to intervene, and the PKK called on Turkey's Kurds to join the fight against ISIS.[31]

The battle for Kobane became the first clash against ISIS broadcast live to global audiences. International TV crews set up cameras on the Turkish side of the border – Kobane lies literally across from it – and began broadcasting the ISIS onslaught live. The captivated world audience exponentially became even more aware of ISIS atrocities.

Erdogan, who refused to help the YPG in Kobane, grossly miscalculated his decision. A global outcry to protect the people of Kobane against ISIS, coupled with the opportunity for the USA to bring about a crushing defeat of the jihadist group, led to one of the most consequential American decisions in the Syrian Civil War. The US-led coalition launched aerial attacks on ISIS near Kobane, followed by airdrops of ammunition and arms to the YPG, against Erdogan's wishes.[32]

Despite coalition air strikes and Kurdish resistance, ISIS seized parts of Kobane in early October 2014. As the Kurdish fighters grew weary, Washington pressed Ankara to do more, but Erdogan was unwilling to assist a violent ideology perceived as an existential threat for decades.

Ankara and the PKK were in nominal peace talks at the time. However, Erdogan is a master of electoral politics and often embraces Turkish nationalist sentiments across broader segments of the society to boost his popularity. He could not fathom helping the PKK's Syrian offshoot, especially as talks with the PKK appeared brittle at the time. Equating the YPG with ISIS, Erdogan said Turkey could not be expected to support a terrorist organisation.[33] The USA, which had already started air operations against ISIS, following the group's onslaught against Yezidis on Mount Sinjar in Iraq in the summer of 2014, signalled it would embrace the YPG in Kobane.

To stymie this eventuality, Ankara allowed Kurdish Peshmerga fighters, including those from the Kurdistan Democratic Party (KDP) – Erdogan's friend at the time – from Iraq to cross via Turkey to reach Kobane in late October.[34] Yet, he still refused to allow large amounts of military aid to cross its borders.[35] Meanwhile, 50–200 FSA militants also arrived in Kobane to prevent the fall of the town, which formed the nucleus of what would later become the Syrian Democratic Forces – a coalition of Arab, Kurdish and other Syrian forces, led by the YPG.[36]

After four months of fighting, Kurdish and Arab fighters managed to drive ISIS out of Kobane in January 2015.[37] The US military, which had already reached out to the PKK, PYD and YPG, including pushing back against ISIS during the jihadist group's siege of the Yezidis on Mount Sinjar in August 2014, was more than happy to counsel Obama and finally formalise ties with the YPG. The US relationship with the YPG sprouted by default rather than by an up-front policy decision in Washington, but Erdogan failed to appreciate this progression.

Furthermore, the rise of ISIS and the increase in terror attacks globally, from Paris in January and November 2015 to Orlando in June 2016 to Nice in July that same year, shifted the USA's primary enemy in Syria from the Assad regime to ISIS. Following ISIS atrocities, including the publicised execution of American journalist James Foley in August

2014, a horror that galvanised US public opinion against the jihadist group, the Obama administration changed its Syria strategy to solely focus on wiping out ISIS (contrasting to its initial half-hearted approach of toppling the Assad regime).

Talks between Turkey and the US to form a Turkey-backed militia to fight ISIS stretched; Obama lost patience, and eventually decided that he had found a reliable partner (the YPG) on the ground that could counter the ISIS threat.[38] This was Erdogan's biggest misstep in foreign policy to date: he had just skipped an opportunity to deliver a crushing blow to the jihadist group together with the USA, and simultaneously prevent further growth of the budding YPG–USA relationship.

Enter ISIS

Turkey is no friend of ISIS, whose goal of sweeping away the nation states of the Middle East in favour of a fundamentalist caliphate clearly challenges Ankara. Yet, Ankara delayed action against ISIS.

Beyond his Kobane calculus, a number of other factors slowed Erdogan down in entering into combat against ISIS. On 11 June 2014, ISIS took 46 hostages from the Turkish mission in Mosul, Iraq, including diplomats and their families.[39] Erdogan worked diligently through Arab proxies in Iraq and Syria to secure the release of these hostages in the same month as Turkish citizens were glued to the news. He delayed joining the anti-ISIS campaign until he secured the release of the Turkish citizens in September 2014. This was understandable, because ISIS was busy executing civilians at the time and Erdogan did not want to put Turkish citizens, including children, in harm's way.

Erdogan felt a bit readier to push against ISIS. At this time, a joint US–Turkish 'Train and Equip' programme had been put in place to wrest the ISIS hold of the Manbij pocket along the Turkish–Syrian border, which the group used to smuggle fighters and weapons into Syria and jihadist fighters into Europe. 'The "Train and Equip" program to support the Syrian rebels grew out of the need to close the Manbij pocked without the YPG.'[40]

In September 2014, Turkey joined other NATO countries united against ISIS, pledging political support for the alliance's efforts, but Erdogan delayed real action, realising that Ankara had further vulnerabilities vis-à-vis ISIS, namely a small Turkish exclave, the Tomb of Suleyman Shah, inside Syria.

The 1920 Ankara Treaty delineating the Turkish–Syrian border had left this tomb, where the grandfather of the house of Osman I (the Ottoman founder) had been interred in the thirteenth century, as an exclave inside Syria, designating it as Turkish territory. A number of Turkish troops guarded this tomb. By early 2015, ISIS had encircled the tomb, and Turkish soldiers faced a potential slaughter. Erdogan decided to 'evacuate' the tomb. In February 2015, Ankara carried out an overnight military operation, with US intelligence assistance, alongside support from the YPG (at the time, Turkey was in peace talks with YPG's mother organisation, the PKK). Together, they relocated both the tomb and the Turkish soldiers to a safer spot within Syria, near the Turkish border.[41]

Erdogan had just truly eliminated Turkey's vulnerabilities vis-à-vis ISIS in Syria. During the summer of 2015, he granted the United States permission to use two airbases on Turkish soil – both Incirlik and Diyarbakir were used for carrying out aerial attacks, as well as search-and-rescue missions in operations against ISIS positions in Syria.[42]

ISIS was quick to retaliate – with blood and vengeance. On 10 October 2015, the terror group carried out the worst terror attack in Turkey's history: killing 103 people gathered at a pro-peace and anti-Erdogan rally in front of Ankara's central train station. ISIS attacks became a common occurrence throughout the following year, including the 5 June bombing in Diyarbakir and 24 July bombing in Suruc, both in southern Turkey, killing dozens of people and wreaking havoc in Turkey.

Enter Russia

If Erdogan could be blamed for failing to block the YPG–USA relationship or the ISIS threat, he should, however, be forgiven for failing to predict Russia's military deployment in Syria. He had good company: virtually no one else predicted it. This move changed the direction of the war, resulting in the eventual defeat of Turkey-backed rebels.

At the beginning of the conflict in 2011, few analysts predicted that Russia would interfere in the war through actual military deployment.

During the initial years of the war, Putin seemed content to provide Assad with military and political support without directly deploying troops to the war theatre.

By late 2015, however, the Russian view of the Syrian Civil War changed. The rebels made speedy gains throughout that year, taking control of a majority of Syria. By the summer of 2015, the Assad regime only held onto the coastal region of Syria; even the country's capital, Damascus, risked being sieged by the rebels. In a major blow for the Assad regime, the rebels, including al-Qaeda, kicked the Assad regime in its entirety out of Idlib Province, about 250 kilometres (155 miles) north of Damascus. In July 2015, even Assad admitted that he was having a hard time holding on to Syria.[43]

Putin concluded that the Assad regime would fall unless he interfered. In September of that year, Russia sent in troops and warplanes to Syria, becoming an active participant in the conflict but also changing the course of the war to Assad's advantage. Russian deployment in Syria undermined Turkey's fortunes there. Russian bombing especially targeted supply lines for rebel-held parts of Aleppo, Syria's commercial capital and largest city before the war. Erdogan had envisioned Aleppo as the centrepiece of his Syria policy from day one of the uprising. His hope was that once the rebels took this city in its entirety, they would then gain wide international legitimacy, boosting their support, especially if a US-enforced no-fly zone were placed over the city.[44] Russia's intervention permanently quashed these hopes.

Not surprisingly, when in November 2015, Turkey downed a Russian plane from Syria that had briefly violated its airspace, a crisis erupted in Ankara's relations with Moscow. In the aftermath of this crisis, Putin slapped economic sanctions on Ankara and implicitly threatened to target TAF incursions into Syria to combat the YPG or back rebels fighting Assad. Suddenly, Turkey was in a bind in Syria against its historic nemesis – seemingly without an exit strategy.

Diverging priorities

Concurrent with Turkey's deteriorating relations with Russia, and making things more difficult for Erdogan in Syria, his relations with Washington started decaying rapidly. Although Turkey and the United States both formally wanted Assad to leave power, the two countries were in different positions by the end of 2015. The conflicting attitudes of Ankara and Washington on combatting ISIS made full-scale cooperation with the United States difficult.

For the United States, Syria was a smouldering conflict and Washington, of course, was not happy with the Assad regime. However, Obama feared the unknowns of a post-Assad Syria and was reluctant to be dragged into a war in another Muslim-majority country. Therefore, the United States took baby steps in Syria, avoiding robust military engagement. The American strategy was designed in anticipation of a soft landing in Syria. The hope was that the opposition would coalesce, take over the country gradually and eventually depose Assad; or, that with enough military pressure, Washington could precipitate a leader, but not regime change, in Damascus. In both cases, avoiding the anarchy that would ensue if the Assad regime were to evaporate overnight.

Overall, Turkey preferred a 'comprehensive approach' to Syria and Iraq (from where the 'core of ISIS' had emerged in 2013), and not just a strategy targeting ISIS. In this regard, Ankara can be faulted for simply wanting to topple Assad, and put its own proxies, linked to the Muslim Brotherhood, in power in Damascus. However, Turkey also took a more global view of addressing the jihadist problem. This is because Ankara believed that the emergence of the militant group was related to the broader conflicts in the region and could not be addressed solely by sheer use of force.[45]

In this regard, Erdogan, indeed, deserves credit. The fact remains that, notwithstanding the grotesque crimes committed by ISIS, Assad, rather than ISIS, is the greater evil in Syria's war. According to the Syrian Observatory for Human Rights report from December 2018, during the 93 months of ongoing civil war, 560,000 people have died, many of them Sunni Arabs.[46] The Assad regime is responsible for nearly 500,000 of these deaths, while ISIS is responsible for about 20,000.

The Assad regime is of Alawite persuasion, belonging to a syncretic offshoot of Islam, sometimes considered closer to a Shi'ite branch of Islam. The persecution which Syria's Sunni Muslims faced at the hands of the Assad regime, and the fact that no outside power came to help them, has allowed al-Qaeda, which brands itself as the 'protector of Sunni Muslims globally', to be gradually welcomed as 'the savior', even if evil, of Syria's brutalised Sunni Muslim population. Assad did not create al-Qaeda, but his persecution fuelled its growth in Syria, which morphed into ISIS there (boosted by forces from Iraq). Thus, Erdogan is correct: Syria cannot be 'fixed' without deposing Assad – or at the very least, making him pay for his war crimes. However, at the same time, Syria cannot be 'fixed' just with the forces that Turkey has been supporting.

Although Erdogan recalibrated his policy by closing Turkey's borders to ISIS activity after 2015–16, Ankara remained intent on toppling Assad despite Obama's continued indecision on that front. To this end, Ankara has sought to maintain support for non-ISIS elements of the radical Syrian opposition, much to Washington's frustration.

Turkey's second priority in Syria after Assad, has been fighting the YPG. Especially after the Turkish–PKK peace talks broke down in July 2015, the PKK and its Syrian franchise, the PYD–YPG, climbed up fast in Turkey's threat perception.

Ever the consummate politician, Erdogan put the PKK in bullseye in Turkey, and the YPG in Syria. Targeting the PKK, a goal shared by constituencies broader than Erdogan's base in Turkey, helped him at the ballot box. In the parliamentary elections of June 2015, Erdogan's AKP lost its legislative for the first time since 2002, winning 40.9 per cent of the vote, and falling 18 seats short of a legislative majority. Turkey entered a period of uncertainty at this stage, with no party able to receive a vote of confidence from a majority of the deputies in the legislature in order to form a government. Erdogan's newly hardened stance against the PKK and the YPG alike at this stage, burnished his Turkish nationalist credentials, successfully widening his base. In the repeat parliamentary elections of November 2015, the AKP won 49.5 per cent of the vote, once again gaining a majority of the seats in the Turkish legislature.

By 2016, as Obama prepared to leave office and Erdogan comfortably entrenched in power, Turkey and the USA did not share primary objectives in Syria. Ankara opposed any US strategy that would bolster the YPG. Although Erdogan offered to provide Turkish troops as well as FSA combatants to fight ISIS, instead of the YPG forces, the Obama administration, which had already bought into working with the YPG, did not budge.

For his own part, Erdogan feared that any weapons provided to the YPG to fight ISIS could one day be used against Turkey. Ankara also increasingly doubted US assurances that assistance to the YPG did not constitute a long-term political commitment to the group. Accordingly, while US policy aimed to degrade ISIS without completely eliminating the Assad regime, Turkish policy aimed to degrade ISIS and eliminate Assad alike, while also subjugating the PKK.[47] Turkey and America had just ended up having completely divergent policies and priorities in Syria.

In 2019, these priorities had still not converged: Ankara saw the YPG as its primary threat, Assad as secondary and ISIS as tertiary, while Washington considered ISIS as its primary threat in Syria, followed by Iran and, lastly, the Assad regime as a distant third.

Erdogan's (and Davutoglu's) Syria report card

Washington's failures notwithstanding, the list of burdens, problems, risks, and threats related to Erdogan's (and Davutoglu's) Syria policy is long, and, as discussed below, it includes: floundering visions; security problems; demographic pressures; growing prejudices; ideological burdens; failed bridges; poor proxies; ill adjustments; and broken pieces.

Floundering visions

First and foremost, Erdogan's Syria war policy, which Davutoglu helped build and frame, has been poorly executed.

His policy evolved without securing concrete and long-term US and NATO support, necessary for pushing the Assad dictatorship, which was backed by both Moscow and Tehran. In addition, with this policy, Turkey has become exposed to threats posed by its two historically adversarial neighbours: Russia and Iran. Remarkably, Erdogan (and Davutoglu) also failed to take into account Russia's veto power at the UN Security Council. The two men should also have realised earlier that, short of a NATO-backed intervention, the only path to ousting Assad was through a UN-approved military intervention, similar to the international intervention against the Gaddafi regime in Libya. This was, however, an impossible feat in Syria, given Russia's commitment to preserving Assad's regime. Remarkably, Erdogan and Davutoglu also failed to take into account Russia's nuclear and military deterrence capability vis-à-vis Turkey in Syria, or elsewhere. Recently, however, Erdogan has started to broker ad hoc deals with Putin in Syria, Moscow's military superiority vis-à-vis Ankara limits the Turkish leader's space for manoeuver.

Security problems

Erdogan's Syria policy has exposed Turkey to the wrath of its most problematic neighbour, Syria, this time controlled by the Assad regime and connected with at least one terror attack in Turkey during the war – the 2013 bombing in Reyhanli that killed 51 people. Erdogan's policy has also failed to predict threats such as the rise of ISIS, which has targeted Turkey on numerous occasions in 2015 and 2016, including an attack on Istanbul Ataturk Airport in 2016 that killed 45 people and injured more than 250. Altogether, over 200 Turks have died in ISIS attacks between 2015 and 2016. The fallout of Erdogan's Syria policy in the security realm is simple, but sad: in 2019, Turkey has the distinction of being hated by all three key actors fighting Syria's civil war: the Assad Regime, the YPG and ISIS, all of which are linked to terror attacks in Turkey.

Demographic pressures

Turkey hosts about 4 million refugees from Syria, who constitute a nearly 4 per cent addition to its 2019 population of 82 million. While Erdogan (and Davutoglu) should be commended for providing a safe haven for persecuted civilians, the influx of Syrian refugees since 2011 is Turkey's most significant demographic shift since the 1923–4 'population exchange' with Greece.[48] This has given rise to significant social and economic tensions across the whole of Turkish society. The country's southern provinces bordering Syria have faced particular economic and social tensions due to the number of Syrian refugees, in some areas constituting 10–50 per cent of the population in these provinces.[49] Most notably, in Kilis, a small province in southern Turkey, Syrian refugees now constitute over half of the population, becoming the majority there.

Growing prejudices

Existing racist views towards Arabs in Turkey have been compounded by the arrival of large number of Syrian refugees in key cities, and especially across the country's southern provinces. Syrians are one of the main targets of hate speech and hate crimes in Turkey today.[50] An overwhelming majority of Turkey's citizens want the Syrians to return home, with a 2017 poll showing this number at 86 per cent, and this issue will be an Achilles Heel in Erdogan's power base going forward.[51]

Ideological burdens

In Syria, as in other Arab countries experiencing uprisings, Erdogan has exclusively backed the Muslim Brotherhood and like-minded movements. While a crafty and pragmatic politician, in this regard Erdogan has perhaps been a captive of his ideological convictions. Erdogan and his fellow travellers see supporting political Islamist movements (such as the Muslim Brotherhood) or Islamist Syrian rebels (such as Ahrar al-Sham) not just as a Machiavellian political choice in power politics, but also, and more importantly, as a 'moral' obligation. In October 2013, Davutoglu said that Turkey's involvement in the Syrian conflict constituted doing the 'morally right thing' by striving for 'democracy for neighbouring Arab people'.[52] Erdogan, too, has shrouded remarks in moral references. 'Turkey is with the people and among the righteous in the Middle East,' he declared in 2014.[53]

Failed bridges

This moralistic stance has made it difficult for Erdogan to dial back in his support for the Sunni rebels in Syria – not of the al-Qaeda ilk, but those factions that listen to him. Accordingly, he has failed to build bridges with the diverse ethnic and political groups across its border beyond the Brotherhood's base. For instance, Ankara has been unable to make friends among the country's secular Muslim elites and urban classes, and to this day cannot count any real allies among Syria's large Alawite,

Assyrian, other Christian, Druze, Shi'ite and Kurdish communities – the FSA remains an army manned mostly by Syria's rural Sunni Arab population, by all accounts a minority of Syria's population.

Poor proxies

It should also have been clear to Erdogan, judging from the FSA's early failure, and lacking American military support after 2013, that he would face an uphill battle to build a powerful and cogent proxy army in Syria, even with Qatari funds flowing through Turkey to boost the anti-Assad rebels. Take, for instance, the FSA. This alliance, composed of many factions that have fought as much among themselves as they have battled the Assad regime, proved an ill match for Damascus and its allies. With the exception of Idlib Province abutting Turkey, Erdogan's allies in Syria have failed to make gains against the Assad regime. The truth is, Turkey's proxies were never as good as those of other countries. For instance, Iran's proxies have among them the Lebanese Hezbollah, which has 30,000 well-trained fighters, and they also have experience fighting in many key battles, such as in 2013 in Qusayr against rebels, where they made strategic gains for the Assad regime.[54]

Ill adjustments

The conflict in Syria has evolved from a pro-democracy uprising in 2011 to a civil war involving jihadists in 2015 that have directly targeted Turkey. Still, Ankara's stated primary goal, for the most part, remained ousting the Assad regime. The result of Turkey's failure to adapt to the dynamic conditions of the conflict empowered mostly radical political Islamists, some of whom have morphed into radical jihadists. Turkey adopted a more flexible approach after 2016, including a more pragmatic outreach to Russia and greater engagement in diplomatic efforts in Geneva and Astana, but the cost of delay has been great.

The Astana Process, led by Moscow, has brought Ankara and the Assad regime to the negotiating table, yet it has not produced concrete results in terms of completely ending hostilities in Syria as of 2019. On a slightly more positive note, this process has produced temporary ceasefires involving Turkey-backed forces, such as in Idlib in September 2018, awarding Ankara some room to breathe.

Broken pieces

The war in Syria has been Turkey's most consequential foreign policy entanglement in decades. Erdogan's support for the rebels to oust Assad and shape Syria's future was the centrepiece of his neo-Ottomanist pivot in foreign policy. Yet, with the Assad regime consolidating its control across large swathes of Syria in 2019, it seems fair to say that Erdogan has failed in this endeavour.

Problems with America

Except for a brief period at the beginning of the war when he coordinated his policies with those of Washington, Erdogan tried to implement his Syria policy without America by his side. What is more, Erdogan's travails in Syria have undermined Turkey's most important strategic relationship since the Second World War: Ankara's ties with Washington (where the blame also lies with Obama).

Squandered dream

The Syrian war has been a test case for Erdogan's attempt to make Turkey a stand-alone power. On its own, Ankara failed to determine the outcome of the conflict. Overall, Erdogan's (and Davutoglu's) Syria policy has squandered Turkey's credibility in the Middle East. By 2010, many people in the Middle East believed that Turkey was a country that could get things done without using force. By 2015, many had started to believe that Turkey was a country that could not get things done in the Middle East, neither by force nor by any other means.

8
MENACING RUSSIANS

Erdogan's involvement in the Syrian conflict has not only failed to deliver Turkey greatness as per his vision, as a stand-alone power, but has also left Ankara exposed to the vicissitudes of its historic archenemy, and the Assad regime's patron: Moscow.

During six centuries of Ottoman rule (1299–1922), the Ottoman Turks reigned over all twelve of their present-day neighbours, with the exception of Russia and Iran. This resilience by the Russians and Persians elevates the two populous countries in contemporary Turkish views and in the Turkish foreign policy *weltanschauung*. Historically speaking, Ankara avoids confrontation with Russia and Iran.

Compare this with Turkey's patronising attitude towards its other neighbours, such as Syria. This is also the case regarding Ankara's other neighbours, such as Iraq, where, between 2007 and 2017, Erdogan sided with the Kurds in the north of that country against the central government in Baghdad. In addition, in Bulgaria in 2016, he supported the establishment of a pro-Turkey political party, Democrats for Responsibility, Solidarity and Tolerance (DOST), among that country's ethnic Turkish minority.

'If you scratch a Turk, you get a Circassian'

Russia is unique among Turkey's neighbours, even when compared to Iran. Ankara does not fear Tehran, but it certainly is afraid of Moscow.

There is a reason why Turks fear Russians so deeply. By my count, the Ottomans and Russians fought nearly fifteen major wars between the late fifteenth century, when they became neighbours, and the end of the Russian Empire, prompted by the Bolshevik Revolution in 1917. In each encounter, Russia was often the instigator, and usually the overall victor of military confrontation. To put it simply, the story of the rise of the Russian Empire has been, in reverse, the story of the demise of the Ottoman Empire. As tsars expanded their rule southwards during the eighteenth and nineteenth centuries, they grabbed vast territories belonging to the Ottomans, including the southern and northern Caucasus, eastern and southern Ukraine, parts of southern Russia, as well as Crimea.

More broadly, Russian policies contributed to the decline of the Ottoman Empire, especially from the nineteenth century onwards, resulting, explicitly or implicitly, in the breakaway of Serbia, Greece and Bulgaria from the Ottoman Empire, as well as in helping Montenegro and Romania gain recognition internationally and expand territorially. In their more direct setbacks, the Ottomans lost vast, and often solidly, Turkish and Muslim territories to the Russians, swathes of land, spanning from Crimea along the Black Sea to Circassia in the northern Caucasus. The Russians killed many inhabitants of these Ottoman lands and expelled the rest to Ottoman Turkey. So many Turks descend from refugees from Russia that the adage in Turkey is: 'If you scratch a Turk, you get a Circassian,' persecuted by Russians underneath.

Similar to the Poles, Romanians, and other nations historically brutalised by the tsars, who even today act based on a deep-rooted fear of Russia, Turkey's leaders, too, have often tended to view their foreign policy through the lens of Russia's expansionist proclivities. In fact, deep-rooted fear of Russia is among the most permanent drivers of Turkish foreign policy. This was the reason, for instance, why Ottoman sultans sought security with Great Britain for much of the nineteenth century, a strategy that staved off Russian advances toward the Ottoman capital for what was left of the empire's history.

The perceived Russian threat also explains Turkey's pivot to the United States after the Second World War and subsequent embrace of NATO. This strategic shift came after Joseph Stalin demanded in 1945–46 that Ankara hand over a portion of north-eastern Turkey and allow the Soviet Union to establish bases on the strategically located Turkish Straits. Acquiescing to these demands would have jeopardised Turkey's very existence as an independent state. Thus, Ankara clamoured for US friendship, and NATO membership, the latter of which it gained in 1952, notably three years before West Germany and thirty years before Spain. Fear of the Russians made Turkey one of the most committed Cold War allies to the United States.

Turkey links with Azerbaijan and Central Asia after the fall of communism

During the Cold War, fearing the Soviet superpower next door, Ankara maintained a distance from the Turkic and Muslim republics under Russian control inside the Soviet Union. This was especially the policy regarding Azerbaijan, whose inhabitants speak a Turkic language, which is among the closest to Turkish of all the Turkic languages – Azeri and Turkish are mutually mostly intelligible.[1]

Fear of Russia even trumps Ankara's proclivity to follow policies to help Turks' ethnic kin overseas. Compare Ankara's Cold War Russia policy to its policy towards communist China in the same period, where Turkey has supported and harboured Uyghur nationalists (explained in Chapter 15).

Traditionally, Turkey pushes back against Moscow's control of Turkic nations only when the latter is weak. Thus, following the fall of the Soviet Union, Ankara quickly moved into Central Asia and the Caucasus to build influence among the Turkic republics. As Moscow's grip on the former Soviet Union weakened further in the 1990s under Russian President Boris Yeltsin, Ankara spread its networks across Turkic and Muslim republics of the rump Soviet Empire. In doing this, it also recognised vast business opportunities that the post-Soviet space offered to its burgeoning economy, which had undergone a massive transformation and liberalisation process in the 1980s under Ozal.

Turkish–Russian spring of the 1990s

As it happened, throughout the 1990s, Ankara was growing frustrated with its never-ending courtship of the EU. Heralding this disappointment, and animated by a desire for gaining influence over new regions opening up to the world, in May 1992 Turkey's then Prime Minister Demirel made a historic visit to Moscow. In the Russian capital, he signalled Ankara's intent to start a new chapter in their countries' relationship.[2] This was a historic trip: a first visit of a Turkish prime minister to Moscow since the establishment of modern Turkey in 1923.[3]

A few years later, Russian Prime Minister Viktor Chernomyrdin reciprocated the gesture, visiting Ankara and declaring, 'If Turkey shakes the hand extended by Russia, we shall become strategic partners in the economy in the twenty-first century.'[4] The 1997 visit produced the first underwater trans-Black Sea natural gas pipeline between Turkey and Russia: Blue Stream, which was inaugurated in the next decade, in 2005.

In the 1990s, Russia often accused Ankara of ignoring the activities of Chechen activists, whom it said used Turkey, home to large immigrant communities from the North Caucasus including Chechnya, as a safe haven. Ecevit, the Turkish prime minister at the time, tried to appeal to Russia, visiting Moscow in 1999, when he declared that the Chechen War was 'strictly domestic business' for Russia, calming Russian fears about Ankara's support for the Chechens against Moscow.

Thus, a new door opened to revitalising bilateral ties with Russia, and Turkish construction companies, representing a vibrant sector in the Turkish economy since the Ozal reforms, as well as other businesses, such as retail giants, rushed in, making fortunes in the process. The Gulen movement also moved into these regions, arriving in Central Asia and other post-Soviet republics with their signature schools and businesses, and then setting up political and social networks.

Willing to take risks, and benefiting from familiarity with emerging markets from experience in their own country, Turkish businesses took advantage of the new business opportunities in the former Soviet republics in Moscow's periphery, as well as Russia, especially in the construction sector. Following this, Turkish–Russian business ties improved significantly, a historical first. However, this also meant that a pro-Russia business lobby emerged in Turkey – another historical first.

Overall, Turkish–Russian ties have noticeably improved after the end of the Cold War. Moscow became Turkey's fourth major trading partner in 2001, after Germany, the United States and Italy.[5] Tourism and personal contacts took off, with 3–4 million Russians vacationing in Turkey annually by the turn of the century, and almost every year since.

In 2017, the number of Russian tourists surpassed the Germans, traditionally the largest nationality among visitors to Turkey since the beginning of mass tourism in the country in the 1980s under Ozal.[6]

At the same time, Turkish businesses have been thriving in Russia. In 2018, the volume of construction contracts of Turkish companies in Russia stood at roughly $65 billion.[7] Symbolising the improvement in Turkish–Russian ties, Turkish Airlines, Turkey's national flag carrier, offered regular flights to eleven Russian cities from Istanbul in early 2018.[8]

The Erdogan boost

After the AKP came to power, the presence of Erdogan's personality added further momentum to Turkey's reset with Russia.

Putin and Erdogan share a mutual affinity as two leaders with authoritarian styles, who see themselves on a mission to make their nations great again. Political courtship ensued after Erdogan's rise in Turkey. His three-day visit to Moscow in 2005 was followed by Putin's trip to Turkey – the first by a Russian head of state since Russia and the Ottoman Empire established relations in the fifteenth century – excluding a 1972 sojourn by Nikolai Podgorny, the titular head of state of the former Soviet Union at the time. Although Erdogan's sojourn in Moscow fell short of finalising a number of pipeline construction and gas export deals, twin Erdogan–Putin visits heralded a new era of improved Turkish–Russian relations.[9]

During Putin's visit to Turkey in December 2004, Ankara and Moscow signed agreements for cooperation in the defence and energy industries. In addition, the two countries issued a declaration for 'deepening friendship and multidimensional partnership'. In a gesture before Putin's visit, Istanbul police detained a number of people believed to be Chechen militants. In return, Russia said it was examining Turkish demands to put the PKK on its list of terrorist groups.

Erdogan's ambition was to orchestrate new bilateral ties with Russia as he did with Iran (explained in Chapter 9) through impressive-sounding intergovernmental bodies such as the Turkish–Russian Joint Strategic Planning Group between Ankara and Moscow, a boost in trade ties and a removal of visa restrictions, among other initiatives. A trade boom followed; for instance, in the first eleven months of 2004, Russian–Turkish trade was worth $9.4 billion, 50 per cent more than in 2003.[10] This upward trend has continued ever since. In 2018, the bilateral trade volume had reached $17 billion, increasing the billions of dollars earned by Turkish companies doing business in Russia.[11]

Inevitably, this has had political ramifications. Turkish business groups benefiting from booming bilateral trade, including those in the construction, retail, banking, telecommunications, tourism, food and beverage, glass and machinery industries are now pushing for stronger political ties with Moscow to increase their access to the Russian market and take advantage of further energy deals (Russia provides nearly half of Turkey's natural gas and oil imports).

And the Putin snub

While the interests of Turkey's business community and the personal rapport that Erdogan enjoyed with Putin reinforced the reset with Russia, some of those inside the AKP wrongfully started to think that unlike the EU or the United States, Russia saw Turkey as an equal partner. Some even viewed enhanced relations with Russia as a counterweight to ties with the EU and the United States as Ankara ran into problems with Washington during the war in Iraq or with Brussels during the EU accession talks.

Moscow, the historically the dominant side in the Russian–Turkish relationship, has the opposite and very different view of Turkey. For the Russians, Turkey has been and is the 'annoying southern neighbour' that has to be frequently reminded of its inferior status compared to Moscow, and then 'put in its place'.

Erdogan has always tried to court Putin, but the latter has often used such outreach to snub the Turkish leader, and the Turks. In 2003, for instance, Erdogan invited Putin to his son Bilal's wedding in Istanbul. This showed the importance Erdogan gave to Putin: together with then Italian Prime Minister Silvio Berlusconi, Putin was one of the top two dignitaries invited by Erdogan to attend his older son's glamorous wedding ceremony held in Istanbul on 10 August 2003.[12]

Simply broadcasting historical Russian views of Turks, however, Putin declined the invitation. While Berlusconi attended the Istanbul wedding, Putin merely sent a gift. The fact is that Russia and Putin do not see Turkey and Erdogan, respectively, as partners, let alone equals. Erdogan (and Davutoglu) would have to find this out the hard way in Syria.

Crossing pipelines

A product of the Cold War, Putin has made the revival of Russian power in its traditional sphere of influence his life's work. Moscow has sought to tighten its grip on its neighbours using oil and natural gas supplies and the politics of building pipelines in order to build power in its near abroad. To this end, Putin has courted Turkey through energy deals, even when Ankara and Moscow split on other issues. Moscow's historic energy-related objective concerning Ankara has been to gain Turkey as a key client, which consumes large amounts of Russian natural gas, until they become overwhelmingly reliant on Moscow – Putin even wrote about using Russian fossil fuels to gain leverage over nearby countries in his university thesis.

Bulgaria–Turkey connection

Turkey first started buying Russian natural gas during the Cold War, under a contract signed by Ozal in 1984. At this time, the Soviet Union agreed to extend the existing Cold War-era Soviet Union–Romania–Bulgaria pipeline into Turkey. The first Russian gas deliveries through this pipeline started in 1987.[13] Turkey gradually transitioned its infrastructure, heating a vast majority of cities and fuelling its power stations and industries with natural gas.

BTC

Seeing Russia's big game, but becoming more reliant on natural gas imports than ever before, Ankara fears that Moscow could use its position as a 'weapon' by cutting much needed deliveries. Accordingly, Ankara has tried to decrease its dependency on Moscow for imports. It has tried to balance each Turkish–Russian and north–south natural gas connector with an east–west pipeline, not involving Russia.

In the late 1990s, with US support, Turkey began envisioning the Baku–Tbilisi–Ceyhan (BTC) pipeline, a transit corridor, bypassing Russia. The BTC was inaugurated in 2005. It made Turkey a key country on the east–west axis of the energy corridor between the Caspian Sea and the Mediterranean, and decreased Turkish dependence on imported Russian gas.[14]

Blue Stream

The BTC took the sting out of Moscow's threats of shutting off the tap during disputes with its neighbours. Moscow pushed back with the aforementioned Blue Stream pipeline running north to south from Russia, across the Black Sea bed and into Turkey. Conceived in the late 1990s, this pipeline became operational in 2005, making Ankara the second-largest consumer of Russian gas after Germany, as well as creating another north–south and Russia–Turkey connector.[15]

Turk Stream

Amidst his war with Ukraine, Putin aggressively promoted the Turk Stream pipeline, running from Russia across the Black Sea to Turkey, skirting Ukraine. Construction of this pipeline ended in November 2018, establishing another north–south gas pipeline between Turkey and Russia.

TANAP

While Erdogan has worked with Putin to bring the Turk Stream to fruition, he has not abandoned Ankara's traditional policy of building east–west pipelines to balance the north–south ones. In June 2018, Turkey inaugurated another connector to this end, the Trans-Anatolian Pipeline (TANAP), bypassing Russia and bringing Azeri gas, this time directly to European networks, through an interconnector in Greece. The interconnector was completed in November 2018.[16]

Akkuyu Nuclear Power Station

Just when Turkey seems to be winning against Russia in one place, it ends up losing in another. Therefore, what should have been Turkish efforts to diversify its energy sources through the development of nuclear energy come with an unfortunate catch. The construction of Turkey's first nuclear plant, in Akkuyu in southern Turkey, broke ground in 2010. The company building this strategic energy plant: Russian state-owned Rosatom.

The Syrian chessboard

However, even platitudes, such as Akkuyu, have not helped completely fix Erdogan's 'Russia problem' in Syria.

In 2013, Putin dispatched a permanent naval unit to the Mediterranean and in September 2015, Russia intervened decisively in Syria, spoiling Erdogan's goal of bringing down Assad. With Obama deciding to stay out of Syria, Erdogan soon concluded that Putin calls the shots in Syria. Consequently, Erdogan has decided to enter into ad hoc deals and de-confliction efforts with Putin. In doing this, Erdogan believes that he can deal with Russia as an equal partner.

This is, of course, not how Putin sees his relationship with Erdogan. Putin appreciates that Erdogan's go-alone policy in Syria has left him susceptible to Russia's grandiose schemes. For instance, as of 2019, Turkey controls parts of northern Syria, though Ankara has been able to occupy these areas only thanks to Russia's green light. It is far from certain that Putin will allow a permanent Turkish presence in Syria.

Erdogan's Syria policy has increasingly been eclipsed by Putin's own ambitions. For instance, following Ankara's November 2015 downing of a Russian SU-24 fighter jet, which had violated Turkish airspace from Syria, Erdogan had to reach out to Putin to express his regrets on 27 June 2016.

The events following the November 2015 incident were also a reminder that Turkey's fear of Russia had not dissipated, nor has Ankara's dependence on the West as tensions between Ankara and Moscow rose after the plane was shot down. Immediately after the incident, Erdogan called for an emergency NATO meeting in panic.[17] He was shocked when NATO responded, in his view, tepidly, to Ankara's request for assistance to defend itself against potential Russian aggression in the aftermath of the plane incident. Doubts about NATO (and US) support for Turkey have led Erdogan to conclude that playing nice with Putin has its benefits.

Woefully open to the Russian menace, and believing that Washington does not have its back any more, Erdogan concluded that he should start listening to Russia, and Putin has taken advantage of this strategic opening.

Realising that the US relationship with the YPG would persist, Erdogan started his pivot even more strongly to Russia in Syria, so that Putin would allow him to undermine the YPG in Syria. The Russian leader, who wants to see NATO weakened, knows that one way to enfeeble the alliance is by diluting Ankara's commitment to it. Putin leapt at the chance to shape the narrative to his own advantage.

The failed coup that changed everything

Analysts anticipated that the 2016 understanding between Erdogan and Putin regarding Syria could eventually result in Turkish–Russian proximity in Syria. The July 2016 failed coup attempt significantly accelerated this process. The putsch attempt against Erdogan occurred only two weeks after Ankara and Moscow began to patch up a seven-month crisis, triggered by Turkey's 2015 downing of the Russian plane. Putin called Erdogan the day after the coup attempt and wished him well, days before Erdogan received a similar message from the USA – and not from Obama, but his secretary of state, John Kerry.

Erdogan, who later gushed that Putin's phone call reminded him of his solidarity, never completely recovered from the fact that Turkey's closest ally, Washington, took days to reach out to him after a coup, one that nearly cost him his life.

In fact, many in the AKP circles believe to this day that the West's condemnation of the coup was weak, and too late, fuelling theories about the involvement of Washington and NATO in the unsuccessful coup attempt. Bekir Bozdag, the Turkish minister of justice at the time, insinuated that Washington and NATO knew what was coming and did nothing, after the United States refused to immediately extradite Fethullah Gulen, the founder and leader of the Gulen movement whom many Turks blame for the coup.[18] These convictions were echoed by the pro-government media in Turkey, who framed the coup-related events as part of 'America's grand plan', fuelling widespread anti-American sentiment.[19] Boosted by Erdogan's rhetoric since the early days of the AKP administrations and often ignored by many in Washington as mere politicking or electioneering, anti-Americanism in Turkey reached a new level in 2016.

Subsequently, Erdogan made his most important move towards Moscow. He announced, to America and NATO's consternation, that he would buy a Russian-made S-400 missile defence system. Calls in the US Congress to sanction Turkey if Ankara went ahead with its decision to purchase the Russian missile system soon followed. Putin finally had the Turkish–US relationship just where he wanted it: the Americans angry at Turkey, and the Turks angry at the United States.

On 9 August 2016, Erdogan made his first foreign visit after the coup attempt – to Russia.[20] Putin greeted him at the Konstantinovsky Palace near St Petersburg, a monument to Putin's vision of reborn Imperial glory.[21] During this visit, Putin restated his support for Erdogan after the failed coup and the two leaders announced their dedication to elevate their bilateral relations to new heights.

Since then, Putin has softened his policy toward Ankara in Syria, expertly noting and taking advantage of growing anti-Western sentiment in Turkey. Further raising his stock in Turkey, after the coup attempt, Erdogan launched a campaign of political purges with ferocity. While the United States and Europe voiced concern over the rampant human rights violations committed amid the purge, Moscow was steadfast beside Erdogan. Following the coup, the frequency of phone calls between Erdogan and Putin spiked, surpassing the frequency of calls between Erdogan and Trump, as seen below, signalling a new era in the Erdogan–Putin relationship.[22]

Erdogan's Putin crush

The rising frequency of phone calls between Erdogan and Putin and notably longer duration of these conversations since July 2016 is not surprising: Putin's style of governance has a special appeal for Erdogan, who was noticeably scarred by the 2016 coup attempt.

In addition to his coup fears, Erdogan also knows that given the corruption charges pressed against him and his family members, he cannot afford to be voted out (another similarity he shares with Putin). Accordingly, the Turkish leader's political strategy has been to end democracy in Turkey. This is not because he is irrational, but rather because he is aware of the tremendous consequences that await him if he were to be voted out by nearly half of the population who oppose him vehemently. His tactic for political survival, therefore, follows the Putin model.

Over the last two decades, Putin has stripped the Russian opposition of nearly every one of its leaders, forcing many of Russia's thinkers and civil society organisers and media figures into self-imposed exile overseas. Erdogan seeks to muzzle the educated and business classes that fervidly oppose him, in the same way in which Putin pushed out educated and wealthy Russian citizens.

In following this model, Erdogan continues his efforts to silence and drive out Turkey's civil society opposition and free media, paving the way for Putin-style landslide electoral victories.

The basis of the Erdogan–Putin connection after the failed coup has been clear. It is as if the former is telling the latter: 'The US and Europe want you to fight your internal enemies with one hand tied behind your back, but Russia is more than happy to support your use of my handbook against your internal rivals. Welcome to the club.'

Syrian 'deals'

Erdogan's growing rapport with Putin notwithstanding, the differing interests of Russia and Turkey in Syria are bound to be a significant obstacle to the real deepening and ongoing rapprochement. In this regard, Ankara's policy in Syria has failed thus far, whereas Moscow's has succeeded.

Erdogan's post-2016 move has been to broker ad hoc deals with Putin, focus on the YPG and slowly shift away from pressing so hard against Assad. This trend, which explains the spike in Erdogan–Putin phone calls, has set in place a pattern in Turkish–Russian ties: almost every time the leaders speak, Putin takes something from Erdogan in Syria in return for allowing him to undermine the YPG.

In 2016, for instance, when Erdogan wanted to send Turkish troops into Syria to take the Jarablus area from ISIS and drive a wedge between YPG-held territories in northern Syria, he had to accept Moscow's (and Damascus') assault on rebel-held east Aleppo. In the end, Erdogan got Jarablus, while Putin took east Aleppo through Turkish pressure on the rebels to abandon the city and Ankara's behind-closed-door mediation between the rebels and the Assad regime.

Similarly, Putin gave Erdogan the green light in 2018 for Ankara to operate its air force over the YPG's Afrin enclave in north-western Syria, and then occupy it, in exchange for Erdogan's tacit approval for an Assad-regime assault on east Ghouta. In yet another deal, this time Erdogan got Afrin and Putin (and Assad) got east Ghouta.

In 2018, when it looked as if Russia, the Assad regime and Iran were going to invade Idlib Province, the last significant rebel-held area in northern Syria, Erdogan and Putin cut a deal again. Ankara forced Turkey-backed rebels to vacate the border zones of southern Idlib Province, abutting Assad-regime-held areas, and in return, Putin put off the invasion. Practically speaking, Turkey got most of northern Idlib, and Russia and its allies got parts of southern Idlib.

In 2019, Turkey's Syria policy aimed to secure Ankara a seat at the table when negotiations are held for Syria's future. This can happen if Turkish-backed rebels continue to hold on to strategic zones in northern Syria. Here is the problem for Erdogan: Putin is eventually going to help Damascus take over control of the Syrian territory. This means that it is not a question of if, but when, Putin will ask Turkey to vacate the Syrian territory that it occupies. However, Erdogan will have some leverage over Moscow as well. Putin wants to bring the war in Syria to an end through his own political track, the Astana Process, and needs Ankara's participation on this platform for it to have any kind of international legitimacy.

Limits to Turkish–Russian rapprochement

Religion

History has tangled Russia and Turkey together in many ways, some of which will continue to undermine the Erdogan–Putin Russian relationship beyond Syria. In the nineteenth century, the Caucasus was a cradle of Islamic revivalism, embodied in the Naqshbandi and Qadiri *tariqats*, or religious brotherhoods, that spread across the Middle East and Central Asia. These *tariqats* eventually became very popular in the Ottoman Empire. Incidentally, Erdogan and many of his companions in the AKP come from branches of the Naqshbandi *tariqat*, still in existence today in Turkey. What is more, Erdogan's entrée into politics as a teenager came through his membership in the aforementioned National Turkish Student Union (MTTB), an organisation first established in 1916 to rally opposition in the Ottoman Empire against Russia for its mistreatment of Turkic peoples and other Muslims within its borderlands.

Political Islam

Russia's population is about 10–15 per cent Muslim and there are deep historic and ethnic ties between Russian and Turkish Muslims. A majority of Russia's Muslims are Turkic Tatars and many non-Turkish Muslims in Russia, such as the Circassians and Chechens, have deep-rooted connections with Turkey due to diaspora communities currently living there. Given these ties, Putin is aware that the success of Erdogan's experiment with political Islam in Turkey will animate and politicise Russia's Muslim communities more than the success of political Islamist movements anywhere else, such as in Iran, Libya, or Gaza.

Chechens

Periodic reports of Russian intelligence services assassinating Chechens and North Caucasus Salafi diaspora in Istanbul, both fiercely loyal to Erdogan and opposing Putin, serve as a reminder of the deep undercurrents that will burden the Turkish–Russian relationship – even one guided by Erdogan's political affinity with Putin. Moscow has, for the most part, brought the Chechen insurgency under control with Putin-appointed Ramzan Kadyrov, whose government is respectful of Putin. Recently, the North Caucasus community in Istanbul and across Turkey, including Chechens, became a way station for militants from the North Caucasus as they travelled to Syria to battle Russia and Assad, with many of these fighters joining ISIS. These intersections are a constant irritant to Turkish–Russian relations. Turkey ultimately does hold a Chechen card in its hand, given the tight Chechen networks that transcend Turkish–Russian borders. If relations between Ankara and Moscow sour, Erdogan could consider activating support for the Chechen diaspora and rebels opposing Moscow.

PKK

Similarly, Russia has its own cards vis-à-vis Erdogan. Part of Russian imperial policy during the nineteenth century included forging ties with the Kurds of the Ottoman Empire. The tsars helped pioneer the anthropological study of the Kurds, an academic tradition that persists in Russia to this day. Between the 1870s and the Ottoman collapse in the First World War, Russia twice pressed deeply into the heartland of Anatolia, and both times, while many Kurdish tribes sided with the Ottoman sultan, others fought for the tsars. In modern times, the Soviet Union supported the PKK after the group's establishment in the Syrian-occupied Lebanese Beqaa Valley in the early 1980s, and once when the group ensconced itself in the mountains of Iraq, bordering Turkey in the late 1980s. Today, official opinion in Russia does not regard the PKK as a terrorist organisation, setting it apart from both the USA and Europe, which formally designate the PKK as a terror group. Russia has carried the same attitude to its relations with the PKK-affiliated PYD in Syria, Erdogan's mortal enemy. Putin personally invited the PYD to open an office in Moscow and Russia has lobbied to give the PYD a place at the table in negotiations over Syria's future, a stance that Turkey stridently opposes.

Does Putin want to see Erdogan succeed?

Despite their recent deals in Syria, it is obvious that Putin is not interested in making things easy for Erdogan. In the run-up to the April 2017 Turkish referendum, which significantly increased Erdogan's political powers, for instance, Sputnik Turkiye, a Russian state-owned

Turkish-language news outlet, produced exponentially more articles than the combined output of other foreign media in Turkey – and unlike these other outlets, campaigned almost exclusively against Erdogan during the referendum.[23] This clearly made a difference in the political environment, in which Erdogan has control of nearly all media outlets, except for foreign-owned media, such as Sputnik Turkiye. Erdogan barely won the referendum, with a thin majority of 51 to 49 per cent.

Sputnik Turkiye also campaigned against Erdogan throughout Turkey's 2018 Afrin operation, although Putin formally gave Erdogan the green light to carry out this military incursion.[24]

His overarching goal is to see a weak NATO, and fuelling Turkish internal discord between pro- and anti-Erdogan camps reinforces that goal. Putin wants neither side to enjoy a sweeping victory in Turkish politics. Nor does he want to replace Erdogan with a liberal or leftist alternative. Rather, knowing that Turkey is split in the middle between Erdogan's supporters and opponents, he wants to exacerbate and prolong Turkey's profound political crisis. Turkey has NATO's second largest military and is an important US ally in the Middle East and South-East Europe. Paralysing Turkey by exacerbating and prolonging its state of crisis serves Putin's ultimate goal in his relationship with the West.

No, but he does not want him out either

However, this does not mean Putin will turn the screws too tight on Erdogan. Russia plays the long game. Since the end of the Cold War, Russian policy toward Ankara has been consistent on a key guiding principle: never completely alienate Turkey. Especially starting with Putin's rise, the strategy has been to keep Ankara as close to Moscow as possible, and simultaneously as far away from NATO as possible.

Putin knows that turning the screws too forcefully will push Turkey back to NATO – a repeat of Stalin's misstep in the period 1945–6. At the same time, however, Putin does not necessarily want to see Turkey leave NATO. Rather, he wants to see Ankara remain in the alliance, albeit as a disgruntled member. This arrangement would dilute the alliance's effectiveness, thereby serving Putin's desire for a debilitated NATO.

Wedging Turkey and the United States

In line with this strategy, Putin wants to widen the schism between the USA and Turkey. Accordingly, he has repeatedly encouraged Ankara to purchase the S-400 system, worth its weight in gold in the triangular Turkish–Russian–American relationship. Putin has insisted to sell this Russian-made system to Ankara, knowing that if Turkey purchased it, the US Congress would, without doubt, sanction Ankara. During a 2018 visit to Ankara, Putin announced that he would be moving up the delivery of the system by a year from 2020 to 2019, while also presenting Ankara with financing options for the purchase of the $2.5 billion system.[25]

This development has added to Washington's unhappiness regarding Turkey. The US Senate responded, demanding that the Pentagon prepare a report detailing whether Turkey's purchase would jeopardise its participation in the F-35 jet project. Furthermore, many in Congress believe Turkey's purchase of the S-400 system[26] exposes Ankara to sanctions under the Countering America's Adversaries Through Sanctions Act (CAATSA), which already provides specific sanctions targeting Russian companies that manufacture the S-400 system.[27] However, in a positive step and pushing back against Putin, on December 2018, the US government announced the sale of the Patriot system to Turkey, suggesting that Congressional blockage regarding this issue had been overcome.

When Russia howls, Turkey moves

Considering its policy regarding Turkish–Russian ties, Washington should take note of a historic dynamic: Turkey reacts to Russian military might.

Russian military prowess has historically acted as a catalyst in the formation of Ottoman and Turkish policy in profound ways. When Russians captured Crimea in 1783, the first Muslim-majority territory the Ottomans lost to a Christian power, for instance, this effectively triggered the Ottoman Turkish Westernisation: the sultans felt so humiliated by

Russia that they consequently decided to adopt European ways to counter the tsars. In fact, the first proponents of Turkic and Turkish Westernisation emerged not in the Ottoman Empire, but among Tatar populations of Imperial Russia. This includes such people as Ismail Gaspirali, a late nineteenth-century thinker from Crimea, who propagated the idea of the modernisation of Turks, Tatars and other Turkic populations to face the Russians. That modernisation movement eventually found its way through the Ottoman Empire, producing Mustafa Kemal Ataturk, the father of the Turkish republic.

Contemporary Turkish fear of Russia is grounded also in economic reality. Turkey is dependent on Russia for its energy needs, although the other side of the coin is that Moscow needs Turkey as a market for its natural gas, too. Nevertheless, the fact remains that despite being a large economy, Turkey has neither significant natural gas and oil deposits nor nuclear power stations of its own. Ankara is therefore bound to Moscow, which has often used natural gas supplies as a means to punish countries, such as Ukraine, that cross its foreign policy goals.

There is also a security component: Russian–PKK ties. The PKK, which became a formidable military force under Russian tutelage in Lebanon's then Syrian-occupied Beqaa Valley during the 1980s, has enjoyed intermittent Russian support ever since.

In addition, in Syria, Moscow will do everything to ensure that Turkey does not emerge a winner from the Syrian Civil War. Regardless of his political romance with Erdogan, Putin ultimately wants to humiliate Ankara *and* Erdogan in order to remind the Turks why they should continue to fear the Russians.[28]

Overall, Russia has returned as Turkey's historic nemesis because of Erdogan's failed strategy. The former's nuclear arsenal and sizable military continue to menace Turkey more than any other nation. Following its military deployment in Latakia, Syria, Russia now encircles Turkey with Anti-Access/Air Denial (A2D2) bubbles to Turkey's north in Crimea, east in Armenia and south in Latakia. Although Erdogan will do his best to placate Moscow, a resurgent Russia remains the biggest threat to Turkey. When Russia growls, Turkey takes note: so should Washington.

9
COMPETING PERSIANS

Erdogan's quest to remake Turkey into a regional power in the Middle East might have stood a chance were it not for the other giant elephant in the region: Iran.

Turkey's geopolitical boundaries have historically hemmed its imperial ambitions. So, while Ottoman (and recent Turkish) imperial rhetoric entertained the fiction of Turkish preponderance, the country's diplomats and political leaders remained keenly aware of the realities of realpolitik.

As mentioned before, during six centuries of Ottoman rule, the Turks defeated and reigned over each of their neighbours, with the exception of Russia and Iran. Iran's position in Turkish history is different from that of Russia. Brutalised by Moscow historically, the Turks simply fear Russia. Iran was never as powerful as Russia and did not inflict suffering on Turks in a similar fashion to the Russians, but historically the shahs managed to put up a valiant defence against the sultans, sometimes even pushing back and, in the end, avoiding Turkish domination. Russia being in a different category, Iran is Turkey's only neighbour that escaped Ottoman rule. Accordingly, in modern times, Turks view the Persians with respect and caution.

Inventing Mutually Assured Destruction (MAD)

The Ottoman and Safavid empires became neighbours in the fifteenth century, at which point they started to push against each other for control of what is now Iraq, eastern Turkey, western Iran and the South Caucasus. This resulted in 166 years of debilitating and inconclusive wars between 1473 and 1639, with bankrupt treasuries, especially for the Ottomans. Princeton University Ottoman historian Professor Norman Izkowitz aptly labelled the Ottoman–Persian wars as the, 'Ottoman Vietnam'.[1] Following mutually devastating losses, the two empires settled on historic power parity, agreeing to avoid future conflict at any cost. This is since both had to face the fact that, in a seventeenth-century version of Mutually Assured Destruction (MAD), neither could destroy the other without completely wrecking themselves in the process. Accordingly, in 1639, Ottoman Sultan Murad IV and Safavid Shah Safi signed the Qasr-e Shirin (Zuhab) Treaty, agreeing to avoid future conflict at any cost.

Surely, the two sides have quarrelled and fought, most notably in the late eighteenth and early nineteenth century, a time of Ottoman weakness, including the 1745 Battle of Kars, in which the Persians crushed the Ottomans. The fact is, however, that the Turkish–Iranian border itself has almost not changed since 1639. As a result, it is the Middle East's oldest and, in fact, after the Spanish–Portuguese and Spanish–French borders, also among the world's oldest permanent borders, running today quite close to its original early seventeenth-century contours.

The Turkish–Iranian detente transferred Ottoman–Persian rivalry mostly to the Arab majority borderlands of these empires and to the mountainous regions of Kurdistan, where Turkey and Iran continue to compete for influence to this day. Viewing each other through the prism of power parity and as historic rivals, Turkey and Iran have avoided fighting each other, except for cases where one perceives the other to be weak and vulnerable. This tradition continued well through the collapse of the Ottoman Empire and into the twentieth century.

Next up: Turkey vs Iran?

The 1979 Islamist Revolution threatened to upset the historic power parity between Turkey and Iran. Ankara saw Iran's 1979 Revolution, after which Tehran's Supreme Leader, Ayatollah Ruhollah Khomeini, sent emissaries into eastern Turkey to convert the country's liberal

Muslim Alevi community to Shi'ism – where he failed – as a new twist in the old threat of Persian 'Shi'ite' expansionism.[2]

In addition, the revolution cast Iran and Turkey as two diametrically contrasting models for the Middle East – an authoritarian anti-Western theocracy versus a pro-Western secularist democracy. Likewise, Ankara feared that Iran might exploit divides within Turkish society, working through local political Islamists and the PKK to destroy Turkey's secular regime and national unity inside out.[3]

Since the 1979 Revolution in Iran, officials in Tehran have relentlessly threatened Turkey. Take, for instance, the warnings to Ankara in 2011 by Major General Yahya Rahim Safavi, the Commander of the Iranian Revolutionary Guard Corps (IRGC) and military advisor to the Supreme Leader: 'Turkey must radically rethink its policies on Syria, the NATO missile shield, and promoting Muslim secularism in the Arab world, or face trouble from its own people and neighbours.'[4]

This is no surprise. Turkish–Iranian rivalry briefly subsided in the twentieth century, when Turkey became an inward-looking nation state, leaving a vacuum in the Middle East. During which, in the early twentieth century, Iran was under the rule of its own modernising leader, Reza Shah, whom Ataturk considered a peer. Iran, which was going through its own secular phase, similarly felt little reason to compete against Turkey in the early part of the twentieth century. Following the 1979 Revolution in Tehran, the competition between the two countries was recalibrated. Moreover, in the past decade, Turkey's economic growth and emergence as a regional giant, coupled with Erdogan's foreign policy, have revived its Middle Eastern posturing. From the Syrian uprising to Iraq's sectarian convulsions, Ankara has emerged as the main challenger to Tehran's desire to dominate the region.[5]

In terms of relations with Iran, while the old fissures remained, even before the rise of Erdogan, Ankara had sought areas of common interest with President Mohammad Khatami's (1997–2005) politically moderate government in Iran, and in June 2002, Turkey's President Ahmet Necdet Sezer, a secularist, made a historic visit to Iran. That Sezer, a politician famous for his unyielding commitment to Ataturk's secularist precepts, was willing to set foot in the Islamic Republic became a testament to the determination of Ankara to refashion a better working relationship with its neighbour.

First Act: Enter Erdogan

Five months later, Erdogan's AKP was in power. While previous Turkish governments recognised the merits of re-engagement with countries like Iran (and Russia), Erdogan pushed this outreach into overdrive.

Finding that a personal touch was difficult with Iran, where power rests with the aloof Supreme Leader Ayatollah Ali Khamenei. Nonetheless, Erdogan took the first step towards cordiality with Mahmoud Ahmadinejad, who took office as president in 2005. In August 2008, Erdogan hosted him in Istanbul, where he heaped compliments on his counterpart. Later on, in a March 2012 visit, Erdogan even addressed him as 'my dear brother'.[6] This soliloquy was not an exaggeration. When I attended Islamic Friday prayers with Erdogan and Ahmadinejad at Istanbul's Blue Mosque in August 2008, I had witnessed the two leaders entering the mosque's prayer hall, walking side by side, like two brothers.

Cocktail of interests and ideals

Erdogan's embrace of Shi'ite-majority Iran resonated with Turkey's Sunni political Islamist constituency, but also created tensions.

Turkey's political Islamists have been deeply torn regarding their opinion of Iran. On the one hand, as a Shi'ite power, it is a constant source of suspicion. Turkey's firebrand clerics never tire of casting aspersions on the 'perfidious' Persian and the 'heretical' Shi'ite on Twitter or TV. On the other hand, Turkish political Islamists cannot help feeling a bit of envy of, and even admiration for, the 1979 Islamist Revolution. In this way, deepening ties with Iran allowed Erdogan (and Davutoglu) to indulge in a grand dream first propounded by Necmettin Erbakan – the father of political Islam in Turkey – in which Ankara leads an anti-Western bloc of Muslim nations to rival the USA and Europe in its political might.

Buoyed by these ambitions, Erdogan set about applying his repertoire of instruments for fashioning new bilateral ties with Iran. He removed visa restrictions on visitors from Iran, and announced bold plans to boost bilateral trade and investment with both countries by astounding proportions, despite the snickers of serious economists. The loftiness of these goals and the rhetoric that surrounded them sent shivers down the spines of Turkey's more experienced diplomats.

Consider, for instance, Ankara's policy on international economic sanctions against Iran: before Erdogan came to power, Turkey used its geostrategic location to squeeze commercial advantage from its neighbours when they faced international sanctions: as Ankara did during the Iran–Iraq War of 1980–8, trading with both sides, making money and sometimes even violating sanctions against Tehran, such as by buying Iranian oil.

This meant occasionally helping them skirt international restrictions, but only when risks accepted by Ankara for such an undertaking proved worthwhile. Erdogan took this practice in an entirely new direction, making it somewhat a pillar of his foreign policy. In May 2010, following the failure of his efforts with Brazilian leader Luiz Lula da Silva to broker a US–Iran nuclear deal, Turkey became slightly friendlier towards Iran. Ankara began to assist Iran in evading the sanctions regime, using its public banks to provide the unpopular state with a critical lifeline to foreign markets.[7]

By the end of the last decade, relations between Ankara and Tehran seemed to be booming. In the Middle East, shared objections to the Iraq War had already bound the two capitals. Turkey was also among the first countries to legitimise Ahmadinejad's contested presidential victory in 2009.

Second Act: Arab uprisings

Then came the Arab revolts. The 2011 uprising in Syria put Ankara and Tehran at polar opposite ends of the regional political spectrum, including in Syria, where Erdogan's support for anti-Assad rebels put him at odds with Tehran, Assad's closest ally.[8]

The Syrian war soon became a zero-sum game: either Assad would win or the demonstrators would triumph. Hence, all was fair game now between Ankara and Tehran. Encouraged by Iran, Assad ignored Erdogan's advice to give in to the demands of the demonstrators. Turkey began supporting, then hosting, and then reportedly arming the Syrian opposition. Iran's response was to turn to the PKK: Tehran entered a ceasefire with the PKK's Iranian branch, the Kurdistan Free Life Party (PJAK). This allowed the PKK to focus its energies against Turkey, without having to watch its back. Subsequently, the PKK launched dozens of deadly attacks, killing more than 150 Turks in one year alone in 2011, the greatest toll of causalities since the height of the PKK insurgency in the mid-1990s.[9]

Competition over Syria has also refreshed historic rivalries in Iraq, where Turkey and Iran have been supporting opposing camps. Since Iraq's first democratic elections in 2005, Iran has supported the Shi'ite-backed parties, while Turkey backed Sunni Arabs, and then the secular pan-Iraqi movement of Ayad Allawi in that country's 2010 elections. Following months of contention after the 2010 vote, Iranian-supported Nouri Maliki formed a Shi'ite-dominated government in Baghdad, with help from the USA, scoring a victory for Tehran.[10]

Maliki cracked down on Ankara-backed factions, issuing an arrest warrant for Tariq al-Hashimi, Iraq's vice president and a prominent leader of the country's Sunni Arab community. Hashimi initially took refuge in the Kurdish-controlled part of Iraq before finally settling down in Ankara in 2012. Iraqi Kurds, who had always blamed Sunni Arabs in the country for the persecution they faced under Saddam Hussein's Sunni Arab-dominated Baath Party, made amends with them. To balance Iranian influence inside Iraq, the Kurdish Regional Government (KRG) also began closely aligning with Turkey.[11] Ankara welcomed rapprochement with the KRG, which helped Turkey diversify its energy sources, namely through oil imports from the KRG – uncoordinated with Baghdad. Through rapprochement with Iraqi Kurds and Sunni Arabs alike, Ankara aimed to push back against what it perceived to be solidifying Iranian influence in Baghdad and rising Shi'ite Arab power in the Iraqi capital.

The Turkish–Iranian rivalry in Iraq resulted in a period of fraught rhetoric. Erdogan slammed expansionist 'Persian nationalism' for leading to sectarianism in Iraq.[12] Iranian leaders attacked Turkey's 'secular Islam' for undermining the spread of the Islamic Revolution. Even more, threats ensued as an IRGC commander, in 2011, asserted that Iran would strike NATO's missile defence shield in Turkey if the USA or Israel attacked the Islamic Republic's nuclear facilities. Even though, Ali Akbar Salehi, the former Iranian foreign minister, said that this statement did not reflect official policy.[13] From Tehran's perspective, with the politically more powerful IRGC targeting Ankara, Turkey appeared to be upsetting the traditional power parity between the two nations. Looking from Tehran, Erdogan's Turkey anchored in NATO but also newly oriented towards the Middle East is, indeed, a greater threat to Iranian interests in the region than Ataturk's pro-Western Turkey of the late twentieth century, with its face turned to Europe.[14]

Third Act: Learning to get along

Both countries were slowly showing their hand in the region's oldest power game.[15] Proxy war in Syria became a stark reality, and yet Turkey-supported rebels had not produced the speedy collapse of the Assad regime as Ankara had hoped. Once it looked like negotiations between Iran and the P5+1 group (made up of the five permanent members of the UN Security Council and the EU) could reach an agreement on Iran's nuclear program in 2014, Erdogan grew unsettled. He feared that as part of negotiations, Washington would purposefully ignore Shi'ite advances in Syria, which would boost Tehran's ambition for a so-called Shi'ite crescent, running through Tehran, Baghdad and Damascus.[16]

The United States increased engagement with Tehran under Obama, signalling to Ankara that Washington had agreed to disagree with Iran on the nuclear issue and in Syria. Erdogan feared a repetition of what had happened in Iraq, when the United States had backed the Shi'ite-dominated party of Maliki, following which he had concluded that Washington had surrendered Iraq to the Shi'ites, and for that matter to Iran.[17]

When a US-led 'Iran deal' was finally reached in 2015, Ankara welcomed it, having felt the negative economic effects of the sanctions on Iran, a vital trading partner and source of oil. Nevertheless, the deal also increased Turkey's uneasiness about the potential of Iran's re-emergence as a regional power that could compete with Turkey.[18]

The US–Iran deal reinforced a valuable lesson: Turkey should not place all its eggs in America's basket. Taking cues from Erdogan's vision, Ankara therefore decided it would boost its efforts to look for additional partners, such as the Russians and the Chinese, while continuing to court the Americans. This explains, among other reasons, Ankara's decision in late 2017 to buy the S-400 air defence system from Russia, as well as its announcement in 2013, from which Erdogan backtracked following US pressure, to purchase a Chinese missile defence system.

Fourth Act: Tehran takes advantage of the coup against Erdogan

The botched 2016 military coup in Turkey provided an unexpected boon to the tripartite that was slowly being forged between Turkey, Russia and Iran. Exploiting the fact that Gulen continues to live in the USA, a plethora of AKP opinion-makers allege that the United States and other NATO allies were behind the coup.[19] Two days after the coup attempt, Suleyman Soylu, Turkey's then Minister of Labour and Social Security and Minister of Interior in 2019, announced that the USA was behind the coup attempt.[20] The narrative that is followed in Turkey is simplistic, but convincing for Erdogan's nativist base: the failed coup was part of a 'cosmic war' between the Turkish nation (with Erdogan as its leader) and a vast conglomerate of its enemies, one of which is the United States.[21] This narrative, of course, tallies perfectly with the image of the world that leaders in Iran and Russia have long sought to instill in the minds of their own people.

Tehran immediately capitalised on the opportunity presented by Turkey's failed coup. Iranian officials reportedly initiated contact with Ankara as the coup unravelled, and Iran's foreign minister, Javad Zarif, following the coup attempt, boasted that Iran was the first country to publically stand by Erdogan during the crisis.[22]

Kurdish intermission

Their transitions out of imperial moulds have left Iran and Turkey with large minority communities whom the central state has been unable to assimilate into its preferred model of national citizenship. About half of Iran's population is not ethnically Persian, and roughly 10 per cent does not adhere to Shi'ite Islam as espoused by the Islamic Republic. The Supreme Leader himself is an ethnic Azeri Turk, alongside many of Iran's top military chiefs – a holdover from previous great Iranian empires, including the Safavids, which were led by Turkic dynasties. Moreover, nearly 10 per cent of Iran's population is Kurdish, many of whom practice Sunni Islam.

In fact, the first modern Kurdish state in the Middle East was established in today's Iran. The short-lived Mahabad Republic, finding support from the Soviet Union, pronounced its creation in north-west Iran just after the Second World War while turmoil within Iran's central government ensued. The successors to this entity, including the Kurdish Democratic Party of Iran (KDPI), have waged an on-and-off war against Tehran ever since, mounting a major insurrection against the Islamist regime in 1979, and continuing to strike at Iran from outposts in northern Iraq to this day. Another current of Kurdish nationalism, the PKK, similarly attempts to undermine Ankara. The PKK has, with limited success, tried to extend its influence into Iran, with the emergence of a sister organisation, the PJAK, formed in 2003.

The shared threat of Kurdish secessionism provides incentives for bilateral cooperation and aligns the foreign policies of the two governments. During the 1920s, the infant Kemalist Turkish republic and the Iran's nascent Pahlavi dynasty pledged to take joint action against Kurdish rebellions. The pair have periodically repeated this commitment ever since. Since 2003, PKK attacks against Turkey and PJAK attacks against Iran led Ankara and Tehran to hold numerous *tête-à-têtes* security discussions focused on deepening their cooperation. More recently, in 2017, Ankara and Tehran signed a protocol for intelligence sharing between the Turkish Gendarmerie and IRGC border security units, in an effort to sever connections between the PKK and PJAK.[23]

However, Iran ultimately does not want Turkish–PKK peace. In 2013, Turkey came closer than ever to cementing a peace deal with the latter. The PKK leader, Abdullah Ocalan, who has been imprisoned in Turkey since 1999, publicly endorsed a roadmap for peace, setting in motion a potential withdrawal of PKK fighters from Turkey.

At this crucial moment, allegations surfaced that Iran's infamous spymaster, Qasem Soleimani, reportedly met personally with PKK leaders in the mountains of northern Iraq, urging them to quit the peace process, even promising them sophisticated weaponry in return. Additional rumours also emerged that Iran saved the life of PKK leader Murat Karayilan by 'taking him into custody' as Turkey was bombing PKK camps across northern Iraq.[24] Iran's efforts to spoil Ankara's peacemaking attempts should come as no surprise, considering Turkey's dream of resolving its Kurdish problem is Iran's nightmare. Turkish peace with the Kurds will allow for the transnational PKK to focus its energies against Iran, while at the same time greatly strengthening Turkey's hand in Syria and Iraq, where Iran wishes to limit Turkey's influence.

Most recently, though, the two countries have, once again, found common ground concerning Kurdish nationalism, more specifically regarding the KRG's ambitions for statehood in Iraq. Worried that this attempt, if it succeeded, could mobilise their own Kurdish populations towards independence, both have denounced the KRG's September 2017 independence referendum.[25] Fierce opposition to Kurdish independence, shared by Iran, Turkey, Iraq and Syria alike, explains why Kurdish independence remains elusive for the landlocked Kurds between the Turks, Persians and Arabs – even if the Kurds were able to overcome their linguistic, political, ideological and historic differences.

Fifth Act: Facing the Saudis and their allies

Recently, Turkey's relations with Iran have improved again in the wake of the Saudi-led boycott of Qatar. On 5 June 2017, Saudi Arabia, the UAE, Bahrain, Egypt, Yemen, the Maldives and Libya's eastern-based government severed relations with Qatar, citing Doha's support for the Muslim Brotherhood and accusing them of supporting terrorism.[26] Turkey and Iran both oppose the Gulf Cooperation Council (GCC) bloc, which includes Saudi Arabia, the UAE and Bahrain, among other countries. Egypt supports the GCC bloc regionally, as does Israel occasionally, but almost always behind the scenes.

When Riyadh and its allies broke ties with Doha, Ankara and Tehran both opposed the isolation of Qatar, and in the early days of the crisis, Iranian Foreign Minister Zarif paid a rare visit – rare for any Iranian foreign minister, that is, since the beginning of the war in Syria – to Ankara to discuss solidarity on the Qatar issue.[27]

The increase in diplomatic contacts between Ankara and Tehran following the Qatar crisis cannot be ignored. These senior-level meetings include Erdogan's visit to Tehran, the Iranian vice president's visit to Ankara (a first in history), and Turkish Defence Minister Hulusi Akar's visit to Tehran, another first by a Turkish defence minister since the 1979 Islamist Revolution in Iran, all occurring in October 2017. The exceptionally frequent meetings within this period demonstrate the eagerness of both countries to establish senior-level military ties.[28] However, it is still unclear whether these developments will lead to the formation of a long-term partnership between Turkey and Iran. After all, the two countries continue to have significant conflicts of interest in Syria and Iraq, and these contacts right now seem to be more accurately attributed to short-term ad hoc concerns rather than a long-term alliance.

Sixth Act: Energy affairs

An enduring aspect of Turkey–Iran relations is regarding energy ties. Iran (as well as Russia) benefit from Turkey's dependence on energy imports, of which natural gas is an important component. About 35 per cent of Turkish energy consumption comes from natural gas, nearly all of it imported. In 2017, almost 70 per cent of this natural gas came from Russia and Iran (52.9 per cent and 16.6 per cent, respectively). Though new natural gas coming into Turkey from Azerbaijan, among other routes via the Trans-Anatolian Pipeline, could change this imbalance in Turkey's favour, the fact is that Turkey is woefully dependent on its two historic rivals for its energy needs.

Despite many opportunities, such as those in the Eastern Mediterranean, Ankara has been slow to diversify its suppliers and move toward alternative energy sources. To be sure, Iran (and Russia) are wary of the political and economic costs that would arise from them seriously disrupting gas flows to Turkey. Iran, even more than Russia, has demonstrated its willingness to use energy deliveries as a strategic lever tool vis-à-vis Ankara. Tehran has, in the past, turned off natural gas deliveries to Turkey in the middle of harsh Anatolian winters. Taking into account that an overwhelming majority of Turkey's cities are heated on natural gas, this indicates that Ankara could someday be a strategic target, especially if Erdogan provokes Tehran too boldly.

All told, Ankara seems to have made the quintessential error of international relations. Since 2003, it has increased, and not decreased, its dependency on the countries that are most able to harm it, namely Iran (and Russia).

Sequel: A union of sultans, tsars and shahs?

For all his lofty ambitions, and Tehran's post-coup public diplomacy outreach notwithstanding, Erdogan cannot escape the geopolitical realities that have driven Turkey's relations with Iran (and Russia) throughout history. The same forces that have pulled Ankara closer to Tehran (and Moscow) also make lasting harmony impossible, at least for the moment.

It is true that all three countries currently share a deeply felt opposition to a Western-led world order. However, as the successors of former land empires – the sultans, tsars and shahs – each has couched its alternative vision in distinctly imperial terms, and this will eventually rekindle the imperial rivalries of the past. Tehran equates its security with safeguarding its influence in its historic 'hinterlands' such as in Iraq, as well as its modern reach across the Levant towards Israel, through Syria and Lebanon. Iran considers its access to the Mediterranean a cornerstone of its policy to be considered a regional power; without it, Tehran's status is restricted to just a Persian Gulf state. Accordingly, maintaining a presence along the Mediterranean, through a Shi'ite-majority government in Iraq and the Assad regime in Syria, is the driving logic of Iran's Fertile Crescent policy.

Tehran, therefore, views Ankara's support for the rebels in Syria fighting the Assad regime as a breach of its sphere of influence. Indeed, the support given by each side to opposing proxy forces in Syria renders this instance the closest in recent memory to outright conflict between Ankara and Tehran. As of 2019, Tehran, whose fortunes and allies are ascendant in Syria, will attempt to restore its historic power parity with Ankara – on its own terms. From Iran's perspective, this restoration would necessitate a complete cessation of Turkish support for anti-Assad rebels.

In this context, every step Iran takes in Syria concerning Turkey also serves its broader goal of maintaining its hold over Syria, Ankara is keenly conscious of this dynamic. While Erdogan and Putin broker ad hoc deals in Syria, Tehran could play the spoiler in such deals through its proxies, including Shi'ite militias, the Assad regime and the YPG – the latter once the USA withdraws from Syria, leaving it alone and in need of new protectors against Ankara.

For all the florid rhetoric of Turkish and Iranian diplomats, Ankara's relations with Tehran have been and will remain a zero-sum game: at their best, the sides will accept this core truth and do their utmost to avoid allowing competition to escalate dangerously. Former Turkish Ambassador Onur Oymen conveyed his basic reasoning more than two decades ago when he remarked, with reference to Iran, 'we can choose our friends but we cannot choose our neighbours'. In other words, the irreducible conflicts of interest, and the consequential need for cautious policies that underlie relations with Iran and Russia, are consequences of their power and proximity, basic facts that are unlikely to change any time soon.

This guiding principle served Ankara well in the past: from the earliest days of the Turkish republic, it recognised that strategic engagement with Iran (and Russia) has its benefits. A case in point, Ataturk himself sought support from the Soviet Union to address Turkey's desperate need for capital and weapons during the Turkish War of Liberation and soon after as well. Ankara has made friends in distant lands but, at the end of the day, the Turks inevitably cannot ignore their frontiers. It is important to note that these past maneuverings were based on sober realpolitik and did not amount to a realignment of Turkey's international relations.

The novelty of Erdogan's foreign policy is a determination to ignore the geopolitical realities that have shaped Turkey's foreign policy for centuries. Erdogan's (and Davutoglu's) idealism sought to repress the memories of fear and danger associated with its powerful neighbours, but like all repressed memories, they never really went away. As a result, instead of attaining the strategic depth that Davutoglu so proudly boasted of, Turkey has unfortunately backed itself into a corner, bristling at old friends and drifting dangerously close to its enduring rivals. 'Historical antibodies,' how Turks view their neighbours and how their neighbours view them, continue to shape and limit Ankara's foreign policy ambitions. Ankara, and, sadly, the wider Turkish public, might one day have to pay the price for these unfortunate blunders.

10
ERDOGAN'S ARAB FALL

The Turkish leader who transcended racist Turkish views towards Arabs . . .

Not all of Erdogan's policies towards Turkey's neighbours are rooted in problematic world viewpoints. Some have actually worked to counter long-standing prejudices. A little-known fact about Turkey: the relatively high level of racist views held towards Arabs, engrained in the country's popular culture. Unknowingly, many people outside of the Middle East often associate Turks with Arabs due to Islam, a religion shared by a majority of Arabs and an overwhelming majority of Turks. Their common faith between them notwithstanding, many of Turkey's citizens harbour racist sentiments towards Arabs, and very few would wish to be associated with Arab cultures.

Some of these opinions are embedded in recent Turkish history. Once again, the collapse of the Ottoman Empire sheds light on the relationship between Turkey's citizens and their neighbours – in this case, the Arabs. As the empire withered away, a wave of Arab nationalism spread through its Middle Eastern provinces, especially Syria. During this period, the Young Turks running the empire increasingly espoused Turkish nationalism. Specifically, Cemal Pasha, one of the three Young Turk leaders who was appointed governor of Syria during the First World War, spearheaded a wave of persecution of Arab nationalist leaders in 1916. He ordered the execution of these leaders, including seven in Damascus,[1] as well as those involved in uprisings in Beirut. To this day, a main square in the Lebanese capital is named 'Martyrs Square', honouring Arab nationalists sent to the gallows by him. The Young Turk leader is notoriously remembered as 'Jamal Basha as-Saffah' in Arabic or 'Cemal Pasha the Bloodthirsty'.

During the First World War, anticipating the collapse of the Ottoman Empire and subsequently making plans to reconfigure the Middle East in order to maintain control over the seaways to India, Great Britain courted Arab leaders in the region in its quest to gain influence. Enter British policy-makers and spies, including Lawrence of Arabia, who ingratiated himself with Arab leaders, including the Hashemite family in Mecca.

Convinced the British would present them with their own independent state, the Hashemites and their Arab followers rose against the Ottomans in 1916 in a rebellion, stretching from Syria to Yemen (to which Cemal Pasha and his companions responded with a vengeance). Despite the persecution of Arab nationalist leaders under Ottoman rule, this legacy of 'betrayal' by Arabs against the administration in Ottoman Istanbul during the First World War has left a bitter taste in Turkey. To this day, the best known cultural icon of Turkey's citizens commemorating the First World War is *Yemen Turkusu* (Ballad of Yemen), a gloomy recanting of the story of an Anatolian soldier who perished in Yemen – fighting Arabs. Generations of Turks, including Erdogan, were taught in Turkish schools during the twentieth century that the 'Arabs stabbed the Turks in the back,' and at least some have internalised strongly anti-Arab nationalist tendencies.

The Ottoman Empire for centuries faced Europe, treating its Middle Eastern possessions truly as second class. An overwhelming majority of the nearly 300 grand viziers (a political rank at the level of prime minister), who served under the sultans in Istanbul, hailed from the Balkans and the Caucasus. Many were ethnic Albanians, Armenians, Bosnians, Bulgarians, Circassians, Georgians, Greeks and Serbs. There was even a sprinkling of Croats and Italians among the list of grand viziers. Yet, excluding grand viziers whose ethnic origins still cannot be traced, the first Arab grand vizier, Mahmut Sevket Pasha, assumed power only in January 1913, barely five years before the collapse of the six-century-old empire.

The Turkish language bears linguistic signs of a longer history of Arab disenfranchisement in the Ottoman Empire as well as uneasy Turkish–Arab coexistence, beyond the events of the First World War. Anti-Arab expressions, many of them widely circulated in contemporary Turkish popular culture, literature, movies and slang, include: 'like Arab's hair' (a mess from which there is no exit); 'neither Damascene candy, nor the Arab's face' (a situation when one has two bad options to choose from); and others that are even less flattering.

Erdogan (and Davutoglu) deserve huge credit for taking an emphatic and passionate interest in the Arab nations and, more importantly, transcending Turkish racist views toward Arabs.

Turkish spring in Cairo

Notwithstanding his progressive views towards Arabs, Erdogan has been unable to build lasting friendships with Turkey's Arab neighbours. After the 2011 uprising in Cairo's Tahrir Square ended President Mubarak's three-decade long regime, Erdogan became one of the first leaders to visit Egypt in support for the revolution. This was part of a larger North African tour for the Turkish leader, who also visited Tunisia and Libya, both similarly shaken by the Arab uprisings.[2]

Erdogan landed in Cairo in September 2011,[3] and Egyptian crowds greeted him as a hero then. Large billboards featuring his face lined the expanse of highway from Cairo International Airport to the city's downtown area.[4] He presented Turkey as a model of modern Islamic democracy and secularism. Although Erdogan's support for secularism surprised his Egyptian hosts,[5] it was actually an insightful and wise warning – which they ignored – to maintain sufficient public support to deter a military takeover.

Egyptian newspapers suggested that a new alignment with Turkey would put pressure on Israel,[6] and Erdogan publicised the fact that he was considering a visit to Gaza to signal Turkish support for Hamas and the broader Gaza population.[7] In the end, the Gaza visit did not take place, reportedly due to opposition from Egypt's then ruling Supreme Council of the Armed Forces.[8] Following the Cairo visit, Davutoglu called for a Turkish–Egyptian alliance, which he branded 'the axis of democracy'.[9]

Indeed, these close bilateral ties were established with the election victories of the Ikhwan and its candidate, Mohamed Morsi, in Egypt in 2012.

Erdogan visited Cairo a second time in November 2012, this time with a large delegation from his government and the private sector. He delivered a speech at Cairo University, praising Morsi for the decision to withdraw Egypt's ambassador to Israel in response to Israeli airstrikes on Gaza. Erdogan further suggested that an 'Egyptian–Turkish alliance' would ensure peace and stability in the Eastern Mediterranean, implying such an alliance would constrain Israel's ability to use force. Erdogan praised Egyptian youth activists for bringing down Mubarak's 'dictatorship' and proclaimed, 'Egypt and Turkey are one hand,' a play on the Egyptian military's slogan, 'The army and the people are one hand.'[10]

Morsi's fall

Erdogan's ambitions for a strategic partnership with Egypt ran aground as Morsi's handle on ruling began to slip. Soon after taking office, Morsi set in motion a hasty power grab, granting himself judicial control above any Egyptian court, and ramming through a new constitution drafted largely by political Islamists, excluding other groups in Egypt. He argued that his political opponents and the judicial system from the Mubarak government were sabotaging efforts to fulfil the revolution's demands. This was after he had already taken over legislative control from the council of generals who ruled after Mubarak's ouster.[11] The speed with which Morsi was able to establish himself as the sole ruler of Egypt (less than a year) made Erdogan's own gradual accumulation of power in Turkey since 2003 look miniscule.

Anti-Morsi and anti-Ikhwan demonstrations in Cairo became increasingly violent, and attempts at a dialogue between Morsi and the various opposition parties collapsed. By the spring of 2013, the anti-Morsi Tamarod (rebellion) movement began organising mass protests scheduled for 30 June, the first anniversary of Morsi's rule. As reports circulated that Morsi had tried to remove General Abdel Fattah el-Sisi from his position as Defence Minister, Egypt's military leadership issued warnings that the army might have to intervene to 'prevent Egypt from entering a dark tunnel'.[12]

Erdogan's appeal to the Egyptians searching for a new political approach remained strong, mainly because of Turkey's economic success at the time. Unlike Erdogan, who boasted about Turkey's then booming economy, Morsi faced a deepening economic crisis.[13] Thus,

Morsi's 2012 visit to Ankara was significant because it resulted in a $1 billion dollar loan deal from Erdogan, but it was not enough to save the Egyptian economy.[14]

Western and Turkish efforts to help Morsi reach an agreement with the International Monetary Fund (IMF) to help the Egyptian economy also collapsed, and Morsi withdrew support for reforms only hours after his office announced them. Ankara offered Egypt concessionary trade deals and promoted Turkish private investment, but Morsi's administration appeared increasingly paralysed. As the 30 June protests drew nearer, Erdogan sent Turkey's national intelligence chief, Hakan Fidan, to visit the Egyptian leader. Subsequent reports in both the Egyptian and Turkish media suggest that Fidan's mission was to warn Morsi of an impending coup and perhaps even discuss how to avoid it. Whatever the real substance of the visit, the Egyptian military and its civilian allies perceived the visit as final proof of Erdogan's alignment with Morsi – and the Muslim Brotherhood.[15]

As scheduled, millions of Egyptians took to the streets on 30 June, this time to protest the Ikhwan's power grab and its failure to tackle ongoing economic and security problems. The protestors gathered in Tahrir Square, the same square where the 2011 revolution began.[16]

Brotherhood politicians labelled the protests 'a coup attempt' to oust their democratically elected leader from the beginning, echoing the rhetoric often used by Erdogan, who at the time faced the Gezi Park rallies in Istanbul, which took place weeks before the Tahrir protests against Morsi.[17]

After rising protests in Egypt, on 3 July 2013, General Sisi announced that the army had removed Morsi from power to 'save' Egypt from the specter of civil war. Sisi received support from the UAE and Saudi Arabia, which oppose the Ikhwan both in Egypt and regionally. Erdogan's carefully cultivated relationship with the new Egyptian leadership was over. He referred to Sisi as 'a tyrant' and accused the interim Egyptian government of practicing 'state terrorism'. He also started to allow pro-Ikhwan and anti-Sisi Egyptian media networks to operate freely from Turkey.

Sisi retaliated. The Egyptian media accused Ankara of 'supporting the terrorist campaign' against the Egyptian security services in the Sinai Peninsula following Morsi's removal from power. Huseyin Avni Botsali, a seasoned diplomat and Turkey's ambassador to Cairo, went from being embraced across the spectrum of Egyptian politics to facing anti-Turkish demonstrations at the gates of his residence. Ankara and Cairo cancelled plans confirmed during Morsi's tenure to hold joint naval manoeuvers in the Eastern Mediterranean. Finally, in November 2013, the Egyptian Foreign Ministry expelled Botsali, severing Turkish ties.

Erdogan's support for Morsi and the Brotherhood in Egypt after their ouster, cost Turkey dearly. To retaliate, Cairo started talks with Athens to delineate Egyptian and Greek maritime economic areas in the Eastern Mediterranean. In November 2014, Sisi held a three-way summit with the Cypriot and Greek presidents to promote a deal supplying natural gas from undersea fields, off the coast of Cyprus to Egypt. In doing this, he was almost certainly seeking to challenge Erdogan's power in the Eastern Mediterranean.[18] Furthermore, Sisi's government drove out Turkish businesses, which were the source of Ankara's ascendancy in the Middle East and specifically in Egypt. Turkish businesses in Egypt have suffered since, undermining Ankara's cherished soft-power goals.

Primal fears

It was impossible for Erdogan and Sisi to get along. The roots of this problem lie as much in the events of 2013 as in Erdogan's past, that is to say Erdogan's traumatic and conflict-ridden relationship with Turkey's own secularist military, similar to Morsi's struggle with Sisi.

Turkey should be safe from military coups today, but a residual fear of 'the coup' looms in the back of the minds of many AKP members, including Erdogan,[19] even though he has brought the TAF under his authority in the last decade.[20]

Erdogan's primal fear can be traced back to the 'Soft Coup' of February 1997, where the TAF orchestrated a civilian protest movement to oust the democratically elected and AKP predecessor, Welfare Party (RP). After the Turkish courts shut down the RP in 1998, they sentenced Erdogan to a ten-month jail term for reciting a poem that allegedly undermined Turkey's secular constitution. The outside world stood with the Turkish military, castigating the events: the RP, an unwanted Islamist party; Erdogan, a heroic prisoner.[21]

Of course, political Islam in Turkey and Erdogan have come a long way since the Soft Coup. After the RP was forcibly shut down, Erdogan and some other leaders broke away from its successor Virtue Party, also abandoning the RP's anti-democratic rhetoric. After the AKP came to power, by delivering a decade of phenomenal economic growth, Erdogan boosted his popularity. In the 2011 parliamentary elections, 49.9 per cent of the electorate supported his party, up from 34 per cent in 2002.[22] Subsequently, he has become Turkey's most powerful leader in nearly a century.

Awakened by Morsi's ouster

Although he is deeply entrenched in power, Erdogan, nevertheless, continues to fear coups. In this regard, the events of 2013 in Turkey and Egypt represent an inflection point in Erdogan's career.

Even after Erdogan's initial crackdown in Istanbul against the Gezi Park protestors on 30 May 2013, police brutality against the demonstrators sparked mass protests in Istanbul and around the country. Nearly 2.5 million joined these rallies in almost all of Turkey's 81 provinces, which soon turned into massive anti-government protests. Erdogan cracked down on the rallies, resulting in over a dozen deaths of protestors and police officers.

During the summer of 2013, just as Morsi was confronted by a popular wave of resentment that eventually led to his ouster, Erdogan was already grappling with his own popular uprising in Turkey. The ousting of Erdogan's ally and fellow political Islamist by a popular movement backed by a secularist military – while the tremors of Gezi Park rallies were still being felt in Turkey – marked a turning point for Erdogan.

After finally cracking down on the Gezi Park rallies in May–June 2013 and 'taking Taksim Square' back from the protestors who had camped on it for nearly three months, Erdogan became more authoritarian in quashing any similar protest movements that he feared could oust him in the future. Domestically, this decision has increased Turkey's democratic backslide following the events in 2013. Renewed PKK violence against the Turkish government following the collapse of a ceasefire in 2015, provided him more reason to crack down on opposition. Harassment of opposition members and media outlets became increasingly common, as did political interference in judicial processes.[23]

Since the Gezi Park rallies, the Turkish leader's deepest fear has been that he suffers Morsi's fate,[24] a fear that has only been attenuated by the failed coup of 2016. Ironically, just as Erdogan became more comfortable with occupying the public profile of an authoritarian leader, the external factors of Syrian war-linked PKK and ISIS led to terror attacks between 2015 and 2016. This was all coupled with the failed coup and Gulenist split in 2016, providing him a pair of serious security threats that justified authoritarian steps for domestic audiences.

For years, Erdogan had been a master of reading the global zeitgeist and responding to it with a PR executive's craftiness, for instance by portraying his AKP as a 'democracy-loving faction' soon after the 11 September 2001 attacks. However, after the Gezi Park rallies, he lost this magic touch and ability to awe the international community. The image of Erdogan as an authoritarian leader, belatedly, started to take shape in many Western capitals and in financial circles. Investment in Turkey soon started to dry up. Rising anti-Erdogan sentiments in the West only fed into Erdogan's rooted resentment towards the West from his political past.

At this point, Erdogan is not interested in 'looking good' to the West. Erdogan saw parallels between Morsi's ouster in Egypt in summer 2013 by the military, the May–June 2013 Gezi Park rallies in Turkey and the TAF-led 1997 'Soft Coup' in Turkey. He has drawn a key lesson from the 2013 Tahrir protests that ousted Morsi: if the Gezi Park protests had gotten out of hand, the West would have done nothing to stop his opponents from toppling him. Erdogan was appalled by the Western countries' decision not to interfere in a military coup against Morsi, a fellow political Islamist and democratically elected leader.[25] He blamed Washington for the coup that ousted Morsi, and, as explained earlier, this undermined his relationship with Obama.

The fears instilled into Erdogan by the Egyptian coup against Morsi also led to his alienation from Turkey's Middle Eastern friends, who opposed the Ikhwan, and Western allies, and who supported Morsi's ouster. After 2013, Turkish ties with Saudi Arabia, the UAE and other Arab monarchies within the GCC suffered severely because of Erdogan's support for the Ikhwan in Egypt. These Gulf monarchies have a deep aversion to the Brotherhood and see it as their biggest domestic security threat. What happened to Morsi is not and will not be acceptable for Erdogan. This is why even if Ankara one day manages to establish a *modus vivendi* with Cairo – perhaps this 'even' is a tall order – it will be hard for Erdogan to feel completely comfortable with Sisi.[26]

This last, but even more important, bit of tension in the Turkish–Egyptian relationship is shaped by the perceptions that Erdogan and Sisi have of each other. Erdogan is the political Islamist leader who imprisoned secularist generals; Sisi, the secularist general who locked up political Islamists. As long as these two men are in charge of their respective countries, it is hard to imagine Ankara and Cairo establishing (much less maintaining) friendly ties.

Limited success in Libya and Tunisia

Erdogan's pro-Ikhwan stance found somewhat more success in the rest of North Africa, where Ankara fared slightly better results in Tunisia than it did in Libya.

When Libya descended into civil war, Erdogan threw his support behind the political Islamist factions in Tripoli's western-based 'Dawn Coalition', which opposed Libya's internationally recognised 'Dignity Coalition' led by General Khalifa Heftar in Tobruk in the east.

Sisi and his ally, the UAE, worried about the ascent of political Islam in Libya next door to Egypt (and eager to undermine Erdogan), were quick to assist the Tobruk government; they carried out air strikes aimed at the Tripoli factions. Because of its support for the Dawn Coalition and loss of favour with Libya's internationally recognised government, Ankara missed out on many of the pre-war economic contracts and commercial ties it had painstakingly built in Libya over the past decades. What is more, Ankara also failed to build influence in the UN-led peace process regarding Libya, because many Libyans and key international players do not view Erdogan as neutral. That was illustrated by the ostracised Turkish delegation at the Libya conference in Palermo, Italy, on 13 November 2018.[27]

Erdogan invested heavily in Tunisia after Ben Ali's fall to help the political Islamist Ennahda Party, which joined the government in November 2011.[28] A notable initiative in this regard was the establishment of the High Level Strategic Cooperation Council (HLSCC) between Tunis and Ankara, which was signed in Ankara by Erdogan and the then prime minister of Tunisia, Hamadi Jebali, on 25 December 2012. This declaration formed various mechanisms for security, the military, economy and trade. During the first meeting of the HLSCC, the delegations made twenty-one agreements and declared 24 twin cities in both countries. Since then, Ankara has provided half a billion dollars' worth of credit to post-Arab Spring Tunisia, though Turkey's clout in Tunisia decreased after Ennahda stepped down from government in 2014.

No one loves Erdogan, but Qatar

Beyond North Africa, GCC members around Saudi Arabia have a deep aversion to the Brotherhood domestically, which they see as their biggest internal security threat. Jordan, a close GCC ally, has also taken issue with Ankara's support for the Ikhwan. On 15 April 2013, Jordan's King Abdullah II gave an interview to *The Atlantic*, in which he criticised Erdogan for his support for the Muslim Brotherhood in the region.[29]

By 2019, Qatar was Erdogan's only friend in the Middle East. Doha and Ankara have much in common when it comes to their foreign policies. Both countries support political Islamist groups, including the Ikhwan in Egypt, Hamas in Gaza, as well as Brotherhood-affiliated groups in Syria and Libya. The Turkish–Qatari alliance solidified after Turkey sided with Qatar in a GCC dispute in 2017.

Turkey's immediate reaction to the crisis was to try to remain neutral and call for dialogue. Just a few days into the blockade, however, it became clear that Ankara had decided to take a pro-Qatar stance. Erdogan condemned the Saudi-led coalition's blockade of Qatar, saying that the isolation imposed on Qatar was inhumane and against Islamic values, even comparing the blockade to a 'death sentence'.[30] As the blockade dragged despite US efforts at mediation, Turkey's role as a critical lifeline for Qatar became increasingly evident.

The Middle East's new power game: 'Axis' vs 'Bloc'

Regional dynamics in the Middle East have aligned Turkey and Qatar, almost moulding them into a bilateral 'Axis' competing against other regional powers, including Saudi Arabia, the UAE, Bahrain, Egypt and Jordan and Kuwait to an extent, in a 'bloc'-like formation, with Israel often supporting this grouping behind the scenes.

As I see them, the 'Axis' and the 'Bloc' are informal alliances, but competition between them remains fierce. For instance, throughout the Arab uprisings and their aftermath, Turkey and the UAE ended up on the opposite side of almost every conflict. Abu Dhabi, which opposes the Ikhwan, has condemned Ankara and Doha for supporting it.[31] Despite their initial shared hostility towards a common enemy in the form of the Assad regime in Syria, the Turkey–Qatar Axis and the UAE have supported rival groups within the Syrian opposition.

In Palestine, the UAE and Egypt have been trying to broker a deal between the rival Fatah and Hamas movements, while the Axis continues to support Hamas.[32] In Libya, Cairo and Abu Dhabi together supported General Khalifa Haftar's campaign against political Islamist militias and groups backed by Ankara and Doha. The rift between the Axis and the Bloc is already spilling over, beyond Libya and the Middle East's borders. As discussed in Chapter 14, this competition now extends to East Africa, where the Axis is vying for influence against the Bloc along the Nile Valley and around the Horn of Africa in a new 'Great Game'.

Underlying this rift is the visceral reaction that the Ikhwan evokes from the Bloc. For Egyptian leader Sisi, Saudi Crown Prince Mohammad bin Salman and his homologue UAE Crown Prince Mohammed bin Zayed, the term 'Muslim Brotherhood' has become synonymous with Erdogan's Turkey and with radical political Islamism – as they understand it. It bears mention that the Ikhwan is a spectrum movement and not a monolith. There are Brotherhood-related intellectuals and movements that are well within the bounds of democratic politics and radical in neither their view of governance nor their critiques of the West, such as the Ennahda in Tunisia. While Turkey's regional initiatives can be explained also through the lens of nationalism or geopolitics, the Bloc's readiness to ascribe all Turkish motives to the Muslim Brotherhood agenda and all Sunni Muslim extremism to the influence of the Ikhwan have deepened the already severe policy differences between them. The USA is left with a treaty ally (Turkey) considered anathema to several of its other regional allies, and regional allies considered undemocratic and tyrannical by Turkey (and much of the 'Arab street').

Within the GCC Bloc, Turkey's ties are worst with the UAE, Erdogan's archenemy in the Persian Gulf and perhaps the entire Middle East in 2019. Abu Dhabi took a strong stance against Erdogan's support for Morsi and his subsequent opposition to Sisi after the fall of the Brotherhood in Cairo. Erdogan's speech at the UN on 24 September 2014, in which he implied Sisi was an illegitimate tyrant, was the straw that broke the proverbial camel's back regarding Ankara–Abu Dhabi ties.[33]

Following this, the UAE launched a successful campaign in blocking Turkey's bid to join the UN Security Council for the 2015–16 term. Since then, Turkish–UAE ties have hit a historic low, with the two countries using any opportunity to undermine each other's policies – from Syria, where Abu Dhabi opened its embassy in December 2018 to support Assad against Ankara, to Somalia, where Ankara backs the central government in Mogadishu, and UAE Somalia's breakaway Somaliland region and Puntland region in the north, where Abu Dhabi is building influence against the Mogadishu government and Ankara.[34]

Saudi ties with Turkey, however, deserve a separate treatment from the Axis and the Bloc, even when considering the Turkish–UAE spat. A devout Muslim, Erdogan has been deferential towards the Saudi kings, whom he respects as the 'Guardian of Islam's Two Holy Shrines' in Mecca and Medina. In fact, in recent years, Turkish–Saudi ties did improve a bit after Saudi Arabia's vehemently anti-Ikhwan King Abdullah died in January 2015. However, these ties took a nosedive when Turkey sided with Qatar over the 2017 Doha–GCC dispute, only to dip further following the 2 October 2018 murder of Saudi journalist Jamal Khashoggi at the Saudi consulate in Istanbul. Erdogan used this incident well for his own sake, slowly leaking evidence to media, incriminating Saudi Crown Prince Mohammad bin Salman in the murder, and embarrassing him internationally.

Overall, the Khashoggi episode has left bin Salman bitter towards Erdogan. Bin Salman has embraced the Bloc more enthusiastically, bonding with Sisi and bin Zayed even more strongly in their visceral opposition to Erdogan. In 2019, therefore, Erdogan faces an Arab triumvirate composed of Sisi, bin Salman and bin Zayed, who aim to undermine him and his regional policies. With Iran and its allies, namely the Assad regime and Hezbollah, also opposing Erdogan, this leaves the Turkish leader alone in the Middle East, as well as facing pushback from two powerful blocs.

However, Erdogan's biggest problem is located with the UAE: Ankara and Abu Dhabi have become bitter enemies. A case in point is Erdogan's recent spat with Abu Dhabi. In December 2017, UAE Foreign Minister Abdullah bin Zayed al-Nahyan shared a post on Twitter that accused Fahreddin Pasha, an Ottoman general who fought to defend Medina during the Arab Revolt of 1916 in the First World War, of stealing priceless artefacts and bringing them to Istanbul at the time.[35] 'These are Erdogan's ancestors, and their history with Arab Muslims,' the tweet concluded.[36] The taunt sprang from a deep well of bitterness. On the propaganda front, the UAE has turned to sniping at Turkey, casting it as a foreign power seeking to impose its supremacy over the Arabs.[37]

Stung by the insult, Erdogan fired back at the minister: 'While my ancestors were busy defending Medina, you impudent man, what were your ancestors doing?'[38] Erdogan's spokesperson, Ibrahim Kalin, also chimed in, calling bin Zayed's comments a 'propaganda lie that seeks to turn Turks and Arabs against one another'. Erdogan advisor Yigit Bulut piled in, too, deriding the UAE as the '52nd state of the US' (Israel, he said, 'is the 51st state').[39] Pro-Erdogan Turkish press sprang into action, with stories and op-eds glorifying Fahreddin Pasha and excoriating the UAE for insulting his character.

Ironically, Erdogan's Middle East pivot, which aimed to undo the Turks' racist views of Arabs, seems to have not only failed in transcending such prejudices, but also to have encouraged a new generation of unfortunately negative perceptions and tensions towards Arabs.

11
UNCOMFORTABLE OTTOMANS

Erdogan's (and Davutoglu's) hope in pursuing a policy of rapprochement with Ankara's Middle Eastern neighbours was that it would further Turkey's integration in the region, creating something like the 1950s Benelux bloc, i.e. the harmonious political and economic union of Belgium, the Netherlands and Luxembourg in Western Europe after the Second World War. Indeed, during the first decade of the twenty-first century, Ankara built good ties with not only the Assad regime in Damascus, but also the Mubarak regime in Cairo and Gaddafi in Tripoli. Erdogan hoped to benefit from these relationships by establishing Turkish influence across the Muslim Middle East, leveraging his rise as a promising regional leader.

However, the takeaway from Erdogan's foreign policy pivot to the Middle East and involvement in the Syrian Civil War is that the Middle East is not, yet, like the Benelux.

Erdogan's (and Davutoglu's) Arab uprising report card

The main reason that lies behind the failure of Erdogan's (and Davutoglu's) Middle East pivot is their over-reliance on the Muslim Brotherhood during the Arab uprisings.

The roots of this dynamic itself lie in the previous decade. Erdogan's post-2003 Middle East focus brought it closer not only to regional governments, but also to various Ikhwan-style parties across the region.

This is since Erdogan saw the AKP, born out of political Islam and still a self-declared moderate force, as a model for Muslim Brotherhood-related political Islamist parties in the Middle East. While the AKP had moderated, as he saw it, and come to power through democratic elections in Ankara, he believed that like-minded Ikhwan-related parties in Egypt and Syria should be able to do the same in Cairo and Damascus, respectively, and other capitals across the region. This was not just wishful thinking, but part of Erdogan's vision to revive Turkey's greatness in the Middle East through Ikhwan-related and AKP-allied parties, which would look to Erdogan as the region's primary influencer.

At the start of the Arab uprisings, this vision seemed to come to fruition. The Ikhwan rose to power in Egypt and Tunisia, and its fortunes seemed to be ascending in Libya. In addition, in Syria, Ankara (and Doha) aggressively supported the Brotherhood forces in their efforts to become the leaders of that country's opposition.

Erdogan entered the era of Arab uprisings with many reasons to feel confident. Turkey had a positive reputation across the Middle East and had invested in both diplomatic and soft-power presence, regionally and around the world. It seemed at the time that Ankara was destined to play a leading role in the region's transformation, winning power, prestige and wealth in the process. In the 2011 TESEV survey previously discussed, a full 71 per cent of respondents in the Middle East agreed that: 'Turkey should play a greater role in the Middle East.'[1] More so, luminaries of the Arab uprisings, such as co-founder of the Tunisian political Islamist Ennahda Party, Rachid Ghannouchi, spoke positively of Turkey as a model and a guide.[2]

Unfortunately, the Arab uprisings tested the limits of Erdogan's soft-power-driven and Ikhwan-devoted approach to the Middle East, as well as exposing its shortcomings in terms of applying the 'Erdogan model' to the region.

One case in point is his ties with the Ennahda in Tunisia. Following the 2013 Gezi Park rallies and anti-Ikhwan protests in Tahrir Square in Cairo, Ennahda leader Ghannouchi objected to Morsi's majoritarian view of democracy, subsequently also breaking with Erdogan.[3] Perhaps in no small part thanks to avoiding majoritarianism and shying away from a Morsi-style power grab, the Tunisian Ikhwan is the only political Islamist movement that has remained a legitimate force to be reckoned with in its own country's politics – not facing a coup, ban or delegitimisation effort.

Erdogan, for his own part, lost the intimate touch he had with Ennahda because of its attempts, since 2013, to decrease the distance between itself and Erdogan's AKP. A brief bilateral spat in 2015 over Tunisia's accusation of alleged Turkish involvement in facilitating the movement of jihadists from Tunisia and Libya to Syria and Iraq is an indicator of tense Turkish–Tunisian relations in recent years.[4]

Why did Erdogan commit himself so strongly to Ikhwan-style parties across the Arab uprisings? The roots of this phenomenon lie in Erdogan's nativist National Outlook antecedents. He seems to believe that *only* political Islamist parties represent the 'true children of the land', other factions being shaped by, and representing 'foreign' ideologies, Erdogan was, therefore, convinced (and maybe still believes) that in Arab countries, the Ikhwan-related parties will sooner or later repeat his AKP's success in Turkey, finally coming to power in various Arab capitals.

He has especially wished to see this happen in Egypt, the region's most populous Arab nation, with nearly 100 million citizens, the dominant country among the almost twenty Arab-majority states. Egypt is often labelled 'Umm al-Dunya' (Mother of the World). It is, indeed, a key nation among the Arabs: while it does not always originate social or political trends, once embraced, it makes these trends ubiquitous, and even hegemonic, across the Arab nations.

At the start of the Arab uprisings, in Erdogan's view, it was only a matter of time before Turkey's proxy influence would spread far and wide across Arab lands through the Ikhwan, starting from Cairo. When Mubarak fell on 11 February 2011, he saw Turkey as being on the cusp of attaining a degree of influence in Cairo not seized since the Ottoman sultan, Selim I, 'The Grim', toppled the Egyptian Mameluk dynasty in 1517. Erdogan appeared in Cairo to support Morsi, but also to recommend that he slow down in consolidating, lest he trigger a popular backlash suppoerted by the Egyptian military. Erdogan failed in this endeavour, but so did Morsi when he refused to heed Erdogan's advice.

Collapse on the Nile

For his own part, Erdogan's Egypt policy failed because his pro-Ottomanist lenses have distorted the actual circumstances on the ground there for him. Morsi did not listen to Erdogan because, far from wanting to come under Ankara's influence, Egypt, even under the

Ikhwan, has always seen itself as competing against Turkey – as a large Sunni Muslim power of the Eastern Mediterranean.

In fact, Egypt and Turkey alike see themselves as regional powers, and now as the leaders of Sunni Islam. The competition between Turks and Egyptians dates back to the days of the Ottoman Empire, of which Egypt was a province until it became semi-independent in 1867.

Even before the 1860s, Egypt proved to be especially difficult for the Ottomans to control. While a governor appointed by Istanbul ran Cairo and paid taxes to it, the land of the Nile enjoyed de facto autonomy for much of the duration of Ottoman rule.

Egypt retained so much power that in the nineteenth century, it attempted to take over the Ottoman Empire. In the 1830s, under the leadership of Mohammad Ali Pasha, the Albanian-born Ottoman Governor of Egypt, and his son, Ibrahim Pasha, an army commander, an Egyptian force conquered Palestine and Syria, and threatened to overthrow the Ottoman sultan. Ibrahim Pasha penetrated deep into Anatolia, reaching the city of Kutahya, only 196 kilometres (122 miles) from Istanbul.

This incident sparked the debate, which resulted in the 'Eastern Question' in Europe regarding the future of the Sublime Porte, that is, what to do with the decaying Ottoman Empire? London, as mentioned before, decided in favour of preserving the core territories of the empire only to prevent Russia from accessing the Mediterranean and the warm seas. Subsequently, it was mainly thanks to the intervention of Great Britain (and its ally, France) that the sultan's throne was protected and the Egyptian threat was contained, though Mohammed Ali's descendants became Egypt's royal family.

Egypt was independent from the Ottoman Empire, in all but name, throughout the rest of the nineteenth century. While the sultans continued to formally appoint a member of Mohammad Ali's family as Egypt's khedive (viceroy) until the final collapse of the Ottoman Empire, Egypt fell under de facto British rule in 1882. At the same time, however, competing against Istanbul, Cairo emerged as a magnet city under the Westernising khedives, attracting Ottoman talent, including many Young Turk exiles escaping Abdulhamid II. Cairo was also outshining Istanbul in the nineteenth century. Egyptian fashion was being copied in Istanbul, and not the other way around.

Following the end of the Ottoman Empire, Egypt continued to harbour modern Turkey's exiles. Some of Ataturk's key opponents, including poet Mehmet Akif Ersoy, who wrote the lyrics for Turkey's national anthem but opposed the secularist ideology of Turkey's founder, took refuge in Cairo. Ersoy and other political figures who challenged Ataturk or his hard secularism, transformed Cairo into somewhat of an anti-Turkey intellectual hub during the interwar period.

The overthrow of the Egyptian monarchy in 1953 added a further dint to Turkish–Egyptian relations. The ouster by Gamal Abdel Nasser of King Farouk and his Ottoman-sourced elite –descending from Albanians, Abkhazes, Circassians, Crimean Tatars and mostly Istanbul Turks, Egypt's rulers often spoke Turkish among themselves until Nasser. The chasm between Ankara and Cairo deepened when Nasser, Egypt's new ruler, sided with the Soviets in the Cold War. Ankara had just entered NATO a year earlier and assumed its role as a serious pillar of Western power in the Middle East.

In the 1970s, Egypt made a pro-US turn under President Anwar Sadat. In the 1980s, Turkey made its aforementioned pro-Middle East pivot under Ozal. Rather than facilitating warm relations between the two countries, these developments only exposed their competition over the Eastern Mediterranean. For instance, Turkey was disappointed Egypt did not support Ankara on the Cyprus issues. Cairo, for its part, was agitated at the time by Turkey's close partnership with Israel, which outshone Egyptian–Israeli ties.[5]

The point is that, regardless of who is in charge in Cairo, Egypt has always seen itself as powerful enough to stand up to Turkey – a fact Erdogan sorely neglected. This explains why Morsi was unwilling to consider Erdogan's advice to moderate his policies, as well as Sisi's visceral reaction when Erdogan refused to recognise his legitimacy. The feud now runs deep: Ankara attempted to take Sisi's government to the UN Security Council for sanctions after Sisi ousted Morsi from power in 2013. In return, Egypt has played the Cyprus card, building ties with the Cypriot Greeks and conducting joint military exercises with them, as well as with Greece in 2015–17.

Bad bets

Across from Cyprus, in Syria, Erdogan actively sponsored the incipient Sunni-Arab dominated rebellion, even as radical jihadists were incubating in its midst. Early rebel gains made it seem like Assad's grip on power was loosening, portending an Ikhwan-dominated post-Assad Syria that, Erdogan believed, would look to Turkey as its sponsor and model. The equation was deceptively simple: Turkey's soft power – the prestige gained from its commercial success and cultural eminence – would translate into hard political power once the Arab uprisings swept from power the old autocrats, allowing Erdogan- and Ankara-adoring masses in the region to call the shots. Needless to say, this scenario never unfolded.

When the Arab uprisings began, neither Erdogan nor Davutoglu, and most probably no one else, predicted that the Brotherhood-related parties would rise and fall so precipitously. However, the bigger issue at stake here is not that Erdogan and Davutoglu lacked foresight in supporting the Ikhwan, but rather, that they limited Turkey's options by betting big *only* on the Muslim Brotherhood. Had the Ikhwan won, Turkey would have won big, but, because it lost, Ankara ended up losing big. With hindsight, as crafty foreign policy practitioners, Erdogan and Davutoglu should have supported the Ikhwan as they wished, but also kept lines of communications open with a broader spectrum of key actors in countries experiencing the Arab uprisings.

Qatar and Turkey: Shared visions

However, not all is lost for Erdogan in Arab-majority countries. This is since, in recent years, he won Qatar as a staunch ally through a shared pro-Ikhwan stance. In addition to the Muslim Brotherhood, related dynamics, power dynamics and historical legacies are also shaping the Turkish–Qatari relationship.

Turkey has 82 million citizens and Qatar just under 350,000. In fact, Qatar has the smallest number of citizens among all the Middle Eastern nations. Yet, thanks to its ownership of one of the world's largest natural gas reserves, it is many times wealthier in terms of per capita income than Turkey and many other states in the region. This has created the dynamics for a uniquely symbiotic Middle Eastern relationship: Ankara brings its powerful military, skilled diplomats, aid organisations and a seasoned intelligence organisation, the MIT, to the table; and Doha, lots of money.

Ankara and Doha have together supported political Islamist parties in the Middle East, forming de facto alliances opposing the Bloc. These cases include Egypt, Syria (against Cairo, Abu Dhabi and Riyadh – the latter initially supported Ikhwan-related factions in Syria's civil war, but later on switched sides), Gaza Strip (against the wishes of Israel), Libya (against the UAE and Egypt) and, last but not least, East Africa (against the UAE and Egypt; discussed in Chapter 14). In each case, Turkey and Qatar combine their unique strength: Ankara offers a vast human resource pool and powerful institutions, and Doha large funds, which support the Turkish institutions and their operations.

Qatar owes its existence to the Ottoman sultans

But – and yet unsurprising for those who by now in the book have become experts in recognising the sprinkles of Ottoman legacy in Turkish foreign policy – events of the late Ottoman Empire also play a role in shaping today's Turkish–Qatari relationship.

A little-known fact is that the special relationship between Ankara and Doha predates Erdogan, and for that purpose Ataturk's Turkey: Qatar owes its sovereign existence to the late Ottoman Empire. In the late nineteenth century, Anglo-Ottoman rivalry dominated Gulf politics. At the time, Qatar was a district under the Ottoman governorship of Najd, which itself fell under the Ottoman province of Basra. Elsewhere in the Gulf, Great Britain had established special relationships with the rulers of Bahrain, Kuwait and the Trucial States (which later united to form the UAE), drawing them into its sphere of influence and eventually opening the path to British control. A series of events in 1893 set Qatar on a different course, however.

That year, the Ottomans sent troops to Qatar to suppress local ruler Jassim bin Mohammed al-Thani's (a predecessor of Qatar's current ruler by five generations) opposition to Istanbul's proposed administrative reforms. After the Ottoman forces were defeated, Qatar became an autonomous district in the empire, but also agreed to host Ottoman troops. Accordingly, the Ottoman military stayed in Qatar until the empire's collapse in the First World War – longer than in any other Gulf principality. Qatar's autonomous status and subsequent troop-hosting under the Ottomans also prevented its absorption into the expanding Saudi state in the early twentieth century, despite their shared Wahhabi creed.

Turkey 'saves' Qatar: The 'Axis' is reforged

In the autumn of 2016, as countries in the Eastern European Time zone (GMT+2), whose time zone Turkey had shared for decades, added an extra hour to end their daylight savings time, Erdogan decided to eschew the traditional time change in Turkey. This also permanently aligned Ankara with its best friend in the Middle East, Doha, in the Arabian Standard Time zone (GMT+3). Nothing speaks more strongly of Erdogan's desire to lock Turkey with Qatar than this dramatic act, which removed Turkey from Europe overnight, in the chronological sense, and placed it in the Middle East.

In fact, this only scratches the surface of the solidification of the Turkish–Qatari alliance. In 2015, the TAF sent forces to Qatar for joint military exercises. Some of these forces stayed behind to build a Turkish military base there. Some Qataris believe that had it not been for the TAF's presence in Qatar in 2017, Saudi Arabia and their allies would have invaded the small country during the Doha–GCC split. What is more, Erdogan established an air bridge to Doha when Riyadh and its allies broke ties with Qatar, allowing much needed supplies to be flown in.

This allowed Qatar to survive the initial shock of tough sanctions applied by its neighbours. In a further step in November 2017, Erdogan formally inaugurated the Turkish military base in Qatar, putting Ankara informally in charge of protecting Doha. During a speech to Turkish troops there, he stated, 'Our expectations from our heroes in Qatar; you must conquer the hearts of the people of Qatar with our love and respect while performing your military duty with your gun and your heart.'[6] The Qatar–GCC split had the effect – unintended perhaps for Saudi Arabia and the UAE – of cementing the already symbiotic Turkish–Qatari relationship, with Ankara and Doha subsequently taking steps to further coordinate their policies, forging their alliance as the Qatar–Turkey 'Axis'.

'Network error'

Erdogan gained a new ally in Qatar in the 2010s. At the same time, he also lost another: Gulen. The rift between Erdogan and Gulen is important also, as it pertains to Erdogan's soft-power approach to the Middle East as well as his consolidation of power at home.

The movement and its supporters, known as Gulenists, backed Erdogan in his quest to dismantle secular Turkey and its institutions following his rise to power in 2003. Largely, these efforts worked. During initial phases of the Ergenekon–Sledgehammer trials of 2008–9, the Gulen movement helped Erdogan silence his opponents in the media, civil society, academia and business community, who wanted to keep space open for secular civil society in Turkey.

The Ergenekon–Sledgehammer trials also bludgeoned the secularist TAF into submission to Erdogan and Gulen through detentions and public defamation. The Turkish military's top brass resigned in 2011 en masse, throwing in the towel and addressing Erdogan and Gulen with: 'You have won, we are out.'[7]

This marked the high point in a decades-long struggle by Gulen's organisation to infiltrate, subvert and ultimately control the TAF. At this juncture, a dilemma emerged: Gulen and Erdogan each wanted Turkey for themselves. And, what ensued was an inevitable, raw power struggle. The Gulen–Erdogan alliance, therefore, quickly unravelled after 2011 after Erdogan refused to appoint a Gulenist as the head of the MIT, thereby kick-starting the series of events that eventually led to the 2016 putsch, in which Gulen-aligned military officers seem to have played a critical role in the failed coup attempt to overthrow and assassinate Erdogan.

Preceding the split, however, Gulen collaborated with Erdogan on topics including Ankara's foreign policy. During the first decade of the twenty-first century, Erdogan encouraged Turkish businesses and civil society organisations to establish businesses, schools and cultural centres overseas, promoting Turkish culture and influence. These institutions, marketed as supposedly 'moderate' overseas alternatives to fundamentalist variants of Islam, unmistakably boosted the Gulenist network.

Almost without exception, Turkey's soft-power building model followed a similar pattern for each country. Gulen's network cooperated with state institutions under Erdogan's control.

First, the Gulen network would move into a certain Middle Eastern, African or Asian country, setting up a key business there to fund operations. This business would then support high-quality school(s) to educate the children of the said country's elites. Soon after, Turkish Airlines would launch a direct flight from Istanbul to the same country's capital, bringing in more Turkish businesses and civil society people, among whom were numerous Gulenists.

A final step, the Turkish Foreign Ministry would open a diplomatic mission in the country, cementing Turkey's political influence and soft power in the country, but also providing Gulen networks with diplomatic and political muscle. Prior to the fallout between Gulenists and Erdogan, Turkish diplomats were instructed to help Gulen schools in their respective countries.[8]

Erdogan, needing support from Gulen's network in Turkey's bureaucracy, media and judiciary to push back against the secularist Turkish military and their allies during the Ergenekon–Sledgehammer trials at home, ignored the fact that many of these schools and cultural centres overseas were run by Gulen's followers. Eventually however, Erdogan saw in the failed coup attempt that it was his Gulenist 'allies', and not his secular adversaries, who would become his nemeses.

As it happened, at least some of Turkey's soft-power investments made through Gulen's network in the Middle East, Central Asia, Balkans, Africa and beyond have turned into liabilities for Erdogan. Today, Turkey wages a costly global diplomatic and political effort to convince various countries to shut down these schools and cultural institutes and, in some cases, to extradite their staff to Turkey for prosecution.[9] Turkish pressure has led to the closure of hundreds of Gulen schools overseas, dozens of which have been reopened under the administration of semi-official 'Education Foundation' personnel from Ankara; but, hundreds more remain open in dozens of countries.

Power deficiency

Beyond problems related to the Gulen movement, the lessons to be drawn from Turkey's attempt to use soft power and 'Ottoman benevolence' in the Middle East to shape the region and then become a powerhouse, are multiple. By 2010–11, many Turks (especially AKP cadres, including Davutoglu) had become increasingly hubristic, and not just in the Middle East. As Turkey's total GDP more than doubled in the previous decade as measured in current prices, many Turks felt they no longer needed Europe to succeed. Since Turkey's economy was growing much faster than the European average, the argument followed, why beg to be part of Europe's 'anaemic Union?'

While drawing closer to its regional neighbours, Ankara moved further away from Brussels, while also often squabbling with Washington. Yet, Turkey's policies during the Arab uprisings, and more specifically in the Syrian war, have demonstrated a mismatch between Erdogan's (and Davutoglu's) approach to the Middle East, Turkish soft power, Ottomanist ambitions and regional realpolitik.

First, Ankara's hard power has arguably lagged behind its soft power. In terms of hard power assets, Turkey was, and remains, what international relations scholars would call a 'middle power': strong in its own neighbourhood, but not in the same league as the big powers.

Turkey's heavily conscripted military is large, but it has a limited number of units trained and equipped for high-intensity combat. It has the ability to successfully operate in conflicts of limited geographic scope, such as northern Iraq and Syria or south-east Turkey, but has neither sufficient forces nor logistical projection capability to wage war against a nation-state enemy outside of a coalition context.

Turkey's economy under Erdogan has grown at an impressive clip, but remains tiny compared to countries like China, the USA or Germany. In a sense, Turkey is a test case for whether soft power is an adequate substitute for hard power – something that scholar Joseph Nye has long argued as impossible.[10] The appeal of Turkish entertainment programming, businesses, religious outreach and so forth has gained fans and customers in diverse areas, but it is hard to argue that these ties constitute tools that the government can use as hard power in an intentional way.

Also questionable is whether Turkey possessed the necessary resources to channel its social influence into a lasting, appealing brand. In 2010, Turkey's foreign ministry budget stood at 44 per cent of that of Brazil, 29 per cent of Spain's, 13 per cent of Germany's and 0.011 per cent of the United States'.[11] In 2012, only a handful of the hundreds of career civil servants involved in Turkish diplomatic missions in Arab countries qualified as Arabic speakers.[12] In short, while Ankara benefited from economic and cultural tailwinds between 2002 and 2011, it lacked the institutional instruments necessary to shape the narrative in the region when the tides inevitably turned against it.

Instead, Davutoglu and Erdogan mostly armed themselves with platitudes. They ardently believed it was their destiny to create a new Middle East, a blend of the EU and a mythologised Ottoman Empire, where commerce and shared Muslim identity would replace power politics. Placing itself at the helm of this new regional order, Ankara would become a force to be reckoned with in world affairs. Yet, with the advent of the Arab uprisings, power politics returned to the region with a vengeance, shattering these illusions.

Turkey's value

I believe that Turkey is East if you come from the West, and West if you come from the East. In other words, in terms of geopolitics, what makes Turkey special in the West is its Middle Eastern exposure, while Turkey's connections to the West fulfil the same purpose for allies in the 'East'. Turkey's power in the Middle East was driven not by 'moderate Islam *à la* AKP', but rather its membership in NATO, the world's most powerful military alliance, as well as EU vocation, attributes that no Middle East country possesses. With hindsight, by losing track of EU accession and making decisions undermining Ankara's position as a staunch NATO ally, Erdogan (and Davutoglu) severely weakened Turkish power in the Middle East.

In the end, Erdogan's hope of transmuting soft power into hard power has made Turkey neither a dominant power nor a secure country. Finally, yet importantly, troubles with the Gulen movement show soft power itself can be messy at times – a hard learned lesson for Erdogan during the 2016 coup.

Davutoglu's demise

Another issue for Erdogan has been evaluating Davutoglu's legacy. By 2015, the Syrian war had resulted in millions of refugees fleeing to Turkey, many of whom attempted to cross the border into Greece to reach Europe. In addition to his function as chief architect of Turkey's

Syria policy, Davutoglu represented Turkey during negotiations with the EU over a deal to stem the flow of Syrian migrants fleeing from violence, which, ironically, his policies aggravated. A deal was reached in March 2016, which included an assertion that Turkey's stagnant EU accession process would be revitalised.[13]

Under the EU–Turkey refugee agreement, Ankara would accept the return of one migrant who had entered Greece illegally by crossing the Aegean Sea in exchange for the EU permanently resettling one Syrian refugee from Turkey. Taking advantage of the refugee crisis that had overtaken the EU, and the panic that ensued, Ankara pressured it into granting concessions. The EU pledged €6 billion in aid to Turkey for hosting nearly 3 million Syrian refugees – as of 2019, the EU had, however, delivered only a portion of this promised aid – and agreed to expedite the process of granting Turkish citizens visa-free travel in the Schengen Area, a demand Erdogan was particularly keen on realising.[14] Since then, Turkey's failure to meet the criteria for visa liberalisation, including its counterterrorism law, has meant that the EU has not granted visa-free EU travel to Turkish citizens.

For his own part, I believe that Davutoglu did not intend to prolong the crisis in Syria by assisting the radicals. He saw supporting opposition groups indiscriminately and allowing foreign fighters to cross into Syria as a worthwhile price to pay so as to precipitate Assad's fall. He believed that even if a few 'bad guys' got into Syria, the 'good guys' would clean them up. However, by 2015, Assad had not fallen, the 'good guys' had not taken over, and the 'bad guys' were busy building the 'Islamic State' in nearly half of Syria and along much of the 900 kilometre (559 miles) Turkish–Syrian border.

The Pandora's box that Davutoglu inadvertently opened in Syria by single-mindedly pushing against Assad presented other surprises. By 2012, at the height of the civil war, as mentioned before, the Assad regime vacated Kurdish areas to devote more resources to other fronts, but also to create trouble for Ankara. The YPG, linked to the PKK, quickly filled the void left by the departure of Assad-regime forces, establishing Rojava. Following the breakdown of a Turkey–PKK ceasefire in 2015, the YPG became Turkey's adversary.

For the five years, 2011–16, Turkey faced a mismatch of its ambitions and its hard power in Syria. Just as the Young Turks pashas were unable to fight on multiple fronts against France, Great Britain and Russia during the First World War, Ahmet Davutoglu could not oust Assad, contain the ISIS, defeat the YPG and push back against Tehran and Moscow, at the same time.

The outcome of the Arab uprisings, too, proved Davutoglu wrong, especially regarding his 'Zero Problems' policy. Thus, it was time for Erdogan to oust Davutoglu. Erdogan's ire rose in early 2016, when Davutoglu took credit for the refugee deal Ankara reached with Europe. The final nail in the coffin came in May that year, when rumours emerged in Washington that Davutoglu had sought contact with the White House to meet US President Obama. Erdogan, who himself was having a difficult time getting an appointment with Obama at this stage, ousted Davutoglu on 5 May 2016. From that point forward, Turkey lowered its ambitions in Syria to better match the limits of its hard power, focusing mostly on the YPG threat.

Unlike Davutoglu, who had a significant impact on Turkey's foreign policy agenda, his successor, former Transport Minister Binali Yildirim, barely registered on the world stage and was unlikely to challenge Erdogan's authority. Davutoglu was the architect of Turkey's ambitious foreign policy gambit in opening itself to the Middle East, Yildirim was an Erdogan proxy rather than a political figure.

Yildirim served as Turkey's prime minister from May 2016 until July 2018, during which time he campaigned for effective termination of his post in the 2017 referendum. At the time, Yildirim's role remained similar to the prime ministers' in monarchies such as Jordan and Morocco: hand-picked and overshadowed by powerful kings. Erdogan formally took over Yildirim's job following the June 2018 Turkish parliamentary and presidential elections. In 2019, Yildirim serves as the speaker of the Turkish Parliament.

The transition from Davutoglu to Yildirim signalled a new style of government in Ankara, marked by consolidation and personalisation of political power in Erdogan's hands. The spotlight promptly left Turkey's most consequential foreign minister in decades. A senior Turkish diplomat friend explained that 'Davutoglu lived in a fantasy world,'[15] whose ripple effects resonate in Turkish foreign policy to this day, often with challenging outcomes for Ankara, especially concerning its relationship with its neighbours. Today, Davutoglu has resumed his teaching career, giving talks at Istanbul's Sehir University, but Turkey's troubles in the Middle East are far from over.

Reluctant *reaya*

Turkey's neighbours, including not just Arabs, but also Greeks and others share a memory of the Ottoman rule much different from that of Davutoglu (or Erdogan).

'No one in Marjayoun would necessarily pine for the days of the Ottoman rulers,' former *New York Times* journalist Anthony Shadid once wrote, describing his family's ancestral village in Lebanon, as follows: 'Massacres occurred, and Jews and Christians faced discrimination in taxes and commerce. There was no such thing as equality.'[16] Indeed, known as *reaya*, non-Muslim Ottoman citizens were given rights by the sultans, but treated as second-class citizens below the Muslims citizens of the empire.

While Davutoglu (and Erdogan) might warmly 'remember' the Ottoman era as a time of peace and tolerance, Turkey's neighbours, among them Arab Muslims, remember the Ottomans, for instance, through the Young Turks hanging to death of Arab intellectuals and leaders during the First World War. The Arabs (and Greeks and other subject nations of the former Ottoman Empire) memorise an 'Ottoman history' through their own nationalist historiographies, which cast the sultans and Turks in a negative light – as colonial overlords. Though it may strike pride in Turkey's leaders and arouse excitement within Erdogan's nationalist base, Turkey's Ottoman flair is simply not always the ideal public relations image abroad, especially in its near abroad.

Another problem with this approach is that Davutoglu and Erdogan failed to take into account the complex nature of 'historical antibodies' – that is to say, mutual political perceptions shaped by past events – between Turkey and its Middle Eastern neighbours. While the two leaders digested traditional, Ottoman-flavoured Turkish views of the country's Middle Eastern neighbours, they failed to recognise the opposing, and often negative, views held in the Middle East, which often castigate the Turks as 'former colonial overlords'.

It did not have to end this way for Erdogan, Davutoglu or Ankara. 'There is a role for Turkey in the new MENA [Middle East and North Africa],' Diana Moukalled, a Lebanese journalist and documentary producer for London-based daily, *Asharq al-Awsat*, wrote more than a decade ago, 'but not as a resurrected Ottoman empire [. . .] The Arabs have not forgotten its large history of abuses and oppression.'[17]

Had Davutoglu heeded this advice when Ankara's regional star was on the rise, he might have been able to cement a public image that would have paid off for Turkey in the long term. Instead, Turkey has sunk deeper into its own neo-Ottoman daydreaming.

12
COURSE CORRECTION

By the middle of the 2010s, Erdogan realised that decade-long dramatic foreign policy adventures influenced by Davutoglu's vision had left behind an isolated Turkey in the Middle East – starkly different from the regional power he had dreamt of as he pivoted Ankara's policies. Using Davutoglu's 2016 ouster as an excuse, Erdogan wisely crafted a new foreign policy agenda, improving ties with various countries nearby. In this regard, three states, namely Iraq, Israel and Greece became priorities.

Flirting with the Iraqi Kurds

In fact, recent developments with Iraq have provided Erdogan with an opportunity to rekindle ties with Baghdad. Over the previous decade, ties between Ankara and Baghdad had crumbled due to the former's flirtation with the Iraqi Kurds.

Ankara initially adopted a hostile position towards the Iraqi Kurds following the 2003 Iraq War, due to the continued presence of PKK camps on their territory and their strong support for the US–led Iraq War. However, Erdogan eventually warmed up to the Kurdistan Regional Government (KRG). The KRG coalesced in Iraq's Kurdish-majority north after the Iraq War of 2003. Erdogan especially felt close to the KRG's dominant and conservative faction, the Kurdistan Democratic Party (KDP), whose power is consolidated in the entity's capital, Erbil. Starting in 2007, rapprochement between Erdogan and the KDP accelerated thanks to energy deals, as well as to cooperation against the PKK, which KDP leader Massoud Barzani offered to Erdogan. Shared conservative social views by the two leaders, though the KDP is not a political Islamist faction, brought Erdogan and Barzani closer.

A Turkish–Iranian condominium

Relations matured further when Barzani's offer of cooperation against the PKK became real. The KDP started intelligence and security cooperation with Ankara to combat PKK presence in the mountainous Kurdish region.[1] At this stage, Barzani saw Ankara as an ally to maintain the KRG's autonomy vis-à-vis the central government in Baghdad. He also saw Ankara as a convenient trading and business partner as the KRG is a landlocked entity, and Turkey was a useful conduit to trade with the outside world.

Tehran, in competition with Ankara for influence in the Middle East, has taken advantage of its historically close ties with the Iraqi Kurds. Iran's now deposed shah cultivated relations with Iraqi Kurds against his rival, Iraq's leader Saddam Hussein, during the 1970s. This policy was kept nearly intact after the 1979 Revolution, which overthrew the shah. Tehran built strong ties with the KRG's other significant political faction, the Patriotic Union of Kurdistan (PUK), whose power is centred in the KRG's second largest city, Sulaymaniyah, close to the Iranian border.

Over the past decade, the KRG has, subsequently, become a de facto Turkish–Iranian condominium, with Ankara holding more sway over the western portions of the Kurdish region, generally across KDP-controlled areas, and Tehran doing the same in the eastern portions of the KRG, across much of the PUK zone.

Erdogan's foray into Iraqi Kurdistan naturally angered Iraq's central government. To leverage against Baghdad, Ankara also sided with Sunni Arabs in the north of the country. This outreach only further angered the Shia-majority government in Baghdad, while also irritating Iran, which considers itself Baghdad's informal patron.[2]

However, it was not until 2010, when Erdogan gambled on the losing horse in the Iraqi elections, that ties between Ankara and Baghdad became completely strained. In these polls, Ankara sided with the pan-Iraqi bloc that lost political power to Nouri al-Maliki's Shi'ite-dominated list during the process of the government formation, following Iraq's March 2010 elections. Consequently, when he became Iraq's prime minister, Maliki shut Turkey out of Iraq. Turkey lost access to non-Kurdish areas of Iraq and Erdogan's influence was limited to the Kurdish region in Iraq's north, specifically the KDP zone.

Subsequently, Turkey was forced to close its consulate in the Iraqi port city of Basra, losing access to large swathes of oil-rich southern Iraq. Maliki also put restrictions on Turkish trade with the Middle East through Iraq, a key truck route. This was a big loss for Turkey. Around that time, with Syria descending into chaos, Ankara was losing its ability to ship its wares to the Middle East through the Syrian highways. These developments put Turkey at risk of losing both of its Middle Eastern access trade routes, a vital lifeline for the transportation of Turkish-made goods.

Erdogan, for his part, chose to ignore Maliki, but also went ahead and criticised him publicly. In April 2012, for instance, he accused the Iraqi prime minister for fanning sectarian conflict between Shi'ites, Sunnis and Kurds through his 'self-centred' behavior.[3] In a clear snub to Iraq, Ankara also started dealing directly with the KRG, bypassing Baghdad. Turkey's leaders, including Davutoglu, started flying directly to Erbil on their official visits to Iraq, without going through Baghdad first, violating diplomatic protocol: an overt insult to Maliki from his neighbour to the north.

Rising Baghdadi fortunes

It looked for a while that the anger between Ankara and Baghdad could become a permanent feature in the geopolitics of the Fertile Crescent. Nevertheless, two recent political dynamics have allowed for a makeover in ties between the two countries. Following the rise of ISIS in 2014, when the jihadi group captured large swathes of Iraq, coming within eight miles of Baghdad, Maliki fell from power.[4] This gave Erdogan the opportunity to deal with his successor, Haider al-Abadi, in a less passionate way. Further shifting Ankara's ties with Baghdad, was the KRG's unilateral 2017 referendum to declare independence from Iraq. This angered Ankara deeply. As a result, Turkish–KRG ties took a nosedive.[5]

Barzani, who led the referendum effort, neglected to notice that strong ties with Erdogan did not necessarily mean that he would support a unilateral declaration of independence by the KRG. This is not because Ankara categorically opposed Iraqi Kurds, but rather because the Iraqi Kurds rushed for independence – as Ankara saw it. Turkey's fear was that if Barzani were to go forward with his move, this unprecedented and unilateral measure could inspire other Kurdish nationalist movements, such as the YPG in Syria or, even worse, the PKK in Turkey, to declare independence similarly through unilateral referenda.

The fact that Barzani had personally led the referendum effort added salt to wound. Accordingly, Erdogan shifted to Baghdad to embarrass and undermine his former ally. Taking advantage of their shared opposition to the KRG's independence referendum, Erdogan and Abadi launched a process of rapprochement in 2017. Abadi reciprocated, by allowing Turkey in October 2018 to reopen its consulate in Basra that had been shut down following the Erdogan–Maliki break-up.[6]

Relying on his newfound relationship with Baghdad, and also taking stock of the improved security environment a little over a year after the military defeat of ISIS in Iraq, Turkey returned to the Sunni Arab heartland around Mosul, in Iraq's north. In October 2018, Ankara announced it was reopening its consulate in the northern Iraqi commercial capital of Mosul – another Turkish recovery in Iraq.[7]

Bring back a broken KRG

After leaving Barzani out in the cold – Ankara not only completely froze Turkey's ties with the KRG, but also suspended the Istanbul–Erbil flight, a lifeline for the KRG – in 2018, Erdogan decided to restore relations with the KRG.

Barzani, too, sought better ties. During his search for rapprochement with Ankara, he was smart to reach out to Erdogan through his nephew, the KRG Prime Minister Nechirvan Barzani, who opposed the KRG's 2017 independence referendum. In return, Erdogan allowed Turkish Airlines to recommence flights from Erbil to Turkey, signalling that he was willing to become friends with the KRG once again. Another promising news item in this regard, is the November 2018 decision by the KRG's other key actor, the PUK, to close off the PKK offices in the PUK capital of Sulaymaniyah.[8] While the PUK has traditionally been friendlier to the PKK than the KDP, these events, put together, provide Ankara with the high ground against the PKK inside the KRG.

Kurdish politics in the Middle East: 101

In 2019, even with the recent Ankara–KRG reset, a Turkish–Iraqi spring is underway, driven by the shared vision by Ankara and Baghdad to snuff the KRG's dream of independence and to centralise Iraqi authority. Erdogan is once more seeking better ties with Baghdad. In return, Baghdad now allows Turkey to carry out operations against PKK targets and its leadership, including the organisation's headquarters in the Qandil Mountain range, straddling Iraq's border with Iran.

As a nation, the Kurds are divided, not only by three main 'dialects' as well as a number of smaller and similarly mutually unintelligible 'dialects', but also by the forces of politics and culture. For instance, Kurds in the Middle East use two different alphabets: a Latin-based one in Turkey, and an Arabic-based one in the rest of Syria and Iraq, as well as across Iran, dividing them orthographically as well as linguistically. Although the Latin-based Kurdish alphabet has somewhat spread to parts of Syria and Iraq, abutting Turkey, ultimately what a Kurdish person writes in Syria is not easily understandable by a Kurd in Turkey, even when both speak the same Kurdish 'dialect'.

Furthermore, while spread amongst four different Middle Eastern countries, the Kurds are influenced, and in return divided, by various political traditions, from secularism in Turkey (embraced by the PKK, ironically thanks to the legacy of Ataturk's secularism) to hardcore political Islam in Iran (shared by a number of Kurdish parties across the region). Together with the legacy of socialist Baath Arab nationalism in Iraq and Syria, these forces have distinctly shaped the political outlook of Kurds in these countries, creating near permanent fissures. In fact, the Middle Eastern Kurds today have nearly a dozen significant, often competing, and sometimes even warring, political movements, ranging from the formerly Marxist, and now leftist, PKK in Turkey to the hard political Islamist, Kurdistan Islamic Group in Iraq.

Deep, cutting imperial lines undermine Kurdish unity, as well. This is especially the case regarding Iranian Kurds, many of whom have lived under a different political system than Turkish, Syrian and Iraqi Kurds since the 1639 Treaty that delineated the Ottoman–Safavid border, permanently slashing across Kurdistan, leaving the previous group under the Persians and the latter under the Turks for nearly four centuries.

A key realpolitik takeaway for Kurdish politics of the Fertile Crescent – but a sad one for Kurdish nationalists – is that the Kurdish nation is divided through the forces of history, culture, politics, intra-Kurd political dynamics and squabbles and, more importantly, geopolitics. In other words, four opposing nation states, three main 'dialects', two imperial legacies, two different alphabets and, finally, yet importantly, around a dozen adversarial political movements undermine Kurdish unity, and for that purpose the dream of a pan-Kurdistan.

And while Iran, Iraq, Turkey and Syria will support Kurdish nationalist movements across their borders as leverage against their neighbours, Tehran, Baghdad, Ankara and Damascus can unite quickly – and rather unexpectedly – if these Kurdish nationalist movements take hasty steps towards independence, to crush those hopes, the KRG's 2017 referendum being a case in point.

Given that, the Kurds are landlocked at the juncture of these four countries, this conclusion effectively nullifies Kurdish dreams for independence – for the moment. In Syria, this conclusion also suggests that, although Erdogan and Assad despise each other, a day may come when they might agree on a deal, whereby Assad stays in power, in return for extinguishing the fire of the YPG in Rojava and bringing them under his control.

However, this does not necessarily mean the complete end of the YPG in Syria. Taking into account the other part of the Middle Eastern Kurdish dynamic, i.e. that regional capitals use Kurdish nationalist movements across their borders against their neighbours, it is also likely that Assad will not destroy the YPG. Instead, he will probably just brush it under the political Syrian carpet. He will save it for a rainy day, to use it against Erdogan and Turkey in the future. Bashar al-Assad's father, Hafez al-Assad, used the PKK to engage in state-sponsored terrorism against Turkey, and there is reason to believe that, going forward, this will be his son's *modus operandi*, as well.

While Erdogan deserves some credit for his manoeuvers regarding Turkey's Kurds in the context of political liberalisation during the first decade of AKP rule and the abortive 'solution process' involving peace talks with the PKK, it cannot be said that he adroitly understands, or fully instrumentalises, Kurdish dynamics across the several regions where they touch upon and influence Turkey's interests. In 2019, he appeared brittle and reactive toward Kurdish nationalism in the Middle East, in much the same way as his Kemalist predecessors had been.

Israel: A country which Erdogan can do neither with, nor without

After firing Davutoglu, Erdogan gained wiggle room for a charm offensive vis-à-vis Turkey's alienated neighbours, including Iraq, and other nations nearby. Reconciliation between Ankara and Baghdad is working, and there could even be some sort of future *modus vivendi* between Erdogan and Assad. Nevertheless, reconciliation with some of Turkey's other neighbours will be an equally steep and uphill battle. For instance, the normalisation effort with Israel has worked out, but ties between the two states face long-term challenges. This is because many Israelis despise Erdogan as much as he opposes Israel: depicted in his unwavering support for Hamas. So long as Erdogan controls Ankara, Turkish–Israeli ties are not likely to recover to how thety were in their golden era of the 1990s, when Israeli military officials described Turkey as their second-best ally after the United States.

Following the 'Flotilla Incident' and left to their own devices, Turks and Israelis were unable to overcome mutual suspicion and domestic obstacles to bridge their differences.[9] In the 2010s, Washington took an active interest in bringing together on talking terms its two most important allies in the Middle East. In March 2013, through Obama's mediation, Israeli Prime Minister Benjamin Netanyahu called Erdogan to apologise for Israeli 'operational mistakes' that resulted in the loss of Turkish lives on the night of the 2010 flotilla (although Israel, to this day, refuses to apologise for the act of stopping the ship, which it regards as a legitimate act of self-defence).

Next, Israel agreed to pay compensation of $20 million to the families of the Turkish victims via a special international fund.[10] In return, Ankara agreed to withdraw and block all indictments or other actions, public or private, against the Israelis involved in the incident.[11] Eventually, in 2016, Erdogan publicly acknowledged that this issue is 'more or less settled'.

At this point, Erdogan opted for normalisation not only because he got the Israelis to agree on some of his key demands regarding the 2010 crisis, but also because he had concluded that Turkey's security environment had changed since the 'Flotilla Incident'.

In 2010, Erdogan could rely on the friendship of Egypt, Syria, Saudi Arabia and even Hezbollah in Lebanon, an ally of Iran, in the Levant region south of Turkey. These actors all, more or less, had a favourable view of Ankara's stance as a country critical of US policies and Israel. By 2013, though, Erdogan was *persona non grata* in Damascus and Cairo. The Saudis began viewing him as a geopolitical threat. In addition, Hezbollah had adopted a hostile view of Turkey, looking at Ankara through the prism of its support for anti-Assad rebels fighting Iran and its proxies, including Hezbollah's own forces in Syria. Erdogan could not afford to fight everyone in the Levant, and therefore decided to normalise ties with Israel.

Israel, too, had its own reasons for normalisation. In 2010, when its ties with Ankara collapsed, Israel had a mostly secure neighbourhood, enjoying stability all around, with the exception of its northern border with Lebanon and Gaza. In 2016, with Hezbollah, Iranian Revolutionary Guards and other Iranian proxies deployed across its border with Syria, Israel's security perception had changed. Just as Erdogan felt he had bigger fish to fry than Israel, Netanyahu also started to think that he could temper some of the policies of his Turkish counterpart by talking to him again.

Alienated in the broader Middle East and more importantly by Israel's neighbours, Erdogan communicated his renewed interest to US officials, including Vice President Joe Biden, who visited Ankara on January 2016 and Jerusalem on March 2016. In addition, the heads of major American Jewish organisations were granted two closed-door meetings with Erdogan: on 9 February in Ankara[12] and on the sidelines of a nuclear summit in Washington on 3 April 2016.[13] On 31 March 2016, in speech at the Brookings Institution in Washington, which I attended, he spent more time discussing reconciliation with Israel than any other regional topic and speculated that the negotiations are on their way to a successful conclusion.[14] Accordingly, following five years of intense negotiations between 2011 and 2016, the two countries finally normalised their ties in June 2016, reinstating full diplomatic relations.[15]

The Hamas split

Yet, one major thorn remains: Erdogan demanded that a deal with Israel must include the removal of Israel's 'blockade of' or 'embargo on' Gaza. Here, the major policy difference between the parties, the source of the Flotilla Incident in the first place, came into play.

Israel disputed the 'embargo' claim, pointing out that hundreds of trucks cross daily from Israel into Gaza, carrying food, medicine and reconstruction materials. Negotiators therefore focused on Turkey's demand for unimpeded access in order to implement housing and infrastructure reconstruction projects. Ankara has also asked to anchor a power-generating vessel offshore to help resolve the territory's acute electricity shortage.

For Israel, these demands are highly sensitive from a security standpoint. Turkey is a staunch supporter of regional movements aligned with the Ikhwan, and openly seeks to empower its Gaza affiliate, Hamas, an entity that officially swore to their commitment to Israel's destruction. Since Hamas' ascent to power in Gaza in 2007, Israel has been drawn into numerous rounds of fighting with Hamas and other armed groups in Gaza, following constant rocket fire and other attacks. Israel is mindful of Hamas' relentless efforts to rearm, including through the diversion of humanitarian assistance. Therefore, Israel insists that all external assistance to Gaza be enveloped within solid security arrangements – if possible in the context of a long-term ceasefire with Hamas, brokered with the Palestinian Authority's involvement.

For its part, Israel has demanded that Ankara shuts down Hamas' headquarters in Istanbul, which Israeli intelligence contends has been guiding violent plots in the West Bank in recent years.[16] The office was still open reportedly as of December 2018. In 2015, Turkey asked Saleh al-Aruri, the office's director and a senior figure in Hamas's military wing, to leave their soil.[17] It is difficult to envision Israel accepting deepening ties with Turkey without the prohibition of such activities. At the bare minimum, Israel will insist on the permanent expulsion of the Hamas leadership from Turkey. Notwithstanding their policy differences over the Palestinian issue, Israel also holds the key to Turkey's role in Gaza, which is meaningful to Erdogan's government for political and ideological reasons.

Economic glue

Before Erdogan, defence cooperation between Turkey and Israel was the bedrock of bilateral ties. In the 1990s, Turkey benefited signifiicantly from Israel, importing Israeli technology to modernise its military, including M-60 tanks. That is no longer the case. In the aftermath of the 'Flotilla Crisis', Erdogan froze a number of defence deals with Israel, and in return, the Israelis have been unwilling to license defence exports to Turkey. Although defence ties have plummeted, the 2010 debacle, interestingly, did not undermine commercial ties, which have continued to develop since.

Turkish–Israeli economic ties took off in the late 1990s as part of a growing strategic convergence. At the time, the two countries viewed each other as natural allies as democracies in a region populated by authoritarian regimes. Deepening defence ties underpinned a series of bilateral agreements, opening Turkish and Israeli markets to each other. In 1996, notable agreements included a Free Trade Agreement (FTA), a double-taxation prevention treaty and a bilateral investment treaty.[18] These agreements ushered in an era of improving political and economic ties. Trade jumped from $447 million in 1996 to more than $1.4 billion in 2002.[19] This remarkable acceleration continued with bilateral trade increasing 16.2 per cent per year, on average, from 2002 to 2008.[20]

Notwithstanding, the political downturn in 2010 did not translate into an economic downturn. Take, for instance, a boycott announced by several Israeli grocery chains in the wake of the Flotilla Incident. Despite the assertions on the part of these retailers, Turkish exports of vegetable products remained steady after 2010, and Turkish exports of prepared foodstuffs, beverages and tobacco more than doubled between 2007 and 2011. Even more interestingly, at the height of tensions following the Flotilla Incident, from 2010 to 2011, bilateral trade increased by an impressive 30 per cent, far surpassing the growth that occurred during the heyday of Turkish–Israeli ties.[21]

What is more, all the aforementioned trade and investment treaties, including the FTA, remained solidly in effect. The mutual reluctance to rupture trade ties is understandable, especially in light of the global economic climate. After all, both countries owe much of their growth in recent years to buoyant exports, a large portion of which goes to European markets. This meant that both countries were vulnerable to a sluggish European recovery. Greater bilateral trade could pick up some of the slack, especially on the Israeli side, where Turkey constituted Israel's sixth-largest export market in 2011 and could climb up the ranks, as Israel's traditional markets remain mostly anaemic.[22]

Some of these economic ties are driven by pure geostratrgic reality: every week, Turkish ships leave the country's Mediterreanean port of Mersin, loaded with cargo destined for the Israeli port of Haifa. This cargo is then loaded onto trucks, driven by Jordanian drivers, who ferry Turkish wares across Israel and Jordan and into the Middle East. This 'surreal' new trade route, binding Turkey and the Persian Gulf through Israel came into existence in the aftermath of the Arab uprisings, when closure of Turkey's land borders with Syria and Iraq forced Ankara to look for new land routes to trade through the Middle East.

Similarly, while tourism from Israel to Turkey has suffered since 2010, more Israelis actually fly to Turkey today than they did before. This is due to the success of Turkish Airlines in penetrating the Israeli air-travel market and connecting it to the rest of the globe through its expansive network. Accordingly, over a million Israelis, constituting nearly one-seventh of the country's population, flew on Turkish Airlines to Istanbul in 2017, where many transferred to flights to continue on their onward journey.[23]

Economics and global networking are not the only areas of Turkish–Israeli cooperation. The two countries have also cooperated in disaster relief, with Turkey helping fight fires near Haifa in December 2010 and Israel sending housing and relief materials after the 2011 Van earthquake. On the public diplomacy front, in January 2012, Turkey's state-run television network aired Claude Lanzmann's famous documentary, *Shoah*, on the Holocaust, marking the first time this eight-hour production has been shown on public television in a Muslim-majority country. Turkey remains to be one of the only Muslim-majority countries that openly air documentaries and movies on the Holocaust. Its small, but active and visible, Jewish population also regularly puts on exhibitions on the tragedy.

Amid many continuing political problems, some friendly political gestures have been exchanged. To facilitate the October 2011 deal that resulted in the release of Israeli Corporal Gilad Shalit from Hamas captivity, Ankara took in a number of the Palestinian prisoners who were part of the swap.

Bonding pipelines?

While economic ties help the bilateral relationship, collaboration in the energy field could provide another set of shock absorbers – if Turkey and Israel can manage to establish cooperation. For its own sake, Israel wants to reap the economic and political benefits of exporting natural gas from its offshore fields to Turkey. Any such deal would give Ankara an additional supply of gas, the opportunity to re-export some of it to Europe, and diversification from their energy reliance on Russia, which currently supplies about half of Turkey's natural gas consumption.

Washington supports the export of Israeli gas through Turkey as a potential catalyst of normalisation, among other reasons. During his visit to Israel in April 2016, then US Energy Secretary Ernest Moniz highlighted how such a deal could help diversify European gas supplies away from Russia.[24] This option is not without its challenges, however, including the fact that Israeli gas would only add a miniscule portion of the total natural gas passing through Turkey to Europe – Israel would not have the leverage in establishing significant profits if a contract was to be signed.

There are also political obstacles. Israel has opted to intensify its relations with Nicosia and Athens in recent years, including in energy cooperation. On 28 January 2016, the leaders of the three countries met in Nicosia and announced the formation of a trilateral committee to explore the possibility of laying a gas pipeline, the 'EastMed', connecting Israeli and Cypriot fields via Greece to Europe.[25] In practical terms, this option is challenging due to topographical challenges along the Mediterranean seabed, where such a pipeline would be built. Even if these difficulties can be overcome, the fact remains that such a long and costly pipeline would likely not be economically feasible.

Yet, a pipeline to Turkey would have to cross Cypriot waters, requiring agreements between the two countries, potentially with US mediation. In the meantime, Israel's gas potential is held up by domestic regulatory challenges. Israel would also have to carefully weigh Russia's potential sensitivities to its gas exports through Turkey to Europe, even in modest quantities, which would defy Putin's desire to keep a near monopoly on natural gas imports flowing into Europe from the east.

Significant challenges and policy differences persist, creating the impression in both Turkey and Israel that a deal may not be within reach. What is more, even if a natural gas agreement were to materialise, it is unlikely to lead to the bilateral intimacy in Turkish–Israeli ties seen in the 1990s. Political tensions will continue to run high, and it will be inaccurate to describe Turkish–Israeli relations as good or great.

The Greek knot

The Cyprus issue not only complicates a potential Turkish–Israeli natural gas deal, but also presents new challenges for ties between Ankara and its EU-member Greek neighbours, Nicosia and Athens. Erdogan is increasingly bellicose in his vision to undermine Greek Cypriot efforts to explore and exploit natural gas deposits off the Cypriot coastline. It continues to refuse recognition of Nicosia's Exclusive Economic Zone that Cypriot Greeks claimed to take ownership of potential natural gas fields around the island. At the same time, Turkish ties with Greece are wrought with tensions, including most recently an April 2018 dogfight between the air forces of both countries that resulted in the crash of a Greek fighter jet and the death of its pilot.[26]

All this is surprising, given how much Greek and Cypriot Greek politicians welcomed Erdogan's ascent to power as Turkey's prime minister in 2003. At the time, these policy-makers took a deep breath when Erdogan, a non-Kemalist, had taken Turkey's reigns. They believed that since he challenged Ataturk's legacy, Erdogan would be less of a Turkish nationalist, paving the way to more favourable terms in Ankara's ties with Greece and Cyprus. When I met friends from the Greek and Cypriot foreign ministries at the time, they simply could not hide their happiness over Erdogan's electoral victory.

Initially, Erdogan proved his Greek fans right, moving to resolve the Cyprus conflict, for instance by backing a 2004 UN plan to unify the island. The plan, which was born out of UN-sponsored negotiations between Turkey, Greece, Cypriot Turkish and Cypriot Greek leaders, foresaw the unification of Cyprus as a federal state ahead of 1 May 2004, when Cyprus was scheduled to join the EU as a whole island.[27]

A Cypriot drama that ends well – for Greeks

Erdogan was shocked by the outcome, though, when the plan was put to a vote on the island on 24 April 2004. The elusive Cyprus issue, once again, evaded solution. Although 65 per cent of Cypriot Turks voted to accept the Annan plan, 76 per cent of Cypriot Greeks opposed it[28] – in no small part thanks to Cypriot Greek President Tassos Papadopoulos, who supported the plan during UN talks, but then openly campaigned against it on the island, to the point of crying on national TV, and urging Greek voters to reject the UN plan to unify the island.[29]

The Annan plan enjoyed support in Turkey and was accepted by Cypriot Turks because both saw it as increasing their prospects of EU accession.[30] Hoping to take advantage of the pro-EU drive, one of the most potent forces in Turkish politics at the time, Erdogan put his full support behind the Annan plan.

Cypriot Turks backed the plan, knowing that if they agreed to unify their island, this would make them EU citizens, ending the international isolation since 1974. Following Turkey's intervention in Cyprus, the international community slapped strict trade, economic and diplomatic sanctions on the Cypriot Turk community, currently organised as the Turkish Republic of Northern Cyprus (TRNC). To this day, only Turkey recognises the TRNC, which declared independence in the north of the island in 1983. For decades, Cypriot Turk citizens faced daily inconveniences because of the sanctions, such as having to fly to Istanbul or another Turkish city or take a ship to Turkey in order to leave the island.

In 2004, while Cypriot Turks overall wanted unification, the dynamics looked different from the Cypriot Greek perspective. The 1974 war, which resulted in the division of the island, and the subsequent imposition of sanctions on the Turkish north, has produced two 'Cypruses': a wealthy ethnically Greek south, which thrives on tourism and offshore banking (mostly dealing with Russian money), and an ethnically Turkish, monetarily poor north, cut off from the world.

Most people in the TRNC saw the Annan plan as a promise of EU membership, access to the outside world and prosperity. For them, it made complete sense to support it.[31] In due course, then TRNC Prime

Minister Mehmet Ali Talat of the formerly communist Republican Turkish Party (CTP) on the island, allied with Turkish Prime Minister Erdogan's AKP to push ahead with EU accession – a most unlikely alliance of former communists and former political Islamists trying to embrace European liberal democratic values and free markets!

For the Cypriot Greeks, the practical added benefits of unification were rather limited compared to Cypriot Turks, and therefore their resolve toward a settlement of the conflict was much weaker. Then Greek Prime Minister Costas Karamanlis in Athens was also tepid in his support for the Annan plan. As mentioned, Cypriot President Papadopoulos at the time called on his constituents to reject the reunification plan. The Cypriot Greeks, who were set to enter the EU on 1 May, regardless of how they voted in the referendum, had little incentive to accept the plan. Although the EU made some last-minute statements in favour of the Annan plan, it had long since lost its leverage with the Cypriot Greeks in the referendum by guaranteeing them membership, whatever the outcome of their vote.

In due course, even though they voted against ending the Cyprus conflict, Cypriot Greeks were allowed to join the EU, while the Cypriot Turks, who voted to end the conflict, remained outside the union. This was a hand well played by Cypriot Greeks, allowing them to become the gatekeepers of Turkey's EU accession process, which they subsequently used to their advantage – to block Ankara's accession process with France's backing.

Greeks have leverage over Turkey – if it believes EU accession is real

Despite the Cypriot turn, Erdogan initially pursued good ties with Greece and Cypriot Greeks, driven by his opinion that if he were nice to them, maybe they would not block Ankara's EU membership path. However, this scenario quickly proved wishful thinking, and Erdogan's willingness to be nice to Athens and Nicosia soon began to depreciate. Once it looked like EU accession was not going to happen for Turkey, Greeks and Cypriots lost their leverage in Erdogan's eyes. What is more, as Ankara pivoted to the Middle East, Erdogan's appetite to court his European neighbours, such as Greece, diminished further.

Recently, the Cyprus issue once again became a sticking point between Turkey and Cyprus as natural gas deposits were discovered off the shores of the island, throwing into question whether Nicosia had the right to explore and exploit these fields on its own. Turkey refuses to recognise natural gas exploration licenses granted by Nicosia to international energy companies around Cyprus in areas near the TRNC coastline. In recent years, Erdogan has declared no-go zones for Cypriot Greeks, leading to regular confrontations between Turkish naval ships and natural gas exploration vessels sailing around Cyprus.

Failed Armenian dreams

Just as Greek policy-makers in 2003 welcomed Erdogan because he was a 'non-Kemalist' Turkish leader, in Washington as well, many policy-makers were elated when he came to power – for the same reason. Many American politicians hoped that by turning away from traditional Kemalism, Erdogan would also embrace normalisation of Ankara's ties with Armenia, an important issue in US domestic politics, given the politically active nature of the Armenian-American community.

Although Turkey recognised all fifteen republics of the former Soviet Union, including Armenia, in 1991, Ankara and Yerevan to this day have not established formal diplomatic ties.[32] While there are historical differences between Turkey and Armenia – for instance, Ankara objects to the Armenian Declaration of Independence referring to eastern Turkey as 'Western Armenia' – the real reason that accounts for the absence of diplomatic ties between the two nations is a current conflict: Nagorno-Karabakh, an autonomous region of Azerbaijan under Armenian occupation since 1993.[33] Azerbaijan, a Turkic state that became independent after the collapse of the Soviet Union, is Ankara's closest ally (together with the TRNC). In a long-established tradition, upon taking office, Turkish leaders make their first official visits overseas to the TRNC capital of Lefkosa and Azerbaijani capital of Baku. Erdogan, who has broken many traditions in Turkish foreign policy, has kept this tradition alive.

Various factors account for political proximity between Ankara and Baku, from linguistic affinity to historic solidarity against Armenia to the power of the pro-Azerbaijani lobby in Ankara. In 2008, when Erdogan,

COURSE CORRECTION   **215**

with then Turkish Foreign Minister Gul's support, launched an initiative to establish ties with Armenia, not only did the Azerbaijani elites object to this opening, but they also succeeded in vehemently lobbying to convince Erdogan and Gul against it, through their contacts in the Turkish business and foreign policy communities. In the end, Ankara and Baku agreed that in order to re-establish ties with Turkey, Yerevan would need to make concessions to Azerbaijan in Nagorno-Karabakh.[34]

The strong ties and kinship between Turks and Azeris will limit the opportunity for Turkish rapprochement with Yerevan in the future. It is a common saying in both countries that Turkey and Azerbaijan are 'two governments, but one people'. Pro-Azerbaijani views hold great weight in Ankara under Erdogan (as do pro-Cypriot Turkish views), and absent of an Armenian promise to withdraw from occupied Azerbaijani territory, no Turkish leader, including Erdogan, will agree to normalise ties with Yerevan.

Erdogan is a Turkish nationalist – and a staunch one, too

With too much disappointment in Greek and Cypriot Greek, and some American, policy-makers of the past decade, Erdogan has proven to be just as much a Turkish nationalist as the country's past Kemalist leaders were, and maybe even more than them. This undermines his public portrayal as a simple 'Ikhwan cheerleader' or 'Eurasianist autocrat'. But, prickly nationalism, of course, does not make Turkey any easier a partner for the USA. It certainly makes Erdogan an even more potent foe for America's other regional partners.

For instance, Erdogan seems to have little patience to provide Greeks with wiggle room on the many issues that divide Ankara and Athens, from the Cyprus conflict to territorial airspace and other disputes concerning the Aegean Sea. Furthermore, for him, the Greeks seem to have a less favourable place in the new Turkish *weltanschauung* than before, even less than his Kemalist predecessors had given them. This was amply demonstrated when he raised the prospect of an 'update' of the Treaty of Lausanne of 1923. The treaty, which defined Turkey's current borders with its neighbours, including Greece, was defended by generations of Kemalist leaders as a sacred text that cannot and ought not to be revised.[35] Erdogan is happy to provoke and irritate the Greeks, even to the point of suggesting that he is ready to revise the 'sacred' Lausanne Treaty to this end.

Even more alarmingly for my Greek friends who welcomed Erdogan in 2003, there has been a surge in new disputes added to the relationship between Ankara and Athens. These include Turkish army officers, who took refuge in Greece in the aftermath of the 2016 coup attempt against Erdogan. Greece initially declined to extradite eight Turkish service members who had fled there following the failed coup. And so, in response, the Turkish government arrested two Greek border guards, who had accidentally crossed Greece's border into Turkey – they were released later on in August 2018.[36] In 2017, many predicted that the potential for a military conflict between Greece and Turkey has never seemed as great since the 1990s.

13
ERDOGAN VS TRUMP

While Erdogan can afford to ignore Athens, he cannot do the same regarding Washington. Complicating things for him after Trump took office in 2016, growing policy differences and problems added to rifts in Ankara's relationship with Washington, thereby undermining Erdogan's relationship with US President Trump.

Trump entered the White House with a nearly blank slate on foreign policy, and initial commentary in pro-Erdogan media in Turkey suggested that Ankara was happy to see him in power.[1] However, differences between the two countries, including those in Syria, soon undermined the Erdogan–Trump relationship. This became more apparent while, after swearing in as US president in January 2017, Trump endorsed and maintained Obama's policy of arming and working with the YPG, out of necessity to use it as a proxy to fight ISIS.

The issue of the YPG is a big and sour pickle in US–Turkey relations. Even taking into account Turkey's polarisation between pro- and anti-Erdogan camps, there is near universal opposition in the country towards US policy regarding the YPG. The PKK has led a brutal terrorist campaign in Turkey for decades killing thousands of people. On 1 August 2018, another attack rocked Turkey, when the PKK killed the wife and infant child of a Turkish soldier via a remote detonated bomb. These bloody attacks, in return, have caused a harsh all-out war by Ankara against the group since their emergence.

Beyond the PKK's violent attacks, Ankara has a key fear concerning the US–YPG relationship. By early 2019, the PKK, through its Syrian franchise, was fast evolving into a governing entity in Syria – an unacceptable development not only for Erdogan, but also for an over-whelming majority of Turkey's citizens. Ankara seemed determined to do everything in its capacity to undermine and eventually debilitate the YPG's Rojava, or at least force it to fall under Assad's power.

'The poor cleric who lives in the Poconos'

Augmenting bilateral tensions in American–Turkish ties are Ankara's demands for the extradition of Fethullah Gulen, a US-based cleric, whose followers in the TAF are blamed for playing an integral role in the failed coup in 2016 against Erdogan.[2]

As of 2019, Gulen continues to live in the USA as a permanent resident, in his compound along the Pocono Ridge in Pennsylvania. The Turkish Government, thus far, has not provided concrete evidence that Gulen personally ordered the coup. Such verification is difficult to obtain: I doubt that Gulen, who is known to rely on verbal and personal communications, sent a written text message or email to his followers, stating 'Do the coup.' Therefore, it is unlikely that the US courts will issue a decision in favour of his extradition to Turkey. New tensions in US–Turkish relations rose in 2017 as Turkish prosecutors began investigations into some 17 Americans, from a former CIA chief to US Senators, accused of participating in the putsch.[3]

'Euphrates Shield'

Realising that developing ties between Washington and YPG threatened to create a PKK-controlled state across Turkey's southern frontier with Syria, Erdogan decided to act. Taking advantage of his 2016 make-up with Putin, he sent troops into Jarablus in Syria to drive a wedge between the YPG-held territories. Dubbed 'Euphrates Shield', this operation allowed Turkey to capture ISIS-held territories before the YPG could lay its hands on them. Erdogan was aware that the latter scenario would have allowed the PKK ally to connect its two already contiguous cantons in north-eastern Syria, Kobane and Jazirah, with that in the north-west, Afrin, hence creating a nearly 650 kilometre-long (400 miles) PKK belt across Turkey's southern border.[4]

Accordingly, he acted to pre-empt this development. After the capture of Jarablus, Ankara pushed further to take land stretching from the Euphrates River in the east, A'zaz in the west and Al-Bab to the south. After more than seven months of fighting, Turkey achieved a victory against ISIS – but in the long-term, really against the YPG – with over 70 Turkish troops killed in combat. Despite the loss of life, the operation can be considered a tactical success for the TAF. It undertook this mission in less than two months after the failed coup, in which factions within the Turkish military fought each other, and after thousands within its ranks were purged. The coup attempt was a de facto, and debilitating, civil war inside the TAF, but despite that, the Turkish military bounced back.

Operation Euphrates Shield enabled Turkey to have a foot in the door of Syria. Ankara also secured a seat at the table of any future talks or summits discussing a political settlement to the conflict in Syria. Overall, although the operation was a success, Turkey eventually had to call in US air support to complete it. Nevertheless, Erdogan's determination to handle the YPG threat by himself proved to the USA that he had not given up on his vision to act independently of the Americans to guard Turkey's interests, when he sees it necessary.

'Battle of Sheridan Circle'

On 16 May 2017, Erdogan paid his first visit to Trump at the White House. Trump's election victory had initially been met with much euphoria in pro-Erdogan media in Turkey, with sympathetic headlines saying: 'A November to Remember by Its Shock'.[5]

Not only was Erdogan hopeful about the potential to reset bilateral ties between Turkey and the USA in the new era, but so, too, was Trump. During Erdogan's May 2017 visit, Trump stated: 'we support Turkey in the first fight against terror and terror groups like ISIS and PKK and ensure they have no safe quarter'. In response, Erdogan congratulated Trump's electoral win by calling it a 'legendary triumph'. However, for all its positive gains, in the end, the trip turned out to be a public diplomacy debacle for Erdogan. As he was wrapping up his visit following a meeting with Trump, a melee ensued at Sheridan Circle, outside the Turkish ambassador's residence in Washington, DC, in which Erdogan's bodyguards fought with and beat up pro-PKK demonstrators, some of whom were US citizens.

Video footage circulating on the event found on the internet show the protestors hurling insults, throwing cups and water at the faces of

Turkish bodyguards.[6] However, many of those outside the consulate, including Erdogan's bodyguards, began attacking the protestors. In what became a terrible public relations debacle, broadcast on American media for days, over a dozen of Erdogan's bodyguards were later indicted by US courts in August 2017.[7]

Iran sanctions and Halkbank

Another issue that has soured relations was the discovery of the Turkish evasion of the US-led sanctions on Iran. In 2013, during a corruption probe against Erdogan launched by Gulen's followers in the judiciary in Turkey, it became apparent that, reportedly with Turkish government knowledge, Halkbank, a state-owned Turkish financial institution, colluded in a scheme to trade with Iran.[8] The alleged plan was devised to bypass the international SWIFT payment system by trading in gold, using shell companies and Dubai in order to conduct trade with Iran.

In March 2016, Reza Zarrab, an Iranian–Turkish dual citizen and a billionaire, who played an integral part in the alleged scheme, was arrested while entering the USA to vacation in Miami, Florida.[9] Then another arrest occurred, this time of Mehmet Atilla, Halkbank's deputy chief executive, who was taken into custody by US law enforcement officials when he travelled to the USA in March 2017.[10] Soon after, in November that year, with both culprits under arrest, Zarrab began cooperating with the United States government, whereby he agreed to appear as a witness in a case against Atilla.[11]

On 3 January 2018, a New York court convicted Atilla of colluding in a multibillion-dollar money-laundering scheme to bypass US sanctions on Iran.[12] He was sentenced to 32 months in prison. The crux of the issue at this point is the fine that the USA will be putting on Halkbank. With the Turkish economy having suffered a downturn in 2018, in early 2019 Ankara was pushing hard to limit the expected amount of the fine.

Erdogan regards the case against Halkbank as being political in nature. The Turkish authorities opposed the January 2018 verdict that found Halkbank and its executive, Atilla, guilty of violating sanctions against Iran, claiming that the US courts have not brought similar actions against other banks and executives for violating the sanctions (e.g. BNP Paribas of France) – although, the USA Department of

Treasury has fined BNP Paribas and other similar institutions for this.[13] Erdogan also believes that the US court case against Halkbank personally targets him since Halkbank is a state-owned Turkish financial institution.

'Olive Branch'

Yet again, displeased with US efforts to help the YPG and driven by his fears of it solidifying its control in north-west Syria, Erdogan opted for another incursion into Syria in January 2018, this time into the YPG's own Afrin canton.[14] Dubbed Operation 'Olive Branch', this incursion went more smoothly than Euphrates Shield. It took just over two months and fewer casualties than Euphrates Shield for the TAF (and their Syrian allies) to capture the YPG's Afrin bastion.[15] High-level visits between Turkey and Russia in January 2018 provided the green light necessary for the TAF to begin their next operation in Syria.

Turkey's blitzkrieg victory against the YPG in Afrin shattered a number of American myths regarding Erdogan's Syria policy, namely that the TAF would not dare enter Syria after the difficulties it faced in Jarablus; that the YPG would stall Turkish forces in direct combat; that Russia would not allow Ankara to, again, enter Syria; and finally, that the Assad regime would protect the YPG.

The first of these conclusions led the USA to seek a solution with Turkey over the issue of YPG control of Manbij – one of the last YPG-dominated areas of Syria west of the Euphrates River. In order to address the pressing differences with Turkey regarding its relationship with the YPG and mitigate the rhetoric of Ankara to capture Manbij next, the United States made commitments to Ankara in June 2018 to draw up a plan to transfer Manbij from YPG control to its local inhabitants, including Kurds, but excluding those affiliated with the YPG.

The S-400 and F35 crisis

Ever since Obama's proposal to arm the YPG through the Syrian Democratic Forces (SDF), which Trump approved after taking office, US–Turkish ties have been fraught with deep crises, mostly initiated by

Ankara, as though Erdogan is telling Washington: 'Stop arming the YPG, and I will stop creating problems.'

Frustrated with Washington's refusal to provide Patriot missile defence systems on favourable terms, Ankara considered the purchase of Russian S-400 missile defence systems. Among other reasons, Erdogan wanted to use this as leverage to achieve a deal with Washington regarding potential Turkish Patriot purchases from the USA, including technology transfers, at an optimum price.

Many in Washington believe that if the S-400 system was to be integrated in Turkey, then Moscow could gather highly critical intelligence data on NATO's military equipment. Far worse, there are fears that leaks could provide confidential information on the F-35 stealth fighter jet, a US-led project, in which Turkey and a number of other NATO allies have come together since the 1990s to build the Alliance's next generation of fighter planes.[16] Not only has Ankara invested hundreds of millions of dollars in the project, but it is also the sole source supplier for multiple parts of the F-35.

With the S-400 issue brewing in June 2018, the US Senate passed legislation requiring the Department of Defense to submit a report regarding potential conflict between Turkey's participation in the F-35 project and its S-400 purchase.[17] Outraged, Ankara argued that there was no conditional agreement on acquiring the F-35 jets.[18] During this period, Moscow pushed the delivery date of the S-400s from 2020 to 2019, to deepen the chasm between Erdogan and the US Congress. Then, US Defense Secretary Jim Mattis emerged as one of the key champions of maintaining good ties with Turkey. In early 2019, even with the Senate threatening to block the eventual transfer of F-35s to Turkey,[19] Turkish Air Force pilots were still receiving their required training flying F-35s in Arizona.[20]

Although Congressional anger with Erdogan should not be underestimated, those arguing that the USA should adopt a tough 'Putin-style' approach tend to get the Russia–Turkey relationship wrong on two levels. First, despite their intimate energy relations, Moscow and Ankara are still on opposite sides of most regional issues, from Syria to Ukraine – hardly a surprise, given their historical rivalry. In contrast, the US–Turkey relationship remains grounded in the NATO alliance and decades of bilateral military cooperation, notwithstanding their disagreements. Washington's treatment of this ally therefore has repercussions throughout the American-led security system, reaching out beyond its immediate relationship with Ankara.

'Brunson Crisis'

By the summer of 2018, the set of divergences between Ankara and Washington, ranging from the S-400 to the F-35s to Gulen and the YPG issue, catapulted bilateral ties between Turkey and the United States into its worst state since the Cyprus War of 1974. That conflict, in the 1970s, had ended with the US Congress slapping sanctions against Ankara, a hurdle that took US–Turkish relations several years to recover.

It took another set of US sanctions for US–Turkish ties to hit rock bottom in 2018, and then make a comeback. Starting with the aftermath of the failed coup in 2016, Turkey arrested a number of US citizens, most notably American Pastor Andrew Brunson, alleging that they were linked to the failed coup plot, or that they had ties to the Gulen network and the PKK.

Because Brunson was, indeed, a pastor of an evangelical church, not much different from that of US Vice President Mike Pence's congregation, this increased the fury towards Erdogan in the US capital. A perception arose in Washington that Erdogan was engaging in 'hostage diplomacy', that is to say, arresting US citizens to use them to extract favourable terms from Washington on issues where America and Turkey diverged. To add fuel to fire, Erdogan even publicly suggested trading 'clergy for clergy', the American Christian pastor for the Turkish Muslim imam, Fethullah Gulen.[21]

The Trump touch

Until this point, Erdogan had dealt with two US presidents: Bush and Obama. Based on his interaction with them, Erdogan had concluded that despite the vicissitudes of Turkey's relationship with the US Congress, he could always count on the US president to preserve America's ties with Turkey. Erdogan, therefore, also concluded that he could stretch negotiations over Brunson's release because no US president would ever take any severe measures against Turkey. In July 2018, a Turkish court moved Pastor Brunson from jail and placed him under house arrest, starting yet another saga about the pastor's fate.[22]

Enter Trump. An unconventional president, Trump has also applied the unconventional path to dealings with Erdogan. In response to Brunson being moved from jail to house arrest in Turkey, he slapped sanctions against two of Erdogan's key ministers, Justice Minister Abdulhamit Gul and Interior Minister Suleyman Soylu, freezing their assets in the USA. In early August 2018, Trump also put in place tariffs on Turkish steel and aluminum exports.[23]

Coupled with a brewing economic crisis in Turkey, driven by its cheap credit boom in recent years, Trump's sanctions had an unintended economic effect: the Turkish lira slid to a historic low against the dollar, reaching an unprecedented TL7.24 to US$1 dollar on 12 August 2018.[24] Erdogan realised that he was not dealing with Bush or Obama, but with Trump, who seemed to have no problem in undermining, or even seriously harming, a NATO ally to get what he wants. Erdogan responded by releasing Brunson, who arrived in the USA on 14 October 2018.[25] The Turkish lira recovered after that, regaining its value previous to Trump's sanctions against Turkey in October 26.[26]

Moving forward

Trump tweeted in the aftermath of Brunson's release, thanking Erdogan and saying: 'There was NO DEAL made with Turkey for the release and return of Pastor Andrew Brunson. I don't make deals for hostages. There was, however, great appreciation on behalf of the United States, which will lead to good, perhaps great, relations between the United States & Turkey!' suggesting that a potential upturn in US–Turkish ties was in the offering.[27]

The US–Turkish relationship hit a new low during the Brunson crisis of summer 2018, but it has had a chance to recover, now that it has seen the worst. In fact, following Brunson's release Trump, in a gesture of goodwill, included Turkey in a list of eight countries, to which he granted waivers from US sanctions against Iran and that went into effect on 5 November 2018.[28] This was a welcome move in Turkey, which heavily relies on Iranian oil imports to fuel its economy.

At the very least, at the end of 2018, President Trump took:

A momentous decision that will have significant policy impacts on the Syrian conflict and on the US–Turkish bilateral relationship throughout 2019. Given that it addressed a central Turkish grievance: Namely, US military support for the PKK's armed Syrian branch, the YPG, as an instrument in the campaign against ISIS. With that campaign in Syria largely concluded, Trump directed the cessation of U.S. military presence in Syria, and as a consequence the end of efforts to sustain a massive military proxy centered on the YPG.[29]

Military problems

Moving forward, even with the US military drawdown in Syria, one of the most important problems in US–Turkish ties, and a legacy of Erdogan for years into the future, are the growing anti-Turkey views inside the US military. In 2002, when I started my work as an analyst in Washington, the US military was Turkey's biggest fan in the American capital. Today, it is Ankara's biggest adversary.

Erdogan is largely responsible for this change, together with policies of the US presidents. On Erdogan's part, his moves, such as the 2003 decision not to help the USA in the Iraq War after promising Washington that he would, or turning a blind eye to jihadist radicals crossing from Turkey into Syria to hasten Assad's fall, have soured the US military towards Ankara. Rising concerns through 2015–18 that Turkey might attack allies to the US military on the ground, i.e. YPG forces in Syria, while the US had military personnel alongside these forces, further turned the US military's view of Ankara – and of Erdogan.

Shifting views of Turkey within the US military can have long-term ramifications for Ankara. Today, sadly, many officers from Central Command (CENTCOM), the US military's wing responsible for fighting in conflicts in the Middle East, simply detest Erdogan, and, sadly, even view Turkey as an adversary. While it is recognised as the 'fighting command' within the US military, more officers from CENTCOM will be promoted within the ranks of US armed forces in the coming years than officers from any other commands – for example, European Command (EUCOM), which is traditionally more sympathetic to Turkey. This is a major problem for Erdogan, and for Turkey, suggesting that the US military's key decision-makers in the coming decades will not necessarily be friendly towards Ankara.

'Muslims, whose men drink beer and whose women fight'

Parts of the US military have played an unwitting role in this transformation. Fighting side by side with the YPG, some troops have become sympathetic towards the PKK–YPG family. This is especially the case for certain units of CENTCOM, as well as for the US Special Operations Command (SOCOM).

Turkey has traditionally fallen into the area of responsibility of EUCOM, which because the latter has dealt with Ankara and Turkish policy-makers for decades, has developed a deeper understanding of PKK- and YPG-related dynamics and Turkey. CENTCOM and SOCOM lack the profound and historically rooted exposure to Turkey that EUCOM possesses. Beginning with the Siege of Kobane in 2014, some in CENTCOM and SOCOM have developed a benign, and sometimes simplistic, but certainly sympathetic view of the YPG, which I could summarise as: 'Muslims, whose men drink beer and whose women fight.' This opinion, coupled with sacrifices made by the YPG against ISIS, has even culminated in some CENTCOM and SOCOM officials speaking favourably about the YPG in public.[30]

Inadvertently, and unfortunately for Ankara and Washington, the policies of Obama and Erdogan together have recrafted the US military's historic perception of Turkey – from a EUCOM and NATO ally to a 'CENTCOM obstructionist' and menacing threat to 'America's Kurdish brothers-in-arms.'

Washington needs to invert the PKK–YPG relationship

In the big picture, in order to salvage its historic tie with Ankara, Washington needs to devise a clear and bold strategy that addresses Ankara's deep security concerns about America's relationship with the

YPG. In this regard, the 2018 plan that was agreed between Ankara and Washington to secure the YPG's withdrawal from the Manbij pocket in northern Syria, abutting Turkey, has been a good step forward.

The issue at stake here is that US policy in Syria regarding the YPG runs against US policy in Turkey regarding the PKK. In Turkey, Washington wants to see peace talks between Ankara and the PKK, but this not possible while the YPG is soaring in Syria.

The YPG is the military wing of the Democratic Union Party (PYD), itself spun out of the PKK in 2003. As the mother organisation in this relationship, the PKK has historically shaped the policies of the PYD and the YPG. Accordingly, the successes of the PKK in Turkey have animated and excited its offspring's base in Syria. However, the 2014 Siege of Kobane has changed that dynamic. In Kobane, the YPG not only successfully pushed back against ISIS, but they also ended up winning the US as an ally in the aftermath of its military victory against ISIS. (At this time, the YPG already had Russia's backing.)

Subsequently, with US support, the YPG took vast swathes of Syrian territory, including nearly 50 per cent of its oil fields, as well as rich gas fields. Taking into account that Syria's pre-civil war oil production was at nearly 2 million barrels a day, the YPG, which has US and Russia as its allies, is confident regarding its future.

This is a source of tension between US policy regarding the PKK in Turkey and US policy regarding the YPG in Syria. In the PKK–YPG orbit, the latter has now become the source of inspiration.

This, in return, has changed the dynamics of the Turkey–PKK relationship, leading to conflict in Turkey. Peace talks between Ankara and the PKK collapsed in July 2015, when the PKK launched a fresh offensive against Turkish security forces. At the time, the PKK hoped to import the 'Kobane Model' into Turkey, and repeat the YPG's successes in Syria, where the latter took control of towns, such as Kobane in 2014, and later declared itself autonomous. Now, in 2015, the PKK was aiming to take over Kurdish-majority towns in Turkey to declare autonomy there. This example, alone, demonstrates the extent to which the YPG's successes have been animating the PKK's policies, and not the other way around. So long as the YPG is soaring in Syria, the PKK is unlikely to end its fight against Turkey. To put it bluntly, Washington's YPG policy in Syria has unwittingly empowered the PKK in Turkey.

Washington needs to find a way to ensure that its Syria policies do not further strengthen the YPG, a development that translates into more robust PKK combat effort against Turkey. In this regard, the US may consider implementing the 'Manbij Model' in the areas in northeast Syria held by the YPG, transferring governance there from the YPG to the local communities, including Syrian Kurds, but excluding formal members of the YPG or its associated political wing, the PYD.

It may turn out that the shrinking US military footprint reduces Washington's influence on political events in Syria, and that events might also take their own course, especially via the risk of a military intervention by Turkey or the Assad regime. However, the statement of intent to transfer control to non-YPG/PYD elements as a matter of US policy will have benefits in the bilateral relationship.

US policies should also help Turkey combat the PKK more directly, including by continuing to provide assistance to Ankara in putting military pressure against the PKK's headquarters in the Qandil Mountains, as well as working with European countries to curb the PKK's criminal operations and fundraising activities in Europe, a key source of income for the group. The PKK will come back to the negotiating table with Turkey only if its wings in Rojava, Qandil and Europe are *simultaneously* clipped.

Renewed peace talks between the Turkish government and the PKK are in the USA's interests. Dialogue on the Kurdish issue would add to Turkey's stability. It would also disarm a Russian proxy – Moscow helped establish the PKK during the Cold War and has maintained ties with the group ever since – against a US ally.

Finally, talks between the Turkish government and the PKK would prevent a potentially disastrous rupture with Ankara over the issue of the YPG. Turkey and the YPG view each other through the lens of the PKK, and not the other way around. Turkey can come to terms with living with YPG enclaves in Syria, only if there are peace talks between Erdogan and the PKK. This is the sole way to secure good ties between Ankara and the YPG. In other words, if Washington takes the right steps regarding the PKK, it will have created suitable conditions to have, one day, Ankara–Rojava coexistence.

Erdogan may even eventually build a KRG-type friendly relationship, based on economic interests, with the YPG-controlled Rojava, should there be Turkish–PKK peace. This is not an unrealistic goal as Ankara and the PKK were in peace talks until recently, between 2013 and 2015. A case can be made for pragmatic relations with the YPG along the border even if an American military departure results either in a chaotic situation or a regime return in the long term. The alternative is an actively combatant YPG, likely sponsored by the regime and the Iranians, ready to strike against Turkish forces or Ankara-supported Syrian forces and populations in northern Syria or across the border in Turkey.

As mentioned before, Washington also needs to work on transitioning the governance of YPG controlled-areas in Syria to their original inhabitants – large swathes of Rojava cut across Arab-majority or plurality regions. The latter step is also in the interest of America's broader policy to counter ISIS, as well as helping to prevent its return. The YPG, which has a leftist pedigree, is simultaneously also a Kurdish nationalist organisation. Given this ideological cocktail, the group's domination of conservative Arab Muslim areas of Syria could lead to an anti-leftist, Arab nationalist and religious backlash in rural Arab-majority Syria, sprouting the seeds of the sons of a new ISIS: ISIS 2.0.

Beyond the Kurdish issue, in the big picture, Washington needs to provide Ankara with ironclad guarantees against Russian aggression. In the absence of such policies, Erdogan will be forced to come more and more under Putin's influence.

In a way, Turkey's struggles in the Middle East mirror those of Japan in East Asia. Even today, Japan, the consummate soft-power nation, relies on US hard power for its security in East Asia, especially against China and North Korea. After its futile foray into Syria, Turkey, the Middle East's largest economy but not the dominant military power (when considering Russia), needs the United States to protect it against the challenges posed by the Syrian Civil War. If Washington can play this opening to its advantage, it can keep Ankara on its side.

14
ERDOGAN'S EMPIRE
PART I: EAST AFRICA

Not all is gloomy for Erdogan's vision of spreading Turkish influence. This is especially the case beyond the Middle East. In recent years, he has taken relatively successful strides in Africa, especially the eastern part of the continent. He has also been somewhat successful in Eurasia, especially in the Western Balkans and Black Sea Basin and to a lesser extent in Central Asia. Following policy disappointments in the Middle East in recent years, Erdogan has pivoted to these regions, which represent the new low-hanging fruit for his foreign policy.

Erdogan had already prioritised ties with these regions, especially African countries, under Davutoglu. After the latter's departure, when Erdogan pivoted more strongly to these regions, he could, as a result, rely on the pre-existing networks of Turkish companies, diplomats, institutions and businesses to support his outreach. However, Erdogan had a challenge to overcome: at least some of these key networks were aligned with the Gulen movement.

Purging Gulenists

After the 2016 putsch attempt, the Erdogan–Gulen relationship became warlike. Sigmund Freud's thesis of 'Narcissism of Small Differences' best explains this enmity: the more similar two people or entities are, the more they hate each other when they have a fallout. This case in point has shaped Erdogan's political thinking in many ways, including towards Gulen's networks overseas. This is why, in addition to seeking influence, Erdogan's outreach to Africa and Eurasia in recent years has also aimed to persuade countries there to purge Gulenist institutions, and to turn a blind eye to renditions of suspected Gulenists to Turkey by its intelligence organisation, the MIT.

By 2019, Erdogan had, indeed, made some progress towards that goal. Following the coup, for instance, his government applied strong diplomatic pressure on African and Eurasian countries to shut down Gulen-aligned institutions, as well as to close or transfer Gulen's schools to the management of a new Turkish government-run organisation, the Education Foundation, established in 2016.

In Somalia, Mogadishu's immediate closure of Gulen-linked businesses and schools, promptly after the 15 July coup in Turkey, signalled Erdogan's far reach in that country. A number of other African states, namely Chad, Congo, Ghana, Guinea, Ivory Coast, Mali, Mauritania, Morocco, Niger, Senegal, Sierra Leone, Sudan and Tunisia, many of them in East and West Africa, responded positively as well. These states either shut down Gulen schools and institutions in their territory, transferred the schools into the hands of the Turkish government or the Education Foundation, or are currently in the process of closing them down.

Erdogan also experienced success in Eurasia, if less limited, with his de-Gulenification efforts. Gulen-aligned schools have been shut down in Azerbaijan and Georgia. In the Balkans, where Erdogan's appeal to states in the peninsula did not always fall on receptive ears, Erdogan took matters into his own hands. Most recently, MIT extradited a number of Gulen members from Kosovo and Moldova to Turkey, in operations in March and September 2018.[1]

Tell me who attended Erdogan's oath ceremony, I will draw you a map of his empire

Signalling Erdogan's rising influence over parts of Africa and Eurasia, a large number of heads of state from these regions, compared to the Middle East and other parts of the world, attended Erdogan's historic swearing-in ceremony on 9 July 2018.

On this day in Ankara, Erdogan took office as Turkey's new executive-style president, at a ceremony held at his new palace in the Turkish capital. Built on one of Ankara's hills, Erdogan's palace towers over Ataturk's mid-twentieth-century mausoleum tomb, Anitkabir, which resembles a pagan Greek temple. Dominating Ankara's skyline, Erdogan's palace, decorated with elements of Muslim Seljuk and Central Asian imperial architectural styles, symbolises the immense political, religious and imperial power of Turkey's new leader.

On this hot summer evening in the Turkish capital, where temperatures rose as high as 34.4°C (94°F) during the day, Erdogan assumed sweeping new powers, given to him by the referendum of April 2017. This was a historic moment in his career, signalling the end of Turkey's first republic, established by Ataturk, and the start of a second, birthed by Erdogan.

As he was sworn in, becoming the country's most powerful leader in nearly a century, Erdogan could take pride in his empire globally, represented by a disproportionate number of heads of state from East and West African, Balkan, Black Sea littoral and Central Asian countries.

Of the twenty-two presidents and monarchs in attendance, eighteen hailed from these countries, namely Bosnia-Herzegovina, Bulgaria, Chad, Djibouti, Equatorial Guinea, Gabon, Georgia, Guinea, Guinea-Bissau, Kyrgyzstan, Kosovo, Macedonia, Mauritania, Moldova, Pakistan, Serbia, Somalia and Sudan.[2] Also in attendance were presidents of the Turkish Republic of Northern Cyprus (TRNC) and Gagauzia (an autonomous Turkic territory in Moldova).

Erdogan often starts his international speeches with his trademark motto, 'The World is Greater Than Five', suggesting that the rest of the world is more important than the five permanent members of the UN Security Council. Supporting his international reputation as defender of the global south, Venezuela's leader Nicolas Maduro and Zambia's President Edgar Lungu also attended the ceremony.

Lastly, but importantly, signalling the forging of the Qatar–Turkey 'Axis' since the Qatar–GCC split, the emir of Qatar, Tamim bin Hamad Al Thani, too, showed up in Ankara to root for the Turkish president. Poignantly however, and highlighting Ankara's broader isolation in the Middle East, Al Thani was the only Middle Eastern head of state or monarch present in the Turkish capital that day. Also in attendance was President Mamnoon Hussain of Muslim-majority Pakistan, one of Turkey's closest friends internationally – Turks and South Asian Muslims have been tightly bound ever since Abdulhamid II's nineteenth-century campaign to use Islam in the subcontinent to spread Ottoman influence.[3]

On 9 July 2018, in Ankara, a good amount of Islamic symbolism was choreographed into Erdogan's oath-taking ceremony to align with his vision of reviving an Ottoman past, one defined by Islam. Throughout the day, Ali Erbas, head of Diyanet, Turkey's government-run Islamic religious authority, accompanied the Turkish president. As Erdogan was sworn in before a crowd of mostly African and Eurasian dignitaries, and a hand-picked crowd of his most devoted Turkish supporters, as well as the country's roster of generals, admirals, spy chiefs, government ministers and top bureaucrats, Erbas blessed Erdogan, saying:

> Dear God, bestow successes upon our esteemed president, who is embarking upon his new assignment with the mandate given to him by our nation, and who has worked tirelessly and fearlessly for the perpetuity of our state, the prosperity of our nation, and the tranquility of mankind; grant him your grace, do not put him to shame.[4]

Instead of cocktails, fancy and exotic fruit juices were served, and prayers in Arabic were chanted from Erdogan's new palace over Ataturk's Ankara. The new sultan had arrived.

Not all was glory, though. Providing a sample taste of challenges to Erdogan's foreign policy and desire to make Turkey a global power, no presidents or prime ministers from the United States or the EU attended the ceremony. The only exception was Rumen Radev, president of Bulgaria, whose Balkan country came under Turkey's influence in recent years (as discussed in Chapter 15).

Also importantly missing among the dignitaries: the presidents of Russia, Iran and China. This signalled that despite the busy brokering of Syria- or pipeline-related deals with Moscow, energy bargains with Tehran and metro construction agreements with Beijing, Erdogan was experiencing trouble actualising true friendships with these capitals. The stark reality is that Turkey's cooperation with these three countries does not mark the clear geopolitical shift that some experts have argued.

The entire world is a stage

The list of countries whose presidents or monarchs showed up at this July 2018 ceremony should help draw an accurate sketch of Erdogan's empire.

In this regard, credit goes to Erdogan (and Davutoglu) for following a foreign policy in the last decade that transcends Turkey's former Ataturk-shaped European focus that past leaders exercised. The two men made Ankara not only a recognised name, but also a listened-to regional actor especially in Africa, Eurasia and beyond.

Under Erdogan, Ankara set its sights not just on its near abroad region in the Middle East, but also further. Erdogan saw Turkey as a rising global power, somewhat akin to India or Brazil, destined to make a splash across the globe. Therefore, a massive diplomatic outreach effort followed Erdogan's ascent. Between 2002 and 2015, for instance, Turkey increased the total number of embassies, consulates and permanent diplomatic missions from 163 to 228.[5] It nourished Istanbul as a centre of global political and cultural exchange, hosting international summits and civil society conferences on a daily basis, second only to New York in the world for having the greatest number of foreign consulates hosted in any city in 2014.[6] In 2019, Turkey had 266 diplomatic missions overseas, 1.6 times the number in 2002.[7]

However, in the aftermath of the post-coup purges targeting Gulenists, the Turkish Ministry of Foreign Affairs suffered from a dearth of personnel. The Turkish diplomatic corps remains stretched now, having lost hundreds of officers but still serving the nearly 230 Turkish missions overseas, as well as staffing a vast foreign ministry.

A global aid agency

Under Davutoglu, Ankara also worked to enhance its brand through the work of government aid agencies and cultural institutes. Turkey's main government coordinator for foreign aid, the Turkish Cooperation and Coordination Agency (TIKA), was an important instrument of this policy. The agency is a product of the 1990s, when Ankara looked to the Turkic peoples of post-Soviet Central Asia and the Caucasus as a possible sphere of influence.

In its early years, the organisation focused on restoring Turkic historical sites in these transitional countries, but dreamt-of political payoffs never really came to fruition. With Erdogan's rise, Turkey's gaze turned to the Arab countries, Africa and beyond, with TIKA branching out to the Middle East and opening offices wherever its efforts were likely to gain publicity. The agency was especially active in East and West Africa. For instance, it performed surgeries in Uganda[8] and built schools in South Sudan.[9]

Today, the agency has a presence in 170 countries across five continents, although the scale of many of its operations is rather small.[10] In parallel, Turkey's disaster relief organisation, Disaster and Emergency Management Presidency (AFAD), had a visible presence during the Arab uprisings as it conducted extensive aid efforts in Libya, Tunisia, Egypt and Syria, among others. More notably, AFAD launched an operation in 2011 in Somalia to provide famine relief. This marked the first significant effort by a Muslim-majority country to invest in Somalia in decades, also paving the way for later Turkish influence in the country.

A global religious network

Diyanet is another government institution that has accompanied and boosted Erdogan's outreach to build Turkish influence. The Directorate of Religious Affairs, commonly referred to as Diyanet, was founded in 1924 to regulate and direct Islam in Turkey, as per Ataturk's vision to control religion. Ataturk wanted to create a unified, state-sponsored Turkish Islam that could replace small, local, religious groups that are hard for the government to control.

Today in Turkey, Diyanet controls the mosques, employs the imams and pays their salaries, and produces the Friday sermons delivered in every mosque weekly.[11] In 1978, Diyanet began opening offices and mosques abroad in European countries, such as Germany and the Netherlands, where large Turkish communities formed due to migration in the 1960s and 1970s.

In recent years, Erdogan has dramatically boosted the agency's funding, boosting its international presence, as well as networks in Turkey.[12] In 2019, for instance, he increased its budget by 36 per cent, from $1.4 billion to $2 billion, or five times the budget of Turkey's intelligence agency, and six times that of its Parliament.[13] Today, Diyanet operates mosques in over forty countries: it has a significant presence in West European states such as Germany and Austria that contain large Turkish immigrant populations; in East European and Eurasian states such as Azerbaijan that are Muslim-majority; and former Ottoman territories in the Balkans such as Serbia.

Erdogan prioritises the expansion of Diyanet for a couple of reasons beyond the agency's initial mandate: the agency provides him with a lever over Islam in Turkey, helping his vision of boosting Ankara's influence globally, through religion.

During the Cold War and immediately afterwards, European governments initially welcomed Diyanet and its imams as a moderate force to counterbalance the emerging Salafi and Wahhabi movements on the continent. As the Turkish agency became ever more willing and capable to expand its operations into the political sphere under Erdogan, however, a more critical view has emerged. Diyanet imams are now accused of hindering the integration of Turks into Europe by promoting their allegiance to Ankara and undermining links between diaspora Turks and their respective states of residence. Increasingly politicised, the agency is also targeted for allowing officials of recently founded pro-Ankara pro-Erdogan Turkish political parties in Europe, such as Denk (styled DENK; Dutch for 'think' and Turkish for 'equal' in) the Netherlands and Democrats for Responsibility, Solidarity and Tolerance (DOST) in Bulgaria to conduct political propaganda in their mosques.[14]

Erdogan's Africa

Erdogan's (and Turkey's) biggest gains over the course of the past two decades have not occurred in Europe, but in Africa. As he shifted Turkey's attention away from the West, Erdogan started to cultivate ties with the southernmost stretches of the former Ottoman Empire and Muslim-majority states beyond the Middle East, which Turkey's twentieth-century leaders and diplomats largely ignored.

In Africa, Ankara followed a robust and vigorous campaign, constructed in the first decade of Erdogan's ascent so as to boost and maintain economic and political ties. From 2003 to 2017, the number of Turkish embassies rose from 12 to 41 and Ankara's FDI flows to the region increased from $100 million to $6.5 billion, respectively.[15] In 2018, Erdogan's administration set the goal of raising the number of Turkish diplomatic missions on the continent to 54, a number that also includes several consulates in key commercial hubs.[16] In addition, by early 2019, Erdogan had made over thirty-five official visits to the continent since coming to power, far outweighing any previous Turkish leader.[17]

Erdogan's Africa opening came with an especially appealing political tack. During his official visit to Algeria in March 2018, a local reporter allegedly asked him, in French, '*Bonjour, monsieur*, did you come here with . . . sympathy for Ottoman colonization?'[18] To which Erdogan wittily replied, 'If we were colonisers, you would have asked this question in Turkish, not French.' This small, insightful transaction of words is the preface of Turkey's efforts to rebrand its image in Africa. In official state visits to more than 24 African countries, mostly in East and West Africa, between 2004 and 2014, Erdogan has reiterated rhetoric, making it a point to draw a sharp dichotomy between the colonising Europeans and the shared cultural and religious values with Africa that the heirs of the Ottoman Empire possess. One where Turkey is akin to European powers in might but without the historical baggage of colonisation.[19]

Erdogan's rhetoric found receptive audiences, especially in formerly Ottoman-ruled East African countries, such as Sudan and Somalia, where the memory of the sultans' rule – tenuous and spotty in nature in these distant regions of the empire – contrasted with the more indelible and forceful legacy of recent European colonisation by powers such as Great Britain and Italy.[20]

To be fair, just as Turkey's first imperial foray into Africa did not start under Erdogan, so did its modern-era Africa pivot. Turkish efforts to boost bilateral relations with African countries in the 1980s under Ozal predate Erdogan. Later on, an 'Africa Action Plan' was commissioned by Ankara in 1998 to increase the number of its diplomatic missions to the continent. In fact, many facets of what Davutoglu called 'multiaxial diplomacy' grew from the Ozal period, as well as the frustrations of Turkish diplomacy in the 1990s with the EU, finding support outside of the AKP camp.

However, Turkey's political and economic instability of the 1990s, including multiple economic crises, kept Ankara occupied from fully capitalising on these newfound ventures at the time. By emitting immense amounts of soft power, and taking stock of economic growth under Erdogan, Ankara began a drastic overhaul of its diplomatic objectives in Africa after 2002. Erdogan has created enduring relationships for Turkey on the continent.

In 2002, the African Union (AU) granted Turkish embassy officials access to their meetings in their headquarters in Addis Ababa, Ethiopia, and by the next year, the Undersecretariat of Foreign Trade of Turkey hosted the 'Strategy for Enhancing the Economic and Commercial Relations with Africa' initiative. In 2005, Erdogan highlighted his growing ambitions by naming 2005, as mentioned before, 'The Year of Africa' in Turkey, followed by the 'Open to Africa Policy' later that year.

The Gulen network, then an Erdogan ally, was quick to move into Africa with him during this opening period. The Turkish Confederation of Businessmen and Industrialists (TUSKON), a Gulenist business lobby outfit that would later be banned in Turkey after the failed 2016 coup, began to organise the 'Turkey–Africa Trade Bridge' to boost commerce in 2005. As discussed earlier, Gulen helped Erdogan build power in Africa and elsewhere abroad through trilateral cooperation between Gulen networks, Turkish Airlines and the Turkish Foreign Ministry.

These efforts and customised diplomacy helped: Turkey was elevated to observer status in the AU. In 2008, Turkey hosted the second 'Turkey–Africa Cooperation' summit. Accentuating Ankara's growing economic power on the continent, representatives from 49 of the 53 African countries at the time attended the summit. 'The Istanbul Declaration on Turkey–Africa Partnership', signed at the end of the summit, signalled Ankara's cresting economic, diplomatic and political muscle on the continent – a welcome development for the country, given that only five years ago, it had just a dozen embassies on the entire African continent, seven of them south of the Sahara. By 2009, Turkey had thirty-four embassies in sub-Saharan Africa, twenty-nine of them in East and West Africa.

Ankara was able to swiftly win influence and trust in various sub-Saharan African countries. Erdogan's administration treated each official visitor from that part of the continent with the same glamour and hospitality with which the government treated officials from European governments. Likewise, countries that Erdogan visited in Africa treated the leader with as much respect as possible. Erdogan soon started to reap the rewards of its opening to Africa. In 2008, at the UN General Assembly, where Turkey was voted to take a seat as a non-permanent member at the UN Security Council for the period of 2009–10 – the first time since 1961 that Turkey won a seat at the UN's prestigious body – 50 out of the 53 African states supported Turkish membership.

The new 'Great Game' in East Africa

After ousting Davutoglu in 2016, Erdogan invigorated Turkey's foreign policy towards Africa. Tacitly admitting his failure in the Middle East for leadership over the region's Muslim-majority countries, he has vigorously pursued ties with the Muslim-majority states on the African continent. He has strategically targeted countries previously mostly under brief or nominal Ottoman suzerainty (specifically, Somalia and Sudan) to explore new areas for Turkish greatness, often through Muslim kinship.

In this regard, East Africa stands out as the low-hanging fruit for Erdogan. Following the end of the nearly two decades-long Eritrea–Ethiopia conflict in 2018, Somalia and Sudan have emerged as flashpoints of regional competition in East Africa. The Ethiopia–Eritrea peace is creating new alignments around the Horn of Africa, and this includes different proxies for Ankara, Doha, Abu Dhabi, Cairo and Riyadh.

The region's two largest Muslim-majority states, Somalia and Sudan, both suffer from political instability: Somalia has been in state of civil war for three decades, and the central government still struggles to assert control over large swathes of the country, much of which is controlled by the al-Qaeda-linked al-Shabaab.

Somalia also faces separatist forces. It splintered during its civil war, and the central government in Mogadishu has yet to take control of all its pre-civil war territory. In 1991, at the start of Somalia's civil war, Somaliland in the north, previously a British colony, broke away from Somalia, itself a former Italian colony. In 1998, Puntland, another northern region, declared itself an autonomous state within Somalia. Whereas Puntland agreed to recognise the Somali Federal Government (SFG), formed in 2012 to end the civil war, Somaliland did not. To this day, Somaliland remains outside of Mogadishu's control. Although no country recognises Somaliland, it is de facto independent.

Sudan, for its part, lost South Sudan, which produced three-fourths of its oil, in an independence referendum in 2011. South Sudan became an independent country, forcing Sudan's now ousted leader, Omar al-Bashir, to seek allies to support his country against further economic loss and potential domestic instability.

Adjacent to the Middle East, these countries in East Africa and the rest of the region are fast becoming the playground of a new 'Great

Game' by nearby Middle East competitors: the Turkey–Qatar 'Axis' vs the Egypt–Saudi Arabia–UAE 'Bloc'.

The Turkish Navy retruns to the Indian Ocean

In this regard, the recently opened Turkish base in Qatar, inaugurated in April 2016, has provided Ankara and Doha with muscle in the Persian Gulf, as well as the northern reaches of the Indian Ocean, stretching from the Gulf towards East Africa.[21]

The Qatar base is the first permanent Turkish military deployment in the Persian Gulf since the collapse of the Ottoman Empire. It includes Turkey in a small group of nations willing and able to project power in the Gulf. The base reportedly includes army, navy, air force and Special Forces components, as well as trainers for the Qatari military.[22]

The Qatar base will also give the Turkish military the desert-training medium it currently lacks, allow Turkish naval forces to conduct counter-piracy and other operations in the Persian Gulf, Red Sea, Indian Ocean, Arabian Sea and East Africa, and perhaps serve as a hub for future transoceanic Turkish operations. More symbolically, the base will signal the Turkish Navy's return to the Indian Ocean and East Africa for the first time as a deterrent force since the 1550s, when the Ottoman sultans fought the Portuguese kings for dominance there.[23]

Mr Erdogan goes to Mogadishu

The Qatar base is significant in Erdogan's vision to increase Turkey's influence around the Horn of Africa. Luckily for Erdogan (and Qatar) Ankara's presence in Somalia predates the Qatar–GCC split, a fact that has provided Ankara and Doha with an advantage in this part of the 'Great Game' for East Africa. During the Qatar–GCC crisis, Somalia did not yield to Saudi–UAE pressures and refused to break ties with Doha.

Erdogan has built more influence in Somalia than any of his rivals, while the UAE has been establishing itself in Somalia's breakaway Somaliland region, as well as Puntland, an autonomous state within Somalia. Somaliland and Puntland are the two parts of the Somali peninsula closest to Yemen and the Bab al-Mandab Strait, hence the UAE's focus there.

In terms of Turkey's influence in Mogadishu, the credit goes to Erdogan. In 2011, while continuing dialogue on a grandiose scale with African nations and intergovernmental organisations, he took a new step and increasingly began to approach countries on an individual basis. In August 2011, he became the first non-African leader to visit Somalia in over two decades. This was a daring sojourn, indeed. The battle for Mogadishu, fought in 2007–11 between the AU peacekeeping force, named the African Union Mission for Somalia (AMISOM), and the al-Shabaab jihadist group, had just ended. Al-Shabaab had only recently evacuated and abandoned the city, but that did not deter Erdogan and his family and cadre of Turkish officials from arriving in Mogadishu within days of the event, on 19 August 2011.

Erdogan visited a refugee camp in Somalia with his family. Immediately after, he decided to spend $1 billion in humanitarian aid for Somalia. Ankara launched its largest famine relief operation ever attempted, and in the process, became Somalia's single largest foreign donor. These investments continued even after the occurrence of one of the worst terrorist attacks in Somalia's history. On 4 October 2011, an al-Shabaab suicide bomber drove a truck to the gates of Somalia's Transitional Federal Government, killing 100 Somalis and injuring hundreds.[24] Ankara, however, was undeterred, and the Turkish government began building the largest hospital in Somalia, the 200-bed 'Recep Tayyep [sic] Erdogan Hospital', which eventually opened in Mogadishu on 25 January 2015.[25]

Erdogan's visit resulted in a boom in Turkish–Somali economic ties, as well. In 2010, Turkish exports to Somalia totalled just $4.8 million; by 2018, they had reached $140 million.[26] In the space of six years, Turkey has gone from Somalia's seventeenth-largest source of imports to its fifth largest.[27] Notably, a Turkish company began operating Mogadishu's port in 2014.[28] Today, the largest Turkish embassy in the world is located in Mogadishu, which is also the largest embassy of any country in this capital city.

Ankara has also set up its largest overseas military base in the capital, which was established as a training facility in September 2016.[29] The base has a capacity to host 1,500 equipped troops at any one time. Turkish troops train and assist local security forces against al-Shabaab. Turkey is currently helping train the SFG's national security institutions, including the Somali National Army and the police force.

Furthermore, in 2017, Ankara set up a relief programme for 6 million Somalis affected by drought and the outbreak of cholera.[30] This included direct budgetary support for the SFG, based in Mogadishu. As a sign of ever closer ties and binational connection, over 15,000 Somali students are currently studying in Turkey.[31] Without a doubt, Turkey's influence on Somalia remains quite deep.

. . . with Qatari money

In his venture into East Africa, Erdogan has found a helping hand from deep-pocketed Qatar, which owns one of the world's largest sovereign wealth funds. Doha has its own concerns in East Africa. It is worried about rising UAE–Saudi influence around Bab al-Mandab, namely, UAE presence in Eritrea, Somaliland and Puntland and Saudi presence in Djibouti and Yemen.

Qatar sees itself as being locked in a competition with its archrival in this region, the UAE. Accordingly, Doha and Abu Dhabi alike have been making competing multibillion-dollar investments across the Horn of Africa, in the hopes of gaining influence in this area, which contains critical routes for crude oil travelling from the Gulf to the Suez Canal and the Mediterranean. Moreover, the region is significant for the UAE and Saudi Arabia due to its proximity to their operations in the war in Yemen, including through the strategic Bab al-Mandab Strait.[32]

Erdogan's investments in Somalia also benefited Qatar handsomely, keeping Somalia on Doha's side in the Qatar–GCC split. In return, Doha gladly funds Turkish moves in Somalia. Qatari–Turkish investments are mostly centred on Mogadishu, and are focused on supporting SFG President Mohamed Abdullahi Mohamed (nicknamed 'Farmajo'). He and his chief of staff are widely viewed in Somalia and by Western diplomats as loyal to Doha after allegedly receiving funds for their 2017 election campaign. Doha has provided $385 million to the central government for infrastructure, education and humanitarian assistance.[33]

Abu Dhabi pushes back

Somali's internal splits make it an especially fertile area for UAE competition against the Qatar–Turkey 'Axis'. Accordingly, Abu Dhabi has been providing state-level support to security forces in Puntland and the breakaway Somaliland region partly in order to undermine the authority of the SFG, and push back against Erdogan and Doha.

In 2016, a UAE-owned firm took control of the Port of Berbera in the self-declared state of Somaliland, pledging $440 million to develop it. The following year, another UAE-owned company agreed to expand a port in Somalia's semi-autonomous Puntland region for $336 million.[34] The UAE will open a military base in Berbera in 2019. Abu Dhabi, which already trains the Puntland coast guard, is set to start training the Somaliland coast guard, providing the UAE with two naval allies around Bab al-Mandab and across Yemen, but also against the Ankara–Doha 'Axis' and Mogadishu. In 2018, the SFG ended military cooperation with the UAE, further limiting Abu Dhabi's influence in Mogadishu.

'Axis' vs 'Bloc' in Sudan

Sudan is another East African country experiencing Middle Eastern competition. Khartoum is ever in search of economic benefactors, following the loss of the oil fields of South Sudan. It also seeks allies against its historic rival: Egypt. Bashir was keen to play the 'Axis' and 'Bloc' against each other. He supported Saudi Arabia and the UAE in the Yemen War, but also welcomed the forays by Ankara and Doha. This has provided Erdogan with a tempting entry point into East Africa, through Khartoum to counter Sisi's Egypt. Cairo has responded, also reacting to Bashir's opposition to it on various regional issues, including the latter's support for the Great Ethiopian Renaissance Dam (GERD, explained below), by reportedly sending troops in 2018 to Sudan's neighbour, Eritrea.

In Sudan, Erdogan can again claim much of the credit for building Turkish influence as leverage. He courted Sudanese leader Bashir, as soon as he took office in Ankara in 2003, and built strong ties with him.[35] Khartoum's loss of South Sudan has undermined Sudan's economic stability, also putting Bashir's survival into question. In December 2017, Erdogan visited Khartoum, meeting the Sudanese president and underlining his support for him.

While Erdogan's early investments in Somalia helped his ally, Doha, during the Qatar–GCC split, Erdogan's early Khartoum opening has benefited him more directly – providing a lever against Sisi following the Erdogan–Sisi split in 2013.

Ties between Sudan and Egypt have been historically strained due to a number of disputes, including territorial disagreements over the Hala'ib Triangle. Recently, Ethiopia's construction of the GERD on the Blue Nile, which would give Ethiopia control over much of the waters of the Nile Basin, has realigned the power balance along the Nile Valley, pitting upstream nations Ethiopia and Sudan against downstream Egypt. The rivalry between Sudan and Egypt has intensified. In this regard, following the collapse of his ties with Sisi in 2013, Erdogan recognised an opportunity in Khartoum. Just as Sisi flirted with Cypriot Greeks to leverage them against Erdogan, the latter has reached out to Khartoum, where he found a welcome hand to push back against Sisi.

Erdogan was quick to send signals of enhanced ties to Sudan after his split with Sisi. In 2014, a Turkish military frigate docked in Port Sudan. TIKA had also built a 150-bed hospital in Nyala, Sudan, which was scheduled to be handed over to the Sudanese Ministry of Health in 2019.[36] Towards the end of 2017, in his aforementioned three-day visit to Khartoum, Erdogan initiated many lucrative deals with Bashir in the mining, agriculture, oil and health sectors.

In December 2017, Erdogan signed an agreement, allowing a Turkish military presence in Sudanese territorial waters and the leasing of Suakin Island on the west coast of the Red Sea, 50 kilometres (30 miles) south of Port Sudan, in a deal amounting to $650 million.[37] Ankara now had the ability to build up Suakin, a former Ottoman outpost used as a resting station by Muslim pilgrims on their way to Mecca, to create a new military base on the designated land. Renovations of the island were started by TIKA in January 2018.

At the same time, separate from (but presumably related to) the Turkish deal, Sudan awarded a $4 billion deal to Doha to manage the commercial port in Suakin along the Red Sea, providing Qatar with a counterbalance to the UAE's port-development project in the Somaliland city of Assab, situated on the coast of the Gulf of Aden, controlling access to the Red Sea.[38]

Qatar worked with Turkey to peel Bashir – who was generally amenable to the Muslim Brotherhood – away from the UAE and Saudi Arabia. This drive, coupled with Ankara's own East Africa initiative, drew further ire from Saudi Arabia and the UAE, as well as Egypt,[39] which are building influence in Eritrea, Ethiopia, and Somaliland to push back against the influence of the 'Axis' in Mogadishu and Khartoum.[40]

Bashir, however, played all sides until 2019. While his ties with Egypt remained tense – Cairo created a new Southern Red Sea naval command in 2017, responsible for security in the vicinity of Suakin, Bashir cultivated good ties with the UAE and Saudi Arabia, supporting their war efforts in Yemen, and providing himself with room to manoeuver between the 'Axis' and the 'Bloc'.

Bashir's ouster in April 2019 seems to have weakened Ankara's hand in Khartoum for now. It is yet to be seen, if following the fall, whether the influence of Turkey and Qatar in Sudan will remain unchanged. Egypt and its allies have already recognised the post-Bashir government in Khartoum, potentially undermining the Ankara–Doha axis.

Djibouti and Ethiopia

If the Suakin base is yet to be built, Erdogan can take comfort in his rising influence in East Africa and along the Red Sea Coast to counter Egypt. In December 2017, Djibouti's ambassador to Ankara stated that the third-smallest nation on the African continent would welcome a Turkish base on its territory.[41] This adds Turkey to a select list of countries, namely China, France, Great Britain, Japan, Saudi Arabia and the United States, among others, which have established facilities, bases or military installations in Djibouti that they also allow their allies to use.

In December 2018, not wanting to be outdone by Erdogan, Sisi announced that Egypt, too, would build a military facility in Djibouti.[42] Nevertheless, together with rising economic clout in Ethiopia, where direct Turkish investment surpasses $2.5 billion,[43] a base in Djibouti would work to strengthen the Turkish footprint in East Africa, helping Erdogan's vision of building Turkish greatness as a power in this region.

The Sahel and West Africa

The Sahel, a geographic-cultural area, stretching from Sudan to Mauritania, along the southern reaches of the Sahara Dessert and populated mostly by Muslims, is another low-hanging fruit for Erdogan in his recent foreign policy outreach. A lack of historical conflicts involving the Ottoman Empire and Islamic kinship has quickly allowed Erdogan to dig roots in the region, as well as nearby West Africa. His pivot to these regions has found a helping hand from the fact that the US and other powers traditionally active here have decreased their engagement in these areas, creating a void that Ankara has been happy to fill in partially.

Under the added pretext that these regions were once connected to the Ottoman Empire – before the middle of the nineteenth century, Ottoman penetration into sub-Saharan Africa through the vast span of the Sahara Dessert was at best notional – Erdogan has reached out to Sahelian and West African nations, including Chad, Niger, Nigeria, Mali, Mauritania and Senegal. Subsequently, he has opened Turkey's first embassies in Chad, Niger, Mauritania and Senegal. Furthermore, TIKA launched their first West African office in Senegal in 2007,[44] and the agency was also responsible for renovating Mali's National Parliament building in 2016.[45] Ankara also continues to grant full scholarships to students from all these countries to study in Turkey. Without a doubt, this has made a positive impression and Turkish soft power has become a noticeable player in the region, as symbolised by the presence of the Chadian, Guinean, Guinea-Bissauan and Mauritanian presidents at Erdogan's swearing-in ceremony on 9 July 2018.[46]

15
ERDOGAN'S EMPIRE
PART II: 'BAYRAM BELT'

When Erdogan turned to Eurasia to seek influence and restore Turkey's status as an imperial power, he discovered a helping hand in the forces of history.

Turkey's sway as a Muslim power traditionally extends north of the 'Bayram–Eid' line, based on the separate words Turks and Arabs use for the Islamic High Holiday. Nearly all Muslims call the holiday *eid*, but Turks and their kin in other nations in Eurasia know it as *bayram*. These nations and ethnic groups include, among others, Bashkir and Tatars in Russia, Azeris in the south Caucasus, and Kazakh, Kyrgyz, Turkmens and Uzbeks in Central Asia. The same is true for countries in the Balkans that were previously Ottoman domains for centuries, such as Albania, Bosnia, Bulgaria, Greece, Kosovo, Macedonia, Montenegro and Serbia. These naming differences offer an unexpected insight into Ankara's bid for influence in Muslim countries, as it successfully projected soft power through cultural and historic ties to the Balkans, Central Asia and the Black Sea region, meaning the 'Bayram Belt', while failing to expand hard power into the Middle East and North Africa, meaning the 'Eid Belt'.[1]

Across the Bayram Belt, Erdogan has successfully built influence over the Muslim-populated states in the Western Balkans, including Albania, Bosnia and Herzegovina, Macedonia, Montenegro and Serbia. He has also used Ankara's ties with Bulgaria, Georgia, Moldova and Romania (all previously ruled by the Ottomans) to gently push back against a resurgent Moscow in the Black Sea region. Finally, he has pivoted to Central Asia to hold sway in a region where Russia has returned as a chief hegemon.

Strategic gap between Erdogan and Europe

Erdogan's most successful endeavours to establish influence across the Eurasian Bayram Belt occurred in the Western Balkans. The states in this region are relatively small compared to Turkey. Kosovo, the smallest state, for instance, has an economy the size of the south-eastern Turkish province, Sanliurfa, which ranks in the middle among Turkey's eighty-one provinces in terms of economic output. Demographically, too, these are small states. The largest, Serbia, had a population of 7 million in 2018, which is slightly larger than Istanbul's Anatolian suburbs. Just as East Africa – with its weak Muslim states – provides an arena for power competition between Turkey and its Middle Eastern rivals, the Western Balkans region – with its small and Muslim-populated states (none of which are EU members yet) – provides a similar arena for competition, this time between Turkey and Europe.

With Turkey's EU prospects dwindling, Ankara and Brussels increasingly perceive each other as competitors in the Balkans, with Erdogan considering the Western Balkans a target for his foreign policy. History works well in Erdogan's favour: this region was under Ottoman control for hundreds of years. Macedonia, for instance, was under Ottoman rule for almost two centuries longer than parts of modern Turkey, particularly the country's eastern provinces. The Balkan states were shaped politically and culturally by an Ottoman legacy due to their proximity to Istanbul.

Turkey and the Western Balkans also share deep religious ties. Excluding a period of Turkish colonisation in the fourteenth and fifteenth centuries, Islam spread on the peninsula under Ottoman rule, predominantly via voluntary conversions. Accordingly, today, Kosovo's population is over 90 per cent Muslim. Bosnia is on the cusp of becoming Muslim-majority. Albania, which has many non-religious citizens (a legacy of it being the world's only formally atheist state under communism) and a large number of intermarriages between its Catholic and Orthodox Christians, Sunni and Bektashi Muslim citizens – the latter, a community of liberal Muslims related to the Alevis in Turkey – is nominally Muslim-majority.

Two other states in this region, Macedonia and Montenegro, have sizable Muslim populations, constituting nearly 40 and 20 per cent of their populations, respectively. Although Serbia has a smaller Muslim population than the rest of the Balkan states, it is not an EU member and has, therefore, also started to enter Turkey's sphere of influence.

If Erdogan (and Davutoglu) can take credit for almost singlehandedly building Turkey's influence in East Africa, historic credit for the same feat in the Western Balkans goes to the Ottoman sultans and Turkish leaders in the 1990s. Nearly half a millennium of Ottoman rule and amalgamation of Turks and Balkan Muslims in the peninsula has produced a pro-Turkish outlook among its Muslim communities – and a pro-Balkans outlook in Turkey. (Obviously, the reverse is true between Christian Balkans and Turkey, where nineteenth-century conflicts between Christian Balkan nations and the sultans have left a legacy of mostly negative mutual perceptions.)

Ankara has always maintained a regional interest in the peninsula since the fall of the Ottoman Empire, signing the Balkan Pact with Greece, Romania and Yugoslavia in 1934. Turkey also accepted Albanians, Bosnians, Macedonian Muslims and Turks expelled from Yugoslavia in the 1950s after the rise of Tito and communism there, and pushed back against Bulgaria to remedy the plight of that country's Muslim community when they faced a communist government-led campaign in 1989 to change Muslim and Turkish names to Christian and Bulgarian ones.

National security concerns and a shared Ottoman heritage alike played a role in shaping Turkey's policies towards the Balkans. Accordingly, Ankara worked tirelessly to help the Bosnian Muslims during the Bosnian War of 1992–5. Ankara also supported NATO efforts to end the conflict between Serbia and Kosovo, which resulted in the Albanian-majority Kosovar independence in 2008. After the violent fall of Yugoslavia in 1992, Turkey played an integral role in conflict resolution through NATO, and joined the Peace Implementation Council after the Dayton Accords in 1995, guaranteeing peace in Bosnia. In the contest to introduce Islam publicly in post-communist states in the Balkans in the 1990s, thanks to historic affinities stretching to the Ottoman Empire, Turkey and its government office for religion, the Diyanet, successfully pushed back against Saudi Arabian attempts that relied on a brand of Salafi Islam.

Also in the 1990s, Turkish businesses moved in vigorously to establish networks and build up influence in the peninsula, boosting

Turkish–Balkan relations. However, Turkish–Balkan relations are 'not just [about] defense and diplomacy as before, but also [about] trade, investment, infrastructure development, energy, tourism, and popular culture'.[2] For instance, the Turkish Cooperation and Coordination Agency (TIKA) opened offices in Bosnia and Herzegovina as early as 1992, during the war in Bosnia,[3] and Turkish businesses established Bosnia's highest-ranked private university in 2004.[4] Furthermore, Ankara promptly recognised Macedonia after its independence and was the first country to send an ambassador to Skopje, providing Macedonia with political support as well as defence cooperation against Greece, which until 2019 refused to recognise Macedonia under that name.[5] These strategic steps augmented Turkish influence in the Western Balkans.

Erdogan and Davutoglu deserve credit for further building Turkish influence in the Western Balkans during the first decade of the twenty-first century. In 2009, Davutoglu, who was the foreign minister at the time, delivered a keynote speech in Sarajevo, entitled, 'Ottoman Legacy and Balkan Communities Today', which outlined Turkey's commitment to Balkan Muslims.[6] During a trip to the country in 2017, Erdogan declared on Albanian national TV: 'I don't know how many investments have arrived from the EU, but ours will not stop,' after stating that Ankara had invested €3 billion in the country.[7] It was under Erdogan's administration that Albania's national airline became a 49 per cent-owned subsidiary of Turkish Airlines, and Turkey's leading airport management firm, TAV, began operating two airports in Macedonia.

Driven by Erdogan's ambitions and economic growth, Turkish businesses popped up all over the Western Balkans and across the rest of the peninsula. Ankara also pursued rapprochement with Serbia, the largest state in the Western Balkans region, in order to overcome political differences with Belgrade rooted in the Yugoslav Wars of the 1990s – Belgrade opposed Ankara's policies in the 1990s that helped Bosnian and Kosovar independence. To build bridges with Serbia, Turkish President Abdullah Gul visited Belgrade in 2009.

Offsetting Middle Eastern losses

In recent years, Erdogan has started investing more time in cultivating Turkish ties in the Western Balkan states. His visits to the region have increased. After becoming president in 2014, for instance, he visited Albania and Bosnia in 2015, Croatia in 2016, Serbia in 2017 and Bosnia again in 2018.[8] Erdogan's recent pivot to the peninsula is driven by two goals. His first goal is to build stronger economic and political ties there in order to compete against the EU and to demonstrate to key European leaders, such as Angela Merkel (who boycotted Erdogan during the 2017 Turkish referendum by refusing pro-AKP election rallies in Germany), that 'Erdogan *is* welcome in Europe.'

A second goal of his Western Balkans pivot is to establish deeper connections with Muslim communities in order to build Turkish power. He may have failed in the Middle East, but he has not given up his goal to make Turkey great again by and through influencing Muslims and populations in former Ottoman lands.

Accordingly, he has even approached a historically unlikely partner: Serbia. In October 2017, Erdogan made an official visit to Belgrade and delivered a speech at Novi Pazar, a Serbian town with a large Bosnian Muslim community and centre of the historically Muslim region of Sandzak (Sancak).[9] Tantalised by Turkey's economic power, Belgrade reciprocated. Serbian Foreign Minister Ivica Dacic even sang Serbian folk songs for Erdogan at a bilateral banquet during the visit.[10] One month later, on 11 November 2017, Bosnian, Serbian and Turkish foreign ministers held a historic trilateral meeting, a continuation of a diplomatic effort initiated by Davutoglu in 2010.[11] This event was another sign of Ankara's ability to bring its Western Balkan partners together, and the result of Turkish opportunism, cooperating with the two other countries as all three sought to join the EU.

Despite recent successes, however, Erdogan's opening to the Balkans suffers from the fact that 'in the wider region, Turkey continues to be perceived as a patron of the local ethnic groups [usually of Muslim or Turkish extraction] rather than an impartial broker'.[12] In addition, it is yet to be seen if the Western Balkan embrace of Erdogan is genuine, or if this is the political equivalent of embracing a rich uncle bringing gifts. Finally, Erdogan needs to remember that Muslim societies in the Balkans are deeply secular due to the legacy of communism and the legacy of syncretic and an open approach to Islam under the Ottomans – a case in point being Albanian Bektashis and Bulgarian Alevis, both liberal Muslim communities. Turkey's soft power in the region will decrease, not increase, if Erdogan injects more religion into politics at home. In this regard, the 2019 backlash against a massive Turkish-built mosque in Kosovo's capital, Pristina, is another case in point.[13]

At the same time, and on the positive side, Turkey contributes troops to 'Operation Althea', the EU's peacekeeping mission in Bosnia, formally known as European Union Force (EUFOR) Bosnia and Herzegovina. In the big picture, Ankara's inclusion in the EU's Common Security and Defense Policy (CSDP), together with CDSP initiatives elsewhere, previously active in the Congo and Chad for example, suggests that even if Turkey's political ties with the EU are under stress and while Brussels and Ankara compete for influence in the Balkans, Turkey and the EU will continue to cooperate on other areas, including defence.

Central Asia: Where Turks and 'other Turks' do not speak the same language

A second Eurasian region into which Erdogan has recently made stronger forays is Central Asia. Once again, he has benefited from ties established by previous Turkish leaders in this region, but here he also had to fix some recent problems.

After the fall of the Soviet Union in the 1990s, Turkish businesses and diplomats moved into the newly independent states in the southern Caucasus and Central Asia, in the same way as they had done in the Balkans. Although Turkey recognised Armenia, together with all of the other republics emerging from the former Soviet Union in 1991, Ankara has refused to establish diplomatic ties with Armenia, saying that the latter fails to recognise the Turkish–Armenian border. Therefore, excluding Armenia, Turkey bolstered ties with two other states in the southern Caucasus, namely Azerbaijan (by taking advantage of linguistic similarities and political affinities) and Georgia (explained in the next part). However, in Central Asia, this pivot produced less than stellar results. Although many of the states in this region initially welcomed Turkish businesses and diplomats (and the Gulen movement), the welcome soon wore out.

The Turks' view of Central Asian republics played a role in this process. Turkish is part of the Turkic language family, which is generally divided into three distinct geographic clusters: 'Western' (Oghuz), including Azerbaijani, Turkish, Turkmen, as well as Gagauz, spoken by Orthodox Turks in Moldova and Bulgaria; 'Eastern' (Chagatai), including Uzbek and Uyghur, among others; and 'Northern' (Kipchak), including Bashkir, Kazakh, Kyrgyz and Tatar. (Yakut, spoken in Siberia, is considered a separate group of its own.) Like other geographic clusters within language families, such as the Romance languages on the Iberian Peninsula, Germanic languages in Scandinavia or South Slavic languages in the Balkans, there is a great degree of mutual intelligibility – dialect continuum – *within* the clusters of the Turkic family, but less so *across* clusters.

Surprisingly, this was a little known fact to many of Turkey's citizens when Ankara started pivoting towards Central Asia in the 1990s. Turkish historiography treats more than a dozen Turkic idioms spread across distinct Turkic clusters not as languages, but as 'dialects of Turkish', and speakers of Central Asian languages as 'ethnicities of the Turkish nation'. Accordingly, when Turkish diplomats and businesspeople arrived in Central Asia, they had an air of cultural superiority about them, which ultimately backfired. Central Asians, who had suffered under claims of Russian cultural superiority for over a century, saw no reason to accept similar assertions made under a different nation's identity construct, even if that nation was a closer relative in an ethnic sense.

Furthermore, occasional dishonest business practices by Turkish companies – often bringing in low-quality products, missing payments and defaulting on contracts – also eroded Ankara's soft-power appeal in the region. Even more importantly, its meddling in the internal affairs of the Central Asian republics – Ankara even allegedly played a role in trying to orchestrate a failed coup against Uzbek President Islam Karimov in 1999 – eroded favourable Central Asian attitudes.

Rising Russia and suspicious views towards political Islam

After Putin came to power in Moscow in 1999, Russia refocused its energies on Central Asia, soon eclipsing Ankara in the region, further limiting Turkish influence. Simultaneously, Central Asian leaders have cooled to Turkey after Erdogan's rise to power in 2003. These leaders, shaped by Soviet secularism and communist progressivism, do not identify with Erdogan's brand of political Islam and also take issue with his targeting of Ataturk's legacy and secularism in Turkey.

Erdogan had his own vision of politics, which also undermined Turkey's relations. Although he formally paid lip service to Central Asia as part of Davutoglu's Strategic Depth policy, the region actually ranked low among his foreign policy priorities. For instance, between 2004 and 2014, by my count, Erdogan made fifteen visits to Iran and Syria alone, but only nine visits to the four Turkic countries of Central Asia, as well as Tajikistan, whose dominant language is a variant of Persian.

Erdogan's Central Asian pivot

However, recently, Erdogan has started to pay more attention to this region, for instance by increasing the number of his visits there. This is because, after a Middle East failure, Erdogan sees Central Asia as another low-hanging fruit of his foreign policy.

To this end, he has made up with Uzbekistan, Central Asia's most populous country. The death of Uzbek leader Islam Karimov in 2016 presented him with this opportunity.[14] Erdogan's visit to Uzbekistan's new leader, Shavkat Mirziyoyev, in May 2018, resulted in visa-free travel for Turkish citizens as a token of rapprochememt.[15] The region's leaders, too, seemed eager to embrace Erdogan, a development that, among other reasons, appears to be linked to Erdogan's rising sultan-like image in Turkey, and Central Asia's own rising ostentatious culture of leader-worship and authoritarian style of government, which dominates across the region. Take for instance, Turkmenistan's leader, Gurbanguly Berdymukhamedov, who recently released a tape of him lifting a golden bar during a cabinet meeting, with his top aides cheering him.[16] Not surprisingly, Berdymukhamedov received Turkish Foreign Minister Mevlut Cavusoglu warmly during the latter's visit to the Turkmen capital, Ashgabat, on 9 November 2018.[17]

Warming ties between Erdogan and Putin, too, have encouraged the Central Asian leaders to welcome Erdogan. The Central Asian leaders now appreciated that they would not be upsetting Moscow, a regional hegemon, if they were shaking Ankara's hand a bit too strongly. To this end, Erdogan's participation in the Astana Peace Process, organised by Kazakh leader Nursultan Nazarbayev to find a political solution to the Syrian war, encapsulates a new driver of Ankara-Central Asia relations: good Erdogan–Putin ties help Central Asian leaders warm up to Erdogan and vice versa.

Erdogan's newfound sway in the region has allowed him to crack down on Gulenist networks through his relationships with regional leaders. Following the failed coup attempt in Ankara in 2016, Tajikistan and Turkmenistan shut down Gulenist networks at Erdogan's request (weary of all Islamic networks, ultra-secularist Uzbekistan had banned Gulenist networks in early 1997, as had Russia in 2004). Erdogan's recent warm welcome in Central Asia notwithstanding, Moscow, which calls most of the shots in this region, is the main regional hegemon, though Chinese influence in the region is also rising, and the United States has some leverage across Central Asia as well.

Going forward, the Turkic Council, spearheaded by Turkey in 2009, could provide Erdogan with additional leverage over Central Asia and Azerbaijan. Currently, in addition to Turkey, Azerbaijan, Kazakhstan, Kirgizstan and Turkmenistan are members of this council. Uzbekistan declared in 2018 that it would join the organisation. The Council is the only international forum bringing together Turkey and the Turkic states, but excluding Russia and other powers, providing Ankara with a unique platform.

Favourite Christian neighbours

Russia is a hegemon along the Black Sea Basin, although Ankara is able to take better advantage of the dynamics there. Of Turkey's twelve neighbours, five lie around the Black Sea: Bulgaria, Georgia, Romania, Russia and Ukraine. These countries, together with Turkey, encircle the Black Sea, which is a closed body of water, with limited access by international law to non-littoral states.

To summarise Turkey's location on a map of cultural geography, four of Turkey's neighbours (Azerbaijan, Iran, Iraq and Syria – five with the TRNC) are predominantly Muslim and eight are predominantly Christian (Armenia, Bulgaria, Cyprus, Georgia, Greece, Romania, Russia and

Ukraine). With the exception of Russia, Turkey gets along well with all of its Black Sea neighbours – all of them Christian-majority.

It is clear that religion does not shape the Turks' view of their neighbours. In fact, more than faith, historical dynamics play a greater key role in moulding Turkey's ties with its neighbours, including the Christian-majority ones. Enter the collapse of the Ottoman Empire during the First World War and events since then.

During this period, among the country's current neighbours, Bulgaria was an Ottoman ally, while Turkish troops fought against neighbouring Greece and Russia. Ankara then fought against Greece (again) and Armenia during Ataturk's campaign of 1919–22 to liberate Turkey from Armenian, French, Greek and Allied occupation.

Along with the 1974 war in Cyprus, this twentieth-century past left a bitter legacy of mutual hostility between Turkey and Greece, Russia, Armenia and the Greek half of Cyprus. This legacy has been perpetuated in popular culture (film, TV, art and literature) and the education system. Many of the country's citizens, who study a curriculum of nationalist historiography and spend hundreds of hours a year learning Turkey's twentieth-century conflicts, often nurture a fresh memory of resentment towards these countries, a sentiment citizens in these countries often reciprocate towards Turkey.

With the exception of Russia, hostile sentiments among Turkey's citizens towards their Black Sea neighbours are not significant. In fact, many of Turkey's citizens view Bulgaria, Romania, Georgia, Ukraine and nearby Moldova in a mostly benign way due to a lack of conflicts with them during the First World War or later. Overall, recent Turkish history has shaped a friendlier public attitude towards Sofia, Bucharest, Tbilisi, Kiev and Chisinau than towards Athens, Moscow, Yerevan or Nicosia.

During the Cold War, Turkey's ties with its Black Sea neighbours suffered from the impact of global conflict – Ankara was the only non-communist Black Sea littoral state during that period. Sofia and Ankara were especially hostile towards each other in this period. Cold War tensions, including Bulgaria's aforementioned campaign to assimilate its Turkish and Muslim community by forcefully changing their names, resulted in severe tensions between Ankara and Sofia in 1989.

The end of the Cold War, however, presented a chance to turn a new page in Turkey's ties with Sofia and its other northern neighbours, formerly under communist control. Ankara has tried to leverage historically good ties with this region, spearheaded the aforementioned Black Sea Economic Cooperation (BSEC) in the 1990s.

Relations have improved since then. Wide freedoms and liberties currently enjoyed by Turkic and Muslim communities in Turkey's Black Sea neighbours (Turks, Bulgarian Muslims and Roma in Bulgaria; Crimean Tatars and Turks in Romania; Muslim Georgians [Adjara] in Georgia; Crimean Tatars in Ukraine's Crimean Peninsula, which is currently under Russian occupation; and Gagauz in Moldova) cast those neighbours in an increased positive light in Ankara's eyes.

Increased trade and tourism contacts have been a major catalyst for warming ties. In 2017, the four Black Sea nations, namely Georgians, Bulgarians, Ukrainians and Romanians, ranked fourth, fifth, seventh and fourteenth, respectively, among the top fifteen countries sending visitors to Turkey.[18] Whereas Davutoglu aimed to create a 'Shamgen [travel] Zone', uniting Turkey and the Arab Levant, it appears that Turkey has already and effectively created a 'Black Sea Zone' with its neighbours to the north, thanks to the forces of history – and the 'antibody of Russia'.

The Black Sea: A Turkish–Russian condominium

The 1936 Montreux Treaty, which regulates access to the Black Sea, is a sacred document of sorts in Turkey. In addition to Lausanne (Lozan) Square, celebrating Turkey's founding document, the country's third largest city, Izmir, also boasts a Montreux (Montrö) Square, testifying to the equivalent significance of this treaty in shaping modern Turkey's identity.

Ask any Turkish diplomat their views on this treaty and they will tell you it should never be changed or modified – because of how favourable it is to Ankara in the Black Sea.

The sole maritime access to the Black Sea is through Istanbul. Montreux allows free naval access to the Black Sea only for littoral states, and forbids non-littoral states from maintaining a permanent naval presence in the sea. It also restricts the time and tonnage of battleships that non-Black Sea nations can keep in the sea for temporary periods (the weight limitation for these states to sail in the Black Sea can be as low as 15,000 tons, limiting a naval presence to two or three surface combatants). Therefore, effectively, all five Black Sea coastal states (Bulgaria, Georgia, Romania, Russia, Ukraine and Turkey) share it militarily. However, considering that Bulgaria, Georgia, Romania and Ukraine have relatively small navies (Tbilisi's maritime force consists of mostly coast-guard boats), the Black Sea is effectively a maritime condominium, shared by Turkey and Russia.

Taking into account the Russian behemoth to Turkey's north, the Montreux Treaty shapes Ankara's view of its northern neighbours, other than Russia. Accordingly, since the end of the Cold War, Turkey has courted them to build influence around the Black Sea against Moscow. Under Erdogan, Turkish ties with these states have improved considerably. Turkish businesses are currently one of the largest investors in Romania, with figures surpassing $6 billion dollars as of early 2019.[19] Erdogan opened the Baku–Tbilisi–Kars railway with Georgia in October 2017, and increased connectivity in June 2018, by inaugurating TANAP.

Ankara's ties with Tbilisi have especially boomed in recent years, with the two countries even eliminating passport requirements for bilateral visits. Turkish and Georgian citizens can visit each other's country with just their national ID cards. This has led to a boom in tourism and cultural and social visits, and in citizens simply driving across the border for shopping – a model of economic integration also witnessed in the EU. In 2017, over 2 million Georgians visited Turkey, which is nearly half of Georgia's population of 5 million that year.[20]

Crimean conundrum

In reaching out to its Black Sea neighbours, however, Erdogan has been careful not to upset Putin. For instance, when Russia invaded Georgia in 2008, Ankara stayed out of the conflict and did not take Tbilisi's side. Similarly, when Putin annexed Crimea from Ukraine in 2014, Turkey did not rush to criticise Russia, instead choosing to engage on behalf of the Tatars behind the scenes, although these efforts failed to produce results favourable to the Tatars.[21]

The Crimean issue is important to Turkey for a number of reasons. Crimea lies only 270 kilometres (168 miles) from the Anatolian coastline across the Black Sea, and is home to an autochthonous community of Turkic Tatars, who are ethnic and linguistic kin of Turks. Unlike the Tatar language spoken along the Volga River, deep inside Russia, some varieties of the Tatar language spoken along the Crimea's coast are mostly mutually understandable with Turkish.

In addition to historic (the Crimean Khanate joined the Ottoman Empire as a commonwealth and not as an invaded territory) and linguistic ones, ethnic ties also bind Turks and Crimean Tatars. After the Russian tsars occupied the Crimea in 1783, they persecuted and harassed the peninsula's Tatar community, forcing many to emigrate to the Ottoman Empire. Today, Turkey boasts a sizable Tatar diaspora, estimated in the millions. In 1944, Stalin deported the remaining Tatars in the peninsula to Central Asia and other parts of the Soviet Union, and Tatars were the only Soviet nationality not allowed to repatriate to their homeland after his death. Many Tatars returned to Crimea, which became part of independent Ukraine, only after the fall of communism in the 1990s.[22] Russia's arrival in the Crimea as a hegemon threatens Tatars repatriation prospects to their homeland and many again fear persecution. Ankara, therefore, opposes Moscow's annexation of the peninsula.

At the same time, Turkey's dependence on Russia for nearly half of its natural gas imports, historic fears regarding Moscow and Erdogan's desire to get along with Putin in order to secure deals on pipelines and Syria with him have tempered Ankara's reaction to Moscow's takeover of Crimea. This is consistent with Erdogan's policy of compartmentalising Ankara's relationship with Putin: agreeing to disagree (as in Syria after 2016), and instead focusing on areas of overlapping interest.

However, even then, Russia's annexation of Crimea and the build-up of the Russian military and navy in the Black Sea through the deployment of strategic bombers, cruise missiles, new ships and submarines, have changed the balance of power in the Black Sea. Erdogan, who will not confront Putin directly on Crimea, has, therefore, quietly remained steadfast in his support for the Tatars. To this end, he convinced Moscow to send imprisoned Crimean Tatar leadership from Crimea to Turkey in 2017.[23]

Politics of resentment

Around the Black Sea, in addition to Tatars, Ankara also takes an active interest in Bulgaria's Turkish and other Muslim communities, who accounted for nearly 10 per cent of Bulgaria's population in the 2011 national census. After the fall of communism, Bulgaria's Muslim community, composed of Turks, Roma and ethnic Bulgarian Muslims (Pomaks), some of whom consider themselves Turks due to their shared religion, organised the Movement for Rights and Freedoms (DPS). This party, which has generally stood at arm's length from Ankara, represents the interests of Bulgaria's Turks and Muslims, and has participated in successive governments in Sofia.

A key element of Erdogan's policy in recent years has been to support the formation of pro-Turkey political parties in Europe, including the autochthonous Turkish communities in the Balkans and within Western Europe's more recently established Turkish diaspora.

In 2015, a number of DPS deputies in Bulgaria left their party, criticising its leadership for failing to support Turkey over the controversy between Ankara and Moscow regarding Turkey's 2015 shooting down of a Russian plane that had violated its airspace from Syria. These deputies then formed the Democrats for Responsibility Solidarity and Tolerance (DOST, as previously noted, the party's Bulgarian-language initials mean 'friend' in Turkish), an openly pro-Erdogan and pro-Ankara faction.

DOST entered Bulgaria's 2017 elections as a competing faction against the DPS. Although it failed to win seats in Bulgaria's Parliament, it did poach votes from the DPS, whose electoral support dropped in the Bulgarian elections from 14.8 per cent in 2014 to 9 per cent in 2017.[24] In 2017, DOST coalesced with another DPS splinter faction, the National Freedom and Dignity Party (NPSD), led by Kasim Dal, an acquaintance of Erdogan's since the early 1990s, to present a more formidable challenge to the DPS in the future.[25]

In the Netherlands, Erdogan found a similar opening to feed on politics of resentment, when two Turkish deputies of the Social Democratic Labour Party did not agree with their party's integration policy.[26] With Ankara's support, these deputies organised a new faction, the DENK (Dutch for 'think' and Turkish for 'equality'), which entered Holland's 2017 parliamentary elections as an independent party. This new pro-Erdogan force won 2.1 per cent of the vote and sent three deputies to the Dutch Parliament. Along with similar parties in Germany and Denmark, the increase in pro-Erdogan Turkish parties across Europe, which feed on bitterness towards Europe, represents an ever-growing political trend: Turkey and many Turks have a love–hate relationship with Europe.

The Erdogan reign in Turkey can be seen as just another episode of Turkey's centuries-old love–hate relationship with Europe (and the West), in which Turkey is simply reacting to the West in order to seek glory. However, unlike twentieth-century Kemalists or late Ottoman sultans, Erdogan resents the West more than he wants to embrace it.

16

TURKEY AND THE WEST

A NEVER-ENDING LOVE AFFAIR

The failed coup has given birth to a new Turkey – and a new Erdogan

Recently rising resentment in Erdogan's rhetoric and policies towards Europe is not accidental. The failed coup in 2016 has invigorated nativist forces in Turkey. This makes it more challenging for the country's Western allies to keep Ankara on their side.

Davutoglu's firing in May 2016, formally concluded the 'Zero Problems with Neighbours' and 'Strategic Depth' policies his foreign ministerial and prime ministerial tenures had represented. Erdogan now had the opportunity to reemphasise Turkey's ties with the West, but he instead started normalising ties with Russia, ties which had suffered due to the two sides being pitted against each other in the Syrian Civil War.

In June 2016, Erdogan wrote Putin a letter, expressing regrets about Turkey' downing of a Russian jet fighter in November 2015. During the same month, Erdogan and Putin spoke by telephone for the first time after the Russian plane incident. When the coup plotters struck in Turkey, on 15 July 2016, just over a month after Erdogan's letter, Putin was the first leader to call the Turkish leader. Conversely, Turkey's Western allies took days, and sometimes weeks, to offer Erdogan condolences and support. This only encouraged Turkey's upward trajectory with Russia and its downward trajectory with Europe and the United States.

It was not the only impact that the coup attempt had on Turkish–Western ties. On 15 July 2016, Turkey witnessed two consecutive historic developments: the botched coup attempt to oust Erdogan and a political Islamist counter-revolution that blocked the coup. Subsequently, the ideology of political Islam shrouded Turkey to an extent never witnessed before.

As soon as news of the putsch attempt surfaced, Erdogan appeared on FaceTime, appealing to his conservative base to save him. Mobilised by loudspeaker broadcasts from Turkey's nearly 80,000 mosques, thousands of conservative Turks, among them large segments of political Islamists, took to the streets to block the putschists, going so far as to lie under tanks to save Erdogan. Opposition parties in Parliament also swiftly responded to support Erdogan, adding liberals, leftists and nationalists to the coalition of opponents of the coup.

Erdogan was traumatised by the coup – the putschists could have killed him. He knows that his supporters saved his life. This perception has moved political Islam to a more central role in Erdogan's thinking.

Crisis with Europe

Until the coup attempt, Erdogan outwardly maintained Turkey's traditionally strong ties with the West, while simultaneously pursuing his dream of making Turkey a Muslim power, capable of defying the West when personal interests did not align. Following the coup, Erdogan became more vocally anti-European and anti-US. A case in point is his foreign policy towards Europe in the aftermath of the coup, and in the run-up to the April 2017 Turkish constitutional referendum. When various European governments, such as Germany, refused to allow Erdogan and AKP officials to conduct rallies to mobilise support among the Turkish diaspora in Europe for the vote, which aimed to significantly increase Erdogan's executive powers, he lashed out at Berlin, by stating: 'I thought it was a long time since Germany left [Nazi practices]. We are mistaken.'[1] Coupled with similarly incendiary comments targeting other European countries, such as Austria and Netherlands, this threw Turkish–European ties into their worst tailspin in recent memory.

Oldest European embassy in Turkey

In this regard, tensions between Ankara and The Hague are especially telling. Nearly a month before the 2017 referendum, the Dutch Government barred AKP ministers of government from entering the country to hold political rallies. Dutch Prime Minister Mark Rutte's decision to block these rallies came at a time when his own post was being contested by the anti-Islam Dutch politician, Geert Wilders, in Holland's general elections, scheduled to be held on 15 March 2017. Most notably, Rutte refused landing rights for Turkish Foreign Minister Mevlut Cavusoglu's plane. Nevertheless, Turkish Minister of Family and Social Policies Fatma Betul Sayan Kaya illegally entered the Netherlands through Germany, in the car of a Turkish diplomat. She was later expelled from the Netherlands.

Erdogan responded by expelling the Dutch ambassador in Turkey, alleging that the Netherlands was acting like a 'banana republic', and then calling for sanctions against The Hague.[2] He added, threatening: 'If Europe continues this way, no European in any part of the world can walk safely on the streets.'[3]

The breakdown of Ankara's ties with The Hague is a complete anomaly in the context of hundreds of years of Turkish history, shedding light on the newly potent anti-Western and anti-European forces that seem to guide Erdogan's thinking. Established in 1612 in the Ottoman Empire, the Dutch embassy is the oldest permanent European embassy in Turkey, underlining excellent historic ties between the Turks and the Dutch for over four centuries – until Erdogan.

The opening of a permanent Dutch mission in Istanbul in the early seventeenth century not only sheds light on the friendly roots of Ottoman–European relations, but also debunks the shared view of political Islam and the European far right, of history being a Manichean Muslim vs Christian affair. As Europe fell into Catholic–Protestant wars in the sixteenth century, Ottoman leaders shrewdly forged strong ties with the new Protestant powers, including the Netherlands, Britain, Denmark and Sweden so as to undermine their main adversaries, all of whom happened to be Catholic powers at the time. These were namely the Papal States, Venice and the Habsburgs. The Ottoman leadership also responded to the Protestant powers' mercantilist overtures to balance against Venice and Habsburgs.

The Hapsburgs, with their often united, or allied, Spanish and Austrian houses, presented the major obstacle to further Ottoman expansion into Europe at the time, by land and at sea.[4] With Madrid and Vienna being the Ottomans' main European adversary, the sultans eagerly extended an olive branch to the Dutch republic in 1581, after the United Provinces gained independence form the Hapsburg Empire in a revolt.

The Ottomans, strategically continuing their courtships, also invited other rising Protestant nations to open permanent embassies in Istanbul. The Swedes and British soon followed course. This legacy of a warm Ottoman welcome to Christian powers in Europe fundamentally undermines the Kemalist narrative, which Turkey's political Islamists have wrongly internalised, that the Ottoman Empire was a religious state with policies rigidly shaped by Islam. On the contrary, Ottomans were comfortable having ties with Christian powers in Europe at a time when these Christian powers did not have peaceful ties with each other. Poignantly, the Dutch mission in Istanbul, a 'Christian embassy' established in a 'Muslim country', was opened at least three decades before the 1648 Westphalian Peace, which put an end to religious wars in Europe.

Even Erdogan knows Turkey needs the West financially

The breakdown with the Dutch notwithstanding, Erdogan's anti-Western animus has its limits, especially beyond election years. This is because he knows that as a recourse poor country, Turkey needs Western money to grow, and he in order to win further elections on his platform of economic prosperity.

Erdogan also knows that Turkey needs to have good ties with either the United States or Europe to continue attracting Western money. Accordingly, during the 'Brunson Crisis' with the United States in September 2018, as Turkey's ties with Washington collapsed and the country's economy plunged into a crisis, Erdogan launched a charm offensive towards Europe. His goal: to immediately, shift Ankara's geostrategic position in order to maintain at least one of the two anchors that tie Turkey and its economy to the Western financial markets. Only days after Trump slapped sanctions against ministers in Erdogan's cabinet and announced tariffs targeting Turkish products, Erdogan allowed The Hague to reinstate its ambassador in Ankara.

'Closet Kemalist'

Turkey's European friends and Washington still have some political leverage in Ankara, also beyond financial ties. Having been raised in Kemalist Turkey, Erdogan is a 'closet Kemalist' and is still as equally excited as Ataturk and his predecessors, the late Ottoman sultans, by a desire to be recognised by the West as an equal partner.

Not just Erdogan, but also many of Turkey's citizens have a love–hate relationship with the West: they want to be as good as it is, but not necessarily come under its power. Despite Erdogan's nearly two-decade-long anti-Western rhetoric and refashioning of Turkey as a nativist society,

> many of Turkey's citizens still see their country as an integral part of the West, and not the 'East' (Arab countries or Iran) or 'North' (Russia). The Customs Union with the EU, security of NATO membership, and the cultural disposition of much of the population (including mainly the 50 percent who do not vote for Erdogan, but also many of his supporters) all position Turkey inextricably towards the West; it is their reference point. Turkey's citizens are not jealous of, nor do they admire, or want to be accepted by Russia, China, Iran, or the Arab world. However, their track record shows that they are indeed jealous of, admire, or want to be part of the West. Be that as it may, Turks' insecurities as a Muslim-majority population with historic ties to the West in the post-September 11 world, Turkey's geographic location, and Turks' transactional view of foreign policy means their relations with the West is anguished at the best of times.[5]

Turkey's 'choice'

Turkey really does not have a 'choice'. In the best-case scenario for the West, it is a status quo country wedded to the West in many ways: 'In the worst-case scenario, Turkey's weighing of "which alliance to join" is transactional, like Italy's decision to enter World War One on the side of the Allies based on which side would provide it with the most goodies.'[6] Ankara cannot ally with Tehran or Moscow because those powers, in near proximity to Ankara, are anti-status quo states, with unapologetic imperial foreign policy agendas, out to become strong at the expense of everyone else, including Turkey. Erdogan is well aware of this. Turkey's Western allies should depict Erdogan's deals with Putin and Syria as ad hoc decisions, not at all his strategic vision to come under Russian influence or become its 'ally'.

Muslim de Gaulle

This conclusion does not mean that Erdogan is simply ready to come under the Western mantle, or to abandon his mission to make Turkey great again by and through influencing Muslims and confronting the West when necessary. Erdogan will continue to cast Turkey as an activist and autonomous power in the Middle East and across Muslim-majority countries beyond, for instance, by sending troops overseas to create its own footprint. Operation Euphrates Shield (in Jarablus, Syria), Operation Olive Branch (in Afrin, Syria), the Turkish base in Bashiqa (near Mosul, Iraq), a proposed Turkish base on Cyprus, as well as other existing or planned Turkish bases and military installations in the Persian Gulf and East Africa (Qatar, Somalia and Sudan), are some examples of this trend. Erdogan will try to carve out a 'quasi-independent' role for Turkey within the West, but mostly as a stand-alone great power, with influence over the Middle East and other former Ottoman areas like the Western Balkans, often making Washington and Brussels unhappy. An analogy would be de Gaulle's foreign policy to make France a stand-alone power in the West in the 1960s.

Western views

The tendency would be to ascribe that parlous fate fully to Erdogan's 'Zero Problems' policy, but Turkey's Western partners played a leading role by playing fast and loose along Turkey's periphery (Iraq and Syria).

This began by first getting too bogged down in Iraq under Bush, then by pulling out too fast and too far under Obama, continued with the fiasco of Western intervention in Libya and reached a crescendo with zigzagging US and European policy in Syria. Therefore, the real problem is not that Ankara is joining the 'dark side'. Rather, that it is Turkey's geostrategic ambitions, residual great power dreams and other frictions with its 'Western vocation' put it on an inevitable course for occasional (though manageable) collision with the EU and the USA. As they formulate future policies towards Ankara, Brussels and Washington alike have to take into account the fact that Erdogan will not give up trying to make Turkey a stand-alone power.

'Strategic West' and Ankara

An additional challenge for Ankara's Western partners is that, unlike his predecessors, such as Ataturk, Menderes, Demlrel or Ozal, Erdogan does not see Turkey as part of the political or cultural West. The good news, however, is that Erdogan is aware that he needs the West financially, as well as in the security realm. Accordingly, while he may not see Turkey as part of the cultural or political fabric of the West, he is interested to see the country included in the 'Strategic West', which I define as the Venn diagram of the OECD and NATO member states. Erdogan benefits from the Strategic West, much like Polish politician Jarosław Kaczyński, a similarly illiberal and 'anti-Western' leader, who also embraces NATO to seek global and regional security.

NATO

The NATO transatlantic alliance is especially important in Erdogan's vision and perceptions. He will continue to treat NATO as a security outlet, in which he buys into certain NATO programmes and initiatives but not all of them. Poignantly, he does not want Turkey's membership in NATO to end. Brokering ad hoc Syria deals and pipeline bargains with Putin, Erdogan knows that he would be forced to fall completely under Russian influence without NATO's ironclad guarantees.

The US

Washington, for its own part, can increase its leverage in Ankara by showing that it is committed to Turkey's defence, by adopting policies alleviating Turkey's security concerns over the PKK and also by regarding its relationship with the YPG. Washington announced on 6 November 2018, a total $12 million reward for the capture of PKK leaders, Murat Karayilan, Cemil Bayik and Duran Kalkan, marking a positive step.[7] Another positive step was the 2018 deal the USA brokered with Ankara to secure the withdrawal by the YPG, PKK's ally, from the Manbij pocket in northern Syria. To further increase its leverage in Turkey, Washington needs to provide Ankara with ironclad guarantees against Russian aggression beyond those NATO already gives.

The US and Russia

A kneejerk reaction in the USA is threatening Ankara with sanctions to undermine its 'cosy' ties with Russia. In fact, however, any such sanctions are likely to serve Putin's ultimate goal of driving a deeper wedge between Ankara and Washington. Even more, sanctions, aimed at punishing Erdogan for his undemocratic or other transgressions, are, in fact, likely to help him, by fanning rampant anti-Americanism and can only boost his nativist base. Erdogan casts any pushback against Ankara as a pushback against himself and Turkey, repeating his message that he is going to, 'Make Turkey great again and Muslims proud,' and that his adversaries, who do not want to see Turks great and Muslims proud, are trying to undermine him. Consequently, anti-Turkey sanctions will only help boost his popularity at the ballot box.

For the moment, Ankara is an upset NATO ally, which often plays to Moscow's tune, but it is also deeply threatened by Moscow due to Russia's military deployments in Crimea, Armenia and Syria. The sheer military might of Russia scares Turkey: in 2016, Moscow simulated a nuclear attack against Istanbul from Crimea.[8]

To take advantage of this dynamic, Washington should start by providing Turkey with Unwavering. security guarantees. Erdogan was shocked in 2018 to find out that it was not certain that the US Congress would authorise the sale of US-made Patriot missile defence systems to Ankara if Turkey dropped its pursuit to buy the Russian-made S-400 missile defence system.

Second, Washington needs to demonstrate to Turkey, through its policies in Syria, that it will not pick the YPG over Ankara. Finally, and more importantly, through its public diplomacy outreach, Washington should remind the Turks and Erdogan how Russians view their country, as a: 'small, irritating' neighbour that has often been, and will continue to be, at the receiving end of Russia's might, and often punishing policies.

Europe

Europe also has leverage with Erdogan, to the extent that the EU and European countries recognise the depth and spread of their financial influence on Turkey.

Although Erdogan has increasingly cast Europe as Turkey's political 'other', he also knows that his success in winning elections since 2002 has largely been driven by the record amount of (mostly European) Foreign Direct Investment that Turkey has attracted. This foreign cash has mainly driven the country's growth, and this growth, in turn, has boosted Erdogan's voter base – many of his diehard fans are attracted to him because he has lifted them out of poverty.

With that said, European leverage in Turkey is coupled with Europe's financial exposure to the Turkish economy. An overwhelming majority of current Turkish debt (nearly 80 per cent) is owned by the banks in EU member states. For example, the exposure of Spanish and French banks to Turkish borrowing adds up to more than half of all Turkish foreign debt.[9] As such, any financial crisis in Turkey is bound to have significant shocks across Europe. In other words, regardless of their feelings for Erdogan, Europe literally cannot afford to see the Turkish economy collapse.

In this regard, Europe can leverage Turkey's continued reliance to fuel its economic growth. With few natural resources of its own, Turkey relies on the injection of capital from nearby countries and strong ties to international markets, especially those in Europe. This became visible when Trump slapped sanctions against Ankara in the summer of 2018: Erdogan immediately pivoted to Europe, launching an extensive charm offensive, while he toned down his anti-European rhetoric, a year after likening the Germans and the Dutch to Nazis, and picking fights with other European governments, including neighbouring Athens.

Erdogan was as quick to mend ties with European countries as he had been to undermine them. In August 2018, Ankara returned two Greek soldiers who had been imprisoned in Turkey since March 2018 because they had accidentally crossed the Greek–Turkish border.[10] The conflict was resolved with the Greek Prime Minister Alexis Tsipras on the sidelines of a NATO summit. Erdogan had kept the Greek soldiers in retaliation for Athens' refusal to extradite Turkish military officers who had fled to Greece in the aftermath of the failed 2016 coup – as of early 2019, they still have not been extradited.[11]

On 7 September 2018, the Netherlands and Turkey announced the appointment of their ambassadors, who had been withdrawn during the 2017 diplomatic crisis, in an effort to 'normalize bilateral relations'.[12] Later that month, Erdogan visited Berlin, reiterating during his meeting with Chancellor Angela Merkel, his desire for warmer relations and stated: 'We want to completely leave behind all the problems and to create a warm environment between Turkey and Germany – just like it used to be.'[13]

'Russia with Spain in it'

European countries have leverage in Turkey beyond Erdogan. I am often asked if Turkey is like Russia, and whether Erdogan wants to be Putin. While Erdogan wants to govern Turkey with a strong hand, the way Putin controls Russia, the fact is that Turkey is not like Russia.

Unlike Russia, which lacks a legacy of democracy and even the tradition of democratic elections, Turkey has had democratic elections since 1950, longer than that of Spain. In Russia, Putin has won majorities, sometimes reaching up to nearly 80 per cent of the electorate. In Turkey, despite his strongman tactics and nearly complete control of the media,[14] Erdogan barely crosses the 50 per cent threshold. Politics has remained competitive and opposition robust despite Erdogan's ability to dominate in the political sphere for nearly two decades.

The bottom line is that Turkey, a country of 82 million people, remains pluralistic and diverse, and is inherently democratic even under Erdogan, and its citizens opposing Erdogan represent a very sizable block. The citizens of Turkey who do not vote for Erdogan constitute a demographic mass nearly the size of Spain, whose population in 2018 stood at 46 million. What is more, Turkish provinces, which voted against Erdogan in the 2017 referendum that amended the country's constitution and allowed him to become an executive-style president, together represented 73 per cent of the GDP of Turkish economy. At current 2017 prices, this exceeds $1.5 trillion, nearing Spain's GDP of $1.8 trillion at the time.[15] Even if Erdogan's Turkey might look like Russia, it hosts 'Spain' in it.

In 2019, Turkey's EU accession talks were dead in all but name. To put it simply, no European capital sees Turkey becoming an EU member soon. The question is, will the EU and its member states call off the negotiations with Ankara entirely; or will they decide to preserve the talks in order to keep Turkey close to Europe, and send a positive signal to those in Turkish society, who are still fighting for reforms and freedoms despite Erdogan, the 'Spain inside Turkey'. I vote for the second option. Europe has leverage across Turkish society to the extent that it treats Ankara as a key ally and Turkey as a European country.

China vs Turkey

Erdogan probably votes for the second option above, as well. This is true since, following Turkey's 2018 currency crisis, he is aware that only Europe, the USA and the IMF, being the 'Strategic West', can *and* would come to Turkey's rescue in case of a financial meltdown. He is also aware that neither Russia nor Iran would be able to provide Turkey with the financial and foreign direct investment necessary to mitigate an economic crisis. In theory, China could do so, but Beijing has also been unwilling to help Turkey, and Erdogan. This is rooted in historic difference between the two countries regarding the status of Turkic Uyghurs in China's restless Xinjiang region.

During the 2018 'Brunson Crisis' with Washington, faced with tough US economic sanctions, a collapsing lira and the risk of an economic meltdown, Erdogan sent his foreign minister, Cavusoglu, to China to seek economic assistance.[16] The latter, unsurprisingly, returned to Ankara with empty hands.

This is surprising, as China has been courting Turkey and other Middle Eastern and European countries lately through its enticing Belt and Road Initiative (BRI). Beijing has provided soft loans to Ankara for infrastructure construction, such as helping build metro lines.[17] China's infrastructure investments through the BRI are at the core of its Turkey policy, and Ankara has repeatedly expressed the desire to benefit from the programme. Almost all Turkish ministries have developed action plans to boost ties with China, and the BRI became incorporated in the policy papers of Turkish bureaucracy.[18]

At the same time, however, Beijing sent Cavusoglu back to Ankara with no promise of financial help handed because China does not necessarily want to invest in Erdogan's political success. The root of this policy lies in Turkey's deep historic ties with the Turkic Uyghur community in the Xinjiang region in China's far west.[19] Xinjiang, previously known as Eastern Turkestan, was a nominal part, and occasionally a vassal state, of China's nineteenth-century Qing dynasty. Turkey's meddling in ties between the Uyghurs and the Chinese state dates back to that time, when Ottoman sultans instrumentalised Islam to spread their influence. For instance, in 1873, in return for recognition of his suzerainty, Sultan Abdulaziz sent the Uyghurs a shipment of weapons for use against the Qing emperors, who, at the time, were once again, trying to advance deep into Xinjiang, laying the foundations of a domination that would become completely formal and deeply entrenched only in the next century.[20] Neither Beijing nor Ankara has forgotten this history.

Following the 1911–12 Republican Revolution in China, Xinjiang became part of Sun Yat-sen's Republic of China as a restive region, still not completely subjugated by Beijing. Only following Mao's 1949 Communist Revolution, did the Turkic region become firmly and fully integrated into China. Subsequently, Mao initiated a crackdown of nationalist Uyghurs. Many fled in search of political asylum.

Turkey, a newly minted and committed US ally in the Cold War at the time, gladly welcomed its ethnic kin. This helped Ankara and Washington together to oppose and undermine a key US enemy in the Korean War as Ankara also fought in Korea alongside the USA and South Korea, providing a force of over 5,000 troops, under the UN forces umbrella, against the Chinese and North Koreans.

Meanwhile, faced with a communist crackdown, many Uyghurs subsequently fled to Turkey at Ankara's invitation, and soon thereafter, Turkey, and Istanbul in particular, became the global hub for Uyghur nationalists, which it remains to this day.[21]

Throughout the 1950s and 1960s, Ankara resettled thousands of Uyghurs with the support of the United States. Another wave of migrants arrived in the late 1970s, following post-Mao reforms. No official data is available on the number of Uyghurs in Turkey, but it is estimated that there are tens of thousands, many of them in a leadership role in the diaspora, they are well liked and respected by Turkey's foreign policy elites.[22] Linguistic affinities have helped. Although Uyghur is one of the most distant Turkic languages to Turkish geographically (Urumqi, the capital of Xinjiang is almost 4,828 kilometres, 3,000 miles, east of Istanbul), there is a surprisingly high level of mutual intelligibility between Turkish and Uyghur, more than that which exists between Turkish and other languages in the Eastern (Chagatai) branch of the Turkic language family, of which Uyghur is a member.

Ankara maintained a strong support for Uyghurs also under Erdogan, who in July 2009 called Chinese policies in Xinxjiang 'a genocide'.[23] In recent years, the Uyghur issue has emerged as the most serious political challenge to Chinese leader Xi Jinping, who has responded with a police-state-style crackdown on Uyghurs. He has sent hundreds of thousands from this community to 're-education camps' and initiated the mass surveillance of Uyghurs, with the help of smart phones, CCTV, the use of social media and high-tech eavesdropping mechanisms.[24]

Erdogan, however, has recently downplayed the Uyghur issue in the Turkish media, which he dominates and which today carries almost no stories pointing at the suffering of Turks' ethnic kin. With this policy, Erdogan is hoping to curry favour with China. Nevertheless, Uyghur activists are still known to meet regularly with Turkish government officials, and the Uyghur community in Turkey still sits at the centre of the global Uyghur diaspora.[25] Beijing is aware of the deep ties that exist between Uyghurs and Ankara, and will shy away from putting hundreds of billions of dollars in Turkey to help Erdogan in case of an economic meltdown in the country.

Erdogan needs the 'Strategic West'

With the chances of China coming to his assistance being low, Erdogan has a problem: Turkey remains exposed to economic and financial risks. The Turkish economy currently has the largest account deficit among OECD countries, amounting to somewhere between 5 and 7 per cent of its GDP. An energy-poor nation with an annual energy import bill of about $30 billion, Turkey needs tens of billions in foreign investment, or a hot cash flow each year to keep growing at a rate of over 4 per cent annually.[26] In this regard, the structure of the country's economy is a major factor anchoring Turkey to the 'Strategic West'.

To maintain trade ties

Furthermore, the nature of Turkey's economic transactions and trade with China, Russia, Iran and the broader Middle East are quite asymmetrical and are nowhere near a match for the country's economic supply chains from the Strategic West. For instance, Turkey has large trade deficits with China and Russia, while its trade ties with the EU and the USA are more balanced:

- In 2016, Turkey's imports from China amounted to $25.4 billion, while its exports remained at $2.32 billion.[27]

- The same year, Turkey's imports from Russia amounted to $10.4 billion, while its exports to Russia amounted to $1.99 billion.[28]

Erdogan diversified the country's foreign trade partners, but it is premature to speak of a major shift away from the Strategic West economically. In addition, while Erdogan has reconfigured Turkey's foreign trade patterns, this does not mean he has transformed them.

Even with the changes in trade patterns since 2002, other countries or alliance structures are not alternatives to the Strategic West, in terms of Turkey's foreign trade partners. For instance, Turkey's top export destinations in 2016 were: Germany ($16.2 billion),[29] the United Kingdom ($15.2 billion),[30] Italy ($8.26 billion)[31] and the United States

($7.69 billion);[32] while Turkish exports to Russia remained at $2 billion and to China at $2.3 billion.[33]

Although the share of non-Strategic West countries in Turkish trade has increased since 2002, constituting nearly 30 per cent of Turkish trade in 2018, the EU alone still accounted for 42 per cent of Turkish trade in the same year.[34] Overall, the Strategic West accounted for 70 per cent of Turkish foreign trade in 2002 and 41 per cent in 2018. Meanwhile, Russia, China and the GCC member countries made up just 12 per cent of Turkish trade in 2018, up from 10 per cent in 2000.[35] Thus, while Turkey's trade partners have diversified since 2002, this has not happened to the advantage of China, Russia or the Middle East monarchies. Moreover, OECD and NATO members still constitute a plurality of Turkey's foreign trade partners.

Therefore, it seems correct to speak not of an axis shift in Turkish trade, but rather a reallocation. In 2000, Turkey's top ten trading partners were: Germany, the USA, Italy, France, the UK, Russia, the Netherlands, Spain, Belgium–Luxembourg and Japan. In 2018, the same list included: Germany, China, Russia, the USA, Italy, the UK, France, Spain, Iran and Iraq.[36] What is more, in 2018, Turkey was the EU's fourth largest export market and fifth largest provider of imports. The EU itself is by far Turkey's number one import and export partner.[37]

. . . and to attract investment

As a resource-poor country, in terms of its reliance on FDI flows to grow, Turkey needs the Strategic West more today than before Erdogan took office.

Since 2003, Turkey's investment partners have also diversified. At the same time, however, the share of FDI inflows from the Strategic West FDI into Turkey have actually increased, suggesting that even stronger financial ties bond Erdogan and Turkey to NATO and OECD members.

In 2005, two years after Erdogan became Turkey's prime minister, 60 per cent of the country's net FDI inflows came from the Strategic West. In 2018, these investments amounted to 78 per cent. As such, it appears that while Turkey grew at unprecedented rates under Erdogan, its financial dependence on the Strategic West also grew, and even more so, proportionally speaking.[38]

In 2005, the EU was the largest investor in the country, accounting for 58 per cent of net FDI inflows. Thirteen years later, the EU was investing even more significantly in the country's markets, accounting for 61 per cent of net FDI inflows.[39]

The proportion of net FDI inflows from the GCC, Russia, China and the Middle East all decreased during this period, although, during the same term, Turkish investments in these regions did increase. In 2018, Chinese investment flows into Turkey remained at under 1 per cent of net FDI inflows – Beijing is clearly not going to be Erdogan's saviour. Meanwhile, Turkey has managed to diversify sources of investment, with FDI inflows from all other countries increased from less than 1 per cent in 2005 to over 15.6 per cent in 2018.[40]

Turkey and the Strategic West together: Yes, but will it last?

Erdogan knows very well that he cannot ultimately afford to break the economic foundation of Turkey's relationship with the Strategic West. Therefore, the post-2016 anti-European animus in Turkish politics notwithstanding, in the most likely scenario, he is going to play a game of transactionalising Turkish ties to the West, including the EU. This is also why, ironically, although he pummelled the Europeans in the run-up to the 2017 Turkish referendum to boost his base, Ankara was simultaneously trying to deepen and broaden the scope of its Customs Union with the EU, which allows most industrial goods to flow freely across borders without tariffs.

Ultimately, Ankara needs the Strategic West, and especially Europe, economically, and it needs NATO in the security realm. At the same time, the West, especially Europe, needs Turkey politically.

Although the EU is mostly inward looking now, the fact remains that the Union still relies on Ankara's cooperation in its defence policy, for instance in Bosnia and in operations in Africa, as well as in handling refugees flowing out of Syria and across the greater Middle East.

For its own part, Washington needs Turkey in order to implement its policies regarding Ankara's neighbouring countries, from Iran to Russia to Iraq. More importantly, Brussels and Washington rely on access to vital Turkish bases, especially Incirlik, in southern Turkey abutting Syria, to combat ISIS and jihadists in Syria and Iraq, thereby preventing their entry into or return to the West. Unfortunately, these ties will become increasingly transactional as long as populist leaders on both sides continue to polarise their constituents with anti-Muslim and anti-Western rhetoric.

Even if its accession process to the EU is stalled, Erdogan's Turkey can contribute much to Europe. The recent economic slowdown notwithstanding, Turkey has witnessed record-breaking economic growth in the last decade. It is no longer a poor country, desperately seeking accession to the EU. It now has a $2.1 trillion economy as measured according to current prices, a powerful army and aspirations to shape the region in its image.[41] As political turmoil paralyses North Africa, Syria and Iraq and economic problems undermine Mediterranean Europe, Turkey remains a stable nation – even if in the tight grip of Erdogan.

In addition, even the staunchest opponents of Turkey's accession are aware that the EU would be better off with a strong Turkey in close political proximity to the Union than a belligerent power opposing the EU and undermining its policies. After all, today's Turkey is no longer the 'Sick Man of Europe'. As of 2018, the size of the Turkish economy has not only eclipsed Spain's economy (as measured in current prices), but is also on a trajectory to overtake Italy's in the coming years.[42] In other words, Turkey, which is already has the Middle East's largest economy, is also about to become the Mediterranean's largest economy, excluding France. It is simply too hard for the EU to turn Ankara away.

The Syrian Civil War and the large number of refugees fleeing to Europe, deeply affected EU–Turkish relations, in Turkey's favour. Ankara inadvertently became the continent's gatekeeper because of the EU's inability to tackle the refugee crisis and the lack of solidarity among its members. The EU–Turkey deal of 2016 demonstrates Ankara's new leverage in Europe. In the agreement, Turkey was promised €6 billion for blocking the refugees' onward journey to Europe and for keeping them in Turkey. Ankara also sought visa liberalisation and the reopening of the suspended chapters in the accession negotiations. A promise was made to open the suspended chapters in the accession negotiations.

The Strategic West needs Turkey politically, and Turkey needs Europe economically and NATO for its security needs. However, does Turkey really need Europe politically?

CONCLUSION
HOW CAN TURKEY BECOME GREAT?

Shifting identities

In 2003, when Erdogan came to power, I had started a fresh career as a policy analyst at the Washington Institute for Near East Policy that eventually transitioned to becoming a senior fellow. While attending various foreign policy discussions and circles and travelling around the USA, I saw that civil servants, policy-makers, journalists and scholars in Washington, DC, and for that purpose many Americans citizens around the USA, almost without exception, considered Turkey to have a European identity – although there was always some debate.

In the past decade and a half, I have witnessed the transformation of Turkey's international identity, under Erdogan, especially as viewed in Washington, DC, and across America. Today, almost all of my colleagues, including the same people from my initial years in the US capital, consider Turkey to be a Middle Eastern country. With some help from his European counterparts, such as German and French leaders who blocked Turkey's EU aspirations, Erdogan has successfully engineered Turkey's exit from what America's policy-makers perceive to be Europe. This is not a small feat.

However, it is neither shocking nor sad. We often think of a country's identity as being set in stone. Although, in reality, international identities can be fluid, morphing with time, and changing according to trends in global and domestic politics. For instance, Finland, considered Eastern European in the interwar period, is today viewed as a Nordic country.

Similarly, the Czech Republic, labelled an East European country during the Cold War, is now regarded as a Central European state. During the Cold War, Greece and Turkey alike were considered West European countries; following the end of the Cold War, the former became Southern European, and the latter Middle Eastern under Erdogan since 2003.

The point is that Turkey's identity could well change again, but the issue at stake regarding the legacy of Turkish President Recep Tayyip Erdogan is that, for now, even if he has failed to make Turkey a Middle Eastern power, he has managed to make it a Middle Eastern country – at least as perceived by outsider observers. He is the most consequential Turkish leader since Ataturk. There is no doubt that after nearly two decades in power, Erdogan has transformed Turkey politically, with ramifications for Ankara's neighbours and Western allies, including the USA.

Ottomania

Near the Topkapi Palace, the first Ottoman imperial palace in Istanbul's old city, there is a booth where families take pictures dressed in the superfluous, exotic and sumptuous garb of the Ottoman Islamic court. Facing a long line of customers, the photographers churn out glossy photos of visitors grinning through layers of imitation silk, their children wobbling under heaps of oversized robes and ribbon. Most of the families lined up, obviously delight in the quirkiness of it all. But, the purpose of the booth, clearly, is not to make light of the Ottoman past; rather, it is to glorify it, and to allow Turks and tourists, alike, to transport themselves to a lost world of Ottoman splendour.

Before the rise of Erdogan, the received wisdom in Turkey, shaped by Ataturk, denigrated the Ottoman era of decline as a dark age of Islamic backwardness and inferiority. To this end, Ataturk singularly focused his attention and that of his country folks on Europe and secularist politics. Erdogan has turned this narrative on its head. Now, Turks are reconnecting with the Ottoman past and Turkey's Middle Eastern heritage and Muslim identity, and in doing so, they are uncovering a plethora of confused and often contradictory meanings.

Calling neo-Ottomanism an ideology would be an overstatement. It is a fantasy brought to life with often kitschy aesthetics – and this gives it an almost unlimited range for interpretation.[1] Ottoman reveries have justified virtually any political stance and moralising attitude one can imagine. Sometimes, the empire is extolled as a paragon of religious and ethnic tolerance; sometimes, it is used to gin up 'evidence' that non-Muslims, such as Jews and Christians, are treacherous and should never have been granted rights in the first place.

Sometimes, Ottomanism is imagined as a homegrown democracy reflecting the people's will, such as Erdogan's AKP, while at the same time, the empire's most despotic sultans are praised for their iron-fisted rule. Some lionise the Ottomans for 'standing up to the West', ignoring the Westernising reforms of the late Ottoman sultans. It is certain that Turkey's citizens are imagining, and reimagining, the Ottomans, and sometimes even inventing traditions and policies, which they attributed to their Ottoman forbearers. However, one thing is certain: neo-Ottomanism has proven a remarkable marketing device in twenty-first-century Turkey for selling everything from hamburgers to T-shirts and home furnishings.

Sloshing promiscuously into topics of religion, society and foreign policy, the cocktail of 'Ottomania' distills, ultimately, to a single assumption: that Turkey's 'genuine' identity resides somewhere in the recesses of its Ottoman past.

Of palaces, mosques and mausoleums

Closer to reality, Erdogan has personally embraced another Ottoman royal home, the Dolmabahce Palace in Istanbul. Previously a museum, in recent years, parts of the vast Dolmabahce complex, the best known of the Ottoman royal residences after the Topkapi Palace, have been converted into Erdogan's office in Istanbul. Built in the nineteenth century and more modern than the Topkapi Palace, the Dolmabahce provides Erdogan with a convenient backdrop in imperial glory.

Running Turkey from his palace in Ankara and the sultan's Dolmabahce in Istanbul, Erdogan has, indeed, been the driving force behind Turkey's quest for 'self-discovery' over the past decade and a half, cheered on by ideologues, who adore him. Turkey's new cultural and political elites in the Erdogan era have painted a heavy imperial veneer over every aspect of the country's politics, domestically and abroad.

Once upon a time, the Ottomans ruled over a vast and diverse land mass, sweeping from Central Europe in the north to the reaches of the Sahara Desert in the south, the heel of the Italian Peninsula in the west to the Persian-speaking world to the east. When the Ottoman Empire fell, the new state-builders, led by Ataturk, downgraded their involvement in their former imperial domains, to focus on the pragmatic tasks of security and welfare in the new republic of Turkey. Subsequently, twentieth-century Turkey became a simultaneously West-facing and inward-looking country.

Erdogan, who has ended Ataturk's first Turkish republic and established his own, has shattered this mindset. Just as the Ottoman borders were not a sharp line, but a fuzzy set of frontiers along the many islands of the Mediterranean Sea, the vast reaches of Sahara sand dessert and the snow-capped peaks of the Caucasus Mountains in the pre-modern era, Erdogan sees Turkey as casting its benevolent shadow across its former imperial lands.

AKP officials glisten when observers claim that Turkey is 'neo-Ottomanist' or that its foreign policy is influenced by a post-imperial worldview. However, Erdogan's own generous usage of Ottoman references in his rhetoric and actions belie these disavowals. Realising that flourishes of Ottoman grandeur excite his base, and no doubt succumbing to his own personality, he has donned the trapping of a sultan on every occasion.

When greeting foreign dignitaries, he has taken to surrounding himself with ceremonial guards, each dressed in armour that represents the putatively Turkish states of the past, from the Hunnic Empire of the third century to the most recent, Ottomans.[2] State ceremonies, in the past modelled on European customs, are increasingly becoming re-enactments of supposedly Ottoman, Middle Eastern and Islamic traditions – alcoholic beverages have disappeared from receptions at the presidential palace in Ankara, only to be replaced by colourful sherbets and communal-style Muslim prayers. Overall, these signal Turkey's political transformation under its new leader, the first sultan of Turkey's second republic: Recep Tayyip Erdogan.

Erdogan's frenzied building spree has also suffered a heavy dose of Ottomania. One notable example is the massive Sultan-esque, and newly furnished, so-called 'Erdogan Mosque', constructed on the heights of the Camlica Hill, overlooking Istanbul, Turkey's greatest city and former Ottoman imperial capital. A tradition in Turkish and other Islamic empires of the past was for sultans, after particularly great conquests or military victories, to commission grand mosques, dubbed *selatin* (from the word, 'sultan') mosques, as a monument to their exploits – Mughal shahs, such as Jahan who built the Taj Mahal for his wife Mumtaz, were an exception to this Islamic tradition, dedicating edifices to love.

The mosque at Camlica, which dominates the Istanbul silhouette, is without a doubt Erdogan's *selatin* mosque. He intervened in the design of the mosque, and has personally overseen its construction, even remarking obliquely that it is a *selatin*.[3] Ismail Karaman, who previously served as the speaker of the Turkish Parliament on behalf of the AKP and who in past decades headed the conservative National Turkish Student Union (MTTB), where Erdogan first cut his teeth in politics, has been even more explicit, declaring that the mosque should be named the 'Recep Tayyip Erdogan Mosque'.[4]

Determined to break from Ottoman traditions, the founder of Turkey's first republic, Ataturk, refrained from commissioning grandiose monuments to himself. Anitkabir mausoleum, the monument constructed in Ataturk's memory in downtown Ankara, was built and opened in 1953, after his death. In a poignant hat-tip to Ataturk's pro-European and secular ideological leanings, however, the Anitkabir has been laid out in the form of a Roman agora facing a Greek temple-style mausoleum, and with Hittite lions from pre-Islamic Turkey guarding its gates.

All hail the new 'Ottomans'

Erdogan's return to the Ottoman political idiom in state architecture underlines his departure from the tenets of Turkey's first republic. The Kemalists' vision of Turkey as a modern republic, guided their nation-building agenda at home and their foreign policy agenda abroad. The Kemalists accepted that the Ottoman Empire was over and that it was no longer coming back. Ataturk tried to shape Turkey to be great as a republic facing Europe. In contrast, a vision of imperial restoration shapes Erdogan's foreign policy. At home, he has taken steps to eliminate the Kemalist legacy and resurrect the Ottoman past – often in the distorted, Islam-dominated version that the Kemalists have taught him. In foreign policy, too, Erdogan has adopted an imperial attitude, often again taking as reference the distorted version of the Ottomans that the Kemalists taught him – an imperial foreign policy, infatuated with Islam.

This attitude has ensconced itself in Turkey's foreign policy discourse. Almost a decade ago, during the heyday of AKP popularity, Cemil Cicek, then an AKP deputy prime minister, remarked in 2009 that Turkey should enjoy privileges with its former Ottoman domains, similar to those that Britain has with its former colonies.[5] Around the same time, some of Erdogan's most exuberant supporters began to fete him with placards hailing him as, 'The Ottoman Sultan Recep Tayyip Erdogan I'.[6]

More recently, the pro-Erdogan Turkish columnist, Abdurrahman Dilipak, claimed that Erdogan's political ascent was raising him to the status of Caliph – titular head of the Sunni Muslim world, formerly vested in the Ottoman sultan – and that other Muslim countries would begin to open 'offices' in the capacious palace that Erdogan has constructed for himself in Ankara.[7] Even if Ankara insists that nothing about its foreign policy reeks of imperialism, Erdogan has clearly transformed Turkey's foreign policy dynamics, adding a strongly pro-Islamic tilt, Middle Eastern pivot and a patronising imperial stance, blending this new concoction with a popular stance to safeguard Turkey's national security interests.

Three paths

There is no question that despite his grandstanding proposal to revive Turkey's Ottoman-era greatness, and do so through Islam, in 2019, Erdogan's policies have left Ankara overall with fewer allies and friends internationally, especially among key powers.

Far from making Turkey great again – by and through influence over Muslims and allies in the Middle East – this policy has resulted in nearly the opposite outcome. Today, Ankara has just one ally in the Middle East: Qatar. And aside from regional influence among some states in the Western Balkans, Black Sea region and East Africa, it, unfortunately, does not enjoy the wide respect internationally that a great power would recognise. To make matters worse, Ankara cannot take for granted the unconditional support of its traditional friends prior to Erdogan's rise: Israel, US, NATO and Europe. Finally, yet most importantly, Turkey's historic adversaries, Russia and Iran, seek to undermine its policies all around, as well as to force it into accepting foreign policy deals – on the latter's own terms.

There are also domestic considerations to take into account, including Turkey's political crisis between the pro- and anti-Erdogan camps. A deeper internal crisis could undermine his ability to focus on foreign policy, but could also tempt the Turkish leader to engage in adventurism abroad in order to distract attention from troubles at home – a potential undertaking that comes to mind in this regard is throwing more support behind Hamas in Gaza to boost his base, rupturing ties with Israel again.

Erdogan's survival instincts will also shape his decisions. He is well known for turnarounds in foreign policy – breaking ties with Israel in 2010, only to re-establish them six years later – and in domestic politics – entering into peace talks with the PKK in 2013, only to declare it 'enemy number one' two years later. Despite the many challenges he has faced, Erdogan has won successive elections. Finally, under him, Ankara has been able to spread its foreign policy wings, thanks to strong economic growth, until recently.

Taking into account these factors, I see three possible scenarios, which are not mutually exclusive, for Turkish foreign policy under Erdogan.

1. 'Muddle through as a stand-alone power'

In this most likely and immediate future scenario, Turkish foreign policy looks much as it does in 2019. Ankara is stuck between the NATO-led West (where the USA and Europe constitute two, somewhat separate, blocks, at least during the Trump era), the Muslim 'East' (including Iran and its Arab neighbours, constituting two opposing blocks, the latter led by the GCC) and the Russian 'North'. Erdogan could continue to successfully hedge these blocks against each other, as he has been doing, for instance, in Afrin, Manbij and Idlib in north-western Syria, where he has pitted the USA against Russia to get what he wants, more territory and a 'say' in Syria's future.

Erdogan might eventually come to terms with the regime in Damascus, giving Assad the green light to undermine Rojava, which would help eliminate a security risk to Ankara, and to him, in the short term. This is plausible, since, excluding minor skirmishes such as fighting in April 2016 in the Syrian city of Qamishli, the YPG and the Assad regime have been co-belligerents in Syria's civil war. 'Air travel, educational, and certain other links [between Damascus and Rojava] have also continued.' The Assad regime has even has 'maintained a token, tolerated presence in northeastern Syria's two largest cities, Qamishli and Hasaka, both controlled by the YPG-affiliated Democratic Union Party (PYD) throughout the Syrian war'.[8]

The 'muddle-through' scenario would require Erdogan to manage his relations with President Trump and the US Congress well, while simultaneously avoiding being overrun by Russia in Syria. Another challenge is the US military, in whose ranks an anti-Turkish opinion has been brewing in recent years. Erdogan would need to launch a charm offensive towards the Pentagon, also tasking the TAF to win CENTCOM's heart.

Erdogan's predicament is that 'historical antibodies' (i.e. how Turks see their neighbours and how Turkey's neighbours see Ankara) will continue to frustrate his foreign policy ambitions in Turkey's near abroad.

At the same time, though, global trends may help him to sustain this path. Erdogan has been a master politician in reading the global zeitgeist well, also using it to his advantage, for instance in aptly framing his AKP as 'a moderate and conservative Muslim democrat party' in the aftermath of the September 11, 2001 attacks, and making himself politically attractive in the USA and European capitals, even as he was busy locking up dissidents during the Ergenekon–Sledgehammer trials. After the 2013 Gezi Park protests, Erdogan lost his magic touch in terms of reading the international zeitgeist well, and has since been increasingly cast as an authoritarian leader. However, he may now be at an advantage point again. The rise of populism globally will help him find and keep new allies, from Hungarian Prime Minister Viktor Orban in the EU to US President Trump, and even gain sympathy globally.

2. 'Failure'

The challenge posed by the first scenario is that under Erdogan, Turkey suffers from a number of structural weaknesses in the foreign policy realm. The split with the Gulen movement means that well-educated and conservative, if self-serving, Gulen cadres are no longer available to staff Erdogan's offices and key positions in various government ministries. At the same time, personalisation of the foreign policy-making process centred on Erdogan's palace since 2018, has weakened the historically strong Turkish bureaucratic structures, including the Turkish Foreign Ministry, MIT and TAF. The latter are increasingly challenged to offer Erdogan sound guidance and policy options to help him navigate the power blocks flanking Turkey to the west, east and north.

The YPG poses a risk for Erdogan and a challenge for Turkey's stability. Even if Assad takes over Rojava, he will not completely destroy the YPG. Rather, he will continue to secretly harbour the terrorist organisation. Erdogan has tried to destroy the Baath Party regime in Syria, and to kill Assad. The latter will not forget this fact and will make Erdogan pay in the long term – by using the YPG clandestinely against him. Overall, a sharp increase in PKK terror attacks, fuelled by the now militarily better equipped and battle-hardened YPG (backed by Assad) could undermine Turkey's stability.

Domestically, problems associated with Syrian refugees could contribute to building this scenario. The Syrian refugee population in Turkey (nearly 4 million in 2019) constitutes anywhere between 10 and 50 per cent of the population of the country's provinces abutting Syria. Rising economic and social tensions have fanned already existing racist views towards Arabs in Turkey. According to a recent study, Syrians are one of the primary targets of hate speech in the country.[9] What is more, there have been frequent cases of attacks and pogroms against the refugee population, especially in the country's southern provinces, though the Erdogan-controlled media underreports such incidents. Rising violence against Syrians, within the background of Turkey's polarised political environment, could add to instability. Knowing this, Erdogan plans to resettle as many of the Syrian refugees as possible back home, which is why he wants to maintain a Turkish zone in northern Syria. This, among other reasons, forces him to continue brokering deals with Putin.

Overall, the above dynamics could make it increasingly difficult for Ankara to navigate among the power blocks and adversaries, that is, 'West', 'East' and 'North', encircling it. Ankara could, subsequently, end up being squeezed by them, falling under their sway. In this regard, a likely, but potentially distant path, would be a rupture in US–Turkish ties over the YPG in Syria, resulting in Ankara caving into Russian influence.

Potential economic crises could also pave the way towards the second scenario. Alarmed by the increasing frequency of crises between Turkey and the 'Strategic West', international capital could lose its faith in Turkey, abandoning or avoiding it in the midterm. The exodus of educated Turks will only increase the likelihood of this scenario.

A critical and sustained economic crisis would not only undermine Ankara's ability to be a serious foreign policy player, but also erode Erdogan's base of supporters. Many in this base are committed to him, primarily because he has lifted them out of poverty, delivering sustained economic growth and higher living standards. Erdogan has made his supporters wealthy and financially solvent for the moment.

The recent trend in Erdogan's increasingly nationalistic rhetoric, beginning in early 2018, further signals that the economy could be facing troubled times in 2019. An economic meltdown would force Turkey to seek a bailout plan with the IMF, and Erdogan can secure such a bailout only if he is on good terms with the USA, which holds the 'golden vote' at the IMF, allowing Washington to approve or disapprove country bailouts.

3. 'Relink with the West – as an autarchic power'

The bad news for Ankara's Western allies is that Erdogan's Turkey does not consider itself part of the political or cultural West. The good news, however, is that Erdogan is aware of Turkey's financial dependency on the Strategic West. More importantly, he knows that Turkey can benefit from the Strategic West in the security realm.

Accordingly, there is a third plausible path by which Turkey can avoid the chaos of the second scenario. Erdogan can relink Ankara with

NATO, the USA and Europe, that is, the Strategic West, by taking into account the interdependency between these sides, also providing Turkey with security in international affairs – in the mould of his predecessors, the sultans and Ataturk. This scenario has become a bit more likely in the aftermath of the resolution of the 2018 'Brunson Crisis' between Ankara and Washington. The main takeaway of this crisis for Erdogan is that Turkey *has* to remain connected to the global economy by maintaining its ties with the Strategic West.

In this scenario, Washington should not expect Ankara to join any sort of defensive or aggressive alliance against Tehran. Far from it, taking into consideration Turkey's historic power parity with Tehran, Erdogan would opt to maintain Turkey's informal, and historically rooted, non-belligerence pact with Iran.

Washington also should not expect Ankara's reversal to its traditional role in the Western alliance. It is almost certain that, under this potential case, Turkey's ties to the Strategic West would face frequent crises. More notably, he would continue to provide support for political Islamist parties, such as Hamas in Gaza and the Ikhwan across the Middle East, much to the consternation of Israel, the GCC and the United States.

Erdogan would continue to champion Muslims and their causes, such as the Rohingya persecuted in Myanmar. Finally, Erdogan would position himself within the Strategic West as the voice of the global south, including authoritarian regimes in places such as Venezuela, again to the frequent consternation of many of his Western counterparts. He would also maintain strong ties with populist leaders in Europe, such as Orban, this time specifically angering the EU and its non-populist leaders.

For Erdogan, the benefit of this scenario is that it would help his goal of seeking greatness for Turkey. To this end, however, he also needs to take into account the country's brain drain (discussed below). This development can be stymied only if educated Turks feel that their country is connected to the West – a pillar for this outcome is having unfettered access to democratic freedoms. Since 2003, he has made Turkey a middle-income economy. However, Turkey remains a resource-poor country. It can only hope to become an advanced economy, and therefore a great power, *only* if educated Turks stay in the country, building value-added economic sectors, catapulting it to join the desired list of great powers.

Nations that were great powers once, such as Turkey, Russia, China and Iran, never forget it. Erdogan has reminded Turkey's citizens, including many of his opponents, that they should be proud to be the offspring of a great empire that vanished less than a Roman *saeculum* ago.

Therefore, even if Turkey relinks with its traditional Western allies in the final scenario, it will continue to behave like an imperial nation, and its citizens will themselves want recognition of this as such. Most importantly, regardless of whichever path is taken, Turkey will be a difficult foreign policy partner because of the changes ushered in by Erdogan. I believe that these changes are becoming a permanent feature of Turkish political and social life – beyond Erdogan.

Erdogan and Ataturk

In 2019, Erdogan became the longest-serving Turkish leader in modern history, surpassing even Ataturk. By the time he finishes his current term in 2023, Erdogan will have controlled the country for twenty years, as prime minister between 2003 and 2014, and as president since 2014.

He is often cast as the leader intent on eliminating the legacy of Ataturk in Turkey. His critics suggest he wants to do away with the legacy and policies of Ataturk in order to bring back the Ottoman Empire in its place. However, Erdogan's agenda goes much deeper: he wants to rid Turkey of the legacy of the Westernised Ottoman Empire of the 1800s, Ataturk's footprint and the country's decades-old established relationship with the West, whereby the sultans and Ataturk alike had brought the country into the Western-led international system.

Erdogan has rolled back much of this legacy. He and the AKP elites around him claimed that Kemalism's strict separation of religion and state was unnatural and deemed public displays of piety, such as government employees donning the Islamic headscarf (*hijab*), completely acceptable. The elimination of Ataturk's firewall between religion and government means that Islam has flooded Turkish politics. Although it is constitutionally a secular system in practice, Turkey is no longer a secular country.

In the sphere of foreign policy, Erdogan has focused on re-engaging the Middle East and cementing Turkey's status as a regional Muslim power, with global ambitions, with some reach into the Balkans and East Africa.

With Erdogan tightening his grip on Turkish society, thereby stifling the voice of the political opposition, the post-2016 failed coup environment has witnessed a proliferation of pro-Erdogan forces in the Turkish media. News outlets promoting and adoring Erdogan have come to dominate the political landscape, and they have used this new prominence to promote a novel historical narrative, in which Erdogan is the main protagonist.

Mao in China, Ataturk in Turkey

Evidently, Ataturk, who liberated Turkey from Allied occupation at the end of the First World War, adding it to a small club of nations never colonised by Europe, is a towering historic figure in Turkey.

So, what will become of what remains of Ataturk's legacy under Erdogan? The closest analogy is Mao Zedong's legacy in China. Mao is China's founder and liberator from Japanese occupation, and for this his legacy persists in China. Ironically, however, everything in today's China, a diehard capitalist society, screams, 'I hate Mao!' Yet, Mao's pictures are still plastered all over the country. In essence, the country's leaders exploit his image as the country's liberator and a source of legitimacy, but strip the country of his core legacy.

Erdogan is seeking something similar. His Turkey is as far as it can get from being secular in politics and education, European-minded in foreign policy and respectful of gender equality in domestic politics – all parts of Ataturk's vision. Not just Ataturk, but also the late-Ottoman sultans would be shocked if they could visit Erdogan's Turkey.

However, the fact is that Ataturk draws a huge amount of respect in Turkey, regardless of where someone falls on the political spectrum. In this case, the unavoidable elephant in the room is that he saved the country from colonial rule and complete devastation. Erdogan, therefore, wants to appropriate Ataturk's legacy, rather than completely repudiate it – he knows that the latter goal would be nearly impossible to achieve.

At the same time, Erdogan also wants to 'correct' Ataturk's legacy, drawing on his successes, and then impose his own ideological veneer on them. The result is 'Green [the colour of Islam] Kemalism'. Erdogan and his supporters believe that Ataturk took a 'wrong turn' after he liberated Turkey, but, nevertheless, they embrace his legacy as Turkey's liberator. If an Erdogan supporter does not like Ataturk as a reformer and Westerniser, therefore, they can still respect him as their liberator. While Erdogan will continue to chip away at the secular and pro-Western legacy of Ataturk (and the Westernising Ottoman sultans), 'Ataturk the Liberator' statues will, therefore, continue to adorn Turkey's town squares, providing the current government and Erdogan with a facade of legitimacy.

Politics of resentment

Taking into account Erdogan's increasing dominance in Turkish politics since the failed coup in 2016, political Islam and Turkish nationalism have become hybrid segments of his political brand, driven by the narrative that *he* is protecting Turkey and Muslims against foreign attacks by the Westerners. This notion is overtly transparent in a government-owned TRT network's series on Sultan Abdulhamid II, the last Ottoman sultan who ruled the country as an absolute monarch.

Abdulhamid II, reining from 1876 to 1908, has become a stand-in for Erdogan in recent years, under the rubric of neo-Ottomanist revival in Turkey.[10] The series, *Payitaht*, depicts Abdulhamid as a benevolent sultan, a devout Muslim and a staunch Turkish nationalist, who faces nefarious conspiracies to oust him from power or kill him. Airing three-hour episodes each Friday,[11] the blockbuster lionises the sultan – with plenty of artistic license – as a rightful and benevolent ruler, and a father figure, making the best decisions for his 'people', while his scheming opponents, acting as proxies for outsiders and Jews, try to undermine him and distort his people's will.

The series has now gathered a cult-like following by Erdogan's fans, even in the upper echelons of the Turkish government. The former speaker of the country's Parliament, Karaman, said after the failed coup attempt in 2016, 'they [coup plotters] wanted to do the same as they did when they overthrew Abdulhamid II, but this time they couldn't succeed'.[12]

The problem with this blend is that while half the country, which adores Erdogan, happily embraces its narrative, the other half of the country, brutalised by him, loathes and rejects it.[13] Yet, as far as Erdogan and his admirers are concerned, those who oppose Erdogan are guilty, in the sense that they can be considered neither good Muslims nor good Turks.

To the contrary, by opposing him, they behave as agents of Western interests. Since Erdogan 'embodies' the Turkish nation, his opposition is blamed for subverting the people's will, and they are, subsequently, often denied participation in democratic institutions. For instance, while pro-Erdogan Turks are free to organise rallies, those who oppose him are generally denied the freedom to assemble. Most recently, during International Day for the Elimination of Violence Against Women, on 25 November 2018, the police cracked down on a mass women's march in Istanbul with tear gas, while pro-Erdogan groups had their own 'women's marches' in a controlled access setting, celebrated by pro-Erdogan media as a peaceful rally.[14] Erdoganism has set Turkish democracy on a path to self-narcosis and there seems to be no exit from this under Erdogan.

In foreign policy, too, not all is bright for Turkey's citizenry, overall. Erdogan's supporters believe that if Turkey 'fails', the only plausible reason is because Erdogan's domestic and foreign adversaries are trying to undermine him. In this speculation, Jews and Christians have emerged as especially convenient scapegoats to blame for the failures of Turkey and Erdogan.[15] This became visible during the 2018 'Brunson Crisis', when pro-Erdogan pundits attacked the pastor for being a 'Christian', while others grotesquely painted Christianity 'as masonic'.[16]

This is bad news for Turkey's Christian and Jewish citizens, also serving as a sign that even when Erdogan relinks Ankara with the Strategic West, the relationship between the sides will not be smooth at all. Overall, the Erdogan era in Turkish politics has reinforced, rather than weakened, the image of the West as being perfidious in Turkey. This is contrary to the expectations of policy-makers in Washington and Brussels whom I met in 2003, back when I began my career as an analyst at the Washington Institute for Near East Policy. At the time, more than a few had told me that as a 'non-Kemalist' politician, Erdogan would breathe 'much needed fresh air' into Turkish politics, as well as improve Ankara's ties with the West. The end result has been almost the opposite.

Erdogan's choice: For or against educated Turks?

Meanwhile, for Erdogan, the challenge lies at home. Among its population of 82 million, Turkey has a large number of well-educated citizenry and liberal urban professionals, many of whom vehemently oppose him. These people often speak multiple foreign languages, hold advanced degrees from world-renowned universities and have connections to civil society institutions and opinion-makers in the West. Erdogan knows that an opposition led by powerful elites poses a permanent threat to him. If he can force this group to give up on Turkey, it does not matter how many people are left to oppose him. Without their guiding elites, the opposition groups will have no choice but to accept his regime – as the Russian masses have done under Putin.

Turkey has an infamous law that allows sitting presidents to sue citizens who have allegedly insulted them. Sezer, Turkey's tenth president and a secularist Kemalist who was not known for his liberal tendencies, used this law 109 times between 2003 and 2006. Gul, the eleventh president and an AKP member, used it 895 times when he was president between 2007 and 2014, while Erdogan, the twelfth and current president, has used it more than 12,168 times between 2014 and 2017.[17]

This law often disproportionately targets Turkey's creative classes, including writers, filmmakers, composers, artists and scholars. In fact, harassment of academics has become a signature trait of Erdogan's rising authoritarianism. Distinguished professors now find themselves being fired and some have even had their passports revoked. Many are leaving, while they still can, for academic freedom abroad. Like their professors, Turkish students are flocking in droves to leave the country. In my 2017 visit to the UK, I met an alarming number of Turkish graduate students at Oxford University, who had recently left Turkey and were seeking to stay for the long run. According to the UK Home Office, toward the end of 2016, Britain saw a 28 per cent increase in short-term student visas, with Turks making up 40 per cent of this bulk.[18]

The wealthy – many old-money Turks who espouse liberal values – are also in Erdogan's line of fire. Prominent Turkish businessperson Osman Kavala, who has supported many civil society causes, was arrested in October 2017. By early 2019, not only was he still in jail, but also the actual indictment against him had not even been prepared, suggesting an open-ended detention. This was a clear-cut signal to Turkey's wealthy: Stay quiet, receive jail time or leave.

That trend had already begun. In 2016, Turkey was among the top five countries globally to experience the highest outflow of millionaires.[19] While around 1,000 millionaires left the country in 2015, this figure rose to nearly 6,000 by the end of 2016, representing an unprecedented 500 per cent increase from the year before. CS Global Partners, a London-based legal advisory firm that specialises in relocating families globally and which is geared towards the wealthier, said that requests from Turkish clients for assistance in acquiring a foreign passport rose 2.5-fold between January and June 2017.[20] The flight of the elites from Turkey increasingly mirrors the situation in Russia in past decades.

Turkish R&D has suffered significantly because of these trends. For instance, in 2015, three Turkish public universities were ranked in the top 200 by the *Times Higher Education* World University Rankings, but none of them made it to the list in the following year. The number of annual scientific publications decreased by a disconcerting 28 per cent in 2017 compared to 2016.[21]

If Erdogan gets what he wants, he might be able to retain a Putin-like grip on power, silencing and driving out the leaders of Turkey's civil society to pave the way for landslide electoral victories against a hollowed and rudderless opposition. However, this would be ironic, completely countering Erdogan's agenda of reviving Turkey's greatness. Turkey cannot become an advanced economy and a great power if its educated citizens continue to leave in masses.

What is more, in the foreign policy realm, Erdogan's Empire is all but a weak one. His strongest allies are limited to a number of countries, including Azerbaijan, Bosnia and Somalia. At the same time, Ankara cannot rely on Turkey's traditional Western allies.

How to *really* make Turkey Great

Taking these challenges into account, can Erdogan's Turkey still become a great power, not a restored empire, but a wealthy state that is the envy of its neighbours, based on a political system that is embraced by all of its citizens? The answer is 'yes', but it quickly needs to resolve the Kurdish issue and transition itself to a new constitution:

1   *By addressing the Kurdish issue*: Recent developments in Syria have internationalised Turkey's Kurdish issue and a solution for the Kurdish problem is more pressing than ever before. This is especially true since the PKK in Turkey and the YPG in Syria share ties and a joint command structure, allowing Turkish and Syrian political dynamics to become dangerously intertwined, while both organisations have historic ties to Russia and the Assad regime.

    Resolving the Kurdish issue is one way for Turkey to disarm, or at least weaken, the PKK and YPG, in order to prevent them from becoming a long-term proxy of Russian and Assad regimes, or be the cause of a rupture in US–Turkish ties. Erdogan should not and cannot leave the resolution of the Kurdish issue to the US, Assad or Russia.

2   *Through granting broad cultural rights for all*: Erdogan can resolve this problem through a liberal democratic constitution that provides broad cultural and political rights for all citizens, specifically promoting the inclusion of Turkey's Kurdish populous. Addressing the Kurdish issue will relieve Turkey from the perennial pressures and burden of a domestic and regional fight with a pro-PKK and pro-YPG constituency in Turkey and Syria.

    Turkey needs to address the grievances of its Kurdish population, although following the regional examples in Syria, Iraq and Iran, it is not necessarily the best way to go about it. In those countries, an overwhelming majority of Kurds live within the boundaries of their traditional homelands, or 'Kurdistans'. In Turkey, in recent decades, nearly half of the country's Kurds have migrated out of their homeland in the country's south-east, and Istanbul is now the most populous Kurdish city in the world.

    Accordingly, addressing Kurdish demands in Turkey means granting comprehensive cultural rights to all the country's citizens, Kurd or not, irrespective of location. Reforms would include access to education and public services, not only in Kurdish but in other minority languages as well. This can happen with a new liberal democratic constitution, which would increase the cultural rights of every individual citizen.

3   *While providing freedom of religion and freedom from religion*: A new Turkish constitution should also guarantee freedom *of* religion for Turkey's religious half, and freedom *from* religion for the country's secular half, bridging the gap between the country's two starkly disparate parts, which often split as pro- and anti-Erdogan camps. Such a step will finally end the country's crisis, muting the country's domestic stress while turning its energies into the foreign policy realm, so that Ankara can truly soar as a great power.

4   *And keeping as well as attracting talent and capital*: Such a charter is in Erdogan's interests as well. I believe that he wants to make Turkey a great nation. Turkey, a middle-income economy now, can become an advanced economy and a global power only if its educated and wealthy citizens remain in the country. These citizens hold the potential to transform Turkey from an economy that exports cars (a chief export) into one that is a hub for software, IT, finance and services – in other words, a high-powered, information-based economy, driven by value-added production, including software and information technology.

However, Erdogan's policies are having the opposite effect: capital and creative classes alike are fleeing the country. Erdogan cannot rely on international money or talent as substitutes – no one who is educated wants to live or do business in a country where YouTube and Twitter are periodically banned. After nearly two decades of rule by the Turkish leader, the country's educated citizens make decisions on their future, not based on the stigmatisation and persecution of political Islamists in 1999 when Erdogan was sentenced to jail, but rather based on stigmatisation and persecution of liberals and others taking place in 2019.

Turkish capital, the creative classes, outside talent and international capital will flee if the Erdogan administration continues on its current trajectory. At the same time, Turkish and expatriate creative classes alike will avoid the country if its leaders continue to deny unfettered access to the internet and ensure freedoms of expression, media, assembly and association. There needs to be respect for individual rights, environmental concerns, urban spaces and gender equality. If Turkey is an open society, it will continue to rise. If it ceases to be democratic, its fire will be extinguished. Turkey's quest for greatness will be fruitless without these steps – and this is one of the great lessons of the Erdogan era so far.

Erdogan's legacy

Turkey has had nationwide polls (seven altogether) or cataclysmic events (such as the failed coup of 2016) every year since 2014. Noting this climate, 2020 will the first year without elections or potential dramatic events. This gives Erdogan room to maneuver – he is a pragmatist before he is an ideologue. Can Erdogan embrace a different strategy at home and in his foreign policy going forward?

Years from now, in a distant future, when Erdogan is gone, not much will be left of him materially, except for the Camlica 'Erdogan' Mosque overlooking Istanbul, the city of Erdogan's birth and political ascent, from where he rose to become a globally recognised name and voice, and twenty-first-century Turkey's first international brand.

How visitors to this mosque will remember Erdogan in the many decades to come depends on the policy choices that he will make in the following crucial years. I am not holding my breath that he will make all the choices suggested above, which I believe are all good for Turkey, but if he does, I know that he would then make Turkey great again and leave the lasting legacy that he so desires to be written into history.

NOTES

Introduction

1 Ataturk, which means 'Father of the Turks' in Turkish, is Mustafa Kemal's second last name. He would receive this name later in life in 1934, when the Turkish Parliament, then under his control, passed legislation bestowing the title 'Ataturk' on him.

2 Although Erdogan's AKP, which he chaired, won the November 2002 Turkish parliamentary elections, he had to wait five months to become Prime Minister. A criminal conviction in his past – which resulted from reading an allegedly incendiary poem while he was Mayor of Istanbul, prevented him from running for Parliament. It was not until March of 2003, when Turkey's election board allowed him to run in by-elections to enter Parliament that he could move to take the office of Prime Minister, after qualifying for that post as a member of the legislative, in accordance with Turkish law at the time.

3 Soner Cagaptay, *The New Sultan: Erdogan and the Crisis of Modern Turkey* (London: I.B. Tauris, 2017), 120–4.

4 Gareth H. Jenkins, *Between Fact and Fantasy: Turkey's Ergenekon Investigation* (Washington DC: Central Asia-Caucasus Institute & Silk Road Studies Program, August 2009), 45.

5 Sarah Rainsford, '"Deep state plot" grips Turkey', BBC News, website (4 February 2008).

6 Daren Butler, 'With more Islamic schooling, Erdogan aims to reshape Turkey', Reuters, news agency (25 January 2018).

7 Cagaptay, *The New Sultan*, 1–13.

Chapter 1

1 Erol Tümertekin, 'The iron and steel industry of Turkey', *Economic Geography*, 31 (2) (1955), 180.

2 Brock Millman, *The Ill-Made Alliance: Anglo-Turkish Relations, 1934–1940* (Montreal: McGill-Queen's University Press, 1998), 88.

3 Selim Deringil, *Turkish Foreign Policy during the Second World War: An 'Active' Neutrality* (Cambridge: Cambridge University Press, 1989), 135–40.

4 Jim Jeffrey, personal correspondence (25 May 2018).

5 Zia Weise, 'Turkey's Balkan comeback', *Politico*, website (17 May 2018).

6 Soner Cagaptay, *The Rise of Turkey: The Twenty-First Century's First Muslim Power* (Lincoln, NE: Potomac, 2014), *passim*.

7 Patrick Kingsley, 'Erdogan Claims Vast Powers in Turkey After Narrow Victory in Referendum', *New York Times* (16 April 2017).

8 See Chapter 4 for more details on the relationship between Erdogan and Gulen.

9 Erin Cunningham, 'Journalists sentenced to jail in case highlighting media crackdown in Turkey', *Washington Post* (6 May 2016).

10 As far as Erdogan's right-wing and political Islamist supporters are concerned, the coup attempt was not only a domestic attack but also a plot by scheming 'foreign allies' to overthrow Erdogan through their Gulenist proxies. His supporters insist that it was simply the latest in a series of historical attacks the West has launched against the Turkish nation and the *umma*, the collection of all Sunni Muslims, stretching back to the Crusades. According to this line of thinking, by targeting Erdogan and the Turkish state simultaneously, these nefarious foreign interests inextricably linked the future of the country to the fate of the leader. The base believes that without Erdogan Turkey cannot become a great nation again or fulfill its historical mission of restoring the dignity of the global Sunni Muslim community, which they consider to be the true *umma*. See, Soner Cagaptay and Oya Rose Aktas, 'How Erdoganism is killing democracy in Turkey', *Foreign Affairs* (7 July 2017).

11 'Türkiye'de 11 milyon 985 bin 118 kişi şüpheliymiş!', Sol, website (9 December 2018).

12 Cagaptay, *The New Sultan*, 200–6.

Chapter 2

1 In this regard, Turkey was the norm rather than the exception in interwar era Europe, where a majority of countries were undemocratic, with the exception of a cluster of states in the north-western corner of the continent, including Great Britain and Scandinavia. A vast majority of countries in Southern, Central and Eastern Europe were single-party regimes or authoritarian dictatorships in the interwar period.

2 Metin Heper, *İsmet İnönü: The Making of a Turkish Statesmen* (Leiden: Brill, 1998), 136.

3 Cihat Göktepe, 'The Menderes Period (1950–1960)', *Journal of Turkish Weekly* [website] (13 April 2005).

4 Ruhi Sarpkaya, 'Köy Enstitüleri'nden Sonra İmam-Hatip Liseleri', *Toplum ve Demokrasi* 2 (3) (2008), 3. See also, Rıfat Önsoy, 'Cumhuriyetten Günümüze İlk ve Orta Öğretimimiz ve Bazı Meseleleri', *Hacettepe Üniversitesi Eğitim Fakültesi Dergisi*, 6 (1991), 8.

5 Interview with Recep Tayyip Erdogan, *Ustanın Hikayesi*, Beyaz TV 3 (September 2013).

6 Ibid.

7 Svante E. Cornell, 'Erbakan, Kısakürek, and the mainstreaming of extremism in Turkey', Hudson Institute, website (4 June 2018), 18.

8 Ibid.

9 Ibid.

10 Cagaptay, *The New Sultan*, 8.

11 Cornell, 'Erbakan, Kısakürek', 18.

12 Ibid.

13 Harun Alanoğlu (@HarunAlanoglu), Twitter (6 November 2015), 'Devletiniz yıkılmış, yeni devletiniz de eski devletinizi yıkanlarla dost olmuşsa yeni devleti kuranlar hain, ülkeniz de artık bir sömürgedir'.

14 Cagaptay, *The New Sultan*, 52.

15 Ibid., 53.

16 Cornell, 'Erbakan, Kısakürek', 18.

17 Daniel Dombey, 'Erdogan attacks "traitors" and foreign media for Turkey protests', *Financial Times*, website (18 June 2013). See also, Zia Weise, 'Erdoğan, the new Atatürk', *Politico*, website (26 December 2016).

18 Davutoglu has a more historically rooted, but still rather problematic, view of Turkey's relationship to the West. He argues that Westernisation destroyed the Ottoman state, 'eroding its religious legitimacy and creating a society with a weakened historical consciousness and uprooted identity'. See, M. Hakan Yavuz, 'Erdogan's Ottomania', *Boston Review*, website (8 August 2018).

19 Cagaptay, *The New Sultan*, 127–142.

Chapter 3

1 Kareem Fahim, 'Trial of American pastor highlights strained US–Turkish alliance', *Washington Post* (15 April 2018).

2 Mehmet Özkan and Birol Akgün, 'Turkey's opening to Africa', *Modern African Studies*, 48 (4) (2010), 528.

3 Mustafa Akyol, 'The problem with Turkey's "Zero Problems" Plan', *New York Times* (29 June 2016).

4 Ahmet Davutoğlu, *Stratejik Derinlik: Türkiye'nin Uluslararası Konumu* (Istanbul: Küre Yayınları, 2001), 118.

5 Ibid., 119.

6 Ibid., 216.

7 Ibid., 144.

8 'Portre: Ahmet Davutoğlu', *Milliyet*, website (21 August 2014).

9 Yavuz, 'Erdogan's Ottomania'.

10 Ibid.

11 Ibid.

12 'Erdoğan: Millet isterse laiklik tabii ki gidecek', *Hürriyet* (21 August 2001).

13 Metin Heper, 'Kemalism/Ataturkism', in Metin Heper (ed.), *The Routledge Handbook of Modern Turkey* (New York: Routledge, 2012), 139–48.

14 Maarif Vekâleti Muallim Heyeti, *Orta Mektep Tarih III. Kitap* (Istanbul: Devlet Matbaası, 1931) *passim*.

15 Gülru Necipoğlu, 'Süleyman the Magnificent and the representation of power in the context of Ottoman–Hapsburg–Papal rivalry', *Art Bulletin*, 71 (3) (1989), 401–27.

16 Ayla Jean Yackley, 'Rare painting by Turkey's last Caliph sold at auction', Reuters, news agency (6 October 2013).

17 'The German Fountain', Istanbul, website (9 May 2014).

18 Following the collapse of the Ottoman Empire, Turkish–German ties remained positive throughout the twentieth century, improving further during the Cold War. In the aftermath of the Second World War, Western European countries called out for foreign workers to fuel their economic boom. At the time, Germany became the main recipient of Turkish migrants. Millions of citizens of Turkey – a poor country during the Cold War, Turkey was 'exporting' its people at the time – voted with their feet, migrating as 'guest workers' to Germany. Today, constituting nearly 5 per cent of Germany's population, these Turkish–Germans also provide a permanent bridge between Ankara and Berlin.

19 Faiz Ahmed, *Afghanistan Rising: Islamic Law and Statecraft between the Ottoman and British Empires* (Cambridge, MA: Harvard University, 2017), 355. Ironically, these funds ended up in Ataturk's hands. He used the capital raised by Muslim Indian charities to buy Soviet weapons. Although Soviet leader Vladimir Lenin was happy to help, he misidentified Ataturk's national liberation struggle as anti-imperialist and anti-Western. In the end, Ataturk used 'communist' weapons bought with 'Muslim' money to defeat the Allies, but also abolished the Caliphate – one of the ironies of history! Even more ironically, Ataturk, after permitting the formation of the Turkish Communist Party in 1920 to curry favour with Lenin, had members of the Communist Party drowned during their ship journey across the Black Sea in January 1921, as soon as he did not need Lenin any more – an irony, this time for Lenin!

20 'Home page', Turkish Cooperation and Coordination Agency, website (n.d.).

21 Geoffrey Jukes, *The First World War (1): The Eastern Front 1914–1918* (London: Bloomsbury Publishing, 2014), 41.

22 Yavuz, 'Erdogan's Ottomania'.

23 Eric Edelman, personal correspondence (19 January 2019).

24 Jesper Moller Sorensen, personal correspondence (3 January 2019).

Chapter 4

1 See, Joseph S. Nye, Jr. 'Get smart: Combining hard and soft power', *Foreign Affairs*, 88 (4) (2009) 160–3.

2 'The World Factbook: Developed countries', Central Intelligence Agency, website (2010).

3 Nathan Williams, 'The rise of Turkish soap power', BBC News, website (28 June 2013).

4 'Turkey ranks second in TV drama export', *Hürriyet Daily News* (30 September 2017).

5 Shibley Telhami, 'The 2011 Arab Public Opinion Poll', Brookings Institution, website (21 November 2011).

6 'Foreign trade statistics', Turkish Statistical Institute, website (n.d.).

7 Mensur Akgün, Sabiha Senyücel Gündoğar and Jonathan Levack (tr.), 'The perception of Turkey in the Middle East 2012', Turkish Economic and Social Studies Foundation, website (December 2012), 8.

8 Mehmet Erkan Dursun, John F. O'Connell, Zheng Lei and David Warnock Smith, 'The transformation of a legacy carrier – A case study of Turkish Airlines', *Journal of Air Transport Management* 40 (2014), 106–18.

9 Ibid.

10 Ibid. See also, 'Offers & Destinations', Turkish Airlines (n.d.), website.

11 'Turkish Airlines (THY) flies to 7 destinations in Ukraine', *Daily Sabah* (21 March 2016).

12 'The world's largest airlines by number of countries served', World Atlas, website (1 August 2017).

13 Pinar Tremblay, 'Why Erdogan's so quiet about Turkish expansion in Africa', Al-Monitor, website (20 August 2018).

14 İsmail Numan Telci, 'İş Birliğinden Stratejik Ortaklığa: Türkiye–Afrika İlişkileri', Foundation for Political, Economic and Social Research (SETA) (3 March 2018).

15 Harun Öztürkler, 'Türkiye Ortadoğu Ticari İlişkilerinin Ekonomi Politiği', *Ortadoğu Analiz*, 7 (66) (2013), 76–9.

16 Federico Donelli and Ariel Gonzalez Levaggi, 'From Mogadishu to Buenos Aires: The Global South in the Turkish foreign policy in the late JDP Period (2011–2017)', in Emel Parlar Dal (ed.), *Middle Powers in Global Governance: The Rise of Turkey* (Basingstoke: Palgrave MacMillan, 2018), 53–73.

17 'Turkey tries out soft power in Somalia', Reuters, news agency (3 June 2012).

18 'President Erdoğan to embark on new Africa trip, attend BRICS summit', *Hürriyet Daily News* (24 July 2018).

19 Telci, 'İş Birliğinden Stratejik Ortaklığa'.

20 Ilgın Barut, 'Osmanlı döneminde gerçekleşen göçlerin kurumsallaşma ve göç politikaları üzerindeki etkileri', DergiPark, website (2 October 2018), 164.

21 From the money sultans borrowed, only a partial amount was invested in. Ottoman society's modernisation. The sultans used large portions of this money to build ostentatious palaces (four in less than half a century) along the Bosporus, such as the Dolmabahce Palace, which would later become Erdogan's Istanbul office, providing him with a backdrop in imperial glory. Erdogan frequently uses Dolmabahce for work meetings, and since becoming executive-style president in 2014, a wing of the palace has been formally allocated to him for use as his 'Istanbul office'.

22 Gürkan Beriş, 'Osmanli Borçlanma tarihi – Ottoman Debt history', Internet Archive Wayback Machine, website (n.d.).

23 Baskin Oran (ed.) and Mustafa Aksin (tr.), *Turkish Foreign Policy 1919–2006 Facts and Analyses with Documents* (Salt Lake City, UT: University of Utah Press, 2010), 145.

24 Ibid..

25 B. R. Mitchell, *European Historical Statistics 1750–1970* (New York: Columbia University Press, 1976; abridged edn, 1978), 129.

26 Statistical Office of the United Nations, *Demographic Yearbook 1948* (New York: Statistical Office of the United Nations: 1949), 129.

27 Ibid., 142.

28 Ibid., 135.

29 Ibid., 147.

30 Ibid., 155.

31 Ibid., 80.

32 Mitchell, *European Historical Statistics*, 23.

33 Statistical Office of the United Nations, *Demographic Yearbook*, 210.

34 'Turkey: Global development data', World Bank, website (n.d.).

35 'The Soviet Union: GDP growth', Nintil, website.

36 'Turkey: Global development data'.

37 World Bank, International Comparison Program Database, website (n.d.), Statistical Office of the United Nations, *Demographic Yearbook 1948*; Mitchell, *European Historical Statistics*; and 'Field listing: Population', *Central Intelligence Agency*, website (n.d.).

38 Cagaptay, *The Rise of Turkey*, *passim*.

39 World Bank, International Comparison Program Database; and 'Field listing: Population', Central Intelligence Agency.

40 'Field listing: Population', Central Intelligence Agency.

41 World Bank, International Comparison Program Database; and 'Field listing: Population', Central Intelligence Agency.

42 'GDP (Current US $)', World Bank, website (n.d.).

43 'Turkey: Literacy rate from 2005 to 2015, total and by gender', Statista, website (n.d.).

44 Ibrahim Kalin, 'Turkey and the Arab Spring', Al Jazeera, website (25 May 2011).

45 Cagaptay, *The New Sultan*, 162.

46 Burak Kadercan, 'Making sense of Turkey's Syria strategy: A "Turkish Tragedy" in the making', War on the Rocks, website (4 August 2017).

Chapter 5

1 'Association agreements', European External Action Service, website (11 May 2011).

2 Parts of this section draw from an unpublished article I have written with my colleague, Raffaella del Sarto. I would like to thank her for her contribution.

3 Stephen Kinzer, 'Turkey, rejected, will freeze ties to European Union', *New York Times* (15 December 1997).

4 Jesper Moller Sorensen, personal correspondence (3 January 2019).

5 Michael Leigh, personal correspondence (3 January 2019).

6 Ibid.

7 Cagaptay, *The New Sultan*, 87.

8 'AKP'ye kapatma davası', BBC News, website (14 March 2008).

9 For more on the Ergenekon trials, see Cagaptay, *The New Sultan*, 106; and Jenkins, *Between Fact and Fantasy*.

10 European Parliament, 'European Parliament Resolution of 21 May 2008 on Turkey's 2007 Progress Report (2007/2269(INI))' (21 May 2008). Clause 23 of Turkey's 2007 progress report 'encourages the Turkish authorities to resolutely pursue investigations into the Ergenekon criminal organization while closely adhering to the principles of the rule of law, to fully uncover its networks reaching into the state structures and to bring those involved to justice'.

11 Leigh, personal correspondence.

12 Ibid.

13 Martin Kuebler, 'Turkey not fit for EU accession: Sarkozy', Deutsche Welle, website (26 February 2011).

14 Ünal Çeviköz, 'EU–Turkey relations: The beginning of the end?', European Council on Foreign Relations, website (19 September 2017).

15 Leigh, personal correspondence.

16 'FAQ for negotiation process', Republic of Turkey Ministry of Foreign Affairs Directorate for EU Affairs, website (6 June 2017).

17 'Chapters of the acquis', European Commission Neighbourhood Policy and Enlargement Negotiations, website (6 December 2016).

18 'Current situation', Republic of Turkey Ministry of Foreign Affairs Directorate for EU Affairs, website (6 June 2017). The blocked chapters are as follows: 'Free movement of goods', 'Free movement of workers', 'Right of establishment and freedom to provide services', 'Financial services', 'Agriculture and rural development', 'Fisheries', 'Transport policy', 'Energy', 'Judiciary and fundamental rights', 'Justice', 'Freedom and security', 'Education and culture', 'Customs union', and 'External relations, foreign, security and defence policy'.

19 Council of the European Union, 'Press Release No. 16289/06' (11 December 2006).

20 'Current situation'.

21 'Social policy and employment', Republic of Turkey Ministry of Foreign Affairs Directorate for EU Affairs, website (11 May 2018).

22 Leigh, personal correspondence.

23 Soner Cagaptay, 'Turkey's turn from the West', *Washington Post* (2 February 2009).

24 Jane's Islamic Affairs Analyst, 'Turkey: Women's work is in the home?', Washington Institute for Near East Policy, website (January 2010).

25 Ibid.

26 Mustafa Aydın, Sinem Akgül Açıkmeşe, Cihan Dizdaroğlu and Onur Kara, 'Türk Dış Politikası Kamuoyu Algıları Araştırması', Kadir Has University Center for Turkish Studies, website (6 June 2018), 14.

27 Gökhan Kurtaran, 'Regional free zone attempt stillborn', *Hürriyet Daily News* (1 December 2011).

28 Soner Cagaptay, 'The E.U. needs Turkey', *New York Times* (20 December 2013).

29 Ross Wilson, personal correspondence (7 January 2019).

30 For more on this process, see Cagaptay, *The New Sultan*, 119.

31 'Polonya'da tartışmalı yargı yasası İptal', Deutsche Welle, website (18 December 2018).

Chapter 6

1 'Turkey "close" to peace force deal', CNN, website (20 March 2002); and 'Turkey opposes strike against Iraq', BBC News, website (17 July 2002).

2 Deniz Zeyrek, '1 Mart Mesajının Adresi', *Hürriyet* (8 February 2016).

3 Brian Knowlton, 'US warns Iraq on new government', *New York Times* (21 March 2005).

4 These sentiments also built on resentment lingering from the 1991 Gulf War, during which Turkey offered full support to the USA and following which, however, Turkish economic losses ran to the billions of dollars.

5 'ABD Basınından Emine Erdoğan'a Kurtlar Vadisi Eleştirisi', Haber Vitrini, website (15 February 2006).

6 'Global poll slams Bush leadership', BBC News, website (19 January 2005).

7 Amberin Zaman, 'Genocide claim by Muslim ally Turkey', *The Telegraph* (5 April 2002).

8 'Unfavorable views of Jews and Muslims on the increase in Europe', Pew Research Center, website (17 September 2008).

9 Senior Turkish diplomat, personal correspondence (3 January 2019).

10 'Erdoğan'dan İsrail'e "soykırım" suçlaması', Deutsche Welle, website (14 May 2018); and 'Erdoğan: İsrail bir terör devleti', *Sabah* (26 July 2014).

11 'Foreigners don't like Muslims, only their money: Turkish President Erdoğan', *Hürriyet Daily News* (27 November 2014).

12 Katrin Bennhold, 'Leaders of Turkey and Israel clash at Davos Panel', *New York Times* (29 January 2009).

13 Scott Wilson, 'Hamas sweeps Palestinian elections, complicating peace efforts in Mideast', *Washington Post* (27 January 2006).

14 Soner Cagaptay, 'Hamas visits Ankara: The AKP shifts Turkey's role in the Middle East', Washington Institute for Near East Policy, website (16 February 2006).

15 Ibid.

16 Senior European diplomat, personal correspondence (3 January 2019). To get even with Rasmussen, Erdogan would later in 2009 try to block the Danish prime minister's appointment as NATO's Secretary General. Although this effort failed, it speaks volumes about the bad blood between Erdogan and some right-wing politicians in Europe.

17 Ferit Demir, 'Turkey sends special forces to Iraqi border', Reuters, news agency (13 November 2007).

18 Steven Lee Myers, 'Bush pledges to help Turkey on intelligence', *New York Times* (6 November 2007).

19 Sinan Ülgen, 'In search of lost time: Turkey–U.S. relations after Bush', Brookings Institution, website (19 February 2009).

20 Myers, 'Bush pledges'.

21 Ülgen, 'In search of lost time'.

22 Turkish diplomat, personal correspondence (1 August 2009).

23 'Obama to visit Turkey "within weeks"', *The Guardian* (7 March 2009).

24 'President Obama's remarks in Turkey', *New York Times* (6 April 2009).

25 Glenn Kessler, 'UN vote on Iran sanctions not a clear-cut win for Obama', *Washington Post* (9 June 2010).

26 Noah Kosharek, Liel Kyzer and Barak Ravid, 'Israel transfers hundreds of Gaza Flotilla activists to airport for deportation', Associated Press and DPA, news agencies, and *Haaretz*, website (1 June 2010).

27 Soner Cagaptay, 'Obama, Erdogan finds shared interests', *Washington Post* (11 November 2011).

28 'Turkish officials hail Turkey's United Nations Security Council Seat', *Hürriyet* (18 October 2008).

29 James Kanter, 'Gates criticizes Turkey vote against sanctions', *New York Times* (11 June 2010).

30 Cagaptay, 'Obama, Erdogan finds shared interests'.

31 Josh Rogin, 'Obama names his world leader best buddies!', *Foreign Policy* (19 January 2012).

32 Wilson, personal correspondence.

33 Simon Cameron-Moore and Samia Nakhoul, 'Arab rulers must change or risk defeat: Turkey', Reuters, news agency (30 March 2011).

34 Thom Shanker, 'U.S. hails deal with Turkey on missile shield', *New York Times* (September 15, 2011).

35 Soner Cagaptay and Marc J. Sievers, 'Turkey and Egypt's Great Game in the Middle East', *Foreign Affairs*, website (8 March 2015).

36 Tim Arango, 'Growing mistrust between U.S. and Turkey is played out in public', *New York Times* (23 December 2013).

37 'Çek git bu ülkeden', *Yeni Şafak* (21 December 2013).

38 Steven A. Cook, 'Egypt and Turkey: Nightmares', Council on Foreign Relations, website (25 November 2013).

39 Christopher M. Blanchard and Amy Belasco, 'Train and Equip Program for Syria: Authorities, funding, and issues for Congress', Congressional Research Service, website (9 June 2015).

Chapter 7

1 Soner Cagaptay, *Islam, Secularism, and Nationalism in Modern Turkey: Who Is a Turk?* (New York: Routledge, 2006), 37.

2 A sanjak is an Ottoman administrative unit below the level of a province. In addition to the Sanjak of Alexandretta, other former Ottoman administrative units, such as the Sanjak of Novi Pazar, today mostly located in Serbia, are also usually referred to as 'sanjak', using a political shorthand.

3 Soner Cagaptay, 'Syria and Turkey: The PKK dimension', Washington Instituite for Near East Policy, website (5 April 2012).

4 'Timeline: Kurdish militant group PKK's three-decade war with Turkey', Reuters, news agency (21 March 2013).

5 Soner Cagaptay, 'Turkey's fray into the Fertile Crescent', *New York Times* (27 February 2013).

6 'Turkey issues "final word" to Syria', Reuters, news agency (15 August 2011).

7 Cagaptay, *The New Sultan*, 164.

8 Cagaptay, 'Turkey's fray'.

9   'Syria unrest: US calls on President Assad to resign', BBC News, website (18 August 2011).

10 Turkish Foreign Ministry official, personal correspondence (1 August 2011).

11 Liam Stack, "In Slap at Syria, Turkey Shelters Anti-Assad Fighters," *New York Times* (27 October 2011).

12 Liam Stack, 'In slap at Syria, Turkey shelters anti-Assad fighters', *New York Times* (27 October 2011).

13 Aaron Stein, personal correspondence (1 January 2019).

14 Elizabeth O'Bagy, 'The Free Syrian Army', Institute for the Study of War, website (March 2013), 11.

15 'Saudi Arabia, Qatar press for more help to Syrian rebels', Reuters, news agency (20 February 2013).

16 Rania Abouzeid, 'Opening the weapons tap: Syria's rebels await fresh and free ammo', *Time* (22 June 2016).

17 Soner Cagaptay and James F. Jeffrey, 'Can Obama save Turkey from a Syrian quagmire?', *New York Times* (16 May 2013).

18 Aaron Stein, 'The origins of Turkey's Buffer Zone in Syria', War on the Rocks, website (11 December 2014).

19 Following a period of massive civilian casualties in Syria in August 2012, Obama issued his famous 'redline' regarding the Assad regime. Specifically, he declared that if the Syrian president were to use chemical weapons, the USA would respond militarily. Assad did use chemical weapons on his own citizens on 21 August 2013. At the time, the expectation in Washington and globally was that the USA would act militarily, changing the course of Syria's uprising against Assad. During a famous string of events, most notably following his self-reflective walk through the Rose Garden of the White House on 30 October 2015, Obama decided not to act military against Assad. From this point on, it was almost certain that he would not interfere in the war to change the course of the conflict.

20 Chuck Todd, 'The White House walk-and-talk that changed Obama's mind on Syria', NBC News, website (2 November 2015).

21 Ahmet S. Yayla and Colin P. Clarke, 'Turkey's double ISIS standard', *Foreign Policy* (12 April 2018).

22 Tuba Şahin, 'Turkey installs 764 km security wall on Syria border', Anadolu Agency, Turkish state-run press agency (9 June 2018).

23 Deborah Amos, 'A smuggler explains how he helped fighters along "Jihadi Highway"', NPR, website (7 October 2014).

24 Ibid.

25 Aaron Stein, 'Turkey did nothing about the Jihadists in its midst – until it was too late', *Foreign Policy* (1 July 2016).

26 Yayla and Clarke, 'Turkey's double ISIS standard'.

27 Edelman, personal correspondence (10 February 2019).

28 'PYD leader arrives in Turkey for two-day talks: Report', *Hürriyet Daily News* (25 July 2013). See also, Aaron Stein, 'For Turkey, it's all about regime change in Syria', Al Jazeera, website (8 October 2014).

29 Stein, 'For Turkey'.

30 'Battle for Kobane: Key events', BBC News, website (25 June 2015).

31 Daren Butler, 'About 60,000 Syrian Kurds flee to Turkey from Islamic State advance', Reuters, news agency (20 September 2014).

32 'Battle for Kobane'.

33 Kareem Fahim and Karam Shoumali, 'Turkey to let Iraqi Kurds cross to Syria to fight ISIS', *New York Times* (20 October 2014).

34 Anne Bard, 'Reinforcements enter besieged Syrian town via Turkey, raising hopes', *New York Times* (29 October 2014).

35 Fahim and Shoumali, 'Turkey'.

36 'Islamic State crisis: Syria rebel forces boost Kobane defence', BBC News, website (29 October 2014), Aaron Stoin, personal correspondence (1 January 2019).

37 'Battle for Kobane'.

38 Tim Manhoff, 'Turkey's foreign policy towards Syria: From neo-Ottoman adventurism to neo-Ottoman realpolitik', Konrad Adenauer Stiftung, website (3 December 2017), 9.

39 Ceylan Yeginsu, 'Militants storm Turkish Consulate in Iraqi city, taking 49 people as hostages', *New York Times* (11 June 2014).

40 Stein, personal correspondence.

41 Joe Parkinson and Ayla Albayrak, 'Turkey sends troops into Syria to retrieve Ottoman tomb, guards', *Wall Street Journal* (22 February 2015).

42 Ceylan Yeginsu and Helene Cooper, 'US jets to use Turkish bases in war on ISIS', *New York Times* (23 July 2015).

43 'President Assad admits army strained by war in Syria', BBC News, website (26 July 2015).

44 Stein, personal correspondence.

45 Ceylan Yeginsu, 'Turkey votes to allow operations against ISIS', *New York Times* (2 October 2014).

46 'In about 93 months . . . about 560 thousand were killed in Syria since the day of claiming rights to the international human rights day', Syrian Observatory for Human Rights, website (10 December 2018).

47 Soner Cagaptay, 'Turkey to vote on Syria policy', Washington Institute for Near East Policy, website (1 October 2014).

48 As part of the Lausanne Treaty of 1923, Turkey and Greece agreed to 'exchange' their Orthodox and Muslims populations. The treaty covered over 2 million citizens from Greece and Turkey, who subsequently found new homes in Turkey and Greece, respectively.

49 Soner Cagaptay and Maya Yalkin, 'Syrian refugees in Turkey', Washington Institute for Near East Policy, website (22 August 2018).

50 Idil Engindeniz, 'Media Watch on Hate Speech report', Hrant Dink Foundation, website (July 2018).

51 'Türkiye'de Kutuplaşmanın Boyutları Araştırması', Istanbul Bilgi University, website (5 February 2018), 65.

52 'Dışişleri Bakanı Sayın Ahmet Davutoğlu'nun TRT-1 Televizyonunda Yayımlanan Enine Boyuna Programında Yaptığı Açıklamalar', Republic of Turkey Ministry of Foreign Affairs, website (27 October 2013).

53 AK Parti (@akparti),Twitter (21 July 2014), 'Başbakan Erdoğan: Biz Ortadoğu'da hakkın ve haklının yanındayız'.

54 'Hizbullah militanları Suriye'de', *Posta* (18 February 2013).

Chapter 8

1 Taking into account a West–East linguistic spectrum, Turkish spoken in eastern Turkey, such as in Erzurum Province, is closer to the Azerbaijani language than it is to Turkish spoken in western Turkey, such as in Istanbul, on which the dialect of modern Turkish has been standardised. Besides historic linguistic similarities, Azerbaijan has a special place in Turkish nationalist thinking, which puts it closer to Turkey than other Turkic nations. Some of the early fathers of Turkish nationalist thinking, such as Ahmet Agaoğlu (Ahmet Bey Agayev), hail from Azerbaijan. And it was the Azeris who adopted the first Latin-based alphabet for a Turkic language. Stalin imposed the Cyrillic alphabet on Azeris in 1939 as well as on other Turkic nations. This initiative was consistent with Soviet efforts to start a process of cultural alienation, separating Turks from Azeris and other Turkic nations within the Soviet Union – until the end of the Cold War.

2 'Turkey's political relations with Russian Federation', Republic of Turkey Ministry of Foreign Affairs, website (n.d.).

3 Vefa Kurban, '1950–1960 Yıllarında Türkiye ile Sovyetler Birliği Arasındaki İlişkiler', *Journal of Modern Turkish History Studies*, 28 (Spring 2014), 270.

4 Duygu Bazoğlu Sezer, 'Russia: The challenges of reconciling geopolitical competition with economic partnership', in Barry Rubin and Kemal Kirişci (eds), *Turkey in World Politics: An Emerging Multiregional Power* (Boulder, CO: Lynne Rienner, 2001), 157.

5 'Foreign trade statistics', Turkish Statistical Institute, website (August 2018).

6 'Border statistics 2017', Republic of Turkey Ministry of Tourism and Culture, website (July 2018).

7 'New era of Russian–Turkish business relations', Russian–Turkish Business Forum, website (12 November 2018).

8 'Turkish Airlines begins flights to its tenth Russian destination', Airline Network News and Analysis, website (18 April 2017).

9 'New Era of Russian–Turkish business relations'.

10 Soner Cagaptay and Nazli Gencsoy, 'Improving Turkish–Russian relations: Turkey's new foreign policy and its implications for the United States', Washington Institute for the Near East Policy, website (12 January 2005).

11 'Foreign trade statistics' (August 2018).

12 'Erdoğanlar'ın mutlu günü', NTV, website (10 August 2013).

13 Fethi, Füsun Yiğit, Emine Akarsu and Kerim Tuncer Sarıkavak 'Güney Akım Projesi', *MTA Doğal Kaynaklar Ve Ekonomi Bülteni* 14, General Directorate of Mineral Research and Exploration, website, (2012), 26–34.

14 Greg Bruno, 'Turkey at an eergy crossroads', Council on Foreign Relations, website (20 November 2008).

15 Alan Makovsky, 'Turkey's growing energy ties with Moscow', Center for American Progress, website (6 May 2015).

16 'The TAP and TANAP pipelines were connected at the border of Greece and Turkey', Energy Market Price, website (30 November 2018).

17 Melik Kaylan, 'Erdoğan shoots down Putin', *Politico*, website (24 November 2015).

18 'Bekir Bozdağ: ABD darbe girişimini Gülen'in yaptığını çok iyi biliyor', *Habertürk* (24 July 2016).

19 Ergün Diler, 'ABD'nin B Planı', *Takvim* (26 May 2017).

20 Named after Catherine the Great's grandson, Grand Duke Constantine, who was supposed to become the ruler of a restored Byzantine Empire. See, 'How Catherine II wanted to revive the Byzantine Empire', Russian Geography (n.d.), website.

21 Shaun Walker, 'Erdoğan and Putin discuss closer ties in first meeting since jet downing', *The Guardian* (9 August 2016).

22 Selim Koru, 'The resiliency of Turkey–Russia relations', Foreign Policy Research Institute, website (19 November 2018).

23 Naz Durakoglu, 'An unlikely opposition: How Sputnik Turkiye is posing as opposition media & exploiting vulnerabilities in Turkey's narrowing media space', Atlantic Council, website (21 March 2017).

24 Dimitar Bechev, personal correspondence (29 December 2018).

25 'Russian brings forward delivery of S-400 missiles to Turkey to July 2019', *Times of Israel*, website (4 April 2018).

26 Tuvan Gumrukcu and Ece Toksabay, 'Turkey, Russia sign deal on supply of S-400 missiles', Reuters, news agency (29 December 2017).

27 'Pompeo presses Turkey'.

28 For a thorough analysis of Turkish–Russian ties, see, Koru, 'The resiliency'.

Chapter 9

1 Alan Makovsky, personal correspondence (1 February 2019).

2 The Alevis are a community of liberal Muslims, whose belief emphasises spirituality over practice. Practising a syncretic and heterodox faith that mixes elements of the Turks' pre-Islamic faith, Shamanism, Christianity and Islam, Alevis can be considered neither Sunni nor Shi'ite, two similarly orthodox, but historically opposing, branches of Islam. Traditionally, many urban Alevis in the Ottoman Empire organised in the Bektashi tariqat, which served as the official faith of the Ottoman army's elite force, the Janissary order. Alevis revere the Muslim Prophet Mohamed's son-in-law, Ali. From the fifteenth to the seventieth century, during Ottoman wars with Shi'ite Safavids, this stance, shared by Alevis, led the Sunni Ottoman sultans to fear that Ottoman Alevis would support Shi'ites, who adore Ali. These wars witnessed an intense period of Alevi ethnic cleansing under the Ottoman sultans, mostly notably Selim I (The Grim). Many surviving Alevis took refuge in the highlands of Anatolia, only to fully reemerge following Ataturk's secularising reforms. The twentieth century witnessed an intense period of Alevi migration to Turkey's big cities and their integration into the broader Turkish population. Today, Alevis, who constitute 10–20 per cent of the Turkish population, mostly vote for secular parties and oppose Erdogan. For more on the Alevis, see David Shankland, *The Alevis in Turkey: The Emergence of a Secular Islamic Tradition* (London and New York: Routledge, 2007).

3 'Iran: Turkey must rethink stance on Syria, NATO Missile Shield or face "trouble"', Reuters, news agency, and *Haaretz*, website (9 October 2011).

4 Soner Cagaptay, 'Next up: Turkey vs. Iran', *The New York Times* (14 February 2012).

5 Ibid.

6 'Erdoğan kime "kardeşim" dediyse . . .', *Sözcü* (5 May 2016).

7 Nicole Hong, 'Recep Tayyip Erdogan allowed Turkish banks to help Iran make illegal payments, witness says', *Wall Street Journal* (30 November 2017).

8 Soner Cagaptay, 'In U.S.–Iran Deal, Turkey fears a Shiite alliance', *New York Times* (27 March 2016).

9 Cagaptay, 'Next up.

10 Ibid.

11 Ibid.

12 'Erdoğan'dan İran'ı kızdıracak açıklama', Odatv, website (4 April 2017).

13 'Iran: Threat to strike NATO radar in Turkey not official policy', *Haaretz*, website (14 December 2011).

14 Cagaptay, 'In U.S.–Iran Deal'.

15 Ibid.

16 Akın Ünver, 'Iran deal and Turkey: Time for a soft-power reset', Al Jazeera, website (19 July 2015).

17 Cagaptay, 'In U.S.–Iran Deal'.

18 Cengiz Candar, 'How Turkey really feels about the Iran deal', Al-Monitor, website (20 July 2015).

19 'AKP'li Şamil Tayyar: Adil Öksüz ABD Konsolosluğu'nda olabilir, imkân olsa da bakılsa!', T24, website (29 May 2017).

20 David Ignatius, 'The coup attempt dealt a new blow to the strained U.S.–Turkish relationship', *Washington Post* (18 July 2016).

21 İbrahim Karagül, 'Dördüncü İstiklal Savaşı da 'Karşı Darbe' ile kazanılacak. Erken doğum, gizli ortaklar, ekonomide "temizlik" zamanı', *Yeni Şafak* (17 August 2018). See also, 'Yeni Şafak: İkinci 15 Temmuz güneyden gelecek', T24, website (2 August 2017).

22 'Iran FM briefs Parliament on Turkey botched coup: MP', Press TV, website (17 July 2016).

23 Metin Gürcan, 'Turkey, Iran could unite to overcome their Kurdish worries', Al-Monitor, website (10 October 2017); and Safa Haeri, 'Erdogan back home from his Tehran visit empty hands', Iran Press Service, website (31 July 2004).

24 Soner Cagaptay, 'Turkish–Iranian rivalry redux', Washington Institute for Near East Policy, website (17 October 2011).

25 Galip Dalay, 'Is there really a Turkey–Iran rapprochement?', Al Jazeera, website (13 September 2017).

26 'Qatar crisis'.

27　'Iran FM Zarif visits Turkey to find solutions to ease regional tensions', Rudaw, website (6 June 2017); and Dalay, 'Is there really a Turkey–Iran rapprochement?'.

28　Gürcan, 'Turkey, Iran'.

Chapter 10

1　'Syria, Lebanon mark Martyrs Day', United Press International, website (6 May 1966).

2　Ivan Watson and Mohamed Fadel Fahmy, 'Turkish prime minister arrives for visit to Egypt as role widens', CNN, website (14 September 2011).

3　Ibid.

4　'Erdoğan Mısır'da sevinç gösterileriyle karşılandı', BBC News, website (13 September 2011).

5　Nicola Mirenzi, 'Erdoğan and secularism', Reset Doc, website (27 September 2011).

6　'مشاهد لرئيس وزراء تركيا أبهرت المصريين 5,' Masrawy, website (12 March 2012).

7　Cagaptay and Sievers, 'Turkey and Egypt's Great Game'.

8　Ibid.

9　Anthony Shadid, 'Turkey predicts alliance with Egypt as regional anchors', New York Times (18 September 2011).

10　Cagaptay and Sievers, 'Turkey and Egypt's Great Game'.

11　David D. Kirkpatrick and Mayy El Sheikh, 'Citing deadlock, Egypt's leader seizes new power and plans Mubarak retrial', New York Times (22 November 2012).

12　Large parts of this discussion on Egypt draw from my following article with Ambassador Sievers whom I would like to thank. Cagaptay and Sievers, 'Turkey and Egypt's Great Game'.

13　Watson and Fahmy, 'Turkish prime minister'.

14　'Egypt signs $1 billion Turkish loan deal', Reuters, news agency (30 September 2012).

15　Cagaptay and Sievers, 'Turkey and Egypt's Great Game'.

16　'Egypt crisis: Mass protests over Morsi grip cities', BBC News, website (1 July 2013).

17　Shaima Fayed and Yasmine Saleh, 'Millions flood Egypt's streets to demand Mursi quit', Reuters, news agency (29 June 2013).

18　Cagaptay and Sievers, 'Turkey and Egypt's Great Game'.

19 Soner Cagaptay, 'Opinion: Erdoğan's empathy for Mursi', Asharq Al-Awsat, website (14 September 2013).

20 Ibid.

21 Ibid.

22 Ibid.

23 'Turkey – Freedom in the World 2015', Freedom House, website (n.d.).

24 Cagaptay and Sievers, 'Turkey and Egypt's Great Game'.

25 Serkan Ocak, 'Başbakan Erdoğan: Batı, demokrasi konusunda sınıfta kaldı', *Radikal* (7 July 2013).

26 Cagaptay, 'Opinion'.

27 'Turkey withdraws from Libya summit in Italy: Vice President', Reuters, news agency (13 November 2018).

28 'Tunisia coalition agrees top government posts', BBC News, website (21 November 2011).

29 Jeffrey Goldberg, 'The Modern King in the Arab Spring', *The Atlantic* (15 April 2013).

30 Selin Girit, 'Why is Turkey standing up for Qatar?', BBC News, website (14 June 2017).

31 Youssef Sheiko, 'The United Arab Emirates: Turkey's new rival', Washington Institute for Near East Policy, website (16 February 2018).

32 Ibid.

33 'President Erdoğan addresses the UN General Assembly', Presidency of the Republic of Turkey, website (24 September 2014).

34 'UAE reopens Syria Embassy in boost for Assad', Reuters, news agency (27 December 2018).

35 Semih Idiz, 'Turkish–Arab ties marked by fear and loathing', Al-Monitor, website (13 March 2018). See also, T. C. Cumhurbaşk anlığı İletişim Başkanlığı (@iletisim), Twitter (20 December 2017) '#CumhurbaşkanıErdoğan, BAE Dışişleri Bakanı Zayed'in tepki çeken paylaşımına ilişkin: Medine korumasını yaparken Fahreddin Paşa, ey bize bühtanda bulunan zavallı, senin ceddin neredeydi?'.

36 'Retweet by UAE FM about Ottoman commander turns into feud with Erdogan', Al Arabiya, website (21 December 2017). See original here, ABZayed (@ali11iraq), Twitter (16 December 2017).
هل تعلمون في عام1916قام التركي فخري باشا بجريمة بحق أهل المدينة النبوية فسرق أموالهم'
وقام بخطفهم واركابهم في قطارات إلى الشام واسطنبول برحلة سُميت (سفر برلك) كما سرق
الأتراك أغلب مخطوطات المكتبة المحمودية بالمدينة وارسلوها إلى تركيا. هؤلاء أجداد أردوغان
.'وتاريخهم مع المسلمين العرب

37 'UAE: The Arab world will not be led by Iran and Turkey', The National, website (27 December 2017).

38 T. C. Cumhurbaşkanlığı İletişim Başkanlığı (@iletisim), Twitter.

39 'Yiğit Bulut: Amerika'nın 52. Eyaleti Birleşik Arap Emirlikleri', YouTube, video (19 December 2017).

Chapter 11

1   Akgün, Gündoğar and Levack (tr.), 'The perception of Turkey'.

2   'Interview transcript: Rachid Ghannouchi', *Financial Times* (11 January 2018).

3   Monica Marks, 'How Egypt's coup really affected Tunisia's Islamists', *Washington Post* (16 March 2015).

4   Sevil Erkuş, 'Turkey summons ambassador over Tunisian FM's comments', *Hürriyet Daily News* (3 April 2015).

5   Cagaptay and Sievers, 'Turkey and Egypt's Great Game'.

6   Sinan Uslu, Enes Kaplan and Sorwar Alam, 'President Erdogan visits Turkey military base in Qatar', Anadolu Agency, Turkish state-run press agency (16 November 2017).

7   'Turkey: Military chiefs resign en masse', BBC News, website (29 July 2011).

8   Asli Aydıntaşbaş, 'The good, the bad, and the Gülenists', European Council on Foreign Relations, website (23 September 2016).

9   'Turkey sent files on 452 FETO members to 83 countries – Cavusoglu', TRT World, website (14 November 2018). See also, Onur Burçak Belli, Eren Caylan and Maximilian Popp, 'Erdogan's hunt against the Gülen Movement', *Spiegel Online*, website (3 August 2016).

10 Nye, Jr., 'Get smart.

11 Figures are calculated from data presented in Osman Bahadır Dinçer and Mustafa Kutlay, 'Türkiye'nin Ortadoğu'daki Güç Kapasitesi: Mümkünün Sınırları', USAK Ortadoğu ve Afrika Araştırmaları Merkezi (April 2012), 18.

12 Ibid., 19.

13 'Migrant crisis: EU–Turkey deal comes into effect', BBC News, website (20 March 2016).

14 Fadi Hakura, 'The EU–Turkey refugee deal solves little', Chatham House, website (Spring 2016).

15 Senior Turkish diplomat, personal correspondence (3 January 2019).

16 Anthony Shadid, 'Can Turkey unify the Arabs?', *New York Times* (28 May 2011).

17 Sotiris S. Livas, 'Turkey's image in the Middle East via the Arab media', *Turkish Review*, 5 (1) (2015), 14–21.

Chapter 12

1 Stephen Kalin, 'Dispute over Turkish troops throws future of Mosul into question', Reuters, news agency (7 January 2016).

2 Galip Dalay, 'Evolution of Turkey–Iraqi Kurdistan's relations', Al Jazeera Centre for Studies, website (20 December 2017).

3 Barry Malone, 'Iraq summons Turkish envoy over Erdogan broadside', Reuters, news agency (23 April 2012).

4 Elizabeth Palmer, 'ISIS encroaches on ultimate prize in Iraq', CBS News, website (10 October 2014).

5 '"Yes" to Kurdistan: 92 percent of Iraq's Kurds voted for independence, official results show', *Haaretz*, website (27 September 2017).

6 'Turkey to reopen consulates in Mosul and Basra: Turkish FM', *Hürriyet Daily News* (11 October 2018).

7 'Turkey to reopen its consulates in Iraq's Basra and Mosul', Associated Press, news agency (11 October 2018).

8 'KCK denounces PUK for closing PKK-linked party offices in Sulaimani', Rudaw, website (30 November 2018).

9 Soner Cagaptay and Michael Herzog, 'How America can help its friends make nice', *New York Times* (20 June 2012).

10 'Turkey says Israel paid compensation to families of 2010 flotilla raid victims – media', Reuters, news agency (23 June 2017).

11 'Turkish court dismisses *Mavi Marmara* case after deal with Israel', *Daily Sabah* (9 December 2016).

12 'Turkey's Erdogan meets American Jewish delegation in Ankara', *Jerusalem Post*, website (9 February 2016).

13 'Erdogan meets with U.S. Jewish leaders on sidelines of Washington Nuclear Summit', *Haaretz*, website (3 April 2016).

14 Soner Cagaptay and Michael Herzog, 'Israel and Turkey approaching reconciliation amid policy challenges', Washington Institute for Near East Policy, website (19 April 2016).

15 'Turkey, Israel sign deal to normalise ties after six years', Reuters, news agency (28 June 2016).

16 Shlomo Cesana, 'Israel livid over new Hamas headquarters in Turkey', *Israel Hayom*, website (26 November 2014).

17 'Report: Turkey bows to US pressure, expels top Hamas operative', *Jerusalem Post*, website (7 August 2015).

18 'Israil', Republic of Turkey Ministry of Trade, website (n.d.).

19 'Foreign trade statistics', Turkish Statistical Institute (n.d.).

20 Ibid.

21 Soner Cagaptay and Tyler Evans, 'The unexpected vitality of Turkish–Israeli trade', Washington Institute for Near East Policy, website (June 2012).

22 Ibid.

23 'Turkish Airlines carried 1 million passengers to and from Israel in 2017', *Hürriyet Daily News* (11 January 2018).

24 Jonathan Ferziger and Elliott Gotkine, 'US says Israel gas may help Europe diversify from Russian fuel', Bloomberg, website (7 April 2016).

25 Arye Mekel, 'Birth of a geopolitical bloc: The Israel–Greece–Cyprus axis', *Haaretz*, website (13 January 2016).

26 Saim Kurubas, 'Turkey–Greece tensions: What comes next?', TRT World, website (25 April 2018).

27 Warren Hoge, 'Cyprus Greeks and Turks agree on plan to end 40-year conflict', *Washington Post* (14 February 2004).

28 Susan Sachs, 'Greek Cypriots reject a U.N. Peace Plan', *New York Times* (25 April 2004).

29 Helena Smith, 'Former President of Cyprus who scuppered reunification with the Turkish north', *The Guardian* (7 January 2009).

30 'Cypriots welcome UN Reunion Plan', Al Jazeera, website (14 February 2004).

31 For more on the Annan Plan and how it was viewed by Cypriot Greeks and Cypriot Turks, see, Neophytos Loizides and Eser Keskiner, 'The aftermath of the Annan Plan Referendums: Cross-voting moderation for Cyprus?', *Penn State Citeseerx Report*, 5 (2–3) (2004), 158–71.

32 'Relations between Turkey and Armenia', Republic of Turkey Ministry of Foreign Affairs, website (n.d.).

33 Saban Kardas, 'Turkey reacts to Armenian Constitutional Court's decision on Protocols', Jamestown Foundation, website (26 January 2010). See also, 'Nagorno-Karabakh Conflict', Council on Foreign Relations, website (n.d.).

34 'Intel: Why Armenia wants to make peace with Turkey', Al-Monitor, website (11 December 2018).

35 'Before Athens trip, Erdogan urges Lausanne Treaty update', Ekathimerini, website (6 December 2017).

36 'Two Greek soldiers return home after Turkey release', *Hürriyet Daily News* (14 August 2018).

Chapter 13

1 'Erdoğan congratulates Trump in phone call, reiterates commitment to strengthen relations', *Daily Sabah* (9 November 2016).

2 Soner Cagaptay, James F. Jeffrey and Ömer Taşpınar, 'Turkey and the failed coup one year later', Washington Institute for Near East Policy, event (20 July 2017).

3 Patrick Kingsley, 'Turkey investigating 17, some Americans, accused in failed coup', *New York Times* (15 April 2017).

4 Soner Cagaptay and Ed Stafford, 'A Turkish-friendly zone inside Syria', Washington Institute for Near East Policy, website (29 January 2016).

5 'ABD seçim sonuçları açıklandı: Trump başkan', *Yeni Şafak* (9 November 2016).

6 'A violent brawl outside the Turkish Embassy in Washington, DC', ABC News, YouTube video (17 May 2017).

7 'Three more Erdogan guards indicted for Washington brawl', Al Jazeera, website (29 August 2017).

8 Glen Johnson and Richard Spencer, 'Turkey's politicians, gold dealer and the pop star', *The Telegraph* (29 December 2013).

9 Nate Raymond, 'US arrests Turkish businessman accused of evading Iran sanctions', Reuters, news agency (21 March 2016).

10 Brendan Pierson, 'US charges Turkish banker in Iran sanctions probe', Reuters, news agency (28 March 2017).

11 Benjamin Weiser, 'Reza Zarrab testifies that he bribed Turkish minister', *New York Times* (29 November 2017).

12 Devlin Barrett, 'U.S. court convicts Turkish banker in multibillion-dollar scheme to help Iran evade sanctions', *Washington Post* (3 January 2018).

13 'US actions purely political, taken against Turkish state, Erdoğan says', *Daily Sabah* (8 September 2017).

14 Carlotta Gall and Anne Barnard, 'Turkey begins operation against U.S.-backed Kurdish militias in Syria', *New York Times* (19 January 2018).

15 'The trajectory of Afrin Operation', Al Jazeera Centre for Studies, website (28 March 2018).

16 Sebastien Roblin, 'America's big fear: Turkey mixing F-35s and Russia's S-400 Air Defense System', National Interest, website (7 July 2018).

17 Patricia Zengerle, Mike Stone and James Dalgleish, 'US spending bill would halt transfer of F-35s to Turkey', Reuters, news agency (21 June 2018).

18 Uğur Ergan and Cansu Çamlıbel, 'F-35 şerhine Ankara'dan tepki', *Hürriyet* (20 June 2018).

19 Jack Detsch, 'Congress to make determination on F-35'S for Turkey', Al-Monitor, website (23 November 2018).

20 For a timeline of events between the US and Turkey in 2018 related to the F-35 planes, see, 'F-35 savaş uçakları: Teknik özellikleri ve Türkiye'ye teslimatıyla ilgili bilinmesi gerekenler', BBC News, website (13 August 2018).

21 'Turkey's Erdogan links fate of detained US pastor to wanted cleric Gülen', Reuters, news agency (28 September 2017).

22 'Andrew Brunson, U.S. pastor, moved to house arrest in Turkey', *New York Times* (25 July 2018).

23 Jacob Pramuk, 'Why Trump is attacking Turkey with sanctions and tariffs', CNBC, website (10 August 2018). See also, Karen DeYoung and Felicia Sonmez, 'US sanctions two Turkish officials over detention of American pastor', *Washington Post* (1 August 2018).

24 'Turkish lira plunges to new record low in Asia Pacific trade', Reuters, news agency (12 August 2018).

25 Caroline Kelly and Kate Sullivan, 'Released US pastor Andrew Brunson returns to US, meets with Trump', CNN, website (14 October 2018).

26 Frederica Cocco, 'Turkish lira extends rally on back of softer dollar', *Financial Times* (26 October 2018).

27 Quint Forgey, 'Trump thanks Erdoğan for American pastor's release', *Politico*, website (13 October 2018). See also, original tweet, Donald J. Trump (@realDonaldTrump), Twitter (20 May 2018), 'There was NO DEAL made with Turkey for the release and return of Pastor Andrew Brunson. I don't make deals for hostages. There was, however, great appreciation on behalf of the United States, which will lead to good, perhaps great, relations between the United States & Turkey!'.

28 'Turkey among 8 countries granted waiver on US oil sanctions against Iran', *Hürriyet Daily News* (5 November 2018).

29 Rich Outzen, personal correspondence (3 January 2019).

30 Helbast Shekani, 'Exclusive: US general visits Syria's Manbij, confirms support for Kurdish-led forces', Kurdistan24, website (21 June 2018).

Chapter 14

1 Madalin Necsutu, 'Turkish Secret Services nab six "Gulenists" in Moldova', Balkan Insight, website (6 September 2018). See also, Amberin Zaman, 'Turkey snatches "Gülenist" teachers in Moldova', Al-Monitor, website (6 September 2018).

2 'With the awareness that I am the President of all our 81 million citizens, I will work to be worthy of our nation', Presidency of the Republic of Turkey, website (9 July 2018).

3   Pakistan and Turkey are each other's evergreen allies. Turkish military thinkers include Islamabad within the 'Pentagon of Turkey's Military Allies', a list of countries that Ankara considers closest to it militarily, together with the Azerbaijan, TRNC, USA, South Korea, which has had strong ties with Ankara, dating back to Turkish military fighting on its side during the Korean War of 1950–3. Israel, too, was on this informal list, creating a 'Hexagon of Turkish Military Allies', until Erdogan dropped it in 2010.

4   'Cumhurbaşkanı Erdoğan Yeni Döneme Dualarla Başladı', Diyanet Haber, website (10 July 2018).

5   '13 yılda 65 yeni temsilcilik: Türkiye'nin yurtdışındaki temsilcilik sayısı 228'e çıktı', T. C. Başbakanlık Kamu Diplomasisi Koordinatörlüğü, website (2015).

6   Ibid.

7   'Turkish representations', Republic of Turkey Ministry of Foreign Affairs, website (n.d.).

8   'Health support from TİKA to Uganda', Turkish Coordination and Coordination Agency, website (9 August 2018).

9   'TIKA offers education support to South Sudan', Turkish Coordination and Coordination Agency, website (12 January 2018).

10   Senem B. Çevik, 'Narrating Turkey's story: Communicating its nation brand through public diplomacy', in Emel Parlar Dal (ed.), *Middle Powers in Global Governance: The Rise of Turkey* (Cham: Springer International, 2018), 213–30.

11   William Armstrong and Ahmet Erdi Öztürk, 'Ahmet Öztürk on the rising profile of Turkey's religious affairs directorate', *Turkey Book Talks*, podcast (4 September 2018).

12   Ibid.

13   Pinar Tremblay, 'Many Turks outraged by state religious authority's bloated budget', Al-Monitor, website (3 December 2018).

14   Ahmet Erdi Öztürk and Semiha Sözeri, 'Diyanet as a Turkish foreign policy tool: Evidence from the Netherlands and Bulgaria', *Politics and Religion*, 11 (3) (2018), 624–48.

15   'Turkey reaping rewards of "Opening to Africa"', Anadolu Agency, Turkish state-run press agency (27 February 2017).

16   'Turkey aims to open more embassies in Africa, says Erdoğan', *Hürriyet Daily News* (7 September 2018).

17   'Turkey is quietly building its presence in Africa', NPR, website (8 March 2018).

18   Bekir Hazar, 'Bonjour Mösyö', *Takvim* (2 March 2018).

19 The Ottoman Empire did, however, participate in the Berlin Conference of 1884–5, together with eleven other European powers, as well as Russia and the United States. This conference effectively partitioned almost the whole of the African continent among key European powers. It also sparked fresh Ottoman imperial interest in Africa. For more on this, see, Mostafa Minawi, *The Ottoman Scramble for Africa: Empire and Diplomacy in the Sahara and the Hijaz* (Stanford, CA: Stanford University Press, 2016).

20 The Ottomans did show a late imperial interest in the rest of the continent as demonstrated by their participation in the Berlin Conference of 1884–5, which formalised the 'Scramble for Africa'. However, as latecomers to the colonial game in Africa, the sultans failed in their imperial ambitions of permanent territorial gains beyond the Sahara Dessert. This 'failure', nonetheless, has today ascribed Ankara a natural advantage in most Muslim-majority states of East and West Africa, where it is viewed with less suspicion today than are the regions' former colonial overlords.

21 Heather Murdock, 'Turkey opens first Mideast military base in Qatar', VOA News, website (10 May 2016).

22 The Turkish base in Qatar has boosted Ankara–Doha defence ties. Most notably, in March 2018, Doha agreed to procure Turkish armed drones, vehicles and two navy training warships. The deal also allowed Turkey's maritime school, Piri Reis University, to open a campus in Qatar. Talks with Qatar to procure the Altay tank, to be built by a Turkish–Qatari joint venture with a potential programme cost of $30 billion began in late 2018. See also, Fergus Kelly, 'Qatar signs deals for armed drones, armoured vehicles and ships from Turkey', Defense Post, website (14 March 2018). And also, Burak Ege Bekdil, 'Tank deal augments Turkey–Qatar procurement ties', Defense News, website (2 May 2018).

23 Soner Cagaptay and Olivier Decottignies, 'Turkey's new base in Qatar', Cagaptay, website (11 January 2016).

24 Mohammed Ibrahim and Jeffrey Gettleman, 'Truck bomb kills dozens in Somalia's capital', *New York Times* (4 October 2011).

25 Abukar Arman, 'Erdogan: The hero of Somalia', Al Jazeera, website (21 January 2015).

26 Abdirahman Hussein and Orhan Coşkun, 'Turkey opens military base in Mogadishu to train Somali soldiers', Reuters, news agency (30 September 2017).

27 Dominic Dudley, 'East Africa becomes a testing ground for UAE and Qatar as they battle for influence and opportunity', *Forbes* (4 April 2018).

28 'Somalia', Observatory of Economic Complexity, website (n.d.).

29 Hussein and Coşkun, 'Turkey opens military base in Mogadishu'. See also, 'Turkey sets up largest overseas army base in Somalia', Al Jazeera, website (1 October 2017).

30 Afyare Abdi Elmi, 'Ending famine in Somalia, the Turkish way', Al Jazeera, website (19 March 2017).

31 Yusuf Selman İnanç, 'Somalia's long-lost brother Turkey is here to rebuild the country', *Daily Sabah* (9 June 2014).

32 Dudley, 'East Africa'.

33 Maggie Fick, 'Harboring ambitions: Gulf States scramble for Somalia', Reuters, news agency (1 May 2018).

34 'Why Saudi Arabia, Qatar and Turkey are battling over Somalia', *Haaretz*, website (3 May 2018).

35 'Türkiye Cumhuriyeti Hükümeti ile Sudan Cumhuriyeti Hükümeti Arasında Askeri Alanda Eğitim, Teknik ve Bilimsel İş Birliği Çerçeve Anlaşması', Türkiye Büyük Millet Meclisi website (23 November 2011).

36 'Nyala Sudan Turkish Training and Research Hospital inaugurated', Turkish Cooperation and Coordination Agency, website (10 March 2014).

37 Ali Küçükgöçmen and Khalid Abdelaziz, 'Turkey to restore Sudanese Red Sea port and build naval dock', Reuters, news agency (26 December 2017). See also, 'Turkey renovating historic Ottoman-era sites on Suakin Island in Sudan', *Hürriyet Daily News* (24 January 2018).

38 'Sudan, Qatar ink $4 billion deal to develop Suakin seaport', *Daily Sabah* (26 March 2018).

39 Theodore Karasik and Giorgio Cafiero, 'Turkey's move into the Red Sea unsettles Egypt', Middle East Institute, website (17 January 2018).

40 I would like to thank my colleague, James Barnett, for this assistance in fleshing out the 'Great Game' concept in East Africa in this book.

41 Özgenur Sevinç, 'Djibouti is open to Turkey's efforts to safeguard Red Sea, Ambassador says', *Daily Sabah* (29 December 2017).

42 'Djibouti allocates 1M square meters to Egypt for logistic zone', Egypt Today, website (6 December 2018).

43 Tuba Şahin and Gökhan Ergöçün , 'Ethiopia: Turkey's Africa policy shows trade potential', Anadolu Agency, Turkish state-run press agency (10 October 2018).

44 Nilgün Erdem Arı, 'Turkish–Senagalese ties growing stronger: Ambassador', Anadolu Agency, Turkish state-run press agency (22 June 2017).

45 'Turkish Development Assistance Report', Turkish Cooperation and Coordination Agency, website (2016), 15.

46 Umut Aras, 'Erdogan sworn in as Turkey's first executive president', Al Jazeera, website (9 July 2018).

Chapter 15

1 Soner Cagaptay and Nick Danforth, 'Turkey's complicated relationship with the Middle East explained in one word', *Washington Post* (September 2, 2017). I would like to thank my colleague, Nick Danforth.

2 Dimitar Bechev, 'Turkey in the Balkans: Taking a broader view', *Insight Turkey*, 14 (1) (2012), 133.

3 'Bosnia and Herzegovina's bilateral relations with Turkey', Centre for Security Studies, website (December 2008).

4 Michael Birnbaum, 'Turkey brings a gentle version of the Ottoman Empire back to the Balkans', *The Guardian* (2 April 2013).

5 Tom Ellis, 'Relations with FYROM and Turkey's influence', Ekathimerini, website (9 February 2018).

6 Bechev, 'Turkey in the Balkans'.

7 Alon Ben-Meir, 'Albania must choose between EU and Turkey', The Globalist, website (19 May 19, 2018).

8 'Yurt Dışı Ziyaretler', Turkiye Cumhuriyeti Cumhurbaşkanlığı, website (n.d.).

9 'It's not 1389 – Serbia and Turkey are now friends', b92, website (10 October 2017).

10 'Serbian FM sings Turkish song for President Erdogan', TRT World, YouTube, video (11 October 2017).

11 'An excellent level of political ties among Serbia, Turkey, and Bosnia-Herzegovina', Serbia Ministry of Foreign Affairs, website (6 December 2017).

12 Bechev, 'Turkey in the Balkans'.

13 Maxim Edwards and Michael Colborne, 'Turkey's gift of a mosque sparks fears of "neo-Ottomanism" in Kosovo', *The Guardian* (2 January 2019).

14 Fuad Shahbazov, 'How will Erdogan's recent visit to Uzbekistan enhance Turkish–Uzbek cooperation?', The Diplomat, website (15 May 2018).

15 'Erdoğan on three-day official visit to Uzbekistan to strengthen relations', *Hürriyet Daily News* (30 April 2018).

16 'Turkmenistan's president lifts golden weight bar', *The Telegraph* (2 November 2018).

17 'Turkey's FM thanks Turkmen president over support to Turkish companies', *Hürriyet Daily News* (9 November 2018).

18 'Border statistics 2017', Republic of Turkey Ministry of Tourism and Culture.

19 'Relations between Turkey and Romania'.

20 Dildar Baykan and Satuk Buğra Kutluğun, 'Georgian envoy hails excellent relations with Turkey', Anadolu Agency, Turkish state-run press agency (26 May 2018).

21 'Russia and Turkey in the Black Sea and the South Caucasus', International Crisis Group, website (28 June 2018).

22 '72 yıl önce yaşanan trajedi: Kırım Tatarlarının sürgünü', BBC News, website (19 May 2016).

23 'Crimean Tatar leaders "freed", fly to Turkey', Radio Free Europe/Radio Liberty, website (26 October 2017).

24 Kerin Hope and Theodor Troev, 'Former PM Borisov claims victory in Bulgarian election', *Financial Times* (27 March 2017).

25 Bechev, personal correspondence.

26 'Muslim Party leader in the Netherlands tells Dutch to leave their country if they don't like diversity', American Renaissance, website (11 July 2018).

Chapter 16

1 Philip Oltermann, 'Erdoğan accuses Germany of "Nazi practices" over blocked political rallies', *The Guardian* (5 March 2017).

2 Tuvan Gumrukcu and Thomas Escritt, 'Turkey's Erdogan says Netherlands acting like a "banana republic"', Reuters, news agency (12 March 2017).

3 Ece Toksabay and Tuvan Gümrükçü, 'Erdogan warns Europeans "will not walk safely" if attitude persists, as row carries on', Reuters, news agency (22 March 2017).

4 The Ottomans also sought to deepen the Protestant–Catholic divide within the Habsburg Empire by protecting Hungarian Protestants so as to undermine Vienna's power in Central Europe and facilitate Ottoman expansion in that region. This explains the presence of a large Protestant community in modern-day eastern Hungary, which constituted parts of the rump Kingdom of Hungary under Ottoman rule in the sixteenth century.

5 Jeffrey, personal correspondence.

6 Ibid.

7 'Intel: Why Washington is putting a bounty on Kurdish insurgents', Al-Monitor, website (6 November 2018).

8 Senior Turkish official, personal correspondence (12 April 2016).

9 'Consolidated banking statistics', Bank of International Settlements, website (n.d.).

10 'Two Greek soldiers return home'.

11 Ibid.

12 'Turkey, Netherlands appoint ambassadors with normalization message', *Hürriyet Daily News* (7 September 2018).

13 Katrin Bennhold, 'In Erdogan's charm offensive, Germans find offense', *New York Times* (28 September 2018).

14 Ece Toksabay and Ali Küçükgöçmen, 'Erdogan's election rivals struggle to be heard in Turkey's media', Reuters, news agency (20 June 2018).

15 World Bank, International Comparison Program Database.

16 'Interview of H.E. Mr. Mevlüt Çavuşoğlu to *Global Times* (China)', Ministry of Foreign Affairs of the Republic of Turkey, website (18 June 2018).

17 'Demiryolunda Türk-Çin ortaklığı', *Habertürk* (29 May 2018).

18 Altay Atli, 'Making sense of Turkey's rapprochment with China', German Marshall Fund of the United States, website (26 November 2018).

19 I would like to thank my research intern, Deniz Yuksel, for conducting research for and drafting this portion of the book.

20 Kemal Karpat, '"Yakub Bey's relations with the Ottoman sultans: A reinterpretation', *Cahiers du Monde russe et soviétique*, 32 (1) (1991), 23–4.

21 Yitzhak Shichor, 'Ethno-diplomacy: The Uyghur hitch in Sino-Turkish relations', East–West Center, website (2009), 9 and 15.

22 Fehim Taştekin, 'Turkey's tough stance on Uighurs has implications for Syria', Al-Monitor, website (7 August 2017).

23 Ayla Jean Yackley, 'Turkish leader calls Xinjiang killings "genocide"', Reuters, news agency (10 July 2009).

24 Chris Buckley, 'China is detaining Muslims in vast numbers the goal: "Transformation"', *New York Times* (8 September 2018).

25 Shichor, 'Ethno-diplomacy'.

26 'Turkey's energy import bill up by 37% in 2018', Anadolu Agency, Turkish state-run press agency (1 February 2018).

27 'Turkey's economic relations with China', Ministry of Foreign Affairs of the Republic of Turkey, website (n.d.).

28 'Russia', Observatory of Economic Complexity, website (n.d.).

29 'Germany', Observatory of Economic Complexity, website (n.d.).

30 'United Kingdom', Observatory of Economic Complexity, website (n.d.).

31 'Italy', Observatory of Economic Complexity, website (n.d.).

32 'United States', Observatory of Economic Complexity, website (n.d.).

33 'Turkey', Observatory of Economic Complexity, website (n.d.).

34 'Foreign Trade Statistics' Turkish Statistical Institute, website (n.d.).

35 Ibid.

36 Ibid.

37 'Turkey and EU economic relations', European Commission, website (n.d.).

38 'Foreign Direct Investments in Turkey by countries', Central Bank of the Republic of Turkey, website (n.d.).

39 Ibid.

40 'FDI statistics according to BMD3 – FDI inflows by partner country', Organisation for Economic Co-operation and Development, website (n.d.).

41 'GDP, PPP (current international $)', World Bank, website (n.d.).

42 Ibid.

Conclusion

1 For a discussion of the various interpretations of Ottoman history in Turkey during Turkey's republican era, see the scholarship of Nick Danforth, including, 'The Ottoman Empire from 1923 to today: In search of a usable past', *Mediterranean Quarterly*, 27 (2) (2016), 5–27.

2 'İşte tarihteki 16 Türk devleti, Cumhurbaşkanlığı Sarayı'ndaki törende hepsi temsil edildi', NTV, website (12 January 2015).

3 Mehveş Emin, 'Sultan'ın camisi', *Milliyet* (23 July 2012).

4 'TBMM Başkanı Kahraman: Çamlıca Camii'ne ismi Recep Tayyip Erdoğan olsun', *Hürriyet* (10 February 2018).

5 Nora Fisher Onar, 'Echoes of a universalism lost: Rival representations of the Ottomans in today's Turkey', *Middle Eastern Studies*, 45 (2) (2009), 235.

6 'Son Osmanlı Padişahı 1. Recep Tayyip Erdoğan!', *Habertürk* (4 March 2009).

7 'Dilipak: Erdogan başkan seçilirse halife olacak', *Yeni Akit* (25 October 2015). Cited in Danforth, 'The Ottoman Empire'.

8 David Pollock, 'How the United States can still keep faith with its best allies in Syria', Washington Institute for the Near East Policy, website (3 January 2019).

9 Engindeniz, 'Media Watch'.

10 William Armstrong, 'The Sultan and the Sultan', History Today, website (8 November 2017).

11 Aykan Erdemir and Oren Kessler, 'A Turkish TV blockbuster reveals Erdogan's conspiratorial, anti-Semitic worldview', *Washington Post* (15 May 2017).

12 Armstrong, 'The Sultan'.

13 Cagaptay, *The New Sultan*, 178–206.

14 'DHA kareleriyle: Taksim'deki 25 Kasım eylemine izin yok', Diken, website
(25 November 2011); and 'AK Parti'li kadınlardan kadına şiddete karşı
"turuncu çizgi"', Anadolu Agency, Turkish state-run press agency
(25 November 2018).

15 Kudret Bülbül, 'Evanjelizm: Tanrıyı Kiyamete, İnsanlığı Felakete
Sürüklemek', *TRT* (8 August 2018).

16 Hay Eytan Cohen Yanarocak, 'Decoding the Payitaht Abdülhamid', *Turkey
Scope*, 1 (5) (March 2017), 4–7.

17 'Türkiye'de 11 milyon!' (2018).

18 Soner Cagaptay, 'How President Erdogan is turning Turkey into Putin's
Russia', Washington Institute for Near East Policy, website (24 April 2018).

19 'Turkey among top five countries which see most millionaire outflow in
2016: Report', *Hürriyet Daily News* (27 February 2017).

20 Soner Cagaptay, 'How President Erdogan is turning Turkey into Putin's
Russia', Washington Institute for Near East Policy, website (24 April 2018).

21 Cagaptay, 'How President Erdogan'.

BIBLIOGRAPHY

Personal correspondence

Bechev, Dimitar, 29 December 2018.
Edelman, Eric, 19 January and 10 February 2019.
Jeffrey, Jim, 25 May 2018.
Leigh, Michael, 3 January 2019.
Makovsky, Alan, 1 February 2019.
Outzen, Rich, 3 January 2019.
Senior Turkish diplomat, 3 January 2019.
Senior Turkish official, 12 April 2016.
Sorensen, Jesper Moller, 3 January 2019.
Stein, Aaron, 1 January 2019.
Senior European diplomat, 3 January 2019.
Sorensen, Jesper Moller, 3 January 2019.
Turkish diplomat, 1 August 2009.
Turkish Foreign Ministry official, 1 August 2011.
Wilson, Ross, 7 January 2019.

Official documents

Council of the European Union, 'Press Release No. 16289/06' (11 December 2006).
European Parliament, 'European Parliament Resolution of 21 May 2008 on Turkey's 2007 Progress Report (2007/2269(INI))' (21 May 2008).

Documentaries, videos and podcasts

Armstrong, William and Ahmet Erdi Öztürk, 'Ahmet Öztürk on the rising profile of Turkey's religious affairs directorate', Turkey Book Talks, podcast (4 September 2018).

'A violent brawl outside the Turkish Embassy in Washington, DC', ABC News, YouTube video (17 May 2017).
Interview with Recep Tayyip Erdogan, *Ustanın Hikayesi*, Beyaz TV 3 (September 2013).
'Serbian FM sings Turkish song for President Erdogan', TRT World, YouTube, video (11 October 2017).
Ustanın Hikayesi, Beyaz TV documentary (3 September 2013).
'Yiğit Bulut: Amerika'nın 52. Eyaleti Birleşik Arap Emirlikleri', YouTube, video (19 December 2017).

Web pages

'13 yılda 65 yeni temsilcilik: Türkiye'nin yurtdışındaki temsilcilik sayısı 228'e çıktı', T. C. Başbakanlık Kamu Diplomasisi Koordinatörlüğü, website (2015).
'An excellent level of political ties among Serbia, Turkey, and Bosnia-Herzegovina', Serbia Ministry of Foreign Affairs, website (6 December 2017).
Armstrong, William, 'The Sultan and the Sultan', History Today, website (8 November 2017).
'Association agreements', European External Action Service, website (11 May 2011).
Barut, Ilgın, 'Osmanlı döneminde gerçekleşen göçlerin kurumsallaşma ve göç politikaları üzerindeki etkileri', DergiPark, website (2 October 2018).
Beriş, Gürkan, 'Osmanli Borçlanma tarihi – Ottoman Debt history', Internet Archive Wayback Machine, website (n.d.).
'Border statistics 2017', Republic of Turkey Ministry of Tourism and Culture, website (July 2018).
'Bulgaria', Poll of Polls, website (n.d.).
'Chapters of the acquis', European Commission Neighbourhood Policy and Enlargement Negotiations, website (6 December 2016).
'Consolidated banking statistics', Bank of International Settlements, website (n.d.).
'Cumhurbaşkanı Erdoğan Yeni Döneme Dualarla Başladı', Diyanet Haber, website (10 July 2018).
'Current situation', Republic of Turkey Ministry of Foreign Affairs Directorate for EU Affairs, website (6 June 2017).
'Dışişleri Bakanı Sayın Ahmet Davutoğlu'nun TRT-1 Televizyonunda Yayımlanan Enine Boyuna Programında Yaptığı Açıklamalar', Republic of Turkey Ministry of Foreign Affairs, website (27 October 2013).
Ellis, Tom, 'Relations with FYROM and Turkey's influence', Ekathimerini, website (9 February 2018).
'FAQ for negotiation process', Republic of Turkey Ministry of Foreign Affairs Directorate for EU Affairs, website (6 June 2017).
'FDI statistics according to BMD3 – FDI inflows by partner country', Organisation for Economic Co-operation and Development, website (n.d.).

'Field listing: Population', Central Intelligence Agency, website (n.d.).
'Foreign Direct Investments in Turkey by countries', Central Bank of the
    Republic of Turkey, website (n.d.).
'Foreign trade statistics', Turkish Statistical Institute, website (n.d.).
'Foreign trade statistics', Turkish Statistical Institute, website (August 2018).
'GDP (current US $)', World Bank, website (n.d.).
'GDP, PPP (current international $)', World Bank, website (n.d.).
'Germany', Observatory of Economic Complexity, website (n.d.).
Hack, David, 'Vietnam war facts, stats and myths', US Wings, website (n.d.).
Haeri, Safa, 'Erdogan back home from his Tehran visit empty hands', Iran
    Press Service, website (31 July 2004).
'Health support from TİKA to Uganda', Turkish Coordination and Coordination
    Agency, website (9 August 2018).
'How Catherine II wanted to revive the Byzantine Empire', Russian Geography
    (n.d.), website.
'In about 93 months . . . about 560 thousand were killed in Syria since the day
    of claiming rights to the International Human Rights Day', Syrian
    Observatory for Human Rights, website (10 December 2018).
'Interview of H.E. Mr. Mevlüt Çavuşoğlu to Global Times (China)', Republic of
    Turkey Ministry of Foreign Affairs, website (18 June 2018).
'Iran FM briefsPparliament on Turkey botched coup: MP', Press TV, website
    (17 July 2016).
'Israil', Republic of Turkey Ministry of Trade, website (n.d.).
'Italy', Observatory of Economic Complexity, website (n.d.).
Kadercan, Burak, 'Making sense of Turkey's Syria strategy: A "Turkish tragedy"
    in the making', War on the Rocks, website (4 August 2017).
Kardas, Saban, 'Turkey reacts to Armenian Constitutional Court's decision on
    Protocols', Jamestown Foundation, website (26 January 2010).
Manhoff, Tim, 'Turkey's foreign policy towards Syria: From neo-Ottoman
    adventurism to neo-Ottoman realpolitik', Konrad Adenauer Stiftung,
    website (3 December 2017), 9.
'Muslim Party leader in the Netherlands tells Dutch to leave their country if
    they don't like diversity', American Renaissance, website (11 July 2018).
'New era of Russian–Turkish business relations', Russian–Turkish Business
    Forum, website (12 November 2018).
'Nyala Sudan Turkish Training and Research Hospital inaugurated', Turkish
    Cooperation and Coordination Agency, website (10 March 2014).
'Offers & Destinations', Turkish Airlines (n.d.), website.
'Ortadoğu'da hakkın, haklının yanındayız', AK Parti, website (22 July 2014).
'President Erdoğan addresses the UN General Assembly', Presidency of the
    Republic of Turkey, website (24 September 2014).
'Relations between Turkey and Armenia', Republic of Turkey Ministry of
    Foreign Affairs, website (n.d.).
'Relations between Turkey and Romania', Republic of Turkey Ministry of
    Foreign Affairs, website (n.d.).

'Russia', Observatory of Economic Complexity, website (n.d.).
Shichor, Yitzhak, 'Ethno-diplomacy: The Uyghur hitch in Sino-Turkish relations', East–West Center, website (2009), 9 and 15.
'Social policy and employment', Republic of Turkey Ministry of Foreign Affairs Directorate for EU Affairs, website (11 May 2018).
'Somalia', Observatory of Economic Complexity, website (n.d.).
Stein, Aaron, 'The origins of Turkey's Buffer Zone in Syria', War on the Rocks, website (11 December 2014).
'The German Fountain', Istanbul, website (9 May 92014).
'The Soviet Union: GDP growth', Nintil, website.
'The TAP and TANAP pipelines were connected at the border of Greece and Turkey', Energy Market Price, website (30 November 2018).
'The World Factbook: Developed countries', Central Intelligence Agency, website (2010).
'TIKA offers education support to South Sudan', Turkish Cooperation and Coordination Agency, website (12 January 2018).
'Turkey', Observatory of Economic Complexity, website (n.d.).
'Turkey and EU Economic relations', European Commission, website (n.d.).
'Turkey – Freedom in the World 2015', Freedom House, website (n.d.).
'Turkey: Global development data', World Bank (n.d.), website.
'Turkey: Literacy rate from 2005 to 2015, total and by gender', Statista, website (n.d.).
'Turkey's economic relations with China', Republic of Turkey Ministry of Foreign Affairs, website (n.d.).
'Turkey's political relations with Russian Federation', Republic of Turkey Ministry of Foreign Affairs, website (n.d.).
'Turkish Airlines begins flights to its tenth Russian destination', Airline Network News and Analysis, website (18 April 2017).
'Turkish Development Assistance Report', Turkish Cooperation and Coordination Agency, website (2016), 15.
'Turkish representations', Republic of Turkey Ministry of Foreign Affairs, website (n.d.).
'Türkiye Cumhuriyeti Hükümeti ile Sudan Cumhuriyeti Hükümeti Arasında Askeri Alanda Eğitim, Teknik ve Bilimsel İş Birliği Çerçeve Anlaşması', Türkiye Büyük Millet Meclisi, website (23 November 2011).
'Türkiye'de Kutuplaşmanın Boyutları Araştırması', Istanbul Bilgi University, website (5 February 2018).
'United Kingdom', Observatory of Economic Complexity, website (n.d.).
'United States', Observatory of Economic Complexity, website (n.d.).
'With the awareness that I am the President of all our 81 million citizens, I will work to be worthy of our nation', Presidency of the Republic of Turkey, website (9 July 2018).
World Bank, International Comparison Program Database, website (n.d.).
'Yurt Dışı Ziyaretler', Turkiye Cumhuriyeti Cumhurbaşkanlığı', website (n.d.).

Policy analysis and reports

'Bosnia and Herzegovina's bilateral relations with Turkey', Centre for Security Studies, website (December 2008).

Akgün, Mensur, Sabiha Senyücel Gündoğar and Jonathan Levack (tr.), 'The perception of Turkey in the Middle East 2012', Turkish Economic and Social Studies Foundation (2012).

Atli, Altay, 'Making sense of Turkey's rapprochment with China', German Marshall Fund of the United States, website (26 November 2018).

Aydın, Mustafa, Sinem Akgül Açıkmeşe, Cihan Dizdaroğlu and Onur Kara, 'Türk Dış Politikası Kamuoyu Algıları Araştırması', Kadir Has University Center for Turkish Studies, website (6 June 2018).

Aydıntaşbaş, Asli, 'The good, the bad, and the Gülenists', European Council on Foreign Relations, website (23 September 2016).

Blanchard, Christopher M. and Belasco, Amy, 'Train and Equip Program for Syria: Authorities, funding, and issues for Congress', Congressional Research Service, website (9 June 2015).

Bruno, Greg, 'Turkey at an energy crossroads', Council on Foreign Relations, website (20 November 2008).

Cagaptay, Soner, 'Hamas visits Ankara: The AKP shifts Turkey's role in the Middle East', Washington Institute for Near East Policy, website (16 February 2006).

Cagaptay, Soner, 'Turkish–Iranian rivalry redux', Washington Institute for Near East Policy, website (17 October 2011).

Cagaptay, Soner, 'Syria and Turkey: The PKK dimension', Washington Instituite for Near East Policy, website (5 April 2012).

Cagaptay, Soner, 'Turkey to vote on Syria policy', Washington Institute for Near East Policy, website (1 October 2014).

Cagaptay, Soner, 'How President Erdogan is turning Turkey into Putin's Russia', Washington Institute for Near East Policy, website (24 April 2018).

Cagaptay, Soner and Tyler Evans, 'The unexpected vitality of Turkish–Israeli trade', Washington Institute for Near East Policy, website (June 2012).

Cagaptay, Soner and Nazli Gencsoy, 'Improving Turkish–Russian relations: Turkey's new foreign policy and its implications for the United States', Washington Institute for the Near East Policy, website (12 January 2005).

Cagaptay, Soner and Michael Herzog, 'Israel and Turkey approaching reconciliation amid policy challenges', Washington Institute for Middle East Policy, website (19 April 2016).

Cagaptay, Soner and Marc J. Sievers, 'Turkey and Egypt's Great Game in the Middle East', Foreign Affairs (8 March 2015).

Cagaptay, Soner and Ed Stafford, 'A Turkish-friendly zone inside Syria', Washington Institute for Near East Policy, website (29 January 2016).

Cagaptay, Soner and Maya Yalkin, 'Syrian refugees in Turkey', Washington Institute for Near East Policy, website (22 August 2018).

Cagaptay, Soner, James F. Jeffrey and Omer Taspinar, 'Turkey and the failed
    coup one year later', Washington Institute for Near East Policy, event
    (20 July 2017).
Çeviköz, Ünal, 'EU–Turkey relations: The beginning of the end?', European
    Council on Foreign Relations, website (19 September 2017).
Cook, Steven A., 'Egypt and Turkey: Nightmares', Council on Foreign
    Relations, website (25 November 2013).
Dinçer, Osman Bahadır and Mustafa Kutlay, 'Türkiye'nin Ortadoğu'daki Güç
    Kapasitesi: Mümkünün Sınırları', USAK Ortadoğu ve Afrika Araştırmaları
    Merkezi (April 2012).
Durakoglu, Naz, 'An unlikely opposition: How Sputnik Turkiye is posing as
    opposition media & exploiting vulnerabilities in Turkey's narrowing media
    space', Atlantic Council, website (21 March 2017).
Engindeniz, Idil, 'Media Watch on Hate Speech report', Hrant Dink Foundation,
    website (July 2018).
Hakura, Fadi, 'The EU–Turkey refugee deal solves little', Chatham House,
    website (Spring 2016).
'Home page', Turkish Cooperation and Coordination Agency, website (n.d.).
Jane's Islamic Affairs Analyst, 'Turkey: Women's work is in the home?',
    Washington Institute for Near East Policy, website (January 2010).
Jeffrey, James F., 'Possibilities for a Turkish–Iranian rapprochement',
    Washington Institute for Near East Policy, website (May 2016).
Karasik, Theodore and Giorgio Cafiero, 'Turkey's move into the Red Sea
    unsettles Egypt', Middle East Institute, website (17 January 2018).
Koru, Selim, 'The resiliency of Turkey–Russia relations', Foreign Policy
    Research Institute, website (19 November 2018).
Livas, Sotiris S., 'Turkey's image in the Middle East via the Arab media', *Turkish
    Review*, 5 (1) (2015), 14–21.
Loizides, Neophytos and Eser Keskiner, 'The aftermath of the Annan Plan
    Referendums: Cross-voting moderation for Cyprus?', *Penn State Citeseerx
    Report*, 5 (2–3) (2004), 158–71.
Makovsky, Alan, 'Turkey's growing energy ties with Moscow', Center for
    American Progress, website (6 May 2015).
'Nagorno-Karabakh Conflict', Council on Foreign Relations, website (n.d.).
O'Bagy, Elizabeth, 'The Free Syrian Army', Institute for the Study of War,
    website (March 2013).
Öztürkler, Harun, 'Türkiye Ortadoğu Ticari İlişkilerinin Ekonomi Politiği',
    Ortadoğu Analiz, 7 (66) (2013), 76–9.
Pollock, David, 'How the United States can still keep faith with its best allies in
    Syria', Washington Institute for the Near East Policy, website (3 January
    2019).
Sheiko, Youssef, 'The United Arab Emirates: Turkey's new rival', Washington
    Institute for Near East Policy, website (16 February 2018).
Shichor, Yitzhak, 'Ethno-diplomacy: The Uyghur hitch in Sino-Turkish relations',
    East–West Center, website (2009), 49–50.

'Syria, Lebanon mark Martyrs Day', United Press International, website (6 May 1966).

Telci, İsmail Numan, 'İş Birliğinden Stratejik Ortaklığa: Türkiye–Afrika İlişkileri', Foundation for Political, Economic and Social Research (SETA) (3 March 2018).

Telhami, Shibley, 'The 2011 Arab Public Opinion Poll', Brookings Institution, website (21 November 2011).

Ülgen, Sinan, 'In search of lost time: Turkey–U.S. relations after Bush', Brookings Institution, website (19 February 2009).

Tweets

ABZayed (@ali11iraq), Twitter (December 16, 2017). 'قام1916في عام هل تعلمون التركي فخري باشا بجريمة بحق أهل المدينة النبوية فسرق أموالهم وقام بخطفهم واركابهم في قطارات إلى الشام واسطنبول برحلة سُميت (سفر برلك) كما سرق الأتراك أغلب مخطوطات المكتبة المحمودية بالمدينة وارسلوها إلى تركيا. هؤلاء أجداد أردوغان وتاريخهم مع المسلمين العرب.'

AK Parti (@akparti), Twitter (21 July 2014), 'Başbakan Erdoğan: Biz Ortadoğu'da halkın ve haklının yanındayız.'

Alanoğlu, Harun (@HarunAlanoglu), Twitter (6 November 2015), 'Devletiniz yıkılmış, yeni devletiniz de eski devletinizi yıkanlarla dost olmuşsa yeni devleti kuranlar hain, ülkeniz de artık bir sömürgedir.'

T. C. Cumhurbaşkanlığı İletişim Başkanlığı (@iletisim), Twitter (20 December 2017) '#CumhurbaşkanıErdoğan, BAE Dışişleri Bakanı Zayed'in tepki çeken paylaşımına ilişkin: Medine korumasını yaparken Fahreddin Paşa, ey bize bühtanda bulunan zavallı, senin ceddin neredeydi?'.

Trump, Donald J. (@realDonaldTrump), Twitter (20 May 2018), 'There was NO DEAL made with Turkey for the release and return of Pastor Andrew Brunson. I don't make deals for hostages. There was, however, great appreciation on behalf of the United States, which will lead to good, perhaps great, relations between the United States & Turkey!'.

Newspaper, magazine and website articles

'72 yıl önce yaşanan trajedi: Kırım Tatarlarının sürgünü', BBC News, website (19 May 2016).

'ABD Basınından Emine Erdoğan'a Kurtlar Vadisi Eleştirisi', *Haber Vitrini*, website (15 February 2006).

'ABD seçim sonuçları açıklandı: Trump başkan', *Yeni Şafak* (9 November 2016).

Abouzeid, Rania, 'Opening the weapons tap: Syria's rebels await fresh and free ammo', *Time* (22 June 2016).

'AK Parti'li kadınlardan kadına şiddete karşı "turuncu çizgi"', Anadolu Agency,
    Turkish state-run press agency (25 November 2018).
'AKP'li Şamil Tayyar: Adil Öksüz ABD Konsolosluğu'nda olabilir, imkân olsa da
    bakılsa!', T24, website (29 May 2017).
'AKP'ye kapatma davası', BBC News, website (14 March 2008).
Akyol, Mustafa, 'The problem with Turkey's "Zero Problems" Plan', New York
    Times (29 June 2016).
Amos, Deborah, 'A smuggler explains how he helped fighters along "Jihadi
    Highway"', NPR, website (7 October 2014).
'Andrew Brunson, U.S. pastor, moved to house arrest in Turkey', New York
    Times (25 July 2018).
Arango, Tim, 'Growing mistrust between U.S. and Turkey is played out in
    public', New York Times (23 December 2013).
Aras, Umut, 'Erdogan sworn in as Turkey's first executive president', Al
    Jazeera, website (9 July 2018).
Arı, Nilgün Erdem, 'Turkish–Senagalese ties growing stronger: Ambassador',
    Anadolu Agency, Turkish state-run press agency (22 June 2017).
Arman, Abukar, 'Erdogan: The hero of Somalia', Al Jazeera, website
    (21 January 2015).
Bard, Anne, 'Reinforcements enter besieged Syrian town via Turkey, raising
    hopes', New York Times (29 October 2014).
Barrett, Devlin, 'U.S. court convicts Turkish banker in multibillion-dollar scheme
    to help Iran evade sanctions', Washington Post (3 January 2018).
'Battle for Kobane: Key events', BBC News, website (25 June 2015).
Baykan, Dildar and Satuk Buğra Kutluğun, 'Georgian envoy hails excellent
    relations with Turkey', Anadolu Agency, Turkish state-run press agency
    (26 May 2018).
Bekdil, Burak Ege, 'Tank deal augments Turkey–Qatar procurement ties',
    Defense News, website (2 May 2018).
'Before Athens trip, Erdogan urges Lausanne Treaty update', Ekathimerini,
    website (6 December 2017).
'Bekir Bozdağ: ABD darbe girişimini Gülen'in yaptığını çok iyi biliyor', Habertürk
    (24 July 2016).
Belli, Onur Burçak, Eren Caylan and Maximilian Popp, 'Erdogan's hunt against
    the Gülen Movement', Spiegel Online, website (3 August 2016).
Ben-Meir, Alon, 'Albania must choose between EU and Turkey', The Globalist,
    website (19 May 2018).
Bennhold, Katrin, 'Leaders of Turkey and Israel clash at Davos Panel', New
    York Times (29 January 2009).
Bennhold, Katrin, 'In Erdogan's charm offensive, Germans find offense', New
    York Times (28 September 2018).
Birnbaum, Michael, 'Turkey brings a gentle version of the Ottoman Empire
    back to the Balkans', The Guardian (2 April 2013).
Buckley, Chris, 'China is detaining Muslims in vast numbers – The goal:
    "Transformation"', New York Times (8 September 2018).

Bülbül, Kudret, 'Evanjelizm: Tanrıyı Kiyamete, İnsanlığı Felakete Sürüklemek', *TRT* (8 August 2018).

Butler, Daren, 'About 60,000 Syrian Kurds flee to Turkey from Islamic State advance', Reuters, news agency (20 September 2014).

Butler, Daren, 'With more Islamic schooling, Erdogan aims to reshape Turkey', Reuters, news agency (25 January 2018).

Cagaptay, Soner, 'Opinion: Erdoğan's empathy for Mursi', Asharq Al-Awsat, website (14 September 2013).

Cagaptay, Soner, 'In U.S.–Iran Deal, Turkey fears a Shiite alliance', *New York Times* (27 March 2016).

Cagaptay, Soner, 'Turkey's turn from the West', *Washington Post* (2 February 2009).

Cagaptay, Soner, 'Obama, Erdogan finds shared interests', *Washington Post* (11 November 2011).

Cagaptay, Soner, 'Next up: Turkey vs. Iran', *New York Times* (14 February 2012).

Cagaptay, Soner, 'Turkey's fray into the Fertile Crescent', *New York Times* (27 February 2013).

Cagaptay, Soner, 'The E.U. needs Turkey', *New York Times* (20 December 2013).

Cagaptay, Soner, 'Turkey's permanent state of crisis', *Washington Post* (20 December 2016).

Cagaptay, Soner and Nick Danforth, 'Turkey's complicated relationship with the Middle East explained in one word', *Washington Post* (2 September 2017).

Cagaptay, Soner and Olivier Decottignies, 'Turkey's new base in Qatar', Cagaptay, website (11 January 2016).

Cagaptay, Soner and Michael Herzog, 'How America can help its friends make nice', *New York Times* (20 June 2012).

Cagaptay, Soner and James F. Jeffrey, 'Can Obama save Turkey from a Syrian quagmire?', *New York Times* (16 May 2013).

Cameron-Moore, Simon and Samia Nakhoul, 'Arab rulers must change or risk defeat: Turkey', Reuters, news agency (30 March 2011).

Candar, Cengiz, 'How Turkey really feels about the Iran deal', Al-Monitor, website (20 July 2015).

'Çek git bu ülkeden', *Yeni Şafak* (21 December 2013).

Cesana, Shlomo, 'Israel livid over new Hamas headquarters in Turkey', *Israel Hayom*, website (26 November 2014).

Cocco, Frederica, 'Turkish lira extends rally on back of softer dollar', *Financial Times*, website (26 October 2018).

Cornell, Svante E., 'Erbakan, Kısakürek, and the mainstreaming of extremism in Turkey', Hudson Institute, website (4 June 2018).

'Crimean Tatar leaders "freed", fly to Turkey', Radio Free Europe/Radio Liberty, website (26 October 2017).

Cunningham, Erin, 'Journalists sentenced to jail in case highlighting media crackdown in Turkey', *Washington Post* (6 May 2016).

'Cypriots welcome UN Reunion Plan', Al Jazeera, website (14 February 2004).

Dalay, Galip, 'Is there really a Turkey–Iran rapprochement?', Al Jazeera, website (13 September 2017).

Dalay, Galip, 'Evolution of Turkey–Iraqi Kurdistan's relations', Al Jazeera, website (20 December 2017).

DeYoung, Karen and Felicia Sonmez, 'US sanctions two Turkish officials over detention of American pastor', *Washington Post* (1 August 2018).

Demir, Ferit, 'Turkey sends special forces to Iraqi border', Reuters, news agency (13 November 2007).

'Demiryolunda Türk-Çin ortaklığı', *Habertürk* (29 May 2018).

Detsch, Jack, 'Congress to make determination on F-35s for Turkey', Al-Monitor, website (23 November 2018).

'DHA kareleriyle: Taksim'deki 25 Kasım eylemine izin yok', Diken, website (25 November 2011).

Diler, Ergun, 'ABD'nin B Planı', *Takvim* (26 May 2017).

'Dilipak: Erdogan başkan seçilirse halife olacak', *Yeni Akit* (25 October 2015), cited in Nick Danforth. 'The Ottoman Empire from 1923 to today: In search of a usable past', *Mediterranean Quarterly*, 27 (2) (2016), 5–27.

'Djibouti allocates 1M square meters to Egypt for logistic zone', Egypt Today, website (6 December 2018).

Dombey, Daniel, 'Erdogan attacks "traitors" and foreign media for Turkey protests', *Financial Times*, website (18 June 2013).

Edwards, Maxim and Michael Colborne, 'Turkey's gift of a mosque sparks fears of "neo-Ottomanism" in Kosovo', *The Guardian* (2 January 2019).

'Egypt crisis: Mass protests over Morsi grip cities', BBC News, website (1 July 2013).

'Egypt signs $1 billion Turkish loan deal', Reuters, news agency (30 September 2012).

Elmi, Afyare Abdi, 'Ending famine in Somalia, the Turkish way', Al Jazeera, website (19 March 2017).

Emin, Mehveş, 'Sultan'ın camisi', *Milliyet* (23 July 2012).

Erdemir, Aykan and Oren Kessler, 'A Turkish TV blockbuster reveals Erdogan's conspiratorial, anti-Semitic worldview', *Washington Post* (15 May 2017).

'Erdoğan congratulates Trump in phone call, reiterates commitment to strengthen relations', *Daily Sabah* (9 November 2016).

'Erdoğan'dan İran'ı kızdıracak açıklama,' *Odatv*, website (4 April 2017).

'Erdoğan'dan İsrail'e "soykırım" suçlaması', Deutsche Welle, website (14 May 2018).

'Erdoğan: İsrail bir terör devleti', *Sabah* (26 July 2014).

'Erdoğan: Millet isterse laiklik tabii ki gidecek', *Hürriyet* (21 August 2001).

'Erdoğan kime 'kardeşim' dediyse . . .', *Sözcü* (5 May 2016).

'Erdogan meets with U.S. Jewish leaders on sidelines of Washington Nuclear Summit', *Haaretz*, website (3 April 2016).

'Erdoğan Mısır'da sevinç gösterileriyle karşılandı', BBC News, website (13 September 2011).

'Erdoğan on three-day official visit to Uzbekistan to strengthen relations',
  Hürriyet Daily News (30 April 2018).
'Erdoğanlar'ın mutlu günü', NTV, website (10 August 2013).
Ergan, Uğur and Cansu Çamlıbel, 'F-35 şerhine Ankara'dan tepki', *Hürriyet*
  (20 June 2018).
Erkuş, Sevil, 'Turkey summons ambassador over Tunisian FM's comments',
  Hürriyet Daily News (3 April 2015).
'F-35 savaş uçakları: Teknik özellikleri ve Türkiye'ye teslimatıyla ilgili bilinmesi
  gerekenler', BBC News, website (13 August 2018).
Fahim, Kareem, 'Trial of American pastor highlights strained US–Turkish
  alliance', *Washington Post* (15 April 2018).
Fahim, Kareem and Karam Shoumali, 'Turkey to let Iraqi Kurds cross to Syria
  to fight ISIS', *New York Times* (20 October 2014).
Fayed, Shaima and Yasmine Saleh, 'Millions flood Egypt's streets to demand
  Mursi quit', Reuters, news agency (29 June 2013).
Ferziger, Jonathan and Elliott Gotkine, 'US says Israel gas may help Europe
  diversify from Russian fuel', Bloomberg, website (7 April 2016).
Fethi, Füsun Yiğit, Emine Akarsu and Kerim Tuncer Sarıkavak 'Güney Akım
  Projesi', *MTA Doğal Kaynaklar Ve Ekonomi Bülteni* 14, General Directorate
  of Mineral Research and Exploration, website, (2012), 26–34.
Fick, Maggie, 'Harboring ambitions: Gulf States scramble for Somalia',
  Reuters, news agency (1 May 2018).
'Foreigners don't like Muslims, only their money: Turkish President Erdoğan',
  Hürriyet Daily News (27 November 2014).
Forgey, Quint, 'Trump thanks Erdoğan for American pastor's release', *Politico*,
  website (13 October 2018).
Gall, Carlotta and Anne Barnard, 'Turkey begins operation against U.S.-backed
  Kurdish militias in Syria', *New York Times* (19 January 2018).
Girit, Selin, 'Why is Turkey standing up for Qatar?', BBC News, website
  (14 June 2017).
'Global poll slams Bush leadership', BBC News, website (19 January 2005).
Goldberg, Jeffrey, 'The Modern King in the Arab Spring', *The Atlantic* (15 April
  2013).
Gumrukcu, Tuvan and Thomas Escritt, 'Turkey's Erdogan says Netherlands
  acting like a "banana republic"', Reuters, news agency (12 March 2017).
Gümrükçü, Tuvan and Ece Toksabay, 'Turkey, Russia sign deal on supply of
  S-400 missiles', Reuters, news agency (29 December 2017).
Gürcan, Metin, 'Turkey, Iran could unite to overcome their Kurdish worries',
  Al-Monitor, website (10 October 2017).
Hazar, Bekir, 'Bonjour Mösyö', *Takvim* (2 March 2018).
'Hizbullah militanları Suriye'de', *Posta* (18 February 2013).
Hoge, Warren, 'Cyprus Greeks and Turks agree on plan to end 40-year
  conflict', *Washington Post* (14 February 2004).
Hong, Nicole, 'Recep Tayyip Erdogan allowed Turkish banks to help Iran make
  illegal payments, witness says', *Wall Street Journal* (30 November 2017).

Hope, Kerin and Theodor Troev, 'Former PM Borisov claims victory in
    Bulgarian election', *Financial Times* (27 March 2017).
Hussein, Abdirahman and Orhan Coşkun, 'Turkey opens military base in
    Mogadishu to train Somali soldiers', Reuters, news agency (30 September
    2017).
Ibrahim, Mohammed and Jeffrey Gettleman, 'Truck bomb kills dozens in
    Somalia's capital', *New York Times* (4 October 2011).
Idiz, Semih, 'Will Turkey be expelled from NATO?', Al-Monitor, website
    (26 July 2016).
Idiz, Semih, 'Turkish–Arab ties marked by fear and loathing', Al-Monitor,
    website (13 March 2018).
Ignatius, David, 'The coup attempt dealt a new blow to the strained U.S.–Turkish
    relationship', *Washington Post* (18 July 2016).
İnanç, Yusuf Selman, 'Somalia's long-lost brother Turkey is here to rebuild the
    country', *Daily Sabah* (9 June 2014).
'Intel: Why Armenia wants to make peace with Turkey', Al-Monitor, website
    (11 December 2018).
'Intel: Why Washington is putting a bounty on Kurdish insurgents', Al-Monitor,
    website (6 November 2018).
'Interview transcript: Rachid Ghannouchi', *Financial Times*, website
    (11 January 2018).
'Iran: Threat to strike NATO radar in Turkey not official policy', *Haaretz*,
    website (14 December 2011).
'Iran: Turkey must rethink stance on Syria, NATO Missile Shield or face
    "Trouble"', Reuters, news agency, and *Haaretz*, website (9 October 2011).
'Iran FM Zarif visits Turkey to find solutions to ease regional tensions', Rudaw,
    website (6 June 2017).
'Islamic State crisis: Syria rebel forces boost Kobane defence', BBC News,
    website (29 October 2014).
'Israel slams Turkey for hosting Hamas members', *Hürriyet Daily News*
    (3 December 2014).
'İşte tarihteki 16 Türk devleti, Cumhurbaşkanlığı Sarayı'ndaki törende hepsi
    temsil edildi', NTV, website (12 January 2015).
'It's not 1389 – Serbia and Turkey are now friends', b92, website (10 October
    2017).
Johnson, Glen and Richard Spencer, 'Turkey's politicians, gold dealer and the
    pop star', *The Telegraph* (29 December 2013).
Kalin, Ibrahim, 'Turkey and the Arab Spring', Al Jazeera, website (25 May 2011).
Kalin, Stephen, 'Dispute over Turkish troops throws future of Mosul into
    question', Reuters, news agency (7 January 2016).
Kanter, James, 'Gates criticizes Turkey vote against sanctions', *New York
    Times* (11 June 2010).
Karagül, İbrahim, 'Dördüncü İstiklal Savaşı da 'Karşı Darbe' ile kazanılacak.
    Erken doğum, gizli ortaklar, ekonomide "temizlik" zamanı', *Yeni Şafak*
    (17 August 2018).

Kaylan, Melik, 'Erdoğan shoots down Putin', *Politico*, website (24 November 2015).

'KCK denounces PUK for closing PKK-linked party offices in Sulaimani', Rudaw, website (30 November 2018).

Kelly, Caroline and Kate Sullivan, 'Released US pastor Andrew Brunson returns to US, meets with Trump', CNN, website (14 October 2018).

Kelly, Fergus, 'Qatar signs deals for armed drones, armoured vehicles and ships from Turkey', Defense Post, website (14 March 2018).

Kessler, Glenn, 'UN vote on Iran sanctions not a clear-cut win for Obama', *Washington Post* (9 June 2010).

Kingsley, Patrick, 'Turkey investigating 17, some Americans, accused in failed coup', *New York Times* (15 April 2017).

Kingsley, Patrick, 'Erdogan claims vast powers in Turkey after narrow victory in Referendum', *New York Times* (16 April 2017).

Kinzer, Stephen, 'Turkey, rejected, will freeze ties to European Union', *New York Times* (15 December 1997).

Kirkpatrick, David D. and Mayy El Sheikh, 'Citing deadlock, Egypt's leader seizes new power and plans Mubarak retrial', *New York Times* (22 November 2012).

Knowlton, Brian, 'US warns Iraq on new government', *New York Times* (21 March 2005).

Kosharek, Noah, Liel Kyzer and Barak Ravid, 'Israel transfers hundreds of Gaza Flotilla activists to airport for deportation', Associated Press, DPA, news agencies, and *Haaretz*, website (1 June 2010).

Küçükgöçmen, Ali and Khalid Abdelaziz, 'Turkey to restore Sudanese Red Sea port and build naval dock', Reuters, news agency (26 December 2017).

Kuebler, Martin, 'Turkey not fit for EU accession: Sarkozy', *Deutsche Welle*, website (26 February 2011).

Kurtaran, Gökhan, 'Regional free zone attempt stillborn', *Hürriyet Daily News* (1 December 2011).

Kurubas, Saim, 'Turkey–Greece tensions: What comes next?', TRT World, website (25 April 2018).

Malone, Barry, 'Iraq summons Turkish envoy over Erdogan broadside', Reuters, news agency (23 April 2012).

Marks, Monica, 'How Egypt's coup really affected Tunisia's Islamists', *Washington Post* (16 March 2015).

McElroy, Damien, 'Kurdish guerillas launch clandestine war in Iran', *The Telegraph* (10 September 2007).

Mekel, Arye, 'Birth of a geopolitical bloc: The Israel–Greece–Cyprus axis', *Haaretz*, website (31 January 2016).

'Migrant crisis: EU–Turkey deal comes into effect', BBC News, website (20 March 2016).

Mirenzi, Nicola, 'Erdoğan and secularism', Reset Doc, website (27 September 2011).

Murdock, Heather, 'Turkey opens first Mideast Military base in Qatar', VOA News, website (10 May 2016).

Myers, Steven Lee, 'Bush pledges to help Turkey on intelligence', *New York Times* (6 November 2007).

Necsutu, Madalin, 'Turkish Secret Services nab six "Gulenists" in Moldova', Balkan Insight, website (6 September 2018).

'Obama to visit Turkey "within weeks"', *The Guardian* (7 March 2009).

Ocak, Serkan, 'Başbakan Erdoğan: Batı, demokrasi konusunda sınıfta kaldı', *Radikal* (7 July 2013).

Oltermann, Philip, 'Erdoğan accuses Germany of "Nazi practices" over blocked political rallies', *The Guardian* (5 March 2017).

Palmer, Elizabeth, 'ISIS encroaches on ultimate prize in Iraq', CBS News, website (10 October 2014).

Parkinson, Joe and Ayla Albayrak, 'Turkey sends troops into Syria to retrieve Ottoman tomb, guards', *Wall Street Journal* (22 February 2015).

Pierson, Brendan, 'US charges Turkish banker in Iran sanctions probe', Reuters, news agency (28 March 2017).

'Polonya'da tartışmalı yargı yasası iptal', Deutsche Welle, website (18 December 2018).

'Pompeo presses Turkey on S-400 missiles purchase from Russia', Reuters, news agency (27 April 2018).

'Portre: Ahmet Davutoğlu', *Milliyet*, website (21 August 2014).

Pramuk, Jacob, 'Why Trump is attacking Turkey with sanctions and tariffs', CNBC, website (10 August 2018).

'President Assad admits army strained by war in Syria', BBC News, website (26 July 2015).

'President Erdoğan to embark on new Africa trip, attend BRICS summit', *Hürriyet Daily News* (24 July 2018).

'President Obama's remarks in Turkey', *New York Times* (6 April 2009).

'PYD leader arrives in Turkey for two-day talks: Report', *Hürriyet Daily News* (25 July 2013).

'Qatar crisis: What you need to know', BBC News, website (19 July 2017).

Rainsford, Sarah, '"Deep state plot" grips Turkey', BBC News, website (4 February 2008).

Rapoza, Kenneth, 'Schools banned in Russia now under fire in two US cities', *Forbes* (20 December 2015).

Raymond, Nate, 'US arrests Turkish businessman accused of evading Iran sanctions', Reuters, news agency (21 March 2016).

'Report: Turkey bows to US pressure, expels top Hamas operative', *Jerusalem Post*, website (7 August 2015).

'Retweet by UAE FM about Ottoman commander turns into feud with Erdogan', Al Arabiya, website (21 December 2017).

Roblin, Sebastien, 'America's big fear: Turkey mixing F-35s and Russia's S-400 Air Defense System', National Interest, website (7 July 2018).

Rogin, Josh, 'Obama names his world leader best buddies!', *Foreign Policy* (19 January 2012).
'Russia and Turkey in the Black Sea and the South Caucasus', International Crisis Group, website (28 June 2018).
'Russian brings forward delivery of S-400 missiles to Turkey to July 2019', *Times of Israel*, website (4 April 2018).
Sachs, Susan, 'Greek Cypriots reject a U.N. Peace Plan', *New York Times* (25 April 2004).
Şahin, Tuba, 'Turkey installs 764 km security wall on Syria border', Anadolu Agency, Turkish state-run press agency (9 June 2018).
Şahin, Tuba and Gökhan Ergocun, 'Ethiopia: Turkey's Africa policy shows trade potential', Anadolu Agency, Turkish state-run press agency (10 October 2018).
'Saudi Arabia, Qatar press for more help to Syrian rebels', Reuters, news agency (20 February 2013).
Sevinç, Özgenur, 'Djibouti is open to Turkey's efforts to safeguard Red Sea, Ambassador says', *Daily Sabah* (29 December 2017).
Shadid, Anthony, 'Can Turkey unify the Arabs?', *New York Times* (28 May 2011).
Shadid, Anthony, 'Turkey predicts alliance with Egypt as regional anchors', *New York Times* (18 September 2011).
Shahbazov, Fuad, 'How will Erdogan's recent visit to Uzbekistan enhance Turkish–Uzbek Cooperation?', The Diplomat, website (15 May 2018).
Shanker, Thom, 'U.S. hails deal with Turkey on missile shield', *New York Times* (15 September 2011).
Shekani, Helbast, 'Exclusive: US general visits Syria's Manbij, confirms support for Kurdish-led forces', Kurdistan24, website (21 June 2018).
Smith, Helena, 'Former President of Cyprus who scuppered reunification with the Turkish north', *The Guardian* (7 January 2009).
'Son Osmanlı Padişahı 1. Recep Tayyip Erdoğan!', *Habertürk* (4 March 2009).
Stack, Liam, 'In slap at Syria, Turkey shelters anti-Assad fighters', *New York Times* (27 October 2011).
Stein, Aaron, 'For Turkey, it's all about regime change in Syria', Al Jazeera, website (8 October 2014).
Stein, Aaron, 'Turkey did nothing about the jihadists in its midst – until it was too late', *Foreign Policy* (1 July 2016).
'Sudan, Qatar ink $4 billion deal to develop Suakin seaport', *Daily Sabah* (26 March 2018).
'Syria unrest: US calls on President Assad to resign', BBC News, website (18 August 2011).
'Tajikistan closes Gülen-affiliated schools', *Daily Sabah* (21 May 2015).
Taştekin, Fehim, 'Turkey's tough stance on Uighurs has implications for Syria', Al-Monitor, website (7 August 2017).
'TBMM Başkanı Kahraman: Çamlıca Camii'ne ismi Recep Tayyip Erdoğan olsun', *Hürriyet* (10 February 2018).

Telhami, Shibley, 'The 2011 Arab Public Opinion Poll', Brookings Institution, website (21 November 2011).
'The German Fountain', Istanbul, website (9 May 2014).
'The Trajectory of Afrin Operation', Al Jazeera Centre for Studies, website (28 March 2018).
'The world's largest airlines by number of countries served', World Atlas, website (1 August 2017).
'Three more Erdogan guards indicted for Washington brawl', Al Jazeera, website (29 August 2017).
'Timeline: Kurdish militant group PKK's three-decade war with Turkey', Reuters, news agency (21 March 2013).
Todd, Chuck, 'The White House walk-and-talk that changed Obama's mind on Syria', NBC News, website (2 November 2015).
Toksabay, Ece and Tuvan Gümrükçü, 'Erdogan warns Europeans "will not walk safely" if attitude persists, as row carries on', Reuters, news agency (22 March 2017).
Toksabay, Ece and Ali Küçükgöçmen, 'Erdogan's election rivals struggle to be heard in Turkey's media', Reuters, news agency (20 June 2018).
Tremblay, Pinar, 'Why Erdogan's so quiet about Turkish expansion in Africa', Al-Monitor, website (20 August 2018).
Tremblay, Pinar, 'Many Turks outraged by state religious authority's bloated budget', Al-Monitor, website (3 December 2018).
'Tunisia coalition agrees top government posts', BBC News, website (21 November 2011).
'Turkey: Military chiefs resign en masse', BBC News, website (29 July 2011).
'Turkey aims to open more embassies in Africa, says Erdoğan', *Hürriyet Daily News* (7 September 2018).
'Turkey among 8 countries granted waiver on US oil sanctions against Iran', *Hürriyet Daily News* (5 November 2018).
'Turkey among top five countries which see most millionaire outflow in 2016: Report', *Hürriyet Daily News* (27 February 2017).
'Turkey "close" to peace force deal', CNN, website (20 March 2002).
'Turkey is quietly building its presence in Africa', NPR, website (8 March 2018).
'Turkey, Israel sign deal to normalize ties after six years', Reuters, news agency (28 June 2016).
'Turkey issues "final word" to Syria', Reuters, news agency (15 August 2011).
'Turkey, Netherlands appoint ambassadors with normalization message', *Hürriyet Daily News* (7 September 2018).
'Turkey opposes strike against Iraq', BBC News, website (17 July 2002).
'Turkey ranks second in TV drama export', *Hürriyet Daily News* (30 September 2017).
'Turkey reaping rewards of "Opening to Africa"', Anadolu Agency, Turkish state-run press agency (27 February 2017).
'Turkey renovating historic Ottoman-era sites on Suakin Island in Sudan', *Hürriyet Daily News* (24 January 2018).

'Turkey says Israel paid compensation to families of 2010 flotilla raid victims – media', Reuters, news agency (23 June 2017).

'Turkey sent files on 452 FETO members to 83 countries – Cavusoglu', TRT World, website (14 November 2018).

'Turkey sets up largest overseas army base in Somalia', Al Jazeera, website (1 October 2017).

'Turkey to reopen its consulates in Iraq's Basra and Mosul', Associated Press, news agency (11 October 2018).

'Turkey to reopen consulates in Mosul and Basra: Turkish FM', *Hürriyet Daily News* (11 October 2018).

'Turkey tries out soft power in Somalia', Reuters, news agency (3 June 2012).

'Turkey withdraws from Libya summit in Italy: Vice President', Reuters, news agency (13 November 2018).

'Turkey's Energy import bill up by 37% in 2018', Anadolu Agency, Turkish state-run press agency (1 February 2018).

'Turkey's Erdogan links fate of detained US pastor to wanted cleric Gülen', Reuters, news agency (28 September 2017).

'Turkey's Erdogan meets American Jewish delegation in Ankara', *Jerusalem Post*, website (9 February 2016).

'Turkey's FM thanks Turkmen president over support to Turkish companies', *Hürriyet Daily News* (9 November 2018).

'Turkish Airlines carried 1 million passengers to and from Israel in 2017', *Hürriyet Daily News* (11 January 2018).

'Turkish Airlines (THY) flies to 7 destinations in Ukraine', *Daily Sabah* (21 March 2016).

'Turkish court dismisses *Mavi Marmara* case after deal with Israel', *Daily Sabah* (9 December 2016).

'Turkish lira plunges to new record low in Asia Pacific trade', Reuters, news agency (12 August 2018).

'Turkish officials hail Turkey's United Nations Security Council Seat', *Hürriyet* (18 October 2008).

'Türkiye'de 11 milyon 985 bin 118 kişi şüpheliymiş!', Sol, website (9 December 2018).

'Turkmenistan's president lifts golden weight bar', *The Telegraph* (2 November 2018).

'Two Greek soldiers return home after Turkey release', *Hürriyet Daily News* (14 August 2018).

'UAE: The Arab world will not be led by Iran and Turkey', The National, website (27 December 2017).

'UAE reopens Syria Embassy in boost for Assad', Reuters, news agency (27 December 2018).

Ünver, Akın, 'Iran deal and Turkey: Time for a soft-power reset', Al Jazeera, website (19 July 2015).

'US actions purely political, taken against Turkish state, Erdoğan says', *Daily Sabah* (8 September 2017).

'US spending bill would halt transfer of F-35s to Turkey', Reuters, news agency (22 June 2018).

Uslu, Sinan, Enes Kaplan and Sorwar Alam, 'President Erdogan visits Turkey military base in Qatar', Anadolu Agency, Turkish state-run press agency (16 November 2017).

Vedrickas, Ginetta, 'Property in Cyprus: A tale of two Cypruses', The Telegraph (27 September 2008).

Walker, Shaun, 'Erdoğan and Putin discuss closer ties in first meeting since jet downing', The Guardian (9 August 2016).

Wall, Robert, 'Big spending on warplanes spurs aerial arms race', Wall Street Journal (26 September 2016).

Watson, Ivan and Mohamed Fadel Fahmy, 'Turkish prime minister arrives for visit to Egypt as role widens', CNN, website (14 September 2011).

Weise, Zia, 'Erdoğan, the new Atatürk', Politico (26 December 2016).

Weise, Zia, 'Turkey's Balkan comeback', Politico, website (17 May 2018).

Weiser, Benjamin, 'Reza Zarrab testifies that he bribed Turkish minister', New York Times (29 November 2017).

'Why Saudi Arabia, Qatar and Turkey are battling over Somalia', Haaretz, website (3 May 2018).

Williams, Nathan, 'The rise of Turkish soap power', BBC News, website (28 June 2013).

Wilson, Scott, 'Hamas sweeps Palestinian elections, complicating peace efforts in Mideast', Washington Post (27 January 2006).

'World: Middle East Turkey losing patience with Syria', BBC News, website (4 October 1998).

Yackley, Ayla Jean, 'Turkish leader calls Xinjiang killings "genocide"', Reuters, news agency (10 July 2009).

Yackley, Ayla Jean, 'Rare painting by Turkey's last Caliph sold at auction', Reuters, news agency (6 October 2013).

Yavuz, M. Hakan, 'Erdogan's Ottomania', Boston Review, website (8 August 2018).

Yayla, Ahmet S. and Colin P. Clarke, 'Turkey's double ISIS standard', Foreign Policy (12 April 2018).

Yeginsu, Ceylan, 'Militants storm Turkish Consulate in Iraqi city, taking 49 people as hostages', New York Times (11 June 2014).

Yeginsu, Ceylan, 'Turkey votes to allow operations against ISIS', New York Times (2 October 2014).

Yeginsu, Ceylan and Helene Cooper, 'US jets to use Turkish bases in war on ISIS', New York Times (23 July 2015).

'"Yes" to Kurdistan: 92 percent of Iraq's Kurds voted for independence, official results show', Haaretz, website (27 September, 2017).

'Yeni Şafak: İkinci 15 Temmuz güneyden gelecek', T24, website (2 August 2017).

Zaman, Amberin, 'Genocide claim by Muslim ally Turkey', The Telegraph (5 April 2002).

Zaman, Amberin, 'Turkey snatches "Gülenist" teachers in Moldova', Al-Monitor, website (6 September 2018).
Zengerle, Patricia, Mike Stone and James Dalgleish, 'US spending bill would halt transfer of F-35s to Turkey', Reuters, news agency (21 June 2018).
Zeyrek, Deniz, '1 Mart Mesajının Adresi', *Hürriyet* (8 February 2016).

Journal articles and chapters from edited volumes

Balci, Bayram and Thomas Liles, 'Turkey's comeback to Central Asia', *Insight Turkey,* 20 (4) (2018), 16.
Bechev, Dimitar, 'Turkey in the Balkans: Taking a broader view', *Insight Turkey*, 14 (1) (2012), 133.
Cagaptay, Soner and Oya Rose Aktas, 'How Erdoganism is killing democracy in Turkey', *Foreign Affairs* (7 July 2017).
Çevik, Senem B., 'Narrating Turkey's story: Communicating its nation brand through public diplomacy', in Emel Parlar Dal (ed.), *Middle Powers in Global Governance: The Rise of Turkey* (Cham: Springer International, 2018), 213–30.
Danforth, Nick, 'The Ottoman Empire from 1923 to today: In search of a usable past', *Mediterranean Quarterly*, 27 (2) (2016), 5–27.
Donelli, Federico and Ariel Gonzalez Levaggi, 'From Mogadishu to Buenos Aires: The Global South in the Turkish foreign policy in the late JDP Period (2011–2017)', in Emel Parlar Dal (ed.), *Middle Powers in Global Governance: The Rise of Turkey* (Basingstoke: Palgrave Macmillan, 2018), 53–73.
Dursun, Mehmet Erkan, John F, O'Connell, Zheng Lei, and David Warnock Smith, "The transformation of a legacy carrier – A case study of Turkish Airlines," *Journal of Air Transport Management* 40 (2014), 106–18.
Göktepe, Cihat, 'The Menderes Period (1950–1960)', *Journal of Turkish Weekly* website (13 April 2005).
Heper, Metin, 'Kemalism/Ataturkism', in Metin Heper (ed.), *The Routledge Handbook of Modern Turkey* (New York: Routledge, 2012), 139–48.
Karpat, Kemal, 'Yakub Bey's relations with the Ottoman sultans: A reinterpretation', *Cahiers du Monde russe et soviétique*, 32 (1) (1991), 23–4.
Necipoğlu, Gülru, 'Süleyman the Magnificent and the representation of power in the context of Ottoman–Hapsburg–Papal rivalry', *Art Bulletin*, 71 (3) (1989), 401–27.
Kurban, Vefa, '1950–1960 Yıllarında Türkiye ile Sovyetler Birliği Arasındaki İlişkiler', *Journal of Modern Turkish History Studies*, 28 (Spring 2014), ss.253–82.
Nye Jr., Joseph S., 'Get smart: Combining hard and soft power', *Foreign Affairs*, 88 (4) (2009), 160–3.

Önsoy, Rifat, 'Cumhuriyetten Günümüze İlk ve Orta Öğretimimiz ve Bazı Meseleleri', *Hacettepe Üniversitesi Eğitim Fakültesi Dergisi*, 6 (1991), 8.

Onar, Nora Fisher, 'Echoes of a universalism lost: Rival representations of the Ottomans in today's Turkey', *Middle Eastern Studies*, 45 (2) (2009), 229–49.

Özkan, Mehmet and Birol Akgün, 'Turkey's opening to Africa', *Modern African Studies*, 48 (4) (2010), 525–46.

Öztürk, Ahmet Erdi and Semiha Sözeri, 'Diyanet as a Turkish foreign folicy tool: Evidence from the Netherlands and Bulgaria', *Politics and Religion*, 11 (3) (2018), 624–48.

Sarpkaya, Ruhi, 'Köy Enstitüleri'nden Sonra İmam-Hatip Liseleri', *Toplum ve Demokrasi*, 2 (3) (2008), 1–28.

Sezer, Duygu Bazoğlu, 'Russia: The challenges of reconciling geopolitical competition with economic partnership', in Barry Rubin and Kemal Kirişci (eds), *Turkey in World Politics: An Emerging Multiregional Power* (Boulder, CO: Lynne Rienner, 2001), 151–72.

Tümertekin, Erol, 'The iron and steel industry of Turkey', *Economic Geography*, 31 (2) (1955), 179–84.

Waterbury, John, 'Review of *The New Sultan: Erdogan and the crisis of Modern Turkey* by Soner Cagaptay', *Foreign Affairs* (November/December, 2017).

Yanarocak, Hay Eytan Cohen, 'Decoding the Payitaht Abdülhamid', *Turkey Scope*, 1 (5) (March 2017), 4–7.

Books

Ahmed, Faiz, *Afghanistan Rising: Islamic Law and Statecraft between the Ottoman and British Empires* (Cambridge, MA: Harvard University, 2017).

Cagaptay, Soner, *Islam, Secularism, and Nationalism in Modern Turkey: Who is a Turk?* (New York: Routledge, 2006).

Cagaptay, Soner, *The Rise of Turkey: The Twenty-First Century's First Muslim Power* (Lincoln, NE: Potomac, 2014).

Cagaptay, Soner, *The New Sultan: Erdogan and the Crisis of Modern Turkey* (London: I.B. Tauris, 2017).

Davutoğlu, Ahmet, *Stratejik Derinlik: Türkiye'nin Uluslararası Konumu* (Istanbul: Küre Yayınları, 2001).

Deringil, Selim, *Turkish Foreign Policy during the Second World War: An 'Active' Neutrality* (Cambridge: Cambridge University Press, 1989).

Heper, Metin, *İsmet İnönü: The Making of a Turkish Statesmen* (Leiden: Brill, 1998).

Jenkins, Gareth H., *Between Fact and Fantasy: Turkey's Ergenekon Investigation* (Washington, DC: Central Asia-Caucasus Institute & Silk Road Studies Program, August 2009).

Jukes, Geoffrey, *The First World War (1): The Eastern Front 1914–1918* (London: Bloomsbury Publishing, 2014).

Heyeti, Maarif Vekâleti Muallim, *Orta Mektep Tarih III. Kitap* (Istanbul: Devlet Matbaası, 1931).

Millman, Brock, *The Ill-Made Alliance: Anglo-Turkish Relations, 1934–1940* (Montreal: McGill-Queen's University Press, 1998).

Minawi, Mostafa, *The Ottoman Scramble for Africa: Empire and Diplomacy in the Sahara and the Hijaz* (Stanford, CA: Stanford University Press, 2016).

Mitchell, B. R., *European Historical Statistics 1750–1970* (New York: Columbia University Press, 1976; abridged edn, 1978).

Oran, Baskin (ed.) and Mustafa Aksin (tr.), *Turkish Foreign Policy 1919–2006 Facts and Analyses with Documents* (Salt Lake City, UT: University of Utah Press, 2010).

Shankland, David, *The Alevis in Turkey: The Emergence of a Secular Islamic Tradition* (London and New York: Routledge, 2007).

Statistical Office of the United Nations, *Demographic Yearbook 1948* (New York: Statistical Office of the United Nations: 1949).

INDEX